EXODUS

Brazos Theological Commentary on the Bible

EXODUS

THOMAS JOSEPH WHITE, OP

Brazos Press
a division of Baker Publishing Group
Grand Rapids, Michigan

Published by Brazos Press
a division of Baker Publishing Group
P.O. Box 6287, Grand Rapids, MI 49516-6287
www.brazospress.com

Printed in the United States of America

Library of Congress Cataloging-in-Publication Data
Names: White, Thomas Joseph, 1971– author.
Title: Exodus / Thomas Joseph White, OP.
Description: Grand Rapids : Brazos Press, 2016. | Series: Brazos theological commentary on the Bible |
    Includes bibliographical references and index.
Identifiers: LCCN 2015051487 | ISBN 9781587433467 (cloth : alk. paper)
Subjects: LCSH: Bible. Exodus—Commentaries.
Classification: LCC BS1245.53 W45 2016 | DDC 222.1207—dc23
LC record available at http://lccn.loc.gov/2015051487

Nihil Obstat:
Rev. Stephen D. Ryan, OP

Imprimi Potest:
Very Rev. Kenneth R. Letoile, OP
Prior Provincial
February 18, 2015

Nihil Obstat:
Rev. Christopher Begg, STD, PhD
Censor Deputatus

Imprimatur:
Most Rev. Barry C. Knestout
Auxiliary Bishop of Washington
Archdiocese of Washington
January 29, 2015

The nihil obstat and imprimatur are official declarations that a book or pamphlet is free of doctrinal or moral error. There is no implication that those who have granted the nihil obstat and the imprimatur agree with the content, opinions, or statements expressed therein.

In keeping with biblical principles of creation stewardship, Baker Publishing Group advocates the responsible use of our natural resources. As a member of the Green Press Initiative, our company uses recycled paper when possible. The text paper of this book is composed in part of post-consumer waste.

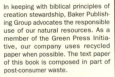

This book is dedicated to my father—mentor and friend.

As a father has compassion on his children,
so the Lord has compassion on those who fear him.

Psalm 103:13

Two errors: 1. To take everything literally. 2. To take everything spiritually.

—Blaise Pascal, *Pensées*

By a prophet the LORD brought Israel up from Egypt,
and by a prophet he was preserved.

—Hosea 12:13

I saw a Lamb standing, as though it had been slain.

—Revelation 5:6

We are apt to treat pretences to a divine mission or to supernatural powers as of frequent occurrence, and on that score to dismiss them from our thoughts; but we cannot so deal with Judaism. When mankind had universally denied the first lesson of their conscience by lapsing into polytheism, is it a thing of slight moment that there was just one exception to the rule, that there was just one people who, first by their rulers and priests, and afterwards by their own unanimous zeal, professed, as their distinguishing doctrine, the Divine Unity and Government of the world, and that, moreover, not only as a natural truth, but as revealed to them by that God Himself of whom they spoke,—who so embodied it in their national polity, that a Theocracy was the only name by which it could be called? It was a people founded and set up in Theism, kept together by Theism, and maintaining Theism for a period from first to last of 2000 years, till the dissolution of their body politic; and they have maintained it since in their state of exile and wandering for 2000 years more. . . . The preaching of this august dogma begins with them. They are its witnesses and confessors, even to torture and death; on it and its revelation are molded their laws and government; on this their politics, philosophy, and literature are founded; of this truth their poetry is the voice, pouring itself out in devotional compositions which Christianity, through all its many countries and ages, has been unable to rival; on this aboriginal truth, as time goes on, prophet after prophet bases his further revelations, with a sustained reference to a time when, according to the secret counsels of its Divine Object and Author, it is to receive completion and perfection,—till at length that time comes.

—John Henry Newman, *A Grammar of Assent*

CONTENTS

SERIES PREFACE

Near the beginning of his treatise against gnostic interpretations of the Bible, *Against Heresies*, Irenaeus observes that scripture is like a great mosaic depicting a handsome king. It is as if we were owners of a villa in Gaul who had ordered a mosaic from Rome. It arrives, and the beautifully colored tiles need to be taken out of their packaging and put into proper order according to the plan of the artist. The difficulty, of course, is that scripture provides us with the individual pieces, but the order and sequence of various elements are not obvious. The Bible does not come with instructions that would allow interpreters to simply place verses, episodes, images, and parables in order as a worker might follow a schematic drawing in assembling the pieces to depict the handsome king. The mosaic must be puzzled out. This is precisely the work of scriptural interpretation.

Origen has his own image to express the difficulty of working out the proper approach to reading the Bible. When preparing to offer a commentary on the Psalms he tells of a tradition handed down to him by his Hebrew teacher:

> The Hebrew said that the whole divinely inspired scripture may be likened, because of its obscurity, to many locked rooms in our house. By each room is placed a key, but not the one that corresponds to it, so that the keys are scattered about beside the rooms, none of them matching the room by which it is placed. It is a difficult task to find the keys and match them to the rooms that they can open. We therefore know the scriptures that are obscure only by taking the points of departure for understanding them from another place because they have their interpretive principle scattered among them.[1]

1. Fragment from the preface to *Commentary on Psalms 1–25*, preserved in the *Philokalia*, trans. Joseph W. Trigg (London: Routledge, 1998), 70–71.

As is the case for Irenaeus, scriptural interpretation is not purely local. The key in Genesis may best fit the door of Isaiah, which in turn opens up the meaning of Matthew. The mosaic must be put together with an eye toward the overall plan.

Irenaeus, Origen, and the great cloud of premodern biblical interpreters assumed that puzzling out the mosaic of scripture must be a communal project. The Bible is vast, heterogeneous, full of confusing passages and obscure words, and difficult to understand. Only a fool would imagine that he or she could work out solutions alone. The way forward must rely upon a tradition of reading that Irenaeus reports has been passed on as the rule or canon of truth that functions as a confession of faith. "Anyone," he says, "who keeps unchangeable in himself the rule of truth received through baptism will recognize the names and sayings and parables of the scriptures."[2] Modern scholars debate the content of the rule on which Irenaeus relies and commends, not the least because the terms and formulations Irenaeus himself uses shift and slide. Nonetheless, Irenaeus assumes that there is a body of apostolic doctrine sustained by a tradition of teaching in the church. This doctrine provides the clarifying principles that guide exegetical judgment toward a coherent overall reading of scripture as a unified witness. Doctrine, then, is the schematic drawing that will allow the reader to organize the vast heterogeneity of the words, images, and stories of the Bible into a readable, coherent whole. It is the rule that guides us toward the proper matching of keys to doors.

If self-consciousness about the role of history in shaping human consciousness makes modern historical-critical study critical, then what makes modern study of the Bible modern is the consensus that classical Christian doctrine distorts interpretive understanding. Benjamin Jowett, the influential nineteenth-century English classical scholar, is representative. In his programmatic essay "On the Interpretation of Scripture," he exhorts the biblical reader to disengage from doctrine and break its hold over the interpretive imagination. "The simple words of that book," writes Jowett of the modern reader, "he tries to preserve absolutely pure from the refinements or distinctions of later times." The modern interpreter wishes to "clear away the remains of dogmas, systems, controversies, which are encrusted upon" the words of scripture. The disciplines of close philological analysis "would enable us to separate the elements of doctrine and tradition with which the meaning of scripture is encumbered in our own day."[3] The lens of understanding must be wiped clear of the hazy and distorting film of doctrine.

2. *Against Heresies* 9.4.
3. Benjamin Jowett, "On the Interpretation of Scripture," in *Essays and Reviews* (London: Parker, 1860), 338–39.

Postmodernity, in turn, has encouraged us to criticize the critics. Jowett imagined that when he wiped away doctrine he would encounter the biblical text in its purity and uncover what he called "the original spirit and intention of the authors."[4] We are not now so sanguine, and the postmodern mind thinks interpretive frameworks inevitable. Nonetheless, we tend to remain modern in at least one sense. We read Athanasius and think him stage-managing the diversity of scripture to support his positions against the Arians. We read Bernard of Clairvaux and assume that his monastic ideals structure his reading of the Song of Songs. In the wake of the Reformation, we can see how the doctrinal divisions of the time shaped biblical interpretation. Luther famously described the Epistle of James as a "strawy letter," for, as he said, "it has nothing of the nature of the Gospel about it."[5] In these and many other instances, often written in the heat of ecclesiastical controversy or out of the passion of ascetic commitment, we tend to think Jowett correct: doctrine is a distorting film on the lens of understanding.

However, is what we commonly think actually the case? Are readers naturally perceptive? Do we have an unblemished, reliable aptitude for the divine? Have we no need for disciplines of vision? Do our attention and judgment need to be trained, especially as we seek to read scripture as the living word of God? According to Augustine, we all struggle to journey toward God, who is our rest and peace. Yet our vision is darkened and the fetters of worldly habit corrupt our judgment. We need training and instruction in order to cleanse our minds so that we might find our way toward God.[6] To this end, "the whole temporal dispensation was made by divine Providence for our salvation."[7] The covenant with Israel, the coming of Christ, the gathering of the nations into the church—all these things are gathered up into the rule of faith, and they guide the vision and form of the soul toward the end of fellowship with God. In Augustine's view, the reading of scripture both contributes to and benefits from this divine pedagogy. With countless variations in both exegetical conclusions and theological frameworks, the same pedagogy of a doctrinally ruled reading of scripture characterizes the broad sweep of the Christian tradition from Gregory the Great through Bernard and Bonaventure, continuing across Reformation differences in both John Calvin and Cornelius Lapide, Patrick Henry and Bishop Bossuet, and on to more recent figures such as Karl Barth and Hans Urs von Balthasar.

4. Ibid., 340.
5. *Luther's Works*, vol. 35, ed. E. Theodore Bachmann (Philadelphia: Fortress, 1959), 362.
6. *On Christian Doctrine* 1.10.
7. *On Christian Doctrine* 1.35.

Is doctrine, then, not a moldering scrim of antique prejudice obscuring the Bible, but instead a clarifying agent, an enduring tradition of theological judgments that amplifies the living voice of scripture? And what of the scholarly dispassion advocated by Jowett? Is a noncommitted reading, an interpretation unprejudiced, the way toward objectivity, or does it simply invite the languid intellectual apathy that stands aside to make room for the false truism and easy answers of the age?

This series of biblical commentaries was born out of the conviction that dogma clarifies rather than obscures. The Brazos Theological Commentary on the Bible advances upon the assumption that the Nicene tradition, in all its diversity and controversy, provides the proper basis for the interpretation of the Bible as Christian scripture. God the Father Almighty, who sends his only begotten Son to die for us and for our salvation and who raises the crucified Son in the power of the Holy Spirit so that the baptized may be joined in one body—faith in *this* God with *this* vocation of love for the world is the lens through which to view the heterogeneity and particularity of the biblical texts. Doctrine, then, is not a moldering scrim of antique prejudice obscuring the meaning of the Bible. It is a crucial aspect of the divine pedagogy, a clarifying agent for our minds fogged by self-deceptions, a challenge to our languid intellectual apathy that will too often rest in false truisms and the easy spiritual nostrums of the present age rather than search more deeply and widely for the dispersed keys to the many doors of scripture.

For this reason, the commentators in this series have not been chosen because of their historical or philological expertise. In the main, they are not biblical scholars in the conventional, modern sense of the term. Instead, the commentators were chosen because of their knowledge of and expertise in using the Christian doctrinal tradition. They are qualified by virtue of the doctrinal formation of their mental habits, for it is the conceit of this series of biblical commentaries that theological training in the Nicene tradition prepares one for biblical interpretation, and thus it is to theologians and not biblical scholars that we have turned. "War is too important," it has been said, "to leave to the generals."

We do hope, however, that readers do not draw the wrong impression. The Nicene tradition does not provide a set formula for the solution of exegetical problems. The great tradition of Christian doctrine was not transcribed, bound in folio, and issued in an official, critical edition. We have the Niceno-Constantinopolitan Creed, used for centuries in many traditions of Christian worship. We have ancient baptismal affirmations of faith. The Chalcedonian definition and the creeds and canons of other church councils have their places in official church documents. Yet the rule of faith cannot be limited to a specific set of words, sentences, and creeds. It is instead a pervasive habit of thought, the animating culture of the church in its intellectual aspect. As Augustine observed, commenting on Jer. 31:33, "The creed is learned by listening; it is written, not on stone tablets nor on any material, but on the heart."[8] This is why Irenaeus is able to appeal to the rule of faith more than a century before the first ecumenical council, and this is why we need not itemize the contents of the Nicene tradition in order to appeal to its potency and role in the work of interpretation.

Because doctrine is intrinsically fluid on the margins and most powerful as a habit of mind rather than a list of propositions, this commentary series cannot settle difficult questions of method and content at the outset. The editors of the series impose no particular method of doctrinal interpretation. We cannot say in advance how doctrine helps the Christian reader assemble the mosaic of scripture. We have no clear answer to the question of whether exegesis guided by doctrine is antithetical to or compatible with the now-old modern methods of historical-critical inquiry. Truth—historical, mathematical, or doctrinal—knows no contradiction. But method is a discipline of vision and judgment, and we cannot know in advance what aspects of historical-critical inquiry are functions of modernism that shape the soul to be at odds with Christian discipline. Still further, the editors do not hold the commentators to any particular hermeneutical theory that specifies how to define the plain sense of scripture—or the role this plain sense should play in interpretation. Here the commentary series is tentative and exploratory.

Can we proceed in any other way? European and North American intellectual culture has been de-Christianized. The effect has not been a cessation of Christian activity. Theological work continues. Sermons are preached. Biblical scholars turn out monographs. Church leaders have meetings. But each dimension of a formerly unified Christian practice now tends to function independently. It is as if a weakened army had been fragmented, and various corps had retreated to isolated fortresses in order to survive. Theology has lost its competence in exegesis. Scripture scholars function with minimal theological training. Each decade finds new theories of preaching to cover the nakedness of seminary training that provides theology without exegesis and exegesis without theology.

Not the least of the causes of the fragmentation of Christian intellectual practice has been the divisions of the church. Since the Reformation, the role of the rule of faith in interpretation has been obscured by polemics and counterpolemics about

8. *Sermon* 212.2.

sola scriptura and the necessity of a magisterial teaching authority. The Brazos Theological Commentary on the Bible series is deliberately ecumenical in scope, because the editors are convinced that early church fathers were correct: church doctrine does not compete with scripture in a limited economy of epistemic authority. We wish to encourage unashamedly dogmatic interpretation of scripture, confident that the concrete consequences of such a reading will cast far more light on the great divisive questions of the Reformation than either reengaging in old theological polemics or chasing the fantasy of a pure exegesis that will somehow adjudicate between competing theological positions. You shall know the truth of doctrine by its interpretive fruits, and therefore in hopes of contributing to the unity of the church, we have deliberately chosen a wide range of theologians whose commitment to doctrine will allow readers to see real interpretive consequences rather than the shadow boxing of theological concepts.

The Brazos Theological Commentary on the Bible has no dog in the current translation fights, and we endorse a textual ecumenism that parallels our diversity of ecclesial backgrounds. We do not impose the thankfully modest inclusive-language agenda of the New Revised Standard Version, nor do we insist upon the glories of the Authorized Version, nor do we require our commentators to create a new translation. In our communal worship, in our private devotions, in our theological scholarship, we use a range of scriptural translations. Precisely as scripture—a living, functioning text in the present life of faith—the Bible is not semantically fixed. Only a modernist, literalist hermeneutic could imagine that this modest fluidity is a liability. Philological precision and stability is a consequence of, not a basis for, exegesis. Judgments about the meaning of a text fix its literal sense, not the other way around. As a result, readers should expect an eclectic use of biblical translations, both across the different volumes of the series and within individual commentaries.

We cannot speak for contemporary biblical scholars, but as theologians we know that we have long been trained to defend our fortresses of theological concepts and formulations. And we have forgotten the skills of interpretation. Like stroke victims, we must rehabilitate our exegetical imaginations, and there are likely to be different strategies of recovery. Readers should expect this reconstructive—not reactionary—series to provide them with experiments in postcritical doctrinal interpretation, not commentaries written according to the settled principles of a well-functioning tradition. Some commentators will follow classical typological and allegorical readings from the premodern tradition; others will draw on contemporary historical study. Some will comment verse by verse; others will highlight passages, even single words that trigger theological analysis of scripture. No reading strategies are proscribed, no interpretive methods foresworn. The central premise in this commentary series is that doctrine provides structure and cogency to scriptural interpretation. We trust in this premise with the hope that the Nicene tradition can guide us, however imperfectly, diversely, and haltingly, toward a reading of scripture in which the right keys open the right doors.

R. R. Reno

ACKNOWLEDGMENTS

I would like to thank friends who helped greatly in the production of this book in various ways. First, for their invitation to contribute to this series and their editorial assistance, R. R. Reno of the Institute of Religion and Public Life and R. David Nelson of Baker Academic and Brazos Press. I also received expert advice from a variety of academic colleagues: Gary Anderson, Shalom Carmy, Bruce Marshall, Fr. Steve Ryan, OP, and Fr. Benedict Viviano, OP. I should offer special thanks to Fr. John Langlois, OP, and Fr. Thomas Petri, OP, the president and dean of the Pontifical Faculty of the Immaculate Conception, for their generous support for this project, and to the Priory of the Holy Spirit, Blackfriars Hall, Oxford, who were most gracious hosts during a time of sabbatical. Other people who have offered generous help are Fr. Dominic Legge, OP, Fr. Dominic Langevin, OP, Sr. Maria of the Angels, OP, Sr. Mary Dominic, OP, and Teresa Vargo. For the fraternal support and friendship of all these kind people I am most grateful.

ABBREVIATIONS

General

ad	adversus	LXX	Septuagint
can.	canon	n.	number
chap(s).	chapter(s)	NASB	New American Standard Bible
corp.	corpus	NIV	New International Version
esp.	especially	NRSV	New Revised Standard Version
ESV	English Standard Version	para(s).	paragraph(s)
i.e.	that is	pr.	prologue to a question

Biblical Books

Acts	Acts	Ezek.	Ezekiel
Amos	Amos	Ezra	Ezra
1 Chr.	1 Chronicles	Gal.	Galatians
2 Chr.	2 Chronicles	Gen.	Genesis
Col.	Colossians	Hab.	Habakkuk
1 Cor.	1 Corinthians	Hag.	Haggai
2 Cor.	2 Corinthians	Heb.	Hebrews
Dan.	Daniel	Hos.	Hosea
Deut.	Deuteronomy	Isa.	Isaiah
Eccl.	Ecclesiastes	Jas.	James
Eph.	Ephesians	Jer.	Jeremiah
Esth.	Esther	Job	Job
Exod.	Exodus	Joel	Joel

John	John		1 Pet.	1 Peter
1 John	1 John		2 Pet.	2 Peter
2 John	2 John		Phil.	Philippians
3 John	3 John		Phlm.	Philemon
Jonah	Jonah		Prov.	Proverbs
Josh.	Joshua		Ps(s).	Psalm(s)
Jude	Jude		Rev.	Revelation
Judg.	Judges		Rom.	Romans
1 Kgs.	1 Kings		Ruth	Ruth
2 Kgs.	2 Kings		1 Sam.	1 Samuel
Lam.	Lamentations		2 Sam.	2 Samuel
Lev.	Leviticus		Sir.	Sirach
Luke	Luke		Song	Song of Songs
2 Macc.	2 Maccabees		1 Thess.	1 Thessalonians
Mal.	Malachi		2 Thess.	2 Thessalonians
Mark	Mark		1 Tim.	1 Timothy
Matt.	Matthew		2 Tim.	2 Timothy
Mic.	Micah		Titus	Titus
Nah.	Nahum		Wis.	Wisdom of Solomon
Neh.	Nehemiah		Zech.	Zechariah
Num.	Numbers		Zeph.	Zephaniah
Obad.	Obadiah			

Modern Editions

ANF	*The Ante-Nicene Fathers*. Edited by Alexander Roberts, James Donaldson, and A. Cleveland Coxe. 10 vols. Repr. Grand Rapids: Eerdmans, 1957
De Malo	Thomas Aquinas. *On Evil* [*Quaestiones disputatae de malo*]. Translated by R. Regan. Oxford: Oxford University Press, 2003
EDP	Thomas Aquinas. *Summa theologica*. Translated by the Fathers of the English Dominican Province. New York: Benziger Brothers, 1947
In Div. Nom.	Thomas Aquinas. *In librum beati Dionysii de divinis nominibus expositio*. Edited by C. Pera. Turin and Rome: Marietti, 1950
In Ioan.	Thomas Aquinas. *Commentary on the Gospel of John* [*Lectura super Ioannem*]. 3 vols. Translated by James Weisheipl and Fabian Larcher. Washington, DC: Catholic University of America Press, 2010
In Rom.	Thomas Aquinas. *Commentary on the Letter of St. Paul to the Romans* [*Super Epistolam ad Romanos*]. Translated by F. Larcher. Lander, WY: Aquinas Institute, 2012

NPNF[1]	*A Select Library of the Nicene and Post-Nicene Fathers.* Series 1. Edited by Philip Schaff. 1886–89. 14 vols. Repr. Grand Rapids: Eerdmans, 1956
NPNF[2]	*A Select Library of the Nicene and Post-Nicene Fathers.* Series 2. Edited by Philip Schaff. 1886–89. 14 vols. Repr. Grand Rapids: Eerdmans, 1956
Quodlibet.	Thomas Aquinas. *Quaestiones quodlibetales.* Edited by Raymundi Spiazzi. Turin and Rome: Marietti, 1949
SCG	Thomas Aquinas. *Summa contra Gentiles.* 4 vols. Garden City, NY: Doubleday, 1955–56
ST	Thomas Aquinas. *Summa theologica.* Translated by the Fathers of the English Dominican Province. New York: Benziger Brothers, 1947
WA	*D. Martin Luther's Werke: Kritische Gesamtausgabe* (Weimarer Ausgabe). Edited by J. F. K. Knaake et al. 57 vols. Weimar: Böhlau, 1883–

INTRODUCTION

The Darkness and Light of God

God calls us out of the limitations of our finite nature, our created lights, into his incomprehensible darkness. We are tempted to restrict our understanding to the sphere of our physical world, our temporal state, and our created condition. But the purpose of the book of Exodus is to call the soul into a deeper union with God. This entails that we look away from creatures and into the divine darkness of God. "Moses drew near to the thick darkness where God was" (Exod. 20:21).[1] "Clouds and darkness are round about him: righteousness and judgment are the habitation of his throne" (Ps. 97:2 KJV). The scriptures, then, speak of God as a darkness that enshrouds the human mind.

The darkness into which God draws the human being can be said to signify four things. First, it symbolizes God's transcendence of all that is sensible. God is the author of the physical world, but the divine nature cannot be perceived under the image of any sensible thing. "You shall not make for yourself a graven image" (Exod. 20:4). Dionysius comments that upon entering the darkness of Mount Sinai, Moses is understood to approach God spiritually by faith, in such a way as to transcend rightfully the mere appearances of the senses.[2]

Second, the darkness of God represents the incomprehensibility of the divine essence on the level of natural knowledge, for God can only be known indirectly through the consideration of his creatures, which are his effects. "Ever since the

1. Citations from the Bible in English in this volume are taken from the Revised Standard Version unless otherwise noted.
2. Dionysius, *Mystical Theology*, chap. 1.

creation of the world his invisible nature, namely, his eternal power and deity, has been clearly perceived in the things that have been made" (Rom. 1:20). And yet even if one comes to think rightly of God as wisdom, goodness, being, and the like, all created limitations that one associates with these very designations must also be removed. In that sense, God is not wisdom, goodness, or being as we know it. Consequently, to rightly contemplate his mystery one must enter not only into a darkness of the senses but also into a darkness of understanding. Gregory of Nyssa teaches that "one who is going to associate intimately with God must go beyond all that is visible and (lifting up his own mind, as to a mountaintop, to the invisible and incomprehensible) believe that the divine is there where the understanding does not reach."[3]

Third, the darkness of God can be seen to represent the nature of God insofar as it connotes a supernatural mystery. That is to say, the illumination of faith not only draws the intellect of man beyond the range of his ordinary sensation and toward a limited natural understanding of God derived from creatures, but it also imparts to him a positive knowledge of a mystery that is utterly inaccessible to unaided human reason as such. In that sense, the person who encounters the unveiled God, the "face" of his love, must also walk beyond the boundaries of all natural intelligence and be illuminated by what is not normally given to human reason. This is why Dionysius speaks of a "ray of the divine shadow."[4] The divine illumination of faith can be said to darken the human intellect insofar as the supernatural mystery that is revealed is obscure to the mind by comparison with all natural knowledge. So Aquinas says, "We attribute to God the darkness of intangibility and invisibility insofar as he is light inaccessible, exceeding all [natural] light that we see, whether by the senses or by the intellect."[5]

Fourth, the darkness of God denotes the mystery of divine love. In creatures the capacity to love is something other than the capacity to know. Human love is determined from within by knowledge of the beloved, but it also moves one person to love another who remains always only partially understood and partially unknown. Consequently, love moves human reason from within toward a reality that reason does not fully comprehend. This is even more the case when one considers the love of God. God is entirely intelligible in himself. But his wisdom and love are infinitely superior to anything found in creatures and therefore evade our perfect understanding. So if the human heart must transcend the realm of

3. Gregory of Nyssa, *Life of Moses* 1.46 (Malherbe and Ferguson 1978).
4. Dionysius, *Mystical Theology*, chap. 1 (Luibhéid and Rorem 1987).
5. Aquinas, *In Div. Nom.* 7.3 (Pera 1950) (my translation).

total comprehension to pursue what is beloved in other creatures, this must be even more the case when it strives to possess God. "By night / I sought him whom my soul loves" (Song 3:1).

This darkness does not connote the mere absence of knowledge but is the sign of a corresponding divine illumination. Accordingly, the book of Exodus denotes the proximity to God by means of the symbols of light. "And the LORD went before them by day in a pillar of cloud to lead them along the way, and by night in a pillar of fire to give them light, that they might travel by day and by night" (Exod. 13:21). The Torah tells us that this light was present at the beginning of the world (Gen. 1:15, 17). Dionysius notes that the creation of physical light is affirmed to be "good" by God (Gen. 1:18) and so manifests the uncreated goodness of God, a goodness that is luminous.[6] When God commands the people of Israel to do what is right according to his law, he likewise enlightens them so that they may partake of his divine goodness.

> The precepts of the LORD are right,
>   rejoicing the heart;
> the commandment of the LORD is pure,
>   enlightening the eyes. (Ps. 19:8)

> Yea, thou dost light my lamp;
>   the LORD my God lightens my darkness. (Ps. 18:28)

Just as the darkness of God can be understood in a fourfold manner so also can the illumination of God be understood.

First, God illumines the minds of men through physical symbols and images drawn from creation. This is especially the case in the divine ordinations of the sacred liturgy, about which the book of Exodus is particularly concerned.

> Oh send out thy light and thy truth;
>   let them lead me,
> let them bring me to thy holy hill
>   and to thy dwelling! (Ps. 43:3)

As Aquinas states, "The condition of human nature ... is such that it has to be led by things corporeal and sensible to things spiritual and intelligible. Now it belongs to divine providence to provide for each one according as its condition

---

6. Dionysius, *Divine Names*, chap. 4.

requires. Divine wisdom, therefore, fittingly provides man with means of salvation, in the shape of corporeal and sensible signs that are called sacraments."[7] Accordingly, Exodus is in great part a book about the institution of the sacraments of the Old Law.

Second, the revelation of God provides a genuine enlightenment to natural human reason. God is "the God of Abraham, the God of Isaac, and the God of Jacob" (Exod. 3:6), but he is also the God of the philosophers. "In the beginning was the Logos" (John 1:1). God is the author of all human intellectual insight. Consequently, divine revelation respects every authentic facet of natural rationality, and it advances the cause of reason in all human cultures. The light of the Torah heals and elevates wounded human reason so that it may discover its own true dignity—both through the contemplation of God and through a complete consideration of the dimensions of the moral law. "And nations shall come to your light, / and kings to the brightness of your rising" (Isa. 60:3).

Third, faith is an illumination that communicates knowledge of the hidden identity and inner life of God. God in his incomprehensible darkness speaks to Moses personally and reveals himself from within the depths of his own being. "I am the One who is" (Exod. 3:14, my translation). Aquinas tells us that the formal object of faith "is nothing else than the First Truth." That is to say, by the light of supernatural faith we come to know in a quasi-immediate way who God truly is.[8] "For with thee is the fountain of life; / in thy light do we see light" (Ps. 36:9).

Fourth, faith illumines the human mind through love. Love creates a bond between the soul and God so that a kind of friendship is established. "My beloved is mine and I am his" (Song 2:16). The soul is given to sense by a spiritual instinct what pertains to the will of God and what is contrary to his will. In this way, the mind is enlightened from within by the movements of divine love; love can answer the question "why" with the gift of itself and thereby become a light to the beloved.

Now, three things should be said about this unique and ultimate form of illumination that pertains to faith.

First, it is a genuine light because it communicates truth about God, but it is simultaneously a light received through trust in the teaching of another, based upon an act of the will. Such knowledge therefore implies some degree of obscurity and darkness. The believer in this world lives simultaneously in both the *claritas* and the *obscuritas* of the faith.

---

7. *ST* 3.61.1. All citations of *ST*, unless otherwise indicated, are taken from the 1920 translation of the English Dominican Province (EDP 1947).
8. *ST* 2–2.1.1.

Second, this light implies an invitation to love, for love is at the heart of personal trust. In turn, love can cause the knowledge of God in us to grow more intense. Consequently, faith is a dynamic process that must develop or fail, depending on Israel's cooperation with love. This helps us understand both the absolute exigencies of the divine commands and the uncompromising response that Israel is expected to give (Exod. 20:6). Such commands and responses need to be understood in light of a deeper mystery of love. Such love is both given and reciprocated in darkness. Faith initiates, then, a new and strange kind of friendship between God and Israel. "Thus the LORD used to speak to Moses face to face, as a man speaks to his friend" (Exod. 33:11). It is a dangerous friendship in which Israel is placed at the mercy of God and continually risks rightful punishment or even death by God's hand (Exod. 4:14, 24). God is incomprehensible, but God is also more morally "sensitive" than man—and infinitely more just. To stand in the darkness of God, then, it is necessary to be illumined in regard to the presence of God's mercy. God proclaims "mercy" in saying his very name to Israel (Exod. 33:19). It is not an accident that the mercy seat of God is placed above the ark of God that contains the law. Believers who wish to progress into the knowledge of the inner life of God must proceed according to the customs of the divine mercy.

Third, this illumination of faith is ordered toward the eternal vision of God, a vision that is beatific.

> The sun shall be no more
>   your light by day,
> nor for brightness shall the moon
>   give light to you by night;
> but the LORD will be your everlasting light,
>   and your God will be your glory. (Isa. 60:19)

What begins for Israel in the exodus from Egypt culminates not in the physical land promised to Abraham, settled by Joshua, and ruled by David, but in the eschaton promised by the prophets. This final illumination consists in the immediate perception of the very life of God. The movement from Egypt to the land promised to Abraham is ultimately an outward symbol of a deeper and more ultimate journey of humanity into the knowledge of the very life of God.

The Torah was composed in order to induct Israelites into the life of faith that is described above. That life is dynamic. It is meant to introduce us into the darkness and obscurity, the illumination and light of the covenant with God. By this same measure it points forward to the mystery of Christ, who opens that same covenant to the Gentiles and so to the whole of humanity. It speaks to each soul, inviting him or her to leave the Egypt of this world—with its moral taint—so that purified, illumined, and protected by the rites of the true religion, that soul might serve God in this life and enter into the light of God in the next. It is these literal and spiritual senses of the book of Exodus that I will treat in this commentary.

The Divisions of the Book of Exodus

The book of Exodus begins with the Israelites in the darkness of slavery, as prisoners to a society of efficiency, cruelty, and idolatry. It finishes with the Israelites in the desert at Mount Sinai, as they enter into the light of God's covenant—recipients of God's laws and of the sacred worship of the tabernacle. As I shall soon make clear, this movement from Egypt into the desert and toward the promised land is a symbol of the Church, who is in pilgrimage in this world, through the power of the grace of Christ and in view of eternal life in the world to come.

The book of Exodus has five main parts.

Exodus 1–12 is concerned primarily with the *deliverance of Israel from Egypt*. First, we are given to see the need for the divine law, which is illustrated by the Egyptians' cruelty and moral blindness, itself reflective of the wider moral condition of humanity. Second, we are told that God is the Lord, who has revealed himself to Moses and commissioned him as his prophet. Third, the liberation of the Israelites from Egypt functions as a kind of catechesis regarding the identity of the Lord as the only true God and Creator of all that exists. Finally, the ceremony of the paschal lamb in Exod. 12 is meant to initiate the reader typologically into the ceremonial law of Judaism, which pertains to the cultic worship of God.

Exodus 13–18 is concerned with the experience of Israel in the *wilderness*, from the Red Sea to the foot of Mount Sinai. This section is meant to illustrate the exodus or going out of Israel from the Gentile nations as a preparation for their eventual instruction in the law and their entry into the land of Israel. This section of scripture is especially symbolic of the later life of Israel (and, by extension, the Church) as a people who must continually recognize their absolute dependence upon God as he sustains them throughout their history.

Exodus 19–24 takes place at Mount Sinai and is concerned with the giving of the *covenant and the law*. In Exod. 19, the central covenant between God and Israel is made manifest for the first time in the Torah. The ten most central precepts of the moral law are then given (the Ten Commandments) in Exod. 20. Exodus 21:1–24:11 spells out particular juridical laws for the governance of the people. Exodus 24:12–18 serves as a transition that closes the Book of the Covenant and prepares for the giving of the ceremonial and cultic laws of the tabernacle and temple.

Exodus 25–31 is concerned with the *cultic rituals* of the people of Israel. In them we are initiated into a theology of the ark and the tabernacle, of sacrifice and the priesthood, and of the accoutrements of Israelite religious ceremonies. This entire section is typologically indicative of the temple and the sacrifices of later Israelite religion, as well as of the one true sacrifice of Christ and the sacramental ceremonies of the New Law.

Exodus 32–40 is concerned with the *fall and restoration* of Israel, which takes place due to Israel's idolatrous worship of the golden calf in Exod. 32. Here we are instructed in the mystery of God's justice and mercy as he not only submits the people to judgment and punishment but also reveals himself as the merciful guardian of an eternal covenant with the people. In Exod. 33–34, the intercession and mediation of Moses are seen to be of central importance, as is the deepening understanding of the "name" of the Lord (3:14–15), which entails the attribute of divine mercy (34:6). In Exod. 34–35 the covenant is restored between God and the people, and in Exod. 36–40 the tabernacle is constructed according to the specifications initially commanded by God in Exod. 25–30 (prior to the golden calf incident). Consequently, the book of Exodus concludes with the people at the base of Mount Sinai, in the presence of the tabernacle. According to the terms of the covenant instituted by the Lord through the mediation of the prophet Moses, the Israelites are in true communion with God. They have passed from the slavery of Egypt to the freedom and nobility of being, in truth, a people uniquely chosen by God.

The Four Senses of Scripture

What does it mean to distinguish the "literal" and "spiritual" senses of scripture? This commentary regularly appeals to the classical distinction of literal, typological, moral, and anagogical senses—of which the latter three are deemed "spiritual." This fourfold distinction is traditional in Catholic thought, but the interpretation of its content is debated.[9] It is useful, then, to give an overview of the approach

9. For an overview of the medieval discussions, see Beryl Smalley, *The Study of the Bible in the Middle Ages* (Notre Dame, IN: University of Notre Dame Press, 1970); Ceslaus Spicq, *Esquisse d'une histoire de l'exégèse latine au Moyen Age* (Paris: Vrin, 1944); Henri de Lubac, *Exégèse médiévale: Les quatre sens de l'Écriture*, 4 vols. (Paris: Aubier, 1959–64).

taken in this commentary by discussing briefly the Thomistic theology of the "four senses" and how it may be applied to Exodus in a modern light, taking into account questions and approaches that arise from modern historical-critical study of the Torah.

Aquinas on the Four Senses of Scripture

This commentary interprets Exodus from within the Catholic Christian tradition. As such, it takes special inspiration from the theological insights of Thomas Aquinas. In a sense, the entire commentary is "Thomist" in character, with many references to Aquinas's theology throughout. This is not due uniquely to the fact that Aquinas commented extensively on the Old Law (though he did). More fundamentally, it stems from the fact that Aquinas is considered the *doctor communis*, or "common doctor," of Catholic theology—a figure of real, if limited, theological authority. Readers should take note that this appeal to the theology of Aquinas is not an exercise in the study of medieval commentary on scripture, nor is it an anachronistic projection of outdated forms of interpretation onto a modern intellectual landscape. The presupposition, rather, is that the theological principles of Thomism constitute a living tradition that has a central vitality in modern Catholic theology, one that engages fruitfully and decisively with typically modern concerns about faith and reason, as well as history and dogma.

My theological appeal to Aquinas begins with his theory of the four senses of scripture. Diverse theories proliferated in the medieval era, and Aquinas's understanding of the subject was fairly original. Subsequently, it has also been influential.[10]

As regards the literal sense, Aquinas makes two fundamental claims. First, the literal sense of the text of scripture pertains primarily to *the realities signified* by the human author of the text, under the inspiration of the Holy Spirit. That is to say, the literal meaning is to be found in the reality the text signifies or indicates.[11] It is not necessary that this reality be historical in kind. For example, if a text articulates a moral precept, then the literal sense of the text is a moral truth: "You shall not murder" (Exod. 20:13 NRSV). If the text directly signifies the eschatological age that is to come (as in Rev. 21–22), then it is the literal sense of the text that denotes this mystery. If the text is poetic, we might ask in turn,

---

10. Most recently, the 1992 *Catechism of the Catholic Church* makes use of Aquinas's theory, appealing specifically to *ST* 1.10.115–18. For analysis of Aquinas on this topic, see John F. Boyle, "St. Thomas Aquinas and Sacred Scripture," *Pro Ecclesia* 4 (1995): 92–104.

11. *ST* 1.1.10 corp.; Aquinas, *Quodlibet.* 7.6.2.

what does it refer to? In the Song of Songs, the literal sense pertains to the nature of human and divine love. In Exod. 15, the poetry signifies the historical event of the deliverance of Israel at the Red Sea.

Second, then, Aquinas claims that the spiritual sense of scripture is *always founded in the literal sense*. This idea is proposed in a complex manner. The literal sense denotes the realities themselves, by way of the inspired text of scripture. The realities themselves, meanwhile, are authored by God, the Creator of all that is and the Redeemer of humanity. Consequently, God can act in a way no human author does, making use of the realities themselves to signify, in turn, other realities. It is this meaning of things that gives rise to the spiritual senses of scripture denoted by the text.[12]

How, then, might we account for the distinctions of the senses of scripture that emerge? Here Aquinas distinguishes between the things that scripture denotes are to be believed and the things that scripture denotes are to be done. Insofar as the realities denoted in scripture act as exemplars for moral instruction (things to be done), they have a moral spiritual sense.

With regard to things to be believed, there is a twofold distinction. If the realities denoted by the literal sense prefigure historically or symbolize mystically things that are to come to pass later, then those realities have a sense that is either typological (also called "allegorical") or anagogical. They are typological when the realities in question denote realities pertaining to Christ and the Church. They are anagogical when they denote the eschatological life of the world to come. The distinction stems from the fact that the Church occupies a midway point between the old covenant and the dawn of the new life of the resurrection. Insofar as the Church stems from the old covenant and from Christ, it can be denoted typologically. Insofar as the Church is itself a sign and anticipatory presence of the life of the world to come, the Church and its teachings (in the New Testament) are indicative of the eschaton and can be interpreted anagogically. That is to say, if the reality signifies the mystery of eternal salvation or eternal damnation, it has an analogical sense. I read this broadly to mean that texts that relate to mystical union with the divine also have an anagogical sense, insofar as they prefigure the final union that is to come in the blessedness of the beatific vision.

12. *ST* 1.1.10: "So, whereas in every other science things are signified by words, this science has the property, that the things signified by the words have themselves also a signification. Therefore that first signification whereby words signify things belongs to the first sense, the historical or literal. That signification whereby things signified by words have themselves also a signification is called the spiritual sense, which is based on the literal, and presupposes it."

So, for example, the account in Exod. 32 of the intercession of Moses on behalf of the people who have sinned is meant to denote literally a reality in Israel's past. But it can also be seen typologically as a prefiguration of Christ, who prays for all of humanity on the Cross, or of the Church, who prays for the salvation of human beings from sin and death. The crossing of the Red Sea in Exod. 13 also denotes literally an event in Israel's past. However, it is employed by the New Testament in Rev. 4:6 as an image of the blessed who stand on the far side of the divide between heaven and earth. Their Passover has led them into the eternal life of God. On this reading, the spiritual sense of Exod. 13 is clearly anagogical and denotes the mystery of eternal life.

It follows from this understanding of the spiritual senses that the Old Testament and the entire life of Christ will typically have four senses. One might question how the moral sense in the Old Testament can be figurative or how the life of Christ might be typological. However, even when the old covenant simply espouses a moral teaching (as the literal sense), this teaching is anticipatory or typologically prefigurative of the recapitulation of the moral law given within the new covenant, by Christ and the apostles. Even when Christ is seen to act in history as the culmination of typologies in the old covenant (in the literal sense of the Gospels), his mystery prefigures typologically in some way the life of the Church. Moral teachings in the New Testament, meanwhile, are anticipatory of the life of glory that is to come, and so they retain an anagogical sense. Only teachings that pertain directly to the eschaton have no other sense than literal because they denote a state that is final and cumulative.

This Thomistic account of biblical interpretation is significant for understanding the finality or ultimate purpose of scriptural inspiration. First, the teaching of the Old Testament has an integral literal signification that must be explored for its own sake. Even within the Hebrew scriptures themselves, however, various texts clearly seek typologically to indicate realities of history that emerge subsequent to one another, so as to demonstrate a pattern of divine intervention. As such, the exodus is understood typologically to foreshadow the exile of Israel in Babylon. The events of the life of Israel foreshadow a definitive eschatological intervention of God, foretold in books such as Isaiah and Daniel. Likewise, then, the events of the Old Testament indicate obscurely and typologically the mystery of the incarnation, passion, death, and resurrection of Christ, as well as the mystery of the Church. The life of the early Church in Acts prefigures the subsequent life of the Church in the postapostolic age, and the whole economy of salvation in both the Old Testament and the New contains prophetic teaching and sacraments that signify the life of the world to come.

In this way, the finality of scriptural revelation and the finality of the grace of supernatural faith are seen to converge. The grace of faith is given to human beings as an anticipation of the immediate vision of God promised in the world to come.[13] First and foremost, it gives us understanding of who God is in himself, but it also permits us to understand creatures in light of God.[14] It teaches us by an inward instinct how to act practically as disciples of Christ and members of his body the Church.[15] Correspondingly, inspired scripture is given to us to nourish our faith, hope, and charity in view of union with God in the life to come. Scripture teaches the knowledge of the identity of God and allows us to understand creatures in light of God. Scripture functions practically, teaching us to live as disciples of Christ by the grace of the Holy Spirit and to avoid all actions that separate us from God and his Church.

Obviously this spiritual reading of scripture should not be employed so as to obscure or ignore the many nuanced and difficult historical and textual topics that modern exegesis brings to light. However, it is a unifying principle for understanding the ultimate purpose of the book of the Bible as a vehicle for divine instruction and grace in the larger life of the Church.

The Literal Sense: Is the Exodus about a Historical Event?

How, then, might we make use of this Thomistic vision of the inspired character of scripture and its several senses when considering the book of Exodus in a modern context? After all, historical-critical study of the Torah suggests with warrant that there are many literary sources within the text, that these stem from diverse traditions with complex histories, and that the work of multiple editors lies behind the book as we have it today.

One way to focus this question is to ask if the literal sense of Exodus, taken in a general way, pertains to a historical event. Or is it primarily a literary construction that serves as a vast metaphor for the Israelite experience of exile in Babylon in the sixth century BC? Without seeking to radically oppose these two options, I lean decidedly toward the former view.

Here I follow moderately conservative modern exegetes and historians such as Roland de Vaux (most especially), Marie-Joseph Lagrange, Walther Eichrodt, and Brevard S. Childs. I take it that the genesis of the ancient Israelite religion

---

13. *ST* 2–2.1.4.
14. *ST* 2–2.1.1.
15. *ST* 2–2.7.2, 2–2.8.1 and 3, 2–2.9.1 and 3.

was due to a movement of slaves that left Egypt, perhaps late in the thirteenth century BC; this movement was led by a seminal religious leader and legislator who provided an initial religious identity and corporate organization. Theologically speaking, the Christian tradition holds that this figure, Moses, was inspired by God as an instrument of revelation to initiate a new monotheistic religion that would eventually have universal import for all humanity. Likewise, I believe in a historical settlement of the land of "Israel" by this people, which gave rise to an eventual tribal confederation and monarchy. This people had a complex social and religious history that is difficult to reconstruct theoretically with certitude. However, we do know a great deal about many of its core beliefs and stable features. The people of Israel were clearly affected in diverse times and places by religious syncretism. Nevertheless, despite all of this complexity, elements of the original exodus tradition were maintained, expanded, and commented upon, presumably and primarily by priests and scribes over the course of hundreds of years.

This movement saw itself as emerging from an original inspiration and leader, but it was also periodically affected by new prophetic revelation, which served to expand the tradition organically and reorient the people of Israel in new circumstances of history. Over time this gave rise to a more ornate and complex theology, bodies of law, customs, and sacerdotal practices. This same tradition had numerous crises and was especially subject to self-examination during the time of the Babylonian exile. During this time and perhaps just afterward, various bodies of law and primal traditions, which had been previously composed, were gathered together and formed coherently into the Torah as we have it today. Exodus is a book, then, composed of diverse, ancient textual sources written largely within the preexilic era, with some elements dating back to the original Mosaic movement itself. These sources may well differ in age but also contain elements of ancient tradition. Consequently, I take the book of Exodus to be a hybrid of traditions but also in some way reflective of ancient events.

Modern scholars since the nineteenth century have typically postulated the possibility of four main bodies of textual tradition in the Torah, based upon the main divisions of the Graf-Wellhausen hypothesis. The Elohist source material is thought to be a mid-ninth-century-BC body of material redacted and reformulated by priests in northern Israel after the settlement, following the early Mosaic movement. The Yahwist source is believed to be a redaction and representation of traditional material that took place in the eighth century BC, during the early stages of the monarchy of the kingdom of Judah. The Deuteronomical material (mostly found in the book of Deuteronomy, though not exclusively) is associated with the religious reformation that took place in seventh- and sixth-century BC Israel prior to the Babylonian exile. The Priestly material is associated with the postexilic priests of the sixth century BC, who were concerned with the preservation and reformulation of Judaism in the wake of the destruction of the first temple of Solomon. One may very well hold to the Graf-Wellhausen hypothesis while also maintaining the following points as historically likely. First, each of these "sources" are postulated not in definitive, fixed terms but rather as likely hypotheses that help us understand in realistic and reasonable terms the conceptual, linguistic, and editorial layering of the text of the Torah. Second, each of these purported "sources" is composed of traditions and can contain much older materials dating back to original events, or stemming from those events. Third, the notion of "sources" is not exclusive to only the four mentioned above, and there can be a broader set of influences in the text as we have it today. Fourth, theologians should make use of hypothetical notions of textual sources with a degree of epistemological reserve since such theories are ultimately unverifiable and are based on conjectures of historical likelihood.

For the purposes of this commentary, I presume a moderate position on historical sources that does not depend essentially upon the definitive truth of any one theory. Some scholars dispute the value of the Graf-Wellhausen hypothesis in an effort to claim that all or most of the material in the Torah is of a much earlier origin, derived from Moses and his initial circle of followers. While I do believe there is material in the Torah that derives from the earliest historical period (including the possibility of Mosaic authorship of some sections), I also think it is evident from any close reading that the text contains a multiplicity of sources. The same events or laws are often recounted several times from different vantage points, even in separate books. Singular events are reported by means of a collage of traditions that have been spliced together. It does not seem to me that the admission of sources in the text in any way compromises a basic commitment to the underlying historicity or inspired character of the Mosaic movement and its universal, world-historical importance.

Meanwhile, other scholars (mostly contemporary) dispute the Documentary Hypothesis on the grounds that it is too artificial and that there are innumerable traditions present in the Torah, most of which were forged together at a later date, in the sixth to fourth century BC, without any real correlation to ancient events that happened at the actual time of the exodus. This viewpoint seems to me not only entirely unverifiable but also excessively skeptical. It is a fool's errand to set out to prove in negative terms that what is purported in scripture as a record of very ancient history must never have happened. Such affirmations can never be demonstrated and may result at most in the skeptical admission that the modern historian cannot say with certitude if something in the past really took place or not. As for the division of the text of scripture, the discernment is more literary than historical in kind. Does there seem to be a set of themes and vocabulary that one might reasonably associate with the Yahwist school as distinct from the Deuteronomist school? It seems to me that one can reasonably perceive patterns in the text according to these "traditional" modern divisions of the Documentary Hypothesis. At the same time, this should be thoroughly qualified. For the purposes of this commentary, I am not presuming the definite validity of the Documentary Hypothesis. On the contrary, my two basic presuppositions are more modest. First, I presume that what is recounted in Exodus has some basis in real events of ancient history. Second, I assume that there are sources in the text and that the text has been heavily redacted so as to show how the ancient event is symbolic of the later historical and spiritual life of the people of Israel. One should note that these two presuppositions could, in principle, be maintained according to any of the three theories mentioned above, which include the early authorship of the Torah by a collection of scribes around Moses, the Documentary Hypothesis (according to a diversity of modalities of qualification), or the later redaction of ancient materials at the time of the Babylonian exile and thereafter.

As for the events of the exodus itself, I take it that there were ancient Hebrews living in Egypt who came to be politically oppressed by the Egyptian government. Some of them were liberated through the "prophetic" work of Moses, a self-designated religious leader who took it upon himself to act on behalf of the people. I believe theologically that there were *mirabilia Dei* involved in the liberation of the people from Egypt, though the character of these divine interventions is difficult to perceive with clarity given the heavily symbolic and markedly folkloric character of elements of the Exodus text. The people liberated did travel in the Sinai Peninsula for an extended time period and were subject to an internal religious ferment, which was characterized by a set of legislative and cultic initiatives on the part of their leaders. I take it then that some of the traditions in the last four books of the Torah do reflect information and belief that come down from the original movement. As for realities that can be attributed directly to Moses, I think it likely that the divine name, the Ten Commandments, the ark, some kind of tent of meeting, and the notion of a covenant with the Lord all stem directly from him.

All this being said, I also take it for granted that the Torah is formed in great part from later tradition, with influences from the ages of the settlement, monarchy, Deuteronomical reform, and the exile. In the redacted text, the event of the exodus is undoubtedly portrayed as prefigurative of the later life of Israel. This means that the events are often depicted in largely symbolic and typological terms and are meant to signify the later religious and cultic life of the people of Israel. The most obvious example in this respect is the tabernacle in the wilderness, which is depicted typologically throughout Exodus as a sign of the temple in Jerusalem. Consequently, the "history" in question is often iconic in kind. It contains elements that may be taken literally to signify historical events, but it also clearly contains elements that are powerfully archetypal, or symbolic, which are meant to denote the perennial mystery of God's covenant with Israel. Moreover, the narrative of the exodus, insofar as it is historical, has a decidedly archaic form. Consequently, we should be cautious when ascribing historical foundations to the event (which I believe we should) and make sure to consider that the mode of signifying history is very different than the mode used in modern or even ancient Greco-Roman history, as is characteristic of the New Testament.

One may ask what gives rise to this extraordinary list of convictions. Here I would like to make clear that what I have just spelled out in the previous paragraphs is presented out of respect to the reader. All interpreters have deep-seated theological (or a-theological) as well as philosophical, exegetical, and historical judgments that inform their work. Stating these clearly is not meant to prohibit other views but rather to make reasoned argument possible. My own views are affected by a combination of theological beliefs about Christian revelation, philosophical views about monotheism, and exegetical and historical judgments that derive from a limited but conscientious textual study of the Bible with the aid of modern exegesis. Although my standpoint is undoubtedly conservative by contemporary standards and the theology in this volume is deeply Catholic in nature, there is no animus toward historical-critical exegesis in this commentary. On the contrary, I am well-disposed toward that field and believe very much in its necessity, even if I also *do not believe* that it is a form of study that operates in pure scientific autonomy, unaffected by any theological views (or lack thereof), or independently from profound philosophical convictions (which are always inevitable, even in the most naïve interpreter).

My basic reasons for treating the exodus as a foundational historical event in the life of ancient Israel derive both from the Catholic faith and from natural reason.

From faith, due to the principles of Christology revealed in the New Testament: The Catholic Church teaches that God has become a man, living in history as a true human being with a human soul and physical body. If God has become incarnate in time and in flesh, then it is only fitting to believe that the Old Testament that bears witness to the mystery of Christ prefiguratively is also grounded in a physical history, albeit one that we know only imperfectly. Here one might make a christological parallel: Irenaeus's understanding of Christ lies at a midpoint between the gnosticism of Valentinus and the "materialism" of the Ebionites. The gnostics retain a spiritual meaning in regard to the event of Christ's life but evacuate the mystery of all physicality and historicity. The Ebionites insist on the fundamental human reality of Jesus but are unable to maintain sufficiently the divinity of the Christ and the inner spiritual nature of Old Testament law. Analogously speaking, one can say that the historical character of the Torah is understood, theologically, in an all too gnostic way, particularly if the document is evacuated of virtually all historicity and understood merely symbolically. Against this view, we must say that the Word has become flesh, beginning with the patriarchs and continuing with the exodus, as a genuine historical event. However, an "Ebionite" literalism that ignores the multiple layers of symbol, typology, and archetype is also unrealistic and overly literalist or materialist. The Torah is primarily given to us not to determine precise historical facts about an ancient event but to introduce us into the mystery of the covenant of God with Israel. The christological balance we are seeking is to understand the divine revelation of God and his law taking place in and through a true historical event, grounded in the flesh, but this event must be understood spiritually in light of God's enduring covenant with Israel through time. Much of the significance of the exodus event was understood retrospectively in light of subsequent prophecy. This spiritual sense of the events is often given to us in the Torah in a highly symbolic form, fashioned by those who transmitted earlier traditions, interpreted them prescriptively, and edited them into a unity. The word is present in the flesh truly, but a materialistic reflection on the factual "flesh" of Israelite history, while warranted and necessary, is not sufficient. One must enter into the deeper "spirit" of the Torah, which is its perennial significance as a revelation of God given to the people of Israel.

A word should be said here regarding metaphysics. At multiple points in this commentary I presume that the text of Exodus literally denotes truths about the mystery of God that are metaphysical or ontological in kind, pertaining to the divine names: God's omnipotence, aseity, and the like. "Literally" here should be understood in a particular way, based primarily upon the object signified rather than the mode of signification. One can denote the attributes of God by use of a metaphor, such as God turning his "back" toward Moses in Exod. 33:23–34:7. Metaphors and intuitive concepts are often pregnant with ontological signification and give rise to subsequent, distinctively philosophical reflection. Consequently, the reader should not be surprised that I will often employ the interpretations of Aquinas or other metaphysical readers of scripture to interpret the text. I do not take this to be a naïve anachronism projected back onto the text. There are implicitly ontological notions latent throughout Exodus that form a central theme in the book. Patristic and medieval theological tradition rightly paid attention to this theme. The presumption, then, is that there exists an organic tradition of reflection on the nature of God both within scripture and subsequent to it, from the Old Testament prophets to the time of the apostles to the modern era. In saying this I am following in my own way the thinking of John Henry Newman on the development of doctrine. Because this is a work of Catholic theology, the interpretations offered make no pretension to being prescriptively normative, but they do presuppose the perennial truth of Catholic doctrine, as well as the possibility of profound coherence between the teaching of scripture, classical Catholic tradition, and the reflections of modern theology.

There are also motives of natural reason to believe in an ancient origin of the Israelite religion by way of the exodus. I will briefly list some of these reasons.

First, it is clear to any mindful reader that the text of the Torah is not merely the product of a postexilic scribal workshop or the product of a single, late-ancient author. The text contains many obvious non sequiturs, stylistic differences, and alternative versions of the same events. Sometimes the latter have clearly been combined or spliced together. The laws of the Torah show strong literary indications of deriving from diverse times and historical settings. An analogy is helpful here: the differences between the four canonical Gospels demonstrate that they cannot all be the work of one person, and yet they share between them preexisting traditions they each received. Likewise, the layers of text in the Torah demonstrate the existence of numerous traditions regarding Moses, his legislation, and the exodus event that were prior to the final redaction. Furthermore, the exodus is referred to clearly by early prophets like Micah and Hosea, the Elijah narratives, a great number of the psalms, and other later prophets. Consequently, we should presume reasonably the existence of some kind of event behind the independent witnesses of so many diverse and independent traditions.

Second, the religion of Israel is striking for its coherence and originality. Many argue that there is a polytheistic or syncretistic religious history hiding behind the text of the Old Testament that has been censored by the later editors. Even if we allow for elements of truth to this theory (due to the syncretism of Yahwism in the earlier epochs), it is impossible to avoid the impression of the Old Testament as a thematically unified text having many core theological themes of a deeply original character. Over the course of hundreds of years, the ancient Israelites clearly maintained the conviction that they had been chosen to have a unique relationship with God, who made an exclusive claim on them as a people. In light of their perseverant convictions about God, they believed themselves warranted to subject the religious behavior of their neighbors and themselves to extreme critique, despite being subjected by superior national powers to severe oppression and persecution for their beliefs. Judging simply from the perspective of natural reason, historical movements with this degree of coherence and intensity are unlikely to come about without a powerful underlying conception that unifies them, and it is simpler to attribute this stimulus to the Mosaic movement (to which the Bible itself ascribes it historically) than to try to identify it elsewhere in some invisible historical agent who remains largely unknown.

Similarly, there is a judgment from philosophical reason. The Torah presents us with an extremely elevated monotheistic understanding of God, one that purifies human reason of all false deification of the physical universe as well as the human political realm. It also contains a profound, noble, and very beautiful moral teaching that has greatly affected the whole of humanity (especially through the medium of Christianity). There is no presence in ancient Greek philosophy of many of the profound insights formulated in the Torah hundreds of years before the epoch of Socrates, Plato, and Aristotle. To this day, the Torah, when rightly understood, casts a ray of enlightenment upon human reason that frees human beings from superstition and idolatry and turns them toward authentic religious and ethical behavior. Consequently, it is reasonable to perceive in the formulation of the Torah no mere historical accident but a kind of profoundly inspired work of God meant to benefit the whole of the human race.

The Typological Sense: The Old Law Prefigures Christ and the Church

In the Catholic tradition, the word "typological" is often used synonymously with the word "allegorical." I employ the former term consistently, in part to distinguish the practices of this commentary from so-called allegorical readings that depart freely from the literal sense of the text. Typological interpretations ought to be well grounded, as Aquinas notes, in the literal sense of scripture.

They may denote how one historical event foreshadows another, but they need not. Often the events of Exodus are portrayed typologically so as to communicate a claim about the ongoing workings of God's grace in the covenant with Israel, and so they foreshadow typologically the life of the elect people that unfolds subsequently. When the Israelites struggle with the Amalekites in Exod. 17 or when Moses is given counsel by Jethro the Midianite priest in Exod. 18, these figures are traditionally seen within Judaism to represent diverse relationships between Israel and the Gentile peoples. Consequently, one's sense of what is typological can be fairly broad because the literal sense of scripture is similarly broad in meaning. That being said, typological reading ought not to drift into a use of allegory that is more or less arbitrary and unconnected from the literal sense of scripture.

Typological readings of scripture can be better understood as both textually warranted and theologically profound precisely because of modern exegesis. Historical-critical interpretation heightens one's sensitivity to natural causalities of authorship that lie behind a given text and to the role that presupposed traditions or beliefs play in the work of human authors. Consequently, modern readings make us more sensitive to the ways that earlier events are often being "reread" by human authors in light of later events, in either the composition of the texts themselves or in their redaction and editing. When Hosea enjoins Judah to "return" to fidelity to God, he makes allusion to an idealized relationship that existed between God and Israel in the wilderness, demonstrating that he has knowledge of some kind of prior tradition (Hos. 12–14). When the Torah is given its final redacted form, the exodus is seen as a prefiguration of the exile. The Gospel of Matthew repeatedly depicts Jesus of Nazareth as a new Moses, who recapitulates in his own life the mysteries of Exodus. Paul makes generous use of typologies in his letters to explain the sense of the Hebrew scripture in light of Christ. The Bible, then, is riddled through with typology. It is a thematic constant that every genuine interpreter must confront.

To this a key theological premise must be added: the belief that the texts of scripture are aligned not only by the ingenuity of human authors but also by the primal causation of God the Holy Spirit. That is to say, God has acted in history to reveal himself and has given a supernatural inspiration to the prophets and apostles to understand in their faith and to communicate truly in their teaching the inward meaning of history and of divine revelation as intended by God. The typologies elaborated by human authors and editors reflect a divine intention to communicate to us divine truth.

It is true that a Christian reading of the typologies of the Old Testament can render obscure the original literal sense of the text, so that the interpreter ignores what the sacred author actually intended to say. However, this need not be the case. On the one hand, the Old Testament books are themselves compiled alongside one another by a harmonious yet open-ended alignment of typologies. The Old Testament prophets are so fundamentally eschatological that their teaching calls out for a resolution beyond itself. This "openness" can be understood in ways that do no violence to the integrity of the Old Testament as revelation but that suggest its integral completion by the New Testament revelation. On the other hand, the New Testament itself provides the main interpretive keys for understanding the "fulfillment" of the types so that the Old Testament is not jettisoned but reactualized in a new way within the Christian era, at the heart of the life of the Church. Indeed, the Old Testament continues to speak to the Church not only about the past but also of the eschaton and in this way actively reveals to the Church what is yet to come, even in the light of Christ.

The Moral Sense: Christian Ethical Teaching in the Old Testament

Catholic theology traditionally divides the laws in the Torah into "moral," "ceremonial," and "juridical" categories. In this commentary, I employ this distinction thematically. The moral laws of the Torah are understood to be of perennial importance within Christianity—particularly the Ten Commandments as reinterpreted and interiorized by Christ and the apostles. The ceremonial law is abrogated by the coming of Christ, his death and resurrection, and the institution of the sacraments of the New Law. These ceremonies foreshadow the mystery of Christ and the Church but also cease to have their living function once Christ appears, who in a real sense supersedes them. The juridical precepts, which concern concrete judgments or social punishments for serious transgressions, are understood by most Christian commentators not only to be inherently morally defensible but also to stem from a particular people and epoch in an ancient social setting. They are sometimes very stern and centered around an ethic of strict religious justice, which is tempered only moderately by clemency. They are historically provisional in nature and need not be adopted in subsequent times and places, but they do contain an inward spiritual content that continues to inspire our moral understanding.

Some modern commentators criticize this distinction, claiming either that it is an arbitrary imposition of divisions from a later era or that it is anti-Judaic and

fails to take seriously the teachings of the Torah on its own terms. To my thinking, both of these claims are seriously erroneous. First, the traditional Christian
analysis of the Torah is grounded in the New Testament revelation itself. In the
teaching of Christ and the apostles, many elements of moral law from the Torah
are retained and intensified. The basic laws of cleanliness and uncleanliness, as well
as the temple rituals, are said to be abrogated or sublimated-by-fulfillment in the
mystery of Christ. Many practical civic judgments and punishments prescribed
by the Torah are seen not to apply to Christians (both Jewish and Gentile) living
under the laws of the Roman Empire.

Moreover, it should be noted that while the Christian interpretation of the
Torah can act as a source of division between Christians and Jews, it is also this
classical interpretation that binds the Church most closely to the people of Israel.
Principally through the Church the Torah has become a "light to all the nations,"
especially in its moral components, and it is in great part due to this profound
connection that Christians and Jews may find ways not only to understand one
another theologically but also to cooperate practically. Talmudic Judaism itself has
ceased to celebrate the parts of the ceremonial laws associated with sacrifice and
the temple and has adapted many of the juridical precepts to the later political,
Gentile epochs in which the Jewish people have lived, in part through a kind of
spiritual interpretation of these precepts. Consequently, the classical Catholic
approach to the moral law of Exodus is in many ways convergent with that of
Judaism, even if there are many nontrivial differences that remain irreducible.
Ecumenism is about recognizing differences as well as similitudes, and the careful
reader will notice that throughout this commentary there is an attempt to engage
in a sustained Catholic theological appreciation of the significance of the Old
Law, Judaism, and the mystery of Israel.

It may surprise some readers, particularly those of a more historical-critical
formation, that I interpret the Ten Commandments in this volume in light of
the contemporary teaching magisterium of the Catholic Church. Furthermore, I
claim that in some real sense this modern Catholic teaching represents the literal
sense of Exodus. This may seem like a historically infeasible affirmation, but I offer
a theological argument for why I take this path of interpretation. Aquinas affirms
that the Ten Commandments (Exod. 20) present what he calls "second-order"
precepts of the moral law.[16] Since human beings can fail to understand or believe
them, they are not inevitably known to human reason, but they are fairly intuitive

16. *ST* 1–2.100.3.

notions that emerge readily from rightly ordered moral reflection. They give rise, in turn, to "third-order" precepts that are more nuanced and developed, which follow organically and logically from them. For example, from the precept that it is always wrong to murder (to take innocent human life) one can derive the precept that it is wrong to take innocent human life at any stage, from conception to natural death. This latter teaching is implied logically by the former, if the former is applied in a consistent and informed manner. Understood in this way, the Torah reveals profound truths of the natural law that may be eclipsed in human culture due to the effects of original and personal sin. However, a developed understanding of this teaching has often taken place gradually, especially in the light of Christian revelation and in the life of the Catholic Church, herself safeguarded and illumined by the Holy Spirit. Therefore, I am working under the presupposition of the moral legitimacy of the ecclesial use of the moral law of the Torah within a Christian landscape.

The Anagogical Sense: The Passover of Israel and the Church into the Eternal Glory of God

The mystical, or anagogical, dimension of scripture is omnipresent and is the "last word" in scriptural interpretation. One might suspect appeals to the anagogical sense are in some way arbitrary and may be projected onto the text extrinsically. Rightly understood, however, the anagogical sense is that which is the most concrete, and in a certain way, that which is most purely identical with the literal sense. The reason for this, as Aquinas notes, is that the spiritual senses are always grounded in the literal sense, but the literal sense pertains to the realities themselves of the economy of salvation. What is most essential to the economy of salvation is the presence of God's divinizing grace acting in human souls. Without this grace there is no salvation history. At its deepest level, the covenant between God and Israel consists "formally" in the mystery of union between man and God, made possible by faith, hope, and love. When Moses is depicted as "seeing God" in Exod. 34, the deepest literal sense of this event is mystical or anagogical. That is to say, it depicts God's intention to unite human beings to himself by grace, bespeaking a deeper mystery of divine inhabitation present among the people of Israel. The text is not merely information. More profoundly, it acts as an invitation to the interior life, as a way of living in covenant with the God of Israel by that same grace denoted in the text.

Furthermore, the revelation given is always teleologically oriented in kind. This formal or essential mystery of union with God, which lies just beneath the surface of the literal sense, is always oriented toward an eschatological horizon. God chose the Hebrew people in ancient Egypt *in view of* the covenant, the elaboration of ancient Judaism, and the formation of the Torah. God inspired the prophets in ancient Israel *in view of* the mystery of the eschaton and the fulfillment of the covenant in Christ. God became human and suffered, died and was buried, rose from the dead in his human nature, and established the Church *in view of* the historical economy of the Christian people and the universal preaching of the possibility of salvation to all the world. The mystery of the Church was established *in view of* the eschaton, and the invitation given to each human being to see God face-to-face and to be raised from the dead to eternal life.

Consequently, the life of grace present in humanity from Abraham to John the Baptist is unitive: it invites the saints of the older covenant into friendship with God. This friendship is implicitly oriented toward Christ and eschatological in its horizon: it leads toward the divinizing life of the beatific vision and the bodily resurrection from the dead. The anagogical sense of scripture, then, is that which is most ultimate and eschatological in nature, as well as that which is most profound or essential. The work of grace in humanity is at the heart of the covenant, but this same work of grace is ordered toward the glorification and transformation of human existence.

When I speak of mystical union in this commentary, the sense of the term is both personal and collective, both actual and eschatological; it pertains to both soul and body. Often I do not overtly distinguish between these different senses of union with God. They are presumed to be interrelated. Union with God in ancient Israel was implicitly related to union with God in Christ. Salvation of the individual is always related in some way to corporate salvation, since our union with Christ relates us intrinsically to his mystical body, the Church. The illumination of the soul and its unitive love for God cannot be divorced from the mystery of the resurrection of the dead and the glorification of the body. Here I am simply presupposing the teaching of the New Testament: that all grace given to human beings, no matter where in the history of the divine economy, is in some way Christ-conforming. Those who live in friendship with God are initiated in some way into union with the life, death, and resurrection of the Son of God, either by way of anticipation (in ancient Israel) or by way of consummation (in the life of the Church). In both ways, the people of God approach the mystery of the Cross and find in it not only their true Passover but also the passage through the sea of this world into that land where God is king forever.

1

DELIVERANCE FROM EGYPT

Exodus 1–12

Pharaoh, Genocide, and Universal Moral Weakness (Exod. 1)

1:1–7 "These are the names of the sons of Israel who went down into Egypt with Jacob" (1:1).

The book of Exodus seeks to portray how the people of Israel became God's own chosen people through their deliverance from Egypt and by a divinely instituted covenant articulated to them through a prophet. Consequently, the opening passage of the book unites the narrative of the people of Israel in Egypt with the prehistory of the patriarchs. It is from this particular people—descendants of Abraham, Isaac, and Jacob—that God will draw forth his elect.

In addition, the book here joins the story of the covenant with the fundamental revelation of the creation of the world in Genesis. The gift of the law occurs against the backdrop of the creation of the physical universe and of the human person made in the image of God as well as the fall of humanity into ignorance of God, which stems from an original disobedience of God's commandments. In this light, the covenant with Israel appears as a gift that repairs the relationship of the human race with God and thus the creation as a whole.

Typologically, Nachmanides says that the descent of Israel into Egypt in the families of the patriarchs prefigures the later exile of the people of Israel into Babylon.[1] This seems to accord with the intention of the final editors of the Torah. First Abraham goes down into Egypt (Gen. 12:10–20) and returns again, prefiguring the subsequent history of Moses and the Hebrews. The subsequent exodus from Egypt prefigures the Babylonian exile. From its inception, Israel lives in this world precariously amidst the powers of the world that may corrupt its calling to fidelity to the law. This allows the faith of the Israelites to shine through amidst the vulnerability of their temporal existence and gives ongoing witness to the power of God to sustain them in history as a sign to the nations.

This descent also foreshadows the voyage into Egypt of Joseph and Mary with the child Jesus (Matt. 2:14–15). The Christ, who is the fulfillment of the mystery of Israel, is taken down into Egypt, recapitulating that mystery in himself. This fulfills the prophecy of Hos. 11:1: "Out of Egypt I called my Son." He who is naturally the Son of God, both God and man, is perfect in his human obedience to the law. He is the source of the grace of adoptive sonship for all other members of the covenant.

Anagogically, this descent represents the souls of men who go down into the material things of this world, living only by sensible knowledge and temporal desires. "Their dead bodies will lie in the street of the great city which is allegorically called Sodom and Egypt, where their Lord was crucified" (Rev. 11:8). Such men must be drawn up out of Egypt and into the life of God by the deliverance of the law and by the redemptive mystery of Christ.

1:8–14 "Now there arose a new king over Egypt, who did not know Joseph" (1:8).

It is reasonable to conjecture from both historical and archeological arguments that the setting of this event might be in the thirteenth century BC, at the beginning of the nineteenth dynasty under Seti I (1308–1290 BC) and Rameses II (1290–1224 BC).[2] At that time the Pharaohs moved their capital from Thebes to Rameses (mentioned in 1:11). The Hebrews of the region presumably came to be seen in a new way as a threat to Egyptian political security. Harsh forms of enforced manual labor were enjoined upon them. The portrayal of these practices in Exodus appears to be consistent with what is otherwise known about practices of that time.[3]

1. Nachmanides, *Commentary on the Torah: Exodus*, preface.
2. De Vaux 1978: 1:388–92.
3. De Vaux 1978: 1:324–27.

The Pharaoh in question is not named in scripture perhaps because his name had been forgotten by the people of Israel down through time or because someone wished to exert a kind of literary discretion. Whatever may be the case, the omission of the Pharaoh's name has the effect of making him a kind of symbol. "Thus the LORD has said, 'I revealed myself to the house of your father when they were in Egypt subject to the house of Pharaoh'" (1 Sam. 2:27). Subsequent Christian tradition understands this biblical symbol of the Pharaoh to stem from the intention of the Holy Spirit. What, then, does he represent?

According to the moral sense of scripture, the Pharaoh is representative of the human person under the influence of excessive pride, that is, an "inordinate desire of one's own excellence."[4] In its most exaggerated forms, pride can lead to "a perverted imitation of God. For pride hates a fellowship of equality under God and seeks to impose its own dominion on fellow men in place of God's rule."[5] Ironically, this terrible possibility exists precisely because of the innately spiritual nature of humanity. Because the human person is made in the image of God, he or she is capable of knowing and desiring the universal good, God himself. Consequently, human beings are also capable of wanting to be like God in ways that transcend the authentic scope of their nature and that are morally distended and unjust.

This tendency is clearly embodied in the Exodus narrative, for the Pharaoh presumes that he has authority to impose unjust political and economic practices upon others, that he has the authority to take innocent human life, and that he may, based on his religious designation, impede the divinely mandated religious activity of others. This attitude is consistent with much of the archaic religion of man, in which the head of state was thought to be an extension of the divinity. It is also consistent with the activity of many human governments in modernity in which human beings do not believe they are divine but either ignore the divine altogether or fail to respect the rights of the Church, which is of divine origin. Such governments may traffic in unjust legal and economic practices, permit or promote the destruction of innocent human life, or trample upon the freedom of the true religion.

Typologically, the Pharaoh represents the powers of the world that strive to eradicate the chosen people, Israel, through the use of temporal power and spiritual intimidation. He is a precursor of the Babylonian Empire that took Israel captive, but also of the Roman Empire at the time of Christ, which persecuted

4. *ST* 2–2.162.2.
5. Augustine, *City of God* 19.12 (Bettenson 1972).

both Israel and the early Church. Thus he represents the powers of the world that oppose the spiritual good of the elect, and the Church.

Anagogically, the symbol of the Pharaoh represents man who resists the truth about God, which introduces the theme of divine reprobation. Paul makes this explicit in his letter to the Romans. "For the scripture says to Pharaoh, 'I have raised you up for the very purpose of showing my power in you, so that my name may be proclaimed in all the earth'" (Rom. 9:17). However, the scriptures teach that God never reprobates a human being unless that person first culpably abandons God, and God is never the cause of moral evil, either directly or indirectly. "Your destruction is your own, O Israel. / Your help is only in me" (Hos. 13:9, my translation). "The omnipotent God wishes 'all men' without exception 'to be saved' (1 Tim. 2:4), even if not all are saved; that some, however, perish is the fault of those who perish."[6] God uses the actions of those who resist the grace and truth of God in order to further glorify his own goodness, justice, and mercy. I will return to this theme at length below.

1:15–22 "Then the king of Egypt said to the Hebrew midwives . . . 'When you serve as midwife to the Hebrew women, and see them upon the birthstool, if it is a son, you shall kill him.' . . . But the midwives feared God, and did not do as the king of Egypt commanded them" (1:15–17).

According to the author of Exodus, the Hebrews multiply both before and after their oppression by the Egyptians (1:7, 12), which is to be understood as a sign of the temporal blessings bestowed upon them by God, due to their election. The author understands this as a fulfillment of the prophecy made to Abraham in Gen. 12. Aquinas argues that the temporal blessings of the old covenant are meant to incite virtue and to teach that God will reward its pursuit. In this way, people are led gradually to a discovery of God as the final good. The new covenant, meanwhile, instructs overtly that the possession of God by grace is man's perfect, final good. The act of charity, whereby we love God above all things, is thus an end in itself. Nevertheless, Aquinas adds:

> There were some in the state of the Old Testament who, having charity and the grace of the Holy Spirit, looked chiefly to spiritual and eternal promises: and in this respect they belonged to the New Law. In like manner in the New Testament there are some carnal men who have not yet attained to the perfection of the New Law; and these it was necessary, even under the New Testament, to lead to virtuous action by the fear of punishment and by temporal promises.[7]

6. Synod of Quiercy, 853 AD, chap. 3 (Denzinger 2012: para. 623).
7. *ST* 1–2.107.1 ad 2.

The two Testaments are in fact united in essence, with the New bringing to perfection what is implicitly present in the Old.

The Pharaoh responds to the threat of the Hebrews by commanding two midwives to kill the male children of the people. According to the Masoretic Text, Shiphrah and Puah are "Hebrew midwives," but according to the Septuagint they are "the midwives of the Hebrews" (1:15, my translation).

Are the midwives righteous Gentiles or righteous Hebrews? The midwives are said to "fear God" (1:17), letting the male children live. In turn, God blesses them: "Because the midwives feared God, he gave them families" (1:21). If they are Gentiles, then the text indicates that there is an inner moral law written on the hearts of all persons and that this law of the human conscience connects even the Gentiles to God (Rom. 2:14), just as it does Israel, who has received the precept, "You shall not murder" (Exod. 20:13 NRSV). However, even if the midwives are Hebrews they are persons who, from the standpoint of the narrative, have yet to receive the divine law. Consequently, the fundamental moral message is similar in either case: human beings have a law written on their hearts that prefigures the gift of the Mosaic law. However, the promulgated, revealed law is necessary on account of human confusion and weakness, as well as the collective social effects of human sin—all of which can be observed in this passage.

Did the midwives lie to the Pharaoh, and if so, is it morally licit to lie in order to save innocent human life? In answer to the first question, the Masoretic Text seems to depict the women as deceiving the Pharaoh. They refuse to obey and tell him, "The Hebrew women . . . are vigorous and are delivered before the midwife comes to them" (1:19). The Septuagint, meanwhile, suggests that they tell the truth. It translates 1:19 in such a way that the midwives merely report a fact: that the Hebrew wives give birth before one can take their children away. Correspondingly, the translation depicts the king ordering them to destroy the children just prior to delivery—presumably through a kind of late-term abortion, which is an order they resist in conscience (1:16 LXX).

Presuming that the midwives are misleading the king, is their deception morally problematic? Some commentators express frustration with the question. After all, the Pharaoh intends a kind of genocide. Clearly extraordinary means are required in order to evade his tactics and protect human life. Can one not lie during a genocide to save human life? To question such a procedure is itself morally problematic.

Against this position, however, consider the following: the portrait of the scriptures is itself more complex than this objection allows. The original sin of the first couple occurs because of the lie of the serpent, whom Christ calls the "father of lies" (Gen. 3:4–5; John 8:44). After the first sin, the couple fails to take honest responsibility before God for what they have done in letting themselves engage with the serpent's way of falsehood. Thus the image of God in them is marred (Gen. 3:12–13). By contrast, the law that is given in a reparative way later tells us, "You shall not bear false witness" (Exod. 20:16). In the New Testament, Christ himself is "the truth" (John 14:6), and 1 John 2:21 (NRSV) states that "no lie comes from the truth." The scriptures in Exodus and elsewhere, then, enjoin upon us an ethic of radical truthfulness.

It follows from this that, at the very least, no lie is morally innocuous. If the midwives were in fact deceptive, even under duress (which is clearly the case), then this act in turn diminished something of their inherent human dignity as beings made for the truth. According to this reading, the oppressive actions of the Pharaoh have the effect of wounding the dignity of those upon whom he places grave burdens of conscience. Those who lie even in order to protect others are in some way morally compromised by the action.

Furthermore, the example of a genocide is of particular importance *not despite, but precisely because* it represents such an extraordinary limit case. The neuralgic character of this example is one that has the potency to unsettle human beings deeply and cause them to reflect and argue much more intricately than usual, which is one of the central functions of scripture: to make human beings more ethically reflective and conceptually nuanced rather than intellectually complacent.

All this being said, there are several ways to respond to the question of deception in a limit case like this one. Some have argued that the prohibition on lying is not an exceptionless norm and that a person has the right to deceive someone when that person has no right to the truth. This answer seems to ignore the intrinsic evil of lying insofar as it deprives the subject who lies of his or her integrity as a being made for the truth.

Others have argued that the moral object of an act of deception in a case like this one is not that of lying but rather that the moral object changes in exceptional circumstances. In a just war it is permissible to take human life as a form of legitimate self-defense, and so certain forms of deception and espionage are possible in a time of grave moral conflict in which there is no reasonable expectation of truth present in human exchanges. This latter view is preferable to the former in that it attempts to maintain the exceptionless character of the prohibition on lying. It does so, however, by creating equivocal definitions of deception that seem to be without legitimate foundation or plausible realism.

It is best to say, with Augustine and Aquinas, that the exceptionless prohibition on lying is a truth of the Catholic faith, revealed by scripture and in accord with right human reason. "Refuse to utter any lie" (Sir. 7:13).

The human person, then, is made for the truth and should avoid lying absolutely. When human beings are confronted with those who would use the truth to do grave harm to others, they should seek prudent means to withhold the truth. "It is not lawful to tell a lie in order to deliver another from any danger whatever. Nevertheless it is lawful to hide the truth prudently, by keeping it back."[8] One may also respond with mental reservation by saying something true that does not aid the immoral cause of an aggressor.

In desperate circumstances, people do sometimes tell lies to save the lives of others. Such acts are morally imperfect. This does not mean that such transgressions should be considered morally grave. Not all acts of deception are equal in moral gravity, nor do all of them necessarily constitute what the Catholic tradition terms "mortal sins" (1 John 5:16–17). Aquinas calls "officious" those lies that are told in order to safeguard the good of another, and among these the least morally disordered are those that are told to spare human life.[9] Such acts are often committed without foresight and are conditioned by panic or fear. If the act is made under duress, its gravity is diminished even more. As for the midwives, Aquinas is clear that he considers their action a venial rather than a mortal sin, that is to say, a sin of weakness that seeks by an imperfect means to safeguard an otherwise noble intention.[10] It is for this intention that they are rewarded by God—not for the act of deception as such. "The midwives were rewarded, not for their lie, but for their fear of God, and for their good-will, which latter led them to tell a lie. Hence it is expressly stated (Exod. 2:21): 'because the midwives feared God, he built them houses.' But the subsequent lie was not meritorious."[11]

Vocation to Prophecy (Exod. 2)

2:1–10 "The woman conceived and bore a son; and when she saw that he was a goodly child, she hid him three months" (2:2).

8. *ST* 2–2.110.3 ad 4. This is also the teaching of Augustine in *Against Lying,* n. 10.
9. *ST* 2–2.110.2.
10. *ST* 2–2.110.4 corp. and ad 4.
11. *ST* 2–2.110.3 ad 2.

Exodus 2 begins with the narrative of what Umberto Cassuto calls "the birth of the savior."[12] In the midst of the most perilous circumstances, God brings forth a person who will deliver the chosen people. He does so through the ingenuity and courage of Moses's mother and sister, as well as through the humane compassion of the daughter of the Pharaoh. The mother puts the child in "a basket made of bulrushes" and "place[s] it among the reeds at the river's brink" (2:3). When the daughter of the Pharaoh finds the child, the sister offers to find a nurse and in turn fetches the mother of Moses, who is then brought up in the house of Pharaoh (2:7–10).

There is a universalistic theme here. The mysterious providence of God unfolds in order to advance the redemption of Israel not only through the ingenuity of righteous Hebrews but also through the moral goodness of Gentiles. God's designs can work mysteriously through the seemingly weak to overcome powerful forms of injustice that abide in the world. This paradox serves to illustrate simultaneously the limitations of the human pretense to be godlike and the very hidden but real power of God, who can bring forth a historically decisive good even in the midst of circumstances marred by evil.

The use of the Hebrew word for "basket" (*tebah*) in 2:3 is significant. This word is only used in one other place in scripture: to denote Noah's ark in Gen. 6–9. Thus Moses, like Noah before him, survives the treacherous waters of death. Moreover, this passage prefigures the crossing of the Red Sea.[13]

Read in the light of the New Testament, Moses is a figure of Christ. As a child, Jesus is taken down into the land of Egypt by Joseph and the Virgin Mary (Matt. 2:13–15). The Mother of Christ must hide him from Herod, who attempts to kill him. Thus the courageous women in Exod. 2 are types of the Virgin Mary and the Church. In Rev. 12:1, "a great portent appear[s] in heaven, a woman clothed with the sun, with the moon under her feet, and on her head a crown of twelve stars." On one level, this figure is clearly the Church of the twelve apostles, who "[cries] out in her pangs of birth" (Rev. 12:2)—that is to say, in giving birth to those who are Christians. On another level, this is the image of a woman giving birth to a messianic child (Rev. 12:5). Given that the symbol is present in a text of the Christian community at the end of the first century, it must also indicate the Mother of Jesus.[14] As such, the Marian archetype and the ecclesial archetype

---

12. Cassuto 2005: 17.
13. Cassuto 2005: 18.
14. For an argument to this effect, see André Feuillet, *Jésus et sa Mère: D'après les récits lucaniens de l'enfance et d'après saint Jean* (Paris: J. Gabalda et Cie., 1974), 30–46.

overlap here; both are symbolized by one collective image. Meanwhile, the devil is portrayed as a dragon standing before the woman "that he might devour her child when she [brings] it forth" (Rev. 12:4). The symbols from Exodus are transposed to denote the eschatological struggle between the Church and the world, between the Virgin Mary and the devil. Those who are aligned with Christ and the Virgin Mary in the life of the Church are leaving behind the world of human selfishness. They "fled into the desert" (Rev. 12:6).

2:11–25 "He killed the Egyptian and hid him in the sand" (2:12).

In his adult life, the prophetic vocation of Moses begins, perhaps maladroitly, from a premeditated act of killing. Seeing an Egyptian who is beating a fellow Hebrew, "He looked this way and that, and seeing no one he killed the Egyptian and hid him in the sand" (2:12). Moses subsequently flees into the Sinai Peninsula of Egypt in order to avoid the punishment of the Pharaoh. There he defends the daughters of Jethro who are drawing water from a well and being threatened by shepherds. He is then inducted into the family of Jethro, a Midianite priest, marries his daughter Zipporah, and has a child, Gershom. All of this serves as a prelude to the deliverance of Israel, whose suffering continues in Egypt (2:22–25) while Moses is set apart in the wilderness, soon to be called by God.

On an ethical level, this episode raises several significant questions. Moses is depicted in Exod. 2 as a man of passionate moral conviction, but there are ambiguities entailed in the premeditated killing of the Egyptian. It is permissible for an oppressed people to rise up politically against an unjust government, and it is permissible to defend the Hebrew who is being beaten from physical oppression. One might ask, however, does Moses have the authority to initiate the kind of action he undertakes? Does he use proportionate force? Does the action come from himself alone, or is it also inspired by God? If the former, is it not an unwarranted usurpation of justice that is itself morally unjust?

The New Testament portrays the action as stemming fundamentally from the righteousness of faith in a person called to act prophetically on the part of God. "Seeing one [of the sons of Israel] being wronged, he defended the oppressed man and avenged him by striking the Egyptian. He supposed that his brethren understood that God was giving them deliverance by his hand, but they did not understand" (Acts 7:24–25). Hebrews 11:24–28:

> By faith Moses, when he was grown up, refused to be called the son of Pharaoh's daughter, choosing rather to share ill-treatment with the people of God than to enjoy the fleeting pleasures of sin. He considered abuse suffered for the Christ

greater wealth than the treasures of Egypt, for he looked to the reward. By faith
he left Egypt, not being afraid of the anger of the king; for he endured as seeing
him who is invisible.[15]

Similar to the New Testament, Maimonides argues that Moses possessed a
first degree of prophecy. "The first degree of prophecy consists in the fact that an
individual receives a divine help that moves and activates him to a great, righteous,
and important action—such as the deliverance of a community or of virtuous
people from a community of wicked people."[16] Aquinas in turn argues that "Moses
seems to have slain the Egyptian by authority received as it were, by divine inspiration. This seems to follow from Acts 7:24–25. . . . Or it may be replied that
Moses slew the Egyptian in order to defend the man who was unjustly attacked,
without himself exceeding the limits of a blameless defense."[17]

Ambrose promotes the latter view in *De Officis* 1.36, making the matter one
of human justice rather than divine inspiration. Augustine, meanwhile, does not
hesitate to characterize the act as sinful: Moses acted without the warrant of
proper authority. By the providence of God, however, his action foreshadowed
the liberation of the people of God. It is an imperfect sign, then, of his later
intervention on behalf of God.[18] Aquinas notes the opinions of Ambrose and
Augustine alongside his own as a diversity of interpretations arranged according
to degrees. Moses was inspired by an initial grace of faith, and his action derived
generally from this faith; it was either specifically inspired by God, or a natural
action of justice, or a morally problematic usurpation of authority. In any event,
his action prefigures the political liberation that ensues, and yet he remains morally imperfect, subject to a series of conversions that are to come.

In the fallen order, violence employed for a just cause always has a note of
moral ambiguity about it. This is the case even (or especially) when we speak of
the legitimate defense of the freedom of true religion. Just rebellion, even when
inspired by God and his justice, is not the deepest theme of the book of Exodus.
Any such rebellion must ultimately be at the service of the restoration of a true
order of justice. The Torah underscores incessantly the fundamental responsibilities of moral life in a political community, as well as the hierarchical nature of that
community. It gives warrant to the legitimate authority of political leaders who are

15. For analysis of these passages in their historical context, see Childs 1974: 33–40.
16. Maimonides, *Guide of the Perplexed* 2.45 (Pines 1963).
17. *ST* 2–2.60.6 ad 2.
18. Augustine, *Reply to Faustus the Manichean* 22.70.

bound to safeguard the common good. Moses eventually becomes a legislator and ruler himself. In subsequent books of scripture, monarchy is subject to profound theological critique but is also vindicated under certain conditions. The office of Caesar is criticized in the New Testament, but we are also told that the king is to be obeyed in all that is just (1 Tim. 2:1–15). In this temporal, fallen order, the Bible promotes no vision of a utopian revolution but advances a vision of just human relations with God and neighbor that is maintained in and through the political life of persons. Human life can be taken by a just authority only for a grave reason and for the purposes of the protection and restoration of the social order.

The Divine Name (Exod. 3)

3:1–12 "And the angel of the LORD appeared to him in a flame of fire out of the midst of a bush; and he looked, and lo, the bush was burning, yet it was not consumed" (3:2).

God reveals his holy name to Moses and commands him to act on his behalf to deliver Israel from Egypt. Here the interpreter is invited to make a fundamental discernment. Is what the scripture portrays something that we should take to be in some way historical, according to the literal sense? Theologically, the answer must be affirmative. The origins of Israelite religion are no doubt historically complex; there were diverse forms of Yahwism in existence in ancient, premonarchic Israel. Furthermore, the Torah is seemingly composed of a variety of ancient Israelite traditions, and its contents were subject to various stages of redaction. Nevertheless, no matter how complex the religious practices of ancient Israelites or the composition of the text, it must be affirmed theologically that ancient Israelite religion in its essence stems from the direct influence of divine revelation. That is to say, it has its historical origins in a revelation given through a primitive religious movement centered on a distinct prophetic figure. "By a prophet the LORD brought Israel up from Egypt, / and by a prophet he was preserved" (Hos. 12:13). It is this initial movement and its traditions that subsequently gave rise to what one might term "biblical Yahwism."

Technically, this historical truth could be affirmed in this text even if there were no direct historical connection between the events that are depicted and the persons recounting the narrative. That is to say, for the sake of argument, even if the text is an idealistic formalization of a long-past history that was composed centuries later, it still necessarily contains the revelatory affirmation of a supernatural truth that natural empirical and archeological study can neither prove nor disprove: at the origins of the Mosaic religious movement, there stood a foundational act of God, who revealed himself personally to the prophet Moses. The idea is not open to definitive historical demonstration, and it cannot be disproven by any merely naturalistic method. It is a truth of faith that is entirely compatible with natural reason and congruent with the best resources of modern historical argument. Here one might draw an analogy to the representation of the original sin of man in Gen. 3:1–7. The author need not have had empirical access to a historical fall in order to rightly affirm, in faith and under the grace of prophetic inspiration, the ontological and historical reality of an original sin and the condition that results from it.[19]

Nevertheless, such a position seems historically minimalistic, since there are good historical reasons to take the account of Exod. 3 seriously as a reflection of ancient Israelite history. While such argument is indirect, inferential, and probabilistic (like all sound historical argument), it takes its point of departure from subsequent traditions of Israelite religion. Eighth-century-BC prophets such as Hosea (in northern Israel) and Micah (in Judah) both claim to be the interpreters of a historical covenant initiated centuries earlier by God the Lord, under Moses, consisting of legal precepts that the people of Israel can be faithful to or not. The terms of this covenant and its legal precepts are not enunciated by these prophets but rather are referred to and presumed to exist already. The worship of the Lord is understood in this context to be exclusive, in contradistinction from the polytheism or false worship of many Israelites as well as their neighbors (concerning this see Hos. 6:7–10; 8:1–3; 1:9, as compared with Deut. 29:12–13; Mic. 2:1–5; 6:1–8).[20]

Likewise, if one follows a reasonable interpretation of the theories of an Elohist strand of tradition in the Torah and of the theologically similar traditions that were employed to compose Deuteronomy, then one can speak of an explicit covenantal theology and of a body of religious legal material in ancient Israel that long predates the Babylonian exile, which Hosea and Micah themselves depend upon or presuppose.[21] Presumably, this body of legal material and traditional theology was both preserved and progressively developed, in large measure by the Levitical priests who predated the Israelite monarchy and these eighth-century

19. Regarding the account of Gen. 3, Karl Rahner offers a similar argument in "Theological Reflections on Monogenism," in *God, Christ, Mary and Grace*, vol. 1 of *Theological Investigations*, trans. Cornelius Ernst (London: Darton, Longmann & Todd, 1961), 229–96, esp. 251–62.

20. See the helpful arguments to this effect by Stephen L. Cook, *The Social Roots of Biblical Yahwism*, Studies in Biblical Literature 8 (Atlanta: Society of Biblical Literature, 2004), 67–120.

21. Ibid., 45–65.

prophets.[22] Based on these starting points, one must conclude that ancient Israelite Yahwism was something with a clear identity, centered around the exclusive worship of the Lord, grounded in a covenant theology, and formulated around a coherent body of religious law.

It is therefore reasonable to posit inferentially, even from a merely natural point of view (by arguments from historical likelihood rather than strict demonstration), that this religion has its origin in an initial historical movement centered around a charismatic leader or initial group of founders. It is reasonable to hypothesize that these people articulated the initial form of the religion and instituted the Levitical priesthood so that the movement could be perpetuated. The best hypothetical explanation for the genesis of the ancient Israelite religion remains that of a historical movement stemming from the Sinai Peninsula in the thirteenth to twelfth centuries BC. This movement claims that the religion has its origin with the prophet Moses, who was inspired by the Lord.

Consistent with what has been said above, Exod. 3:1–12 is most likely composed from diverse traditional sources (for example, Elohist and Yahwist accounts of the call of Moses). Through their preservation and redaction, the final portrait that is given to us presents a simultaneously historical and symbolic account of the origins of the Mosaic religion.

Regarding the symbols in the passage, I would like to note several things.

First, Moses encounters the God of Israel under the appearances of a burning bush. Here an external charismatic miracle (visible to the senses) precedes the address of faith and the internal gift of supernatural prophecy. The bush or shrub is humble in nature and represents the elect people, Israel, in whom God is present or in whom he dwells. Meanwhile, the fire represents the living presence of God among his people, particularly in the truth of his law. "The pillar of cloud by day and the pillar of fire by night did not depart from before the people" (13:22); "And Mount Sinai was wrapped in smoke, because the LORD descended upon it in fire" (19:18a). The initial appearance of God to Moses is probably meant to prefigure the revelation of the law given to the people at Horeb or Sinai. "When you have brought forth the people out of Egypt, you shall serve God upon this mountain" (3:12).

Typologically, the symbolism of the burning bush points toward the incarnation; the living tree represents the Virgin Mary, the daughter of Sion, in whom the incarnate Word is present. God's holiness does not destroy the integrity of the creature in whom he becomes manifest but by his grace preserves and ennobles

22. Ibid., 195–266.

her in proximity to God.[23] The burning tree is also a symbol of God's presence on the Cross and in the Church. Like a shrub, the Church is perceived as lowly in the eyes of the world but is sustained interiorly by the fire of divine truth.

What is denoted by the "angel of the LORD" (3:2)? In Acts 7:35, which comments on this passage, we are given to believe that this phrase denotes an angelic being distinct from God who speaks on behalf of the Lord. However, the Torah sometimes uses this expression to denote the Lord himself speaking or appearing (Gen. 16:10, 13). One might say, then, that God truly reveals himself but that God does so while remaining partially hidden or veiled by the mediating presence of the angelic messenger. The knowledge of God we are given in this life, even by revelation, is given in faith and through mediations, not by immediate perception. The recipient who knows God through his word does truly know God as he is in himself but does not yet perceive God face-to-face.

Typologically, this expression is christophanic. For Justin Martyr the "angel" is Christ. "This same One, who is both angel, and God, and Lord, and man, and who appeared in human form to Abraham and Isaac, appeared in a flame of fire from the bush, and conversed with Moses."[24] The burning bush event foreshadows the unveiling of God in the humanity of Christ. "He who has seen me has seen the Father" (John 14:9). Ultimately, this is the way God will come to his people: in and through his own human life, death, and resurrection.

Moses is told to remove his sandals as a sign of humility before the presence of God (Exod. 3:5). This external gesture symbolizes the interior gift of fear, which, the scriptures suggest, God typically pours into the heart of those he calls to prophesy on his behalf. "Who am I that I should go to Pharaoh, and bring the sons of Israel out of Egypt?" (3:11). Such fear can be "servile" or "filial."[25] Fear is servile when the subject is motivated to obey God primarily out of fear of punishment; it is filial when the soul fears to offend God primarily out of love rather than the possibility of divine retribution.

Catherine of Siena claims that filial fear gives the recipient a reverential sense of his own nothingness before God the Creator and is accompanied by piety, love, and surrender to God. "Do you know, daughter, who you are and who I am? You are she who is not, and I Am He Who Is."[26] Due to God's creation of all

23. Gregory of Nyssa, *Life of Moses* 2.21 (Malherbe and Ferguson 1978).
24. Justin Martyr, *Dialogue with Trypho*, chap. 59 (*ANF* 1:226).
25. *ST* 2–2.19.2.
26. Raymond of Capua, *Life of Catherine of Siena*, trans. C. Kearns (Wilmington, DE: Michael Glazier, 1980), 91.

things from nothing, nothingness is in a certain sense ontologically prior to the gift of being. The free decision of God—who alone is—precedes the creature's being-out-of-nothing. The recipient of the gift of fear is aware of his or her unworthiness not primarily on account of any morbid self-detestation but due to love for the truth about who God is and who the creature is. Furthermore, the Torah here clearly suggests that unless one lives in this state of utter religious surrender to God as the Creator—who alone truly is in the absolute sense—one is not really living in the truth as regards one's own person.

3:13–22 "God said to Moses, 'I AM WHO I AM.' And he said, 'Say this to the people of Israel, "I AM has sent me to you."' God also said to Moses, 'Say this to the people of Israel, "The LORD, the God of your fathers, the God of Abraham, the God of Isaac, and the God of Jacob, has sent me to you": this is my name for ever, and thus I am to be remembered throughout all generations'" (3:14–15).

In 3:14–15 the divine name is revealed to Moses. In fact, it is two names. The first of these is given in 3:14: "I Am He Who Is," or "I AM WHO I AM," abbreviated as "I AM." The second is the tetragrammaton (YHWH), which is mentioned in 3:15. This personal name is often translated into other languages euphemistically under the title "Lord" as a way of designating the God of Israel.[27] This twofold revelation of the intimate name of God serves as an addition to the title "God of the fathers," that is to say, God as he was previously recognized in the age of the patriarchs and designated "the God of Abraham, Isaac, and Jacob."

How ought we to understand the two names, I Am He Who Is and the tetragrammaton?

Aquinas distinguishes here between titles that signify God's deity (the divine nature), titles that signify God's existence, and titles that signify God as an individual. The word "God," when rightly understood, signifies the divine nature. It is not a personal name, like "David" or "Paul," but is an abstract term pertaining to a nature, like "human being" or "angelic person."[28] The divine nature is not comprehensible; it cannot be understood in a fully circumscribed way by mere created human reason. However, one can denote the divine nature of God the Creator indirectly from creatures, by analogy, and may speak appropriately therefore of the one God. "The LORD is God; there is no other besides him" (Deut. 4:35).

---

27. Typically the name is not pronounced within traditional forms of the Christian liturgy, as a way of respecting its sacred character. Often it is not written out in Hebrew or vernacular transliteration but is replaced by the term "Lord," a custom I am following for the most part in this commentary.

28. *ST* 1.13.8.

Furthermore, one can employ the abstract term to address God personally: "O God, come to my assistance."

The tetragrammaton, by contrast, signifies God as a singular individual. This is analogous in human discourse to the title we give a concrete individual we encounter through our sense experience, such as "John" or "Paul." If we encounter a stranger, we cannot know that person's name unless he (or another) discloses it to us. Even less can we know the transcendent God unless he reveals himself to us personally. Consequently, the name here is given freely by God to Moses and pertains to his singular identity. This is also the name by which God identifies himself as the God of Israel, over and against the gods of the other nations and all merely human attempts to name God or the gods, which stem from human ingenuity but do not come from God. The name symbolizes, then, the unique choice that God makes of the chosen people, to whom a privileged knowledge, covenant, and law are given. It is the Lord who acts freely in history to make himself the savior of Israel.

According to Aquinas, the name I Am He Who Is signifies the existence of God. It is given to us so that we may interpret the meaning of the terms "God" and "the Lord."[29] What is utterly different about God (as distinct from every creature) is that it pertains to God necessarily to exist. God in his incomprehensible, divine essence exists simply and eternally. Since it pertains to his essence to exist, there is no real ontological distinction in God the Creator between his essence and his existence. God, by essence, is. By contrast, all creatures that are caused to be depend upon God for the gift of their being and are thus ontologically composite. Their act of being does not pertain to their essence, and so there exists in each creature—from the angel to the smallest material particle—a real distinction between existence and essence. Creatures are capable of not being. They have their existence from God as their first cause and thus participate in being received from God, who is being of a higher and incomprehensible sort. God is the One Who Is.

On this reading, the passage is saying that the God of Israel—who has chosen this people as his particular people and given them alone his name, his deliverance,

29. *ST* 1.13.11 corp. and ad 1:
This name "He Who Is" is most properly applied to God . . . because of its signification. For it does not signify form, but simply existence itself. Hence since the existence of God is His essence itself, which can be said of no other (*ST* 1.3.4), it is clear that among other names this one specially denominates God, for everything is denominated by its form. . . . This name "He Who Is" is the name of God more properly than this name "God," as regards its source, namely, existence; and as regards the mode of signification and consignification, as said above. But as regards the object intended by the name, this name "God" is more proper, as it is imposed to signify the divine nature; and still more proper is the Tetragrammaton, imposed to signify the substance of God itself, incommunicable and, if one may so speak, singular.

his covenant, and his law—is also the God who alone is and who has created all things (Gen. 1:1). This God is the author of all peoples, Gentile and Jew alike, but he intends to bless all nations through the seed of Abraham (Gen. 22:18), and he has chosen to reveal himself personally to Moses in the miracle of the burning bush. God, the author of all reality, has spoken to Israel.

Against this reading of the name of God several objections might be raised. First of all, it seems from textual and archeological studies that the personal name YHWH has a history in ancient Near Eastern religion before the time to which historians typically ascribe the exodus. Additionally, in the monarchical period of Israel this name was employed in diverse religious forms of worship, many of which depart from "normative" biblical Yahwism. If this name was subject to non-Israelite and polytheistic uses, how could it have come from Moses in a discrete occasion in history?

Second, the interpretation given above seems to project back upon an ancient text anachronistically a subsequent Christian metaphysical interpretation. The authors of that archaic cultural period in which Exodus was composed lived and wrote before the age of classical Greek metaphysics and the subsequent Jewish-Christian appropriations of that tradition.

These concerns are treated at greater length in the coda of this book, "The Divine Name and the Metaphysics of Exodus." Here, however, I will respond briefly.

First, it seems likely that the name YHWH was employed both before and after the dawn of the Mosaic religious movement. This was the case both in Near Eastern religious practices that may or may not have been connected historically with biblical Yahwism (such as Kenite religion) and in subsequent Israelite syncretistic religious practices (such as in the monarchic period of Israel's history).

The use of a personal name, however, can refer to a plurality of subjects. "John," for example, can refer to John Locke or John Donne. Likewise any proper name (Peter, Paul, Jesus, YHWH) can be reappropriated to speak of a new subject in a new way. Here, the text is suggesting that the early Israelites discovered God in a new way and therefore made a new use of the (perhaps preexisting) name of the Lord. Subsequently, the new use of the name developed through a movement from the exodus to the Babylonian exile and return. As such, the use of that name attained a canonical form over time. In its scriptural form, it effectively denotes Israel's experience and understanding of the activity and self-revelation of the living God and nothing else. The scripture's exclusive, even jealous, sense of the uniqueness of the name is not based, then, on an absence of influence from other cultural forms of religious expression, other uses of the name of their God. It is based rather on the fundamental and ferocious desire to understand rightly who God is as the Lord, on God's own terms, as God has revealed them exclusively in and through a saving history with Israel, which God himself initiated and which they by grace have understood. Here it is a fundamental question of belief in the living God or of doubt, of conversion or apostasy, of the living God of Israel or the idols of men. No other option is available to one who encounters the Bible on its own terms.

Regarding the second objection, one might respond as follows. It is difficult to discern what if any ontological signification the term "YHWH" might have had in the early Israelite religious movement. Aquinas's interpretation of the term as a personal name diminishes the importance of this question. The tetragrammaton does not need to have an abstract meaning. However, there are good arguments to be made that the word derives originally from the biblical Hebrew root *h-y-h*, "to be," which may have *h-w-h* as an alternative form. If the word is a simple *qal* verb of the latter form, it could mean "he is" or "he exists." Alternatively, based on the way the word is spelled as an element of an Israelite proper name, it may represent a causative *hiphil* verb inflection of the root, in which case it could mean "he causes to exist."[30] If either of these interpretations is correct, then the word has an implicitly metaphysical meaning.

In any event, the term "I Am He Who Is" (*ehyeh asher ehyeh*) can and should be interpreted in an overtly ontological way within the context of Exodus itself. The complete narrative of the redacted text presupposes that the Lord, I Am He Who Is, will deliver Israel from Egypt by extraordinary works of divine power, showing that he is the true God over against the idols of Egypt. One might argue that the early Mosaic movement was implicitly monotheistic, based on its commandments, which enjoin exclusive worship of the Lord and the prohibition of the use of any images for God.[31] This is certainly the understanding one finds in subsequent prophets like Hosea and Micah. The Torah in its mature redacted form certainly understands the God of Exodus to be he who "in the beginning created the heavens and the earth" (Gen. 1:1). This understanding of the Lord's universal causality over creatures is also developed in Second Isaiah, where the Lord is clearly He Who Is, the cause of all that is and the savior of the world.

---

30. De Vaux 1978: 1:338–57, esp. 347–48; F. M. Cross, "Yahweh and the God of the Patriarchs," *Harvard Theological Review* 55 (1962): 225–59, esp. 253. I am grateful to Fr. Paul Mankowski, SJ, for clarifications on this subject.

31. Marie-Joseph Lagrange, *Le judaïsme avant Jésus-Christ*, 2nd ed. (Paris: J. Gabalda et Fils, 1931), 2–3; de Vaux 1978: 1:462–72.

> I am the LORD, and there is no other,
>> besides me there is no God. (Isa. 45:5)

> Turn to me and be saved,
>> all the ends of the earth!
>> For I am God, and there is no other. (Isa. 45:22)

We can perceive in this historical succession of thought an organic, homogeneous development of doctrine, from the Elohist and Yahwist material to Hosea and Micah and then to Second Isaiah and the Priestly redaction. Subsequently, the Septuagint translation of Exod. 3:14 interprets this biblical tradition in more expressly metaphysical terms as a way of promoting the biblical truth within the context of a Hellenistic culture. *Ehyeh asher ehyeh* is interpreted as *egō eimi ho ōn*: "I Am the One Who Is" or "I Am He Who Is Being."

The name is also frequently interpreted either as "I Am Who I Am" or "I will be present to you." The first signification is apophatic; God in his freedom transcends the categorizations of human understanding. The second is a promise of fidelity: "I will be there to deliver you." It may be interpreted as a sign of the divine freedom. God is free to be who God wishes in his fidelity to Israel.

Each of these interpretations is defensible, both etymologically and theologically. However, God transcends the intelligibility of any created thing (and therefore is unknown to us) because God is not a creature; rather, God is he upon whom all created realities depend. The condition of possibility for the God of Israel "freely being present" to Moses throughout the events of the exodus is that God is the one who is present to all that he has created and all that depends upon him. God is free to be present to his creatures in a way that no other is because of who God is in distinction from his creatures. Consequently, these other interpretations of the name seem to presuppose the primary one that has been presented above.

There is a tension present in this text between universality and particularity. On the one hand, God has made a particular choice of Israel to be his own people and to deliver them from other peoples to a land that is promised to them. "I promise that I will bring you up out of the affliction of Egypt, to the land of the Canaanites, the Hittites, the Amorites, the Per'izzites, the Hivites, and the Jeb'usites, a land flowing with milk and honey" (3:17; see also 3:8). On the other hand, the One who intervenes on Israel's behalf is the sovereign Lord who has made all things. He is therefore the author of all human beings, who are made unto his image and likeness (Gen. 1:26–27). God chooses the people who are oppressed, even in their particularity as a people, in part to show in the most universal fashion that all human beings possess an inherent dignity that should not be ignored. The metaphysical reflections on the divine name offered above may seem unrelated to God's revelation that he is concerned with the liberation of slaves from severe injustice and mistreatment. However, these two aspects of the revelation are deeply interrelated. Exodus 3 reveals to us that man's dignity as a rational creature makes him capable of intimacy with God and capable of obeying the commandments of God. This dignity has its grounding in God's own wisdom and activity as the Creator of all and the Savior of Israel. How, then, does the salvation of Israel pertain to God's plan for the salvation of all human beings, all those who are made in his image? Herein lies the tension encoded in the text.

This tension is both intensified and resolved in the mystery of Christ. It is intensified because Christ, who is the God of Israel, is a member of the covenanted people, a Jew according to the flesh (Gal. 4:4). In the most ultimate way this seals the particularity of the Hebraic form that salvation has taken. At the same time, it is precisely the life, death, and resurrection of Christ as not only the Son of David but also the Son of Adam—or the New Adam—that opens the covenant of the people of Israel to all people and makes the salvation of God possible to all.

It is important to underscore this theological truth here because it is manifest in the New Testament in the christological interpretation of the divine names. It is through the death and resurrection of Jesus that he is revealed to the nations as the "Lord," the God of Israel, before whom every knee will bend and that every tongue will confess (Phil. 2:10–11; Isa. 45:23). The ultimate revelation of YHWH is Jesus. He is the eternal Word of God made flesh, who is the name of the Father (John 1:1, 14; 17:6).

At the same time, then, Jesus is He Who Is—"I and the Father are one" (John 10:30). "Hear, O Israel: The LORD our God is one LORD" (Deut. 6:4). This unity of the Son and the Father is revealed ultimately not at the burning bush but at the elevation of Christ upon Golgotha: "When you have lifted up the Son of man, then you will know that I am" (John 8:28). "Before Abraham was, I am" (John 8:58). The metaphysics of Exodus are resolved christologically in a metaphysics of Calvary. There is no opposition between ontological reflection on God as the Creator of all that is and Christ as God become man. In biblical thought, the two reflections are distinct and not reducible to one another, but they are also inseparable, mutually conditioning, and ultimately deeply interrelated.

Introduction to Exodus 4–11: Catechesis on Divine Omnipotence

Having revealed his holy name to Israel, God now reveals his power. The purpose of Exod. 4–11 is to show forth the omnipotence and goodness of God. It is typical of the scriptures that they present the highest and most sublime of realities in language that is accessible even to the simple. The book of Exodus is meant to instruct us in wisdom concerning who God is, but like the four canonical Gospels, it can continually augment the understanding of both the youngest child and the most gifted person of learning.

Because of its archaic style, the initial impression of some readers is that the Torah is primitive and irrational, both morally and philosophically. It is true that the text was composed and edited in an archaic age. It has a particular style that mixes history, folkloric narrative, and symbolic discourse. The teaching is often declarative in kind and is presented in language that is at once terse and intuitive.

However, the intellectual and moral depth of these intuitions is not to be underestimated. The book of Exodus has a unique power to influence all human culture because of its inspired character—not in spite of but in and through the fabric of its very original form. The text is meant to serve as an ongoing source of instruction and of mystagogical initiation for the reader. Without denying the historical dimension of the book, the reader is invited with Israel to depart the Egypt of this world, to offer true worship and sacrifice to the Lord, to ascend the mountain of God, and to enter into the binding covenant of the law.

That being said, one can speak of a biblical enlightenment of reason that is present in the Torah. Historically speaking, one can see in the first five books of the Bible the emergence of a universal human rationality, inspired and prompted by God. This enlightenment pertains to the truth about God the Creator, the reality of the human person made in God's image, and many elements of the natural and the divine law. All of these have a universal character that is applicable to all human beings in every time and place. This emergence of biblical rationality and universalism occurs over against many obscurities and superstitions that were present in ancient human culture, which the Torah criticizes or refutes. However, the Torah is also expressed in the literary forms and concepts of the ancient world, which places it in a time prior to the advent of Hellenism. This literary style does not act as a hindrance to the enlightenment of universal human reason. On the contrary, the Torah is able to communicate truths about God to a broad audience in an intuitive and symbolic way, with a unique profundity that utterly transcends the highest efforts of any merely human philosophy. As Dionysius says, in this way God hides the treasures of his wisdom from the proud and reveals them to the simple and to the lowly of heart who pray for enlightenment.[32]

A typical example is given in Gen. 1, where the creation of the world is depicted over against the irrationalities of ancient Babylonian religion. For the Torah, there is only one God, and God is not a physical body. God is neither male nor female but is transcendent of the physical world. God's deity is incomprehensible, but God's activity is characterized by divine wisdom. God creates all things through his Word or reason, and all that God has created is good. The universe is an ordered, intelligible totality created by God and is not something divine. It should not be worshiped and is not to be confused with the first principle from which all things originate. The universe is composed of a multiplicity of visible beings that are also arranged hierarchically, with the human being standing at the summit. The human person is made in God's image as male and female and is the most noble reality in the visible creation. Due to the human powers of created reason and freedom, he or she is capable of friendship and communion with God. From the beginning, human marriage and the transmission of life form an intimate part of God's plan for the creation. Genesis 2–3 goes on to show that God is not the author of moral evil; rather, evil entered the world through the transgression of rational creatures. Note that none of these teachings is trivial: each of them can be pondered for the duration of a human lifetime. And yet they are all communicated in a brief passage, beautiful to human reason, in a language that is at once simple, accessible, and utterly profound.

Exodus 4–11 is intended to accomplish something analogous. It serves as a kind of basic catechesis regarding the omnipotence and goodness of God in the service of the salvation of Israel. The book is deeply marked here by the character of the setting in which the divine revelation was given; the narrative is simple and at times folkloric. Concurrently, the metaphysical teachings implied by the sequence are deeply insightful and, in their historical context, somewhat revolutionary. In human religious history, the revelation of the Torah here effectuates the passage from the common pagan belief in many gods to the knowledge of God the Creator, from the widespread belief in magic to the spiritually mature confidence in divine providence and the *mirabilia Dei*, and from the erroneous and morally dangerous belief in the divinity of human governments to a rational acceptance of universal human subjection to the moral law and to the law of God.

32. Dionysius, *On the Celestial Hierarchy* 2.136D–145C.

Consequently, there are a number of major themes that emerge in Exod. 4–11. First, it is revealed that God has a transcendent and absolute knowledge of future historical events. Second, we are introduced to the "problem" of the hardheartedness of Pharaoh. How is it that God can sustain in existence a creature that perseveres in moral evil and defies the law of God? In what way is God responsible for or innocent of the evil done by the human agent? Third, we see the movement from archaic magic to revelatory miracles. The wonders of God are signs of God's presence and activity on behalf of the people God has chosen to adopt as his own. Fourth, the plagues of God are meant to show forth the omnipotence and omnipresence of the God of Israel, who as the Creator has a unique form of power over the natural order of creation. Last, the death of the Egyptian firstborn reveals the transcendent justice of God with respect to his creatures, while the salvation of the Israelites reveals God's transcendent mercy. Each of these themes occurs repeatedly in this section of the book, but I will refer to each in greater detail only at various stages.

Mirabilia Dei as a Purification of Human Superstition (Exod. 4)

4:1–17 "The LORD said to him, 'What is that in your hand?' He said, 'A rod.' And he said, 'Cast it on the ground.' So he cast it on the ground, and it became a serpent" (4:2–3).

Exodus 4 begins with Moses's complaint that he will not be believed, either by the Hebrews or the Egyptians. In response, God performs two signs: he turns the staff of Moses into a serpent (4:2–5), and he turns the flesh of Moses white with leprosy (4:6–8). He also promises to change the water of the Nile River into blood (4:9–10). When Moses persists in his refusal, God is angered (4:11–15). He appoints Moses's brother Aaron, "the Levite," as his spokesman: "He shall speak for you to the people; and he shall be a mouth for you, and you shall be to him as God" (4:16). In this way, Moses is assured that he can communicate God's will in both signs and words.

What should be made of all this? Since the text is very archaic in style, is this something we could or ought to consider historical, in its literal sense? I will first address the definition of the miraculous as such and then consider the question of the historical ambiguities presented by the text.

It should be noted that the Bible does not present us with an affirmation of human magic but rather with something entirely opposed to human magic. Magic in its religious forms can be defined as a human attempt to manipulate the divine power or unseen angelic forces by means of occult rituals. Although such practices are less frequently encountered in secularized cultures, they are not rare in the history of religions or even in the current age. As such, religious magic amounts to a form of superstition: that is, it either offers religious honor to that which is not God, or it attempts to approach the divine providence or channel the power of God by means of practices that are unworthy of God and that vitiate the religious dignity of the human person.[33] Miracles, by contrast, are works of God that do not contradict but rather transcend the order of nature and can only have for their cause the author of nature.[34] It is because God alone is the cause of the very being of creation that he is able to act not only upon the formal natures of things (altering them via their properties) as created agents do but also upon the very existence and substance of the thing. Consequently, the genuinely miraculous is only possible for God and (when it occurs) is necessarily a sign of the presence of the power of God acting in an extraordinary way.

Aquinas notes that miracles are a kind of "gratuitous grace" or charismatic phenomena that are intended to show signs of the presence of God to instruct those who are ignorant of the reality of God. As such, they are ordered toward the infused virtues of sanctifying grace: faith, hope, and charity, as well as infused moral virtues and the gifts of the indwelling Holy Spirit.[35] Miracles, then, are always something second and exterior with regard to something infinitely greater—the gift of divine life—which is received only in faith. Furthermore, the mystery of God is something infinitely more profound than the miraculous, and the miracle stands as a partial and necessarily imperfect indication to human reason of the reality of the mystery. Because miracles only have a sign value denoting something else more ultimate and interior, they are only perfectly decipherable in their meaning by the supernatural faith that adheres to divine revelation. This also means, Aquinas

---

33. *ST* 2–2.92.1.

34. *ST* 1.105.8:

> A thing is called a miracle by comparison with the power of nature which it surpasses. So the more the power of nature is surpassed, the greater the miracle. Now the power of nature is surpassed in three ways: firstly, in the substance of the deed, for instance, if two bodies occupy the same place, or . . . if a human body is glorified: such things nature is absolutely unable to do; and these hold the highest rank among miracles. Secondly, a thing surpasses the power of nature, not in the deed, but in that wherein it is done; as the raising of the dead, and giving sight to the blind, and the like; for nature can give life, but not to the dead; and such hold the second rank in miracles. Thirdly, a thing surpasses nature's power in the measure and order in which it is done; as when a man is cured of a fever suddenly, without treatment or the usual process of nature; or as when the air is suddenly condensed into rain, by divine power without a natural cause, as occurred at the prayers of Samuel and Elias; and these hold the lowest place in miracles.

35. *ST* 1–2.111.1.

notes, that the capacity to believe rightly in a miracle always stems from an inward grace of faith. Correspondingly, disbelief in the miraculous sign is only culpable on the part of the one who refuses it on the presupposition that the internal grace of God is being resisted by the one who refuses the outward sign.[36] This means that in the book of Exodus the Pharaoh is only considered culpable in his refusal of the message of Moses (which is accompanied by signs of the power of God) because he is also the subject to whom a divine initiative is made, both externally by word and internally by grace.

Charismatic graces are fitted to proper times and circumstances and have both a divine origin and also a cultural context of intelligibility precisely because they are intended to awaken the intellectual understanding of persons in a given cultural era with its particular symbols. The miracles depicted in these chapters correspond, then, to religious customs and symbols employed in ancient Egypt at the time in which the exodus is traditionally dated. The rod in ancient Egypt symbolized royal authority and power, while the snake represented Wadjet, the Egyptian cobra goddess. It was worn on the forehead of the Pharaohs as a sign of their sovereignty and signified their prerogative to sentence to death enemies of the state.[37] In addition, the Pharaohs were considered avatars of the divine. Seen in this context, the signs that Moses is commanded to perform make sense. They show not that he is invested with power from himself but that the true authority comes from YHWH, the God who has sent him before the Egyptians. Magic was an ordinary part of the religious life of the culture of that age, as was the attempt to manipulate the conditions of nature by means of external rituals. Consequently, the plagues that occur are also considered as signs of contradiction, meant to speak to the Egyptians in terms they can understand while subverting or "decoding" their religious symbols from within and employing them to show the power of the God of Israel. In this sense the signs performed by Moses are meant to invite the Egyptians to a conversion, to open their eyes to the limits of their superstitious practices so that they can see these practices in the light of faith in the living God.

What should be said, however, about the historical character of this passage? Does the archaic, pedagogical style of the text militate against a theological belief that the narrative is historical in kind? Clearly there are features of the text that seem very typological in nature. The introduction of Aaron in this sequence is plainly meant to symbolize and foreshadow the relationship between the

36. Aquinas, *In Ioan.* 15.5.2055.
37. See *Etz Hayim: Torah and Commentary*, ed. David L. Lieber et al. (New York: Jewish Publication Society, 2004), 333.

priesthood and the prophetic revelation of Israel. God has given the law through the prophets, which priests interpret and promote. Perhaps the authors of this passage are presenting theological ideas in symbolic fashion and are not concerned with conveying a historical truth.

However, here I want to mention two errors to avoid when thinking about biblical miracles. The first is a kind of gnosticism that denies the capacity of God to work in the material world and to act in ways that are manifestly miraculous. This kind of thinking must ultimately deny not only the reality of the miraculous as such but also the giving of divine revelation and the mystery of the incarnation. The other error is a kind of theological materialism based on an ideology that treats all miraculous portrayals in the Bible with equal importance and identical historicity. This view falsely presumes that the denial of historicity in any context amounts to a denial of the inerrancy of the scriptures or the power of God to act in history. However, narrative styles in the scriptures are diverse, and it is not always obvious that the text means to denote a historical fact.

There is a hierarchy of the miraculous in both the Old and New Testaments, at the summit of which is the resurrection and glorification of the physical body of Christ. This is more than a miracle since it consists in a new creation of the material order in a higher plane. The resurrection of Christ is the eschatological glory of God creating the world anew, yet it is also miraculous since it entails the activity of God working above the ordinary order of nature by the power that is proper to him as Creator. This ultimate "miracle" serves as the teleological term and reference point by which all other miracles are understood and evaluated hermeneutically. For example, the healing miracles of Christ can be understood as historical events proleptically prefiguring the life of the resurrection and the revelation of Christ as the Son of God.

Something analogous takes place in the Old Testament: the characteristic miracle that stands above all others is the miraculous deliverance of the people of Israel at the Red Sea. That miracle is itself historical and signifies proleptically the historicity of the physical resurrection of Christ that is to come. It exists in view of the incarnation and the universal redemption of humanity in baptism. Yet while the miracle of the resurrection comes last in the order of the actions of Christ, the miracle of the Red Sea comes first in the order of the life of Israel. All other miracles in Israel are in some way signs of the covenant God has established at Sinai/Horeb, either by way of reiteration (renewing a sense of its reality and ongoing significance) or as signifying an eschatological consummation of the covenant that is to come.

If one interprets things in this way, the historicity of these initial "magic-destroying" miracles on the part of Moses is of debatable significance. Perhaps these accounts are primarily symbolic and possess, above all, a typological significance: they show forth the fact that the faith of Israel will bring to an end the power of any magical view of the gods or of the universe.[38] This has effectively come to pass, to a great extent. However, it seems more fitting theologically to say the following. Moses and the early Israelite leadership employed the symbols of the Egyptians to suggest, by prophetic gestures, the limitations and falsehood of their sacral system. God fittingly gave signs to the ancient Egyptians of the reality of YHWH, the God of the Hebrews. Arguing about what exactly is historical in the narrative of Israel's deliverance by miracles is reasonable, but a theologically licit diversity of opinions is possible. Because God was at work in that particular cultural and religious context, the miracles worked at the time were of a particular kind, often physically overt and even brutal in nature. They were meant to speak to a civilization enmeshed in religious superstition and hardened by political brutality.[39] If miracles do truly occur, why are they not more spiritually overwhelming, converting their witnesses as if by necessity? The intentions of God must be the focus here. In the words of Pascal: "There is enough light to enlighten the elect and enough obscurity to humiliate them. There is enough obscurity to blind the reprobate and enough light to condemn them and deprive them of excuse."[40]

4:18–31 "And you shall say to Pharaoh, 'Thus says the LORD, Israel is my first-born son'" (4:22).

The second half of Exodus 4 consists of four segments.

First, Moses asks permission of his father-in-law, Jethro, before departing for Egypt (4:18–20). This may follow from his consent to stay with Jethro in 2:21. A traditional question: Why does Moses not tell Jethro his reason for returning to Egypt? Perhaps the event recounted here is intended to signify the break between the religious customs of Jethro, the Midianite priest (3:1), and the revelation of the Lord given to Israel. The inspired origins of the prophetic religion of Israel should not be interpreted merely in light of its natural cultural context (and this without denying the real influence the Near Eastern religion of the time may have had on the origins and development of early Israelite religion). At any rate,

---

38. Ultimately, as Maimonides notes, the miracles are ordered toward the giving of the law, so that the law is more important and fundamental to the life of Israel. Maimonides, *Mishneh Torah: Yad Hachzakah*, trans. A. Finkel (Scranton, PA: Yeshivath Beth Moshe, 2001), chaps. 7–8 (46–53).

39. Buber 1958: 64–68.

40. Pascal, *Pensées* (Krailsheimer 1966: 236).

the text clearly denotes the moral truth that the revelation of God to one such as Moses cannot be transmitted to others voluntarily. In proclaiming the revealed truth about God, one is dependent upon God to act first by grace in the heart of the other person to engender the receptivity necessary for the word's acceptance.

Second, Moses is told by the Lord to declare to the Pharaoh that Israel is God's firstborn son, that the Lord will slay the firstborn of the Egyptians, and that Pharaoh's heart will be hardened (4:21–22). Note that this is the first time that the Torah refers to Israel as the firstborn son of God. What is last in the order of realization is first in the order of intention. God intends in the exodus to make Israel a people of God who are adopted into a filial covenant of grace.

> But now thus says the LORD,
> he who created you, O Jacob,
>   he who formed you, O Israel:
> "Fear not, for I have redeemed you;
>   I have called you by name, you are mine." (Isa. 43:1)

Typologically, this sonship signifies the coming of Christ, the Son of God, who is at the core of the covenant. Anagogically, it signifies the life of beatitude in heaven, where the life of sonship in grace first manifest among the people of Israel will come to final fruition. "In the LORD all the offspring of Israel / shall triumph and glory" (Isa. 45:25). I spoke above about the fact that the Torah promotes a unique form of religious rational enlightenment to all human civilization, even through the medium of a sometimes archaic set of motifs. Exodus 4:18–31 is exceptional in this respect because it signifies three things: (1) that God knows from himself and in himself all future contingent events, (2) that God can and will realize his intentions for the human race independently of the disobedience and moral evil of human subjects, and (3) that the "hardening of the heart" of those who defect from the plan of salvation is something that God foreknows and can integrate into his providence but that he is also innocent of and does not cause per se. The literary forms of expression in the text are simple (and therefore accessible to all), but the rational consequences of the ideas are very profound. The Torah begins to elaborate a noncompetitive conception of divine and human causality, along with a vibrant insistence upon divine omniscience, human culpability for sin, and divine sovereign goodness. I will return to these ideas below.

Third, God comes to kill Moses at night, due to the fact that his son is not circumcised (4:23–26). The anger of God in scripture is metaphorical and signifies the vehemence of the justice of God. At the same time, the manifestation of the justice of God is based upon God's goodness and is a sign of his mysterious desire that the human person be true and attain intimacy with God by grace. The refusal of God's grace or the terms of God's grace is what most especially makes the human being subject to judgment, not least because by this rejection the human person refuses what is greatest and best in him- or herself.

This archaic text may seem to stand in contradiction to the point that has just been articulated. Is God not portrayed here anthropomorphically as an irrational agent or even as an evil spirit? Against this Manichean reading of the scripture, the Torah here is emphasizing in a very primitive and visceral way the rectitude necessary for a right relationship with God. Obedience to God must be conducted on God's terms and not conventional human terms. Induction into the covenant of God occurs through circumcision. Moses is not excepted from the patriarchal custom or from the law of God but is subject to God like everyone else, and even more so.

The text stands as a warning against the presumption of religious leaders who might come to think they are excused from the observance of the commandments of God. God is far more terrifying than Pharaoh. He is the author of life and death; God is good, but he is also sovereignly just. Here we see a foreshadowing of the coming of the Lord to slay the firstborn, as a punishment of the Egyptians (11:4). The Israelites will be spared because they place the blood of the Passover lamb upon their doorposts (12:7). Typologically, circumcision prefigures baptism, while the Passover lamb signifies the Eucharist.[41] It is true that God works by grace outside of the sacraments of the New Law. However, it is seriously presumptuous for a person to presuppose that he or she can knowingly forgo the means of salvation divinely instituted by Jesus Christ and yet still obtain the grace of salvation. On the contrary, such behavior is liable to judgment since it constitutes a very serious act of disobedience to supernatural faith in Christ.

Fourth, the Lord speaks directly to Aaron and commands him to go out to meet Moses "at the mountain of God" (4:27). The two of them then address the elders of the people of Israel, which is a typological image of the later life of Israel. Down through time, there are both inspired prophets and divinely instituted priests. They continually bring the revelation from Sinai to the people of Israel to renew the covenant. Anagogically, this also signifies Christ in his resurrected glory. Down through the ages, he is both the prophet of the Church and the priest,

---

41. See the argument of Aquinas in *ST* 3.70.1: circumcision inducts a person into the covenant of the Old Law, just as baptism does in the New Law.

mediating all knowledge of salvation to the Church and making intercession on behalf of all men.

Religious Error as Political Oppression (Exod. 5)

5:1–14 "Afterward Moses and Aaron went to Pharaoh and said, 'Thus says the LORD, the God of Israel, "Let my people go, that they may hold a feast to me in the wilderness."' But Pharaoh said, 'Who is the LORD, that I should heed his voice and let Israel go? I do not know the LORD, and moreover I will not let Israel go'" (5:1–2).

Considered from a historical point of view, the confrontation between Moses and the Pharaoh as it is portrayed in Exod. 5–11 is strongly pedagogically contrived, for theological reasons, and is composed in the rhetoric of a popular saga. However, this does not mean that we must discount any historicity to the events that are narrated. In the words of Martin Buber:

> In the Egypt known from history the negotiations between the King and the representative of the slaves cannot possibly have assumed any such forms as those recorded. . . . Yet even here, in this fantastic popular narrative, intended as it is to bring to later generations of the nation a sense of one-time passage of their history from wonder to wonder, we feel the breath of some distant event of which there is no longer any clear-cut recollection. . . . We must adopt the critical approach and seek reality . . . by asking ourselves what human relation to real events this could have been which led gradually, along many bypaths and by way of many metamorphoses, from mouth to ear, from one memory to another, and from dream to dream, until it grew into the written account we have read. It is certainly not a chronicle which we have to work on, but it is equally not imaginative poesy; it is a historical saga.[42]

It is significant to note that Exod. 5 begins with an insistence on the religious freedom of the elect people who are oppressed. Through the prophetic action of Moses, the defiant slave, God alerts Pharaoh to the responsibilities of his people: they must be permitted to worship him in "the wilderness" (5:1). This anticipates the journey to Mount Sinai and the giving of the law. Exodus 5 seems to give an unambiguous warrant for the political autonomy of the people of Israel. They must be free from the superstitions and religious errors of their surrounding neighbors in order to worship the living and true God rightly.

42. Buber 1958: 61.

Sociologically speaking, if one attempts to place this scene in its original ar-chaic context, one sees the sacred leader of an oppressed minority culture—who under the circumstances is their only political representative—asking for some kind of political autonomy by appealing to religious motives. He is promising divine chastisements if the group is not accorded this political-religious liberty. By contrast, Pharaoh, who presumes to hold a kind of absolute religious author-ity of his own, does not recognize the Lord of the Hebrews and believes that his authority gives him warrant for the physical oppression of the people. He is warned by Moses and Aaron of the potential for divine chastisements (5:3) and responds with a revindication of his own. He increases the mandated production of the Hebrews (5:4–9). The taskmasters of the people oblige them to gather more straw for the brick production (5:10–13), and the subjects are beaten when they cannot physically conform to the demands (5:14). According to historians, this show of power by the Egyptian government does correspond to practices of the age in which the exodus is traditionally dated.[43]

The political critique of human government offered in Exod. 5 is clear and profound. The pagan ruler's political omnicompetence over his subjects—and the grave injustice that it entails—stems directly from his religious ignorance and error, allied with human hubris. When rightly understood, belief in the God of Israel (who is the Creator of all human persons) acts as a necessary con-straint upon the pretentions of total political dominance over life and death, which are endemic to cultures both religious and areligious (the difference between the two being in some ways insignificant) in man's fallen state. Man's presumption to have political control over the practice of a true religion that has been revealed by God is also a kind of idolatry and stems from profound moral blindness.

5:15–23 "And they said to them, 'The LORD look upon you and judge, because you have made us offensive in the sight of Pharaoh and his servants, and have put a sword in their hand to kill us'" (5:21).

The pressures of the Egyptian government incite the foremen of the Hebrews to ask the Pharaoh for relief (5:15–19). When they do not receive it, they in turn utter their complaints to Moses and Aaron (5:20–21). Internal divisions erupt within the community. Moses then lodges a complaint to God on behalf of the people: "O LORD, why hast thou done evil to this people? . . . thou hast not delivered thy people at all" (5:22–23).

43. See de Vaux 1978: 1:324–27.

The primary senses of this passage are typological and moral. Typologically, it signifies the moral frailty of the chosen people, either in their journey through the wilderness or in the era of the settlement that is to come. These initial trials of the Hebrews are only a foreshadowing of the purification that they will undergo in the wilderness.

The moral realism of the passage is profound: being chosen by God and receiving both divine revelation and infused prophetic inspiration does not do away with the reality of the experience of evil. There are trying questions regarding the justice of divine providence (theodicy) to which even the saints are subject. The potential for serious tension between initial faith and profound trust is often acute in those who are less ardent in faith. Consequently, God does not spare from trial those to whom he reveals himself. On the contrary, God often wills or allows the multiplication of temporal trials so that believers are encouraged to seek concertedly their refuge in God alone. "For the Lord disciplines him whom he loves, / and chastises every son whom he receives" (Heb. 12:6). This is not due to any masochism on the part of God, who is infinitely just, but is a result of God's preferential love; God chooses to form human beings internally in heart and mind to be close to him. The friends of God are intimately familiar with his express will in a privileged but also utterly demanding way.

By this process, as the epistle to the Hebrews suggests, the grace of God conforms the elect to the image of Christ: "[By faith, Moses] considered abuse suffered for the Christ greater wealth than the treasures of Egypt, for he looked to the reward. By faith he left Egypt, not being afraid of the anger of the king; for he endured as seeing him who is invisible" (Heb. 11:26–27).

The Name of Mercy (Exod. 6)

6:1–13 "I appeared to Abraham, to Isaac, and to Jacob, as God Almighty, but by my name the LORD I did not make myself known to them" (6:3).

In 6:1, God responds to the complaints of Moses with a promise: "Now you shall see what I will do to Pharaoh; for with a strong hand he will send them out, yea, with a strong hand he will drive them out of his land." We then encounter the seeming interjection of a different textual tradition (normally identified with the Priestly source), which runs from 6:2 to 7:7. Despite the apparent textual discontinuity, there is a thematic unity maintained in the overall shape of the narrative and the theology it is meant to convey. Man has failed to deliver Israel, and the Hebrews have despaired of God; God is now going to assert his own authority.

At the heart of this statement is the reassertion of the divine name. The revelation in 3:14–15 is recapitulated: "I appeared to Abraham, to Isaac, and to Jacob,
as God Almighty, but by my name the LORD I did not make myself known to
them" (6:3). However, in the context of the narrative, the name is now given to
Moses in response to the doubts and complaints of the Israelites. God promises
to vindicate his own name by freeing the people from bondage and by establishing them in the land that was promised to the patriarchs. "I will take you for my
people, and I will be your God; and you shall know that I am the LORD your
God, who has brought you out from under the burdens of the Egyptians. And I
will bring you into the land which I swore to give to Abraham, to Isaac, and to
Jacob; I will give it to you for a possession. I am the LORD" (6:7–8).

A kind of commentary on this passage of scripture can be found in Ezek.
20:5–14. There God says that the revelation of the name given to the Israelites
in Egypt (not Sinai!) implies a kind of oath: "I swore to the seed of the house
of Jacob, making myself known to them in the land of Egypt, I swore to them,
saying, I am the LORD your God" (20:5). And then in Ezek. 20:8–9: "But they
rebelled against me and would not listen to me. . . . But I acted *for the sake of my
name*, that it should not be profaned in the sight of the nations among whom
they dwelt" (20:9, emphasis added). According to the prophet, the revelation of
the name itself connotes the eternal foreknowledge of God and his predestination of Israel, even in the face of human unbelief. God acts "for the sake of his
name" when God acts in fidelity to himself, to God's own wisdom and goodness,
to bring forth his designs over and above the limits and vicissitudes of his people.

Moreover, it should be noted that the name of God is associated in Exod.
33:19 with the attribute of divine mercy. There God states: "I will make all my
goodness pass before you, and will proclaim before you my name 'The LORD';
and I will be gracious to whom I will be gracious, and will show mercy on whom
I will show mercy."

Based upon these passages, there is a sound canonical basis for the tradition
of interpreting Exod. 6:2–3 as a new revelation given to Moses of the eternal
mercy communicated implicitly by the name of God. Rather than arguing that
the patriarchs did not know the Lord, Nachmanides argues that the true identity
of God was revealed to Israel more profoundly through time. Exodus 6 offers,
then, the new revelation that it is the eternal mercy of God that forms the basis
for all God's action in the economy. The initial failures of the Hebrews are an
occasion for God not to destroy or abandon human beings but to reveal more
profoundly the mercy that characterizes his divine identity. This mercy is at the

origins of God's covenant with Israel, God's eternal fidelity to that covenant, and God's saving plans with regard to the entire human race.[44]

In 6:12 Moses complains that he cannot speak to Pharaoh for he is a man of "uncircumcised lips." The complaint is reiterated in 6:30. This is the first figurative use of noncircumcision that we find in the Torah. Leviticus 26:41 later speaks of the "uncircumcised heart." In Deut. 10:16 and 30:6 the people are commanded to "circumcise their heart." Ezekiel and Jeremiah, in particular, speak of the uncircumcision of the heart: "Therefore thus says the LORD God: No foreigner, uncircumcised in heart and flesh . . . shall enter my sanctuary" (Ezek. 44:9). "For all these nations are uncircumcised, and all the house of Israel is uncircumcised in heart" (Jer. 9:26). This tradition, in turn, forms the background to Paul's spiritual theology of circumcision in Rom. 2:25–29: "Circumcision indeed is of value if you obey the law; but if you break the law, your circumcision becomes uncircumcision. . . . He is a Jew who is one inwardly, and real circumcision is a matter of the heart, spiritual and not literal. His praise is not from men but from God" (2:25, 29).

6:14–30 "These are the names of the sons of Levi according to their generations: Gershon, Kohath, and Merarʹi, the years of the life of Levi being a hundred and thirty-seven years" (6:16).

Exodus 6:14–25 interjects a mysterious genealogy. Why is it here? Seemingly, it roots the mission of Aaron and Moses within the prehistory of the patriarchal traditions (of significance, Aaron is listed first before Moses in 6:26). In addition, it suggests that the priesthood of the Levites is rooted historically in the mission of Moses and Aaron. Hence, the land that is promised to the Israelites (through the patriarchs) is a land in which the moral, juridical, and ceremonial laws of the Torah are to be observed, especially by those who belong to the Levitical priesthood.

According to this genealogy Moses and Aaron are born into the tribe of Levi only three generations removed from Levi himself (6:16–20), while 12:40 suggests that the exile in Egypt endured 430 years. Such inconsistencies demonstrate that figures and numbers in the Old Testament are often symbolic in character. In their literal sense, the figures are meant to denote symbolically a historical reality: that God has worked in this particular people that he has chosen—in their genealogical history of birth, life, and familial succession. Genealogies also denote that the work of God's providence unfolds successively through history and across generations. Consequently, they communicate the idea that the elect

44. Nachmanides, *Commentary on the Torah: Exodus* 3.14, 6.2.

people ought always to maintain theological hope in their future, despite adversity, as they participate in a history that is open to God.

Exodus 6:26–30 then reintroduces the narrative of Moses's mission. God again commands him to go to Pharaoh and "tell [him] all that I say to you" (6:29).

The Hard-Heartedness of Pharaoh: God and Free Will (Exod. 7:1–7)

7:1–7 "But I will harden Pharaoh's heart, and though I multiply my signs and wonders in the land of Egypt, Pharaoh will not listen to you; then I will lay my hand upon Egypt and bring forth my hosts, my people the sons of Israel, out of the land of Egypt by great acts of judgment" (7:3–4).

In 7:1–7, God commands Moses to speak to Pharaoh anew and tells him that he will "harden Pharaoh's heart" (7:3), after which God will afflict Egypt with extraordinary chastisements and "lay his hand upon [it]" (7:4), so as to bring out the people of Israel but also so that the Egyptians will know that God is the Lord (7:5).

It should be noted that (1) God foretells the future, which God knows, including the future of human contingent decisions; (2) God's knowledge includes infallible divine foreknowledge of human moral evil; and (3) God is seen not only to act in light of human moral evil that he foreknows but also to bring forth a greater good in response to and in spite of it. How is this to be properly understood?

The book of Exodus speaks in many instances of God hardening the heart of Pharaoh. In grammatical terms, the Lord is sometimes depicted as the active agent: 4:21; 7:3; 9:12; 10:1, 27; 11:10; 14:4, 8, and 17. In other passages, the Pharaoh is said to harden his own heart to the signs given by God. As such, Pharaoh is depicted as the principal agent: 8:15, 32; 9:7, 34; and 13:15.

In response to six of the plagues that strike Egypt, we read that Pharaoh's "heart was hardened" or that he "hardened his heart" (7:22; 8:15, 19, 32; 9:7, 34), while in response to four of the plagues, "God hardened Pharaoh's heart" (9:12; 10:20, 27; 14:8).

Those who hypothesize about the textual sources of Exodus sometimes conjecture that the passages where Pharaoh hardens his own heart stem from the J source and those where God hardens the heart of Pharaoh stem from the P source. The first author would be concerned to show the capacity of the human heart to resist God's calling, while the second would be concerned to emphasize God's sovereignty over the history of human free choices.[45] While this idea introduces an

45. See Childs 1974: 170–75.

interesting counterpoint of two true claims, it offers us only a superficial interpretation of the biblical text (even on the presupposition of the accuracy of the source
theory). In reality, there is only one humanly edited, divinely inspired, canonical
biblical text, and in it we are confronted irreducibly both with the agency of God
and the agency of the human person. It is not without reason that this passage of
scripture has become a *locus classicus* for the exploration of the relations of divine
causality and human free will.

Consequently, one should not attempt to evade the important theological questions that the text poses. If God knows the future of human free choices, does this
mean that God causes human free acts, and if so, are those acts genuinely free? If
God has infallible knowledge of future morally evil contingent actions of human
creatures, does this imply that God is the cause of the evil actions themselves? If
so, how might one maintain the innocence and goodness of God? If God is not
the cause of the actions, at least insofar as they are evil, then how does God know
of them beforehand and even from all eternity? Or if God is morally innocent
of the malice of creaturely evil, then does God really foreknow evil events prior
to their occurrence, or must God in fact be incapable of infallibly knowing the
future? If we deny that God knows all things in the creation, do we not implicitly
deny the divinity of God, contrary both to divine revelation and the realism of
sound metaphysical reasoning? Would not a God who is incapable of knowing
the future also be incapable of saving us from moral evils that occur throughout
human history?

Without seeking to answer all of these questions comprehensively, let me
begin with the scriptural teachings themselves, after which I will consider various
theological interpretations of the "hardening of the heart" of Pharaoh on the
part of God.

Beginning with the aforementioned passages within Exod. 7–11, the Torah
promotes here, in a particularly profound way, the form of biblical enlightenment
of human reason that I made reference to above. Through an archaic narrative form
and in a folkloric format, the author (or at least the final redactor) introduces a
number of principles regarding divine sovereignty and human free agency that are
utterly profound. The vision that is offered has implicit metaphysical and moral
depths that are explored in greater length in the subsequent givens of biblical
revelation itself.

Most particularly, the narrative presents us with a consistent pattern of (1) divine foreknowledge of the disobedience of the Pharaoh; (2) the promise made
to Israel that God governs history infallibly toward a good end, even in the face

of the human evil, which God permits; (3) a genuine warning given to the agent
who God foreknows will disobey; (4) an assignment of true culpability to the
human agent who carries out the evil; and (5) an effective realization in history
of the good that God had previously promised to accomplish in response to the
evil action. This may imply, among other things, actions of mercy on behalf of
the elect but also appropriate chastisements directed toward those who are (as
yet) unrepentant.

Of particular importance for understanding the theology at work in this section of scripture are 8:19 and 9:34. In 8:19 we are told, "The magicians said to
Pharaoh, 'This is the finger of God.' But Pharaoh's heart was hardened, and he
would not listen to them; *as the LORD had said*" (emphasis added). The prophecy
of God that is being referred to within the context of the canonical narrative can
only be that of 7:3, where God foretells that he will "harden the heart" of Pharaoh.
Likewise, we read in 9:34–35: "But when Pharaoh saw that the rain and the hail
and the thunder had ceased, *he sinned yet again, and hardened his heart,* he and his
servants. So the heart of Pharaoh was hardened, and he did not let the people of
Israel go; *as the LORD had spoken through Moses*" (emphasis added). Significantly,
this last phrase refers back to 9:12 and 7:3, where we are told that "the LORD
hardened the heart of Pharaoh."

When one considers these texts together the implication is clear. Scripture
is revealing a noncompetitive vision of divine and human freedom. God knows
human free actions from all eternity and is active in sustaining them in being, yet
this does not imply that one must deny the reality of human freedom or deny the
reality of human culpability for morally evil actions.[46] On the contrary, human
beings are free precisely because God does create them and sustain them in being
as free creatures and true causes in their own right, and God knows all future
human actions because God is the cause in very being of those actions. However,

---

46. Augustine offers a similar textual and theological interpretation of these texts in *On Grace and
Free Will*, chap. 45 (*NPNF*[1] 5:464):

> Nor should you take away from Pharaoh free will, because in several passages God says, "I have
> hardened Pharaoh"; or, "I have hardened or I will harden Pharaoh's heart"; for it does not by any
> means follow that Pharaoh did not, on this account, harden his own heart. For this, too, is said
> of him, after the removal of the fly-plague from the Egyptians, in these words of the Scripture:
> "And Pharaoh hardened his heart at this time also; neither would he let the people go" (Exod.
> 8:32). Thus it was that both God hardened him by his just judgment, and Pharaoh by his own
> free will. . . . [For] God will, therefore, certainly recompense both evil for evil, because he is just;
> and good for evil, because he is good; and good for good, because he is good and just; only, evil
> for good he will never recompense, because he is not unjust. He will, therefore, recompense evil
> for evil—punishment for unrighteousness; and he will recompense good for evil—grace for
> unrighteousness; and he will recompense good for good—grace for grace.

if God is the cause of the being of the free human creature, this does not remove the moral culpability for evil on the part of the human agent. On the contrary, God foreknows and permits human evil, even from all eternity, but God does not cause human sinfulness as such; God may justly chastise or remediate human evil in the way that is unique to him as the transcendent God.

Even according to this reading, however, one might ask what it could mean that God "hardened the heart of the Pharaoh." Does this not imply some kind of active complicity in causing the act of evil per se? The question is intensified by Paul's exegesis of this passage in Rom. 9:17–18. Referring specifically to the case of the Pharaoh, Paul exclaims, "So then he has mercy upon whomever he wills, and he hardens the heart of whomever he wills" (9:18). Here, however, the hardening of the heart on the part of God is said to pertain not only to human actions of evil within human history but even to the mystery of eschatological reprobation. Does God actively inflict the hardening of the heart even unto eternal damnation? This portrait of God would seem to undermine any attempt to defend rightly the divine innocence and goodness of God in the face of human evil, as well as its just punishment in this life or the next.

Aquinas notes that the scriptures often speak metaphorically of God hardening human hearts or governing sinful events, both of which are conveyed through rhetorical tropes that were common to ancient Semitic authors. Their purpose is to denote God's sovereign lordship and omnipotence in the face of human history. Yet the same scriptures also insist universally on the absolute innocence and goodness of God in the face of all human history: "A God of faithfulness and without iniquity, / just and right is he" (Deut. 32:4). Particularly, this is to be understood in the light of the crucifixion of God: "This is the message we have heard from him and proclaim to you, that God is light and in him is no darkness at all" (1 John 1:5). Consequently, one must affirm without compromise both the omnipotence of God and God's absolute moral innocence.

In what sense, then, does God "cause" hardening of the heart? God is only an "occasional" cause of moral evil and never a direct or indirect cause. God allows evil by causing inclinations toward a good that, while licit in itself, the human subject misuses to the destruction of the moral order. Regarding Rom. 9:17–18 and Exod. 7:3, Aquinas comments:

> [God] stirs [human beings] to good and to evil in different ways: for he inclines men's wills to good directly as the author of these good deeds; but he is said to incline or stir up men to evil as an *occasional* cause, namely, inasmuch as God

puts before a person, either in him or outside of him something which of itself is conducive to good but which through his own malice he uses for evil: "Do you not know that God's kindness is meant to lead you to repentance? But by your hard and impenitent heart you are storing up wrath for yourself on the day of wrath" (Rom 2:4–5), and "God gave his place for penance: and he abused it unto pride" (Job 24:23). Similarly, to the extent that it depends upon God, God enlightens a man inwardly to good, for example a king to defend the rights of his kingdom or to punish rebels. But he abuses this good impulse according to the malice of his heart. This is plain in Isa. 10:6, where it is said of Assyria: "Against a godless nation I send him, and against the people of my wrath I command him, to take spoil and seize plunder, and to tread them down like the mire of the streets." And further on: "But he does not so intend, and his mind does not so think; but it is in his mind to destroy" (Isa. 10:7). That is the way it happened with Pharaoh, who, when he was prompted by God to defend his kingdom, abused this suggestion and practiced cruelty.[47]

Based upon this reading, a number of problematic theological interpretations can briefly be noted.

First is the interpretation of certain gnostics and of Marcion, who argue that God the Creator is revealed in the Old Testament to be the cause of moral evil and therefore cannot be the true God who saves by grace.[48] On this reading, the Pharaoh might be said to represent all earthly men, those who are not gnostics. Being unenlightened, they live in view of merely temporal ends and are moved to do evil by the prince of this world. This view is absurd since it fails to recognize the existence of free will in all men. Furthermore, freedom derives from the spiritual, voluntary power of the soul; however, the human being is a substantial unity of body and spiritual soul, and human free actions take place in and through the body. Consequently, if God is the transcendent cause of free human actions, God must be the author of both that which is spiritual and that which is physical. Free human actions are sustained in being by the Creator, who is simultaneously the author of all things visible and invisible.

47. Aquinas, *In Rom.* 9.3.782 (Larcher 2012, translation slightly modified).
48. Irenaeus, *Against Heresies* 4.29. The Marcionites based their argument particularly on the hardening of Pharaoh's heart. As Irenaeus points out, there are passages in the New Testament that are equally insistent on God "hardening the heart": Matt. 13:11–16, which quotes Isa. 6:10; 2 Cor. 4:4; Rom. 1:28; 2 Thess. 2:11–12 ("Therefore God sends upon them a strong delusion, to make them believe what is false, so that all may be condemned who did not believe the truth but had pleasure in unrighteousness"). On this point, we see clear continuity. The God of the Old Testament is the same as the God of the New Testament. See also Tertullian, *Against Marcion* 2.14; Origen, *On First Principles* 2.9.5–8, 3.1.8.

There is a profound parallel, then, between God's actions as Creator and God's actions as Redeemer. Creation pertains to the whole person as both body and spiritual soul. Therefore, authentic salvation for the person must pertain to both the body and the spiritual soul. Only God the Creator, who is the transcendent cause of man's entire being, truly can save human beings— precisely because God is the author of their whole being and can act to redeem them both spiritually and physically. Jesus Christ can only be the savior of man, therefore, if he is the same Lord as the Lord revealed in the Torah as the Creator.

Second is the interpretation of Origen, who wrote directly against the gnostic position noted above and desired to emphasize both the moral goodness of God and the reality of human free will.[49] Consequently, he affirms that God's "hardening of the heart of Pharaoh" refers uniquely to God's permission of the sin of Pharaoh.[50] Rightly understood, this affirmation is true. However, Origen does not acknowledge in any clear way that God is the cause of the being of the free act, even when that act is morally deformed. Nor is he clear about the primary role that initiatives of grace have in the process of conversion. At times, he suggests that the just and the unjust receive identical aids or helps from God and are then judged by the ways in which they naturally avail themselves of this assistance.[51] He then goes on to add: God sometimes allows those who sin to linger longer in the error of their misconduct until such time as they have experienced greater misery and spiritual desolation.[52] This experience inclines those who sin to repentance, and once they have begun again their upward ascent toward God, God rewards them with the newly found offer of grace.[53] Such a teaching seems insufficiently sensitive to the primacy of divine grace in the work of human repentance and carries within it a note of Pelagianism.

Third is the error of Martin Luther, who reacted against the teaching of Origen, which was reiterated by Erasmus.[54] In commenting upon the hardening of the heart of Pharaoh in Exodus, Luther accuses Origen of denying the plain sense of scripture. God does not merely permit human sin; rather, God is the cause of the human sinful act and as such the sovereign cause of human agency in both good

---

49. See Origen, *On First Principles* 3.1.7–24. In 3.1.8 Origen makes clear that his analysis of the Pharaoh is meant to counter the interpretations of the "heretics," referring back to 2.9.5–8, where he discusses Marcionite and gnostic positions regarding human free will and evil.

50. Origen, *On First Principles* 3.1.10.

51. Origen, *On First Principles* 3.1.10–11.

52. Origen, *On First Principles* 3.1.11–14.

53. Origen, *On First Principles* 3.1.17.

54. See Martin Luther, *Bondage of the Will*, WA 18:696–709.

and evil acts alike. It is an error to conclude from this, however, that God causes human beings freely to sin. In fact, there is no such thing as genuine free will in the fallen human person. All voluntary actions occur by means of necessity, and such acts are necessarily evil in kind. In this case, there is no purpose to divine forbearance: "Man . . . is necessarily in bondage to sin; because once it is granted that free choice cannot will anything good . . . it is in no way made better by the forbearance of a long-suffering God, but necessarily worse."[55] God chooses to save only some by the mercy of his divine election, moving them to repentance by grace, while God wills to reprobate others, leaving them in their sins.

Domingo Báñez notes rightly that this position is in some respects worse than that of the gnostics,[56] who argued that if the God of Israel is the author of moral evil in human persons then he could not be the true and living God. In that sense, they sought at least to maintain the moral innocence of the true divinity. By contrast, Luther's position, while articulated with some nuance, comes dangerously close to attributing the causality of moral evil directly to God.[57] Even if such an idea is intended to safeguard divine omnipotence, it risks attributing to God the voluntary causality of moral evil, which, as Báñez notes, is blasphemous. Moreover, this latter position was condemned by the Council of Trent.

> If any one says that after Adam's sin the free will of man is lost and extinct or that it is an empty concept, a term without real foundation, indeed, a fiction introduced by Satan into the Church, let him be anathema. If anyone says that it is not in man's power to make his ways evil, but that God performs the evil work just as he performs the good, not only by permitting them, but properly and directly, so that Judas' betrayal no less than Paul's vocation was God's own work, let him be anathema.[58]

Last is the position of Friedrich Nietzsche, who reacts against the position of Luther. Nietzsche does not see the God of the Old Testament as real but as

---

55. Luther, *Bondage of the Will*, WA 18:702–9; trans. P. Watson, *Luther's Works*, vol. 33 (Philadelphia: Fortress, 1972), 170.

56. Domingo Báñez, *Commentarios Inéditos a la Prima Secondae de Santo Tomás*, ed. V. Beltrán de Heredia (Salamanca: Biblioteca de Teólogos Españoles, 1944), 2.79.4, para. 2–4, esp. para. 3, pp. 200–203.

57. Luther, *Bondage of the Will*, WA 18:709–14.

58. Council of Trent, Session 6, *Decree on Justification*, can. 5–6 (Denzinger 2012: para. 1555–56). In effect, Luther explicitly denies the classical theological distinction between the will of God and God's divine permissions of evil. See *Bondage of the Will*, WA 18:614–20, 630–39. In WA 18:709–33, Luther suggests repeatedly that the acceptance of the distinction carries with it the implicit disavowal of the existence of God as the cause of all things: "The omnipotence and the foreknowledge of God, I say, completely abolish the dogma of free choice; . . . If God foreknows a thing, that thing necessarily happens. *That is to say*, there is no such thing as free choice" (Watson, *Luther's Works*, 189, 195; emphasis added).

a literary projection derived from human artistry. The portrait of the justice of God toward human actions in the Torah is in reality an arbitrary construction of man, derived from the will-to-power of its sacerdotal authors. These authors promoted a slave morality that appealed to God in order to privilege the rights of the weak against the strong. In this way, the priests who promoted the Israelite religion surreptitiously sought power for themselves over the politically dominant and were motivated by their *ressentiment* of the temporal privileges of the cultural and political elite.[59] It is not the Pharaoh who is restricting the freedom of the Israelites but rather the Hebrew scribes who have restricted the freedom of Western civilization through their "invention" of the mystery of God.

This view is laden with philosophical errors, both epistemological and metaphysical. The chief error, however, is the denial of the reality and importance of the religious instinct in the human person. Nietzsche's contempt for the virtue of religion is based not on any well-founded rational argument but on the mistaken intuition that the affirmation of the transcendent causality of God inevitably threatens the autonomy of the human agent and his moral and aesthetic development. It is as if Nietzsche, like Luther (whom Nietzsche in certain ways admired), saw a fundamental opposition between the assertion of divine causality and the assertion of the autonomous freedom of the human being and that, in seeming contrast with Luther, he chose to dramatically assert not the primacy of the divine will but the absolute primacy of the human will-to-power over against the existence of God.

None of the abovementioned positions are compatible with the Bible's metaphysical realism and with the Catholic Church's interpretation of scripture. They all fail to acknowledge, at least in a sufficiently nuanced way, either the true nature of divine causality or the true integrity of the created order. Therefore, each position fails to attain a correct understanding of the relation between divine and human agency. In contrast to these diverse positions, one may hold within the Orthodox and Catholic (Eastern and Western) traditions any number of diverse viewpoints, though two basic ideas must be maintained. First, God as the Creator gives being to genuine created freedom in human beings. Second, with respect to the primacy of divine causality, there is not a pure parallelism between good human acts and evil human acts. In good acts, whether these are considered to pertain to the order of nature or of grace, transcendent divine agency is primary and gives being to human free agency. Any good in human agents stems primarily

59. See, for example, Friedrich Nietzsche, *Beyond Good and Evil* 5.195; *On the Genealogy of Morals* 1.7–8; *Twilight of the Idols*, "The Four Great Errors," n. 7; *The Anti-Christ*, 49–50.

from God, who actually causes them to be. In morally evil acts, the human agent is always the principal source of the deficit in the evil act. God is in no way the cause of the moral evil per se, even if God does sustain in being the agent who perpetrates the evil. The influential positions of Thomas Aquinas, John Duns Scotus, and Francesco Suárez on this topic do not agree in many respects, and yet all of them seek to uphold these basic givens of the scriptural faith of the Church. One may commend the position of Aquinas and the Thomist school more generally, which teaches the following ideas.

First, God is the cause of all that exists, including the contingent free actions of rational creatures. God's creative causality is, therefore, the primal origin of all creaturely freedom, not a source of its negation.[60] Free decisions of creatures do not occur by necessity. On the contrary, as Aquinas notes, rational creatures are "free contingent causes." They act through genuinely free and rationally deliberate actions.[61]

Second, God is the author of all that is good in reality, both in the orders of nature and of grace. Therefore, God is also the cause of all positive good in creaturely free actions. Any ethical goodness that a human person has by virtue of human action is truly in and from himself; simultaneously, and more ultimately, that goodness is only in and from the pure gift of the transcendent God, who is the Creator and the Author of grace.[62]

Third, all works of human salvation by grace are both preceded and sustained by the ongoing activity of the grace of God, including what Thomists call the "physical pre-motion" by which God moves the human will from the interior—not by violence, but freely and entirely naturally—so that the created will consents to and cooperates with the ongoing presence and activity of grace in the soul.[63] Consequently, no one may boast of his or her merits before God. Our cooperation with the grace of God is itself a gift that stems from the prior initiative of God.

---

60. *ST* 1.83.1 ad 3:
> Free-will is the cause of its own movement, because by his free-will man moves himself to act. But it does not of necessity belong to liberty that what is free should be the first cause of itself, as neither for one thing to be cause of another need it be the first cause. God, therefore, is the first cause, who moves causes both natural and voluntary. And just as by moving natural causes He does not prevent their acts being natural, so by moving voluntary causes He does not deprive their actions of being voluntary: but rather is He the cause of this very thing in them; for He operates in each thing according to its own nature.

61. *ST* 1.19.8.

62. *ST* 1.19.4, 1.23.6, 1.90.2, 1–2.109.5–10.

63. *ST* 1–2.9.6, 1–2.10.4, 1–2.111.2, 1–2.112.3; Aquinas, *De Malo* 6.1 ad 3 (Regan 2003). On the consent of the will even to the inward movements of operative, justifying grace, see in particular *ST* 1–2.113.7 ad 1.

Fourth, God knows the future of all free, contingent acts of rational creatures, insofar as God is the cause of the very being of all that will come to be in the future.[64] Therefore, God knows from all eternity in himself all that will come to pass in creation. God knows this simply, in the eternity of his divine wisdom, and does not "learn about the future" from the examination of creatures.[65]

Fifth, God knows all future acts of human evil. If God did not know such things, God would not be God, the Creator of all that exists, who sustains rational creatures in being even when they sin and as they sin.[66] Also, were God unable to know the future (an affirmation directly contrary to divine revelation and natural metaphysical reasoning), God would be unable to redeem the world from moral evil because God would be unable to foreknow its occurrence and so to act in his omnipotence to draw good even out of human evil.[67]

Sixth, God is in no way the cause of creaturely moral evil, whether directly or indirectly. God does not will human evil but only permits or allows it, in contradiction to God's express or manifest will that creatures should do the good and avoid evil.[68] Rightly, then, God holds creatures accountable for their evil acts and responds to their actions with mercy and justice.

Seventh, God foreknows all future actions of moral evil from all eternity, but God knows them through the medium of his "eternal permissive decrees."[69] That is to say, God knows from all eternity that he will allow particular creatures at particular times to fall into evil actions by their own fault and culpability. But such divine permissive decrees are in no way causal.[70] Creatures do not sin because God has decided from all eternity to withhold from them the necessary movements of grace or nature such that they must inevitably sin. To claim as much, as Aquinas notes, makes a mockery both of human justice and divine

64. *ST* 1.14.13.
65. *ST* 1.10.3, 1.14.8–9.
66. *ST* 1.14.10. "The knowledge of God is not the cause of evil; but it is the cause of good whereby evil is known [as a privation of the good]" (*ST* 1.14.10 ad 2).
67. *ST* 1.48.2 ad 3.
68. *ST* 1.19.9, 1.49.2, 1–2.79.1.
69. *ST* 1.19.9 ad 3, 1.19.12, 1.22.2 ad 2, 1.23.3.
70. One finds this doctrine in *ST* 1.23.3 corp. and ad 3. Commenting on this passage, Báñez emphasizes rightly that, for Aquinas, those who are lost to eternal life are reprobated only in light of their own culpable sin and that they *could have and should have* done otherwise. *Scholastica Commentaria in Primam Partem Summae Theologiae S. Thomae Aquinatis* (Madrid: F.E.D.A., 1934), 491: "Indeed, as St. Thomas indicates in the third solution to this article, reprobation does not remove anything from the power of willing in the reprobate, nor diminish his freedom, just as we have said that the permission, by which God permits someone to sin, removes nothing from the power and freedom [of that person]. Therefore, he freely sins, he who could have not sinned, had he wished."

goodness.[71] God can give to creatures the infused power to do the good and an initial inclination to perform good actions while at the same time permitting them to misuse this power by their own fault. This is not equivalent to God's causing the fault to occur.

Finally, creatures are able to sin because the rational will, being a feature of creaturely reality, is ontologically capable of failing to be all that it is capable of being or inclined toward being, whether in the natural or supernatural order.[72] This occurs when the rational creature culpably fails to consider the right rule of moral action and then acts anyway, based upon the impulse of the love of an inferior good, to the detriment of rightly ordered love for a superior good.[73] For example, a man who is Pharaoh may fail to examine the duties he has to his subjects (a negation of the rational truth) and then act based on problematic motives of political control or religious superstition. The absence of reference to the moral truth in the act is culpable. This negative absence in turn causes the act itself to incur privation; it is a true human act, though now deprived of right order toward the good.[74] If there is a supernatural motion introduced into Pharaoh's reason and will, inviting him to recognize God and the truth of divine prophecy, and he rejects this inward spiritual instinct that God has infused into his heart, then he is all the more culpable for acting through a negation of the truth and in a voluntary way that is deprived of its right order.

God can be said to "harden the heart" of such an individual in one of two ways: (1) God gives the created will the power to pursue actively the lesser good that the individual culpably has chosen. In this case, God sustains the activity of the immoral creature in being in spite of the negation of the truth and the privation

---

71. Aquinas, *De Malo* 6.1 (Regan 2003):
> Some have held that the human will is necessarily moved to choose things. But they did not hold that the will is coerced, since only something from an external source, not everything necessary, is coerced. And so also some necessary movements are natural but not coerced. For what is coerced is as contrary to what is natural as to what is voluntary, since the source of both the natural and the voluntary is internal, and the source of what is coerced is external. But this opinion is heretical. For it takes away the reason for merit and demerit in human acts, as it does not seem meritorious or demeritorious for persons to do necessarily what they could not avoid doing. It is also to be counted among the oddest philosophical opinions, since it is not only contrary to faith but also subverts all the principles of moral philosophy. For if nothing is within our power, and we are necessarily moved to will things, deliberation, exhortation, precept, punishment, and praise and blame, of which moral philosophy consists, are destroyed. (257)

72. Augustine, *City of God* 14.13 (Bettenson 1972): "But only a nature created out of nothing could have been distorted by a fault. Consequently, although the will derives its existence, as a nature, from its creation by God, its falling away from its true being is due to its creation out of nothing" (572).

73. *ST* 1.49.1.

74. *ST* 1–2.75.1, 1–2.79.2.

of moral rectitude that is in the person.[75] (2) God withdraws the helps of grace from the human person as a punishment because of the disordered act of the individual.[76] However, it is important in this case to add some qualifications. God never deprives a soul of the aids of grace unless that soul first culpably abandons God.[77] Many theologians also hold that God only abandons a soul "economically" as a temporary privation, so as to offer grace in a subsequent moment, after the spiritual misery of the creature has augmented.[78] It is possible, however, for a human person to persevere in the refusal of grace, and so it is also possible for God to reprobate human souls, leaving them over to eternal damnation—not because God causes their sins in any way but only because human persons have culpably refused the truth and grace of God, which has been effectively offered to them in Jesus Christ.[79]

It is possible to hold *that* all of these teachings are true without having a comprehensive understanding of *how* they are simultaneously true. None of the principles listed above is incompatible with any of the others. The perspective presented above is compatible with divine revelation and also harmonious with human metaphysical reason. Even if this is the case, however, any human knowledge of this matter is imperfect and must respect the mystery that is signified obliquely by the kinds of ideas sketched out above. One may affirm with equal vigor both the divine omnipotence of God (who causes human freedom to exist) and the divine innocence of God (who is not the cause of moral evil in any way), even while failing to understand comprehensively the mystery of how God is what God is and why God permits grave evils or accords profound graces in diverse instances. In this way, faith seeking understanding remains open respectfully and realistically to the contemplation of God in his transcendence.

75. *ST* 1.19.6 corp. and ad 1.

76. *ST* 1–2.79.3.

77. Aquinas holds unequivocally that Christ died for all human beings in order to offer grace to all. See, for example, *ST* 3.48.2 and 3.46.6 ad 4. As a seventeenth-century representative of the Thomist school, Jean-Baptiste Gonet offers a thorough defense of Aquinas's teaching against the charge of restrictive atonement (as found in Jansenism) by appealing to a range of such texts. See Gonet, "Depulso Jansenismi" 10.140–44.583–84, in vol. 1 of *Clypeus Theologiae Thomisticae* (Paris: Vivès, 1875). This position is typical of the Thomist school.

78. *ST* 1–2.79.4.

79. *ST* 1.23.3 ad 2: "Reprobation differs in its causality from predestination. This latter is the cause both of what is expected in the future life by the predestined—namely, glory—and of what is received in this life—namely, grace. Reprobation, however, is not the cause of what is in the present—namely, sin [of which God is innocent]; but it is the cause of abandonment by God. . . . But guilt proceeds from the free-will of the person who is reprobated and deserted by grace. In this way, the word of the prophet is true—namely, 'Destruction is thy own, O Israel' (Hos. 13:9)."

The Theological Meaning of the Plagues

The plague sequence in the Torah begins with a confrontation between Moses and Aaron on the one hand and the Pharaoh and his magicians on the other (7:8–13). Following this, ten plagues are depicted in Exod. 7–11. The last of these (the death of the firstborn) is referred to in Exod. 11 but in fact executed only in Exod. 12, consequent to the rite of the Passover. The literary structure of the entire sequence is complex, which suggests that a diversity of sources has been edited and placed together.

The first nine plagues are as follows:

1. Blood (7:14–24)
2. Frogs (7:25–8:15)
3. Gnats (8:16–19)
4. Flies (8:20–32)
5. Animal pestilence (9:1–7)
6. Boils (9:8–12)
7. Hail (9:13–35)
8. Locusts (10:1–20)
9. Darkness (10:21–29)

These events are depicted according to two general patterns. In plagues 1, 2, 4, 5, 7, and 8 (perhaps from the J source), (1) God commands Moses to warn the Pharaoh to let the people of Israel go and to threaten Pharaoh with the plague; (2) God then brings the plague; and (3) the Pharaoh negotiates with Moses to have the plague removed. A second pattern is depicted in plagues 3, 6, and 9 (perhaps from the P source), where (1) God simply commands Moses to execute the plague, and then (2) Pharaoh negotiates with him. In both patterns the final end is typically the same: the heart of the Pharaoh is hardened, and he refuses to let the people of Israel go. This sets the stage for the final confrontation in the tenth and final plague, which strikes down the firstborn of the Egyptians, after which the Pharaoh commands Moses to take the people and leave.

Turning first to the literal sense of this section of the Torah, the entire section is composed in an archaic, folkloric style. It is a narrative drama meant to convey to later Israelite auditors or readers a deep sense of moral trust in God and

God's power to deliver the people of Israel, even in the midst of the most adverse political circumstances.

Despite the very stylized character of this narrative and its significant literary difference from a strictly historical narrative, one should not dismiss the idea of a historical background to the plague cycle in Exodus. The plagues that are listed—however supernatural their literary depiction—also correspond in various ways to events that occurred (either regularly or occasionally) in the natural environment of Egypt. Martin Buber provides a hypothetical description of the events that could make sociological sense within the historical context. Moses acts on behalf of the Hebrews as a kind of *nabi*, or inspired prophet (Hos. 12:14), who goes before the Pharaoh to demand that the Hebrews be allowed to go into the wilderness to worship their God. Moses predicts that catastrophe will ensue if the demand is refused, perhaps by reference to the Nile River, which was red—as it frequently was before the river was about to rise. Subsequent adverse natural events unfold, possibly over multiple seasons: the infestation of frogs after a flood, a winter that brings destructive hailstorms, an eventual plague of locusts, and sandstorms that darken the sky. Competing religious interpretations of these "signs" are given—by the Hebrews, on the one hand, and by the magicians of the Egyptian court, on the other. The Pharaoh remains politically impervious to the religious ambiguities of this situation and refuses to concede to any minority viewpoint that would compromise what he takes to be his divinely warranted governmental authority. Finally, however, there is a wave of illness that takes the life of young children, including the child of the Pharaoh. In the wake of this disaster, he is laid low by the sense of his own impotence and mortality. He cedes to the demands of the "God of the Hebrews" and orders their prophet to take his people and go, perhaps still interpreting the cosmic power of their "god" from within the purview of his pagan superstition.[80]

The scenario presented above is only one possible sketch of how one might understand the historicity of the plague narrative. It could be altered in various ways. For example, one could expand the number of plagues and seek to underscore their miraculous character as *mirabilia Dei* by arguing that these historical weather miracles were in some way manifestly abnormal, terrible, and extraordinary. Nevertheless, even if one were inclined to argue that this is the literal sense of scripture, four theological principles should be kept in mind.

First, the plagues that are depicted in Exodus seem to be primarily natural in character (flies, locusts and frogs, hailstorms, diseases that strike cattle and human

80. Buber 1958: 66–68.

beings), even if they are also depicted as having a particular intensity, quantity, and extension. Therefore, according to Aquinas's definitions that I referenced above, they might be called miracles only in a looser, more attenuated sense. As Aquinas puts it:

> A thing is called a miracle by comparison with the power of nature which it sur-
> passes. . . . [This is the case to the least degree when] a thing surpasses nature's power
> [only] in the measure and order in which it is done; as when a man is cured of a fever
> suddenly, without treatment or the usual process of nature; or as when the air is
> suddenly condensed into rain, by divine power without a natural cause, as occurred
> at the prayers of Samuel and Elias; and these hold the lowest place in miracles.[81]

Second, one must be careful to avoid two theological extremes. If the plagues are depicted too "supernaturally" then they seem to be patterns of weather that compel the consent of faith and leave no room for the authority of the prophet Moses. The word of Moses has to be *believed* and does not pertain to something wholly evident. By contrast, if the plagues are minimized as mere events of nature without any providential connection to the teaching of Moses, then they have no real connection with the faith of the Israelites, and their interpretation as provi-dential events must be seen as the mere imposition of a given people's subjective religious reason upon the external world. The theological message of the scriptures here falls between the two extremes: God does truly work through the events of the physical world, even quasi-miraculously, to demonstrate to the Egyptians that the Israelites worship the true God. And yet this action is also sufficiently discreet that it refers those who witness it to the prophetic word that alone can truly interpret it. They are invited to pass to a higher or deeper level—from the outward miracle to the inward character of theological faith.

Third, then, the principle of Aquinas stated above should be kept in mind: charismatic or tangible graces are only ever given in view of the internal movements of sanctifying grace. External events can only be rightly understood religiously in light of supernatural faith, hope, and charity. It is significant that none of the plagues, arguably not even the last of them (the death of the firstborn), results in an acceptation of the faith of Israel on the part of the Egyptians. The miracles are only effective, then, for the Israelites who receive the message of Moses and the Torah. They serve to condemn the Pharaoh, who is culpable precisely because he refuses to accept the signs given by God and, by doing so, seemingly acts against

81. *ST* 1.105.8.

both reason and the inward movements of grace. Enough light is given to him that he is left without excuse, but not so much light is given to him that his free will is eradicated. The outward miracles one perceives can only be rightly "read from within" by the light of faith. Here they are meant to reveal to Israel that God is the Author and Creator of reality and that God can act in the very being of things in order to be the Savior of Israel. God who made all things can also refashion them in view of the determination of the covenant. God does so, however, in an alliance of faith with the people of Israel so that the outward manifestations of God's power do not encroach upon God's more ultimate purposes: the establishment of a covenant in the sanctifying darkness of faith and the fidelity of supernatural love.

Fourth, it should be noted that in the intention of the Holy Spirit—the principal author of scripture—the archaic character of the plague account is meant to do more than convey a merely historical truth. If one considers subsequent books of the Bible, the dramatic symbols employed in this narrative remain open, in retrospect, to a spiritual interpretation taken by later authors. It is only reasonable, in light of the principles of scriptural interpretation, to take this development in thinking as something willed by God. In this way, even if one were to insist strongly on the miraculous dimension of events in the exodus, it should be borne in mind that, in accord with the plan of the Holy Spirit, these events are themselves depicted in such a way as to be symbolic types; they prefigure the mystery of Israel and the Church, whom God separates from the irreligious Egypt of this world. A uniquely materialistic concern with physical events to the detriment of the inner dimension of scripture distorts the sacred and traditional meaning of Exodus.

An interpretation of the moral sense of the plague sequence is offered in Wis. 11–19, where the blessings of Israel are contrasted with the punishments of the Egyptians. At the center of the drama, the sacred author presents his analysis of the origins of religious superstition (Wis. 13–15). The book of Wisdom treats the exodus, therefore, as simultaneously a liberation of Israel for the true worship of God and a mocking chastisement of the gods of the Egyptians. Those who culpably ignore the Creator and worship creatures in the place of God are punished by God precisely through the medium of such creatures (11:15–16; 16:1). In this way God makes manifest God's absolute transcendence with regard to all his creatures but also reveals his imminent presence and power within creation, in the service of his divine goodness (16:24–25). God can be manifest in a uniquely imminent way *only because* God is the uniquely transcendent Creator (11:21–26). God alone, who truly is the unchanged cause of all that is, can act even at the very heart of existence within the natures of intraworldly causes that depend upon him for their very being in order to newly restore or transform them (12:1; 1:7). This is why the manifestation of the creative power of God in the plagues (which the author of Wisdom recounts with his own creative symbolic embellishments) logically invites an eschatological interpretation of Exodus (depicted particularly in Wis. 19:5–6, 18–22). The deliverance of Israel by the intervention of God acting immediately in his creation is itself a preparation for the end of the world when God will transform all things by his divine power. The exodus teaches us to hope in the transformative power of the Creator to make all things new.

The typological sense of the plagues can be seen as an extension of the moral sense. Augustine perceives a parallel between the ten plagues and the Ten Commandments.[82] The people who are being brought out of Egypt to live under the moral law of the Torah are Israel and the Church. The people who are being chastised are those who continue to live under the tyranny of the vices, symbolized by the ten plagues.

> The frog is very talkative vanity. . . . The locust is malice hurting with the mouth.
> . . . The hail is iniquity taking away the goods of others. . . . By the death of beasts
> was figured . . . the loss of chastity. For concupiscence, whereby offspring do arise,
> we have in common with beasts. . . . The death of the first-born things is the putting
> off of the very justice whereby a man does associate with mankind. But whether the
> figurative significations of these things be so, or whether they are better understood
> in another way, whom would it not move, that with ten plagues the Egyptians are
> smitten, and with ten commandments the tables are inscribed, that thereby the
> people of God should be ruled?[83]

The anagogical sense of the plagues is developed in the book of Revelation, in which the symbols of the Torah are seen to have a hidden eschatological signification. In Rev. 8–9 seven angels blow trumpets to inaugurate the final judgment of God, and there follows hail and fire (8:5–6), a sea of blood (8:9), a darkness that covers the world (8:12), and locusts that are demonic spirits (9:1–11). In Rev. 16, we see angels pouring bowls of punishment upon the world, including boils that incite spiritual revolt (16:2, 11), the turning of the sea into blood (16:4), darkness (16:10), frogs that are demonic spirits issuing from the mouth of the false prophet (16:13–14), and huge hailstones (16:21). The "Egyptians" represent those who refuse the gospel. The plagues of the end-time are above all

---

82. Augustine, sermon 8, *On the Ten Plagues and the Ten Commandments*, in vol. 3 of *The Works of Saint Augustine*, trans. E. Hill (Brooklyn: New City, 1990).

83. Augustine, *Expositions on the Book of Psalms* 78.25 (*NPNF*[1] 8:375).

spiritual in character: "locusts" and "frogs" are symbols of demonic spirits that afflict humankind, who have alienated themselves from God. The plagues that are deepest and worst are those by which human beings strive to turn in on themselves to live without God and apart from God. In the end, history is a proving ground in which the human person is invited into a freely chosen intimacy with God. Only this relationship can truly fulfill the human person, though he can reject the grace of God and seek to build a world of his own, separated from the divine commandments. This is the spiritual Babylon (Rev. 14:8) that threatens the heart of each human person, which can be overcome only with the grace of Christ, the true Passover Lamb (Rev. 5:6).

It is clear that the mentality and literary symbolism in Exodus are very different in character from that of Wisdom, a sapiential book from the Second Temple period, and from Revelation, a first-century AD, Jewish-Christian apocalypse. Nevertheless, all three texts make use of the plague traditions and the symbols they contain to explore an association of theological themes. If one understands the inspired scriptures as a whole, any one of these books should not be reduced to the other by ignoring the differences of historical setting, literary composition, and theological themes. However, one should not interpret them in isolation from one another either. There is in fact a plenary sense to the whole of the scriptures on this theme of "the plagues" that develops over time and that should be alluded to in considering rightly the inspired meaning of Exod. 7:8–11:10.

A final general consideration pertains to the topic of divine "punishment" or "chastisement" by God. Certainly this idea is central to the plague narrative as a whole, though it is also present throughout scripture in various ways. Is the notion of divine punishment for sins morally unreasonable or archaic? Does it result in part or in whole from an all-too-human projection of sadistic characteristics onto the divine and onto cosmic events? Even if not, does such a notion lead us to fear God excessively? I will respond to these queries briefly as follows.

First, the divine punishments in the scriptures are seen to be grounded in divine goodness, justice, and mercy. If God exists and God is good, then the presence of moral evil in rational creatures is something that contravenes the will of God, even though God does allow moral evil to occur.[84] It is just for God to respond to evil by reasserting the deeper metaphysical order of goodness in creation. To do so by punishing human beings in overt but limited ways is understandable and even merciful, since it invites human beings to embrace self-correction and moral

84. *ST* 1.19.6 ad 1, 1.19.9 corp.

rehabilitation. Thus, to deny that God rightly punishes the moral evil of rational creatures is to deny that God exists, that God is just, or that punishment is just. But these affirmations are problematic. The fact that the scriptures repeatedly denote the intention of God to respond to moral evil is evidence of the goodness of God in the face of moral evil.

Furthermore, if God never responds to moral evil through the medium of temporal events and if the reality of God's goodness and justice is never manifest in the internal order of history, then the goodness of God must have purely spiritual effects. In this case the work of God's goodness is utterly divorced from the temporal history of human beings and the physical world. Consequently, the physical world, human history, and the human body would seem to have no ultimate significance before God. In such an interpretation one detects the unmistakable presence of gnosticism (a dualism that opposes spirit and matter), which the Torah reveals to be erroneous. It is utterly befitting that God, because God is just, should manifest his sovereign goodness in various times and ways through the medium of physical creatures so as to denote the omnipresence of God's justice throughout the whole created order.

Third, we should note that the physical chastisements of God in scripture are typically intended for the health of the human soul.[85] Outward physical events can be perceived simultaneously, then, in two different ways, depending on the disposition of the subject. Those who hope in the mercy of God may bear with the deprivations or sufferings of this life with hope of rejoining God in God's goodness. Those who despair of salvation amidst human suffering may view the same events without hope of any spiritual amelioration. "Know then in your heart that, as a man disciplines his son, the LORD your God disciplines you" (Deut. 8:5). "For they disciplined us for a short time at their pleasure, but he disciplines us for our good, that we may share his holiness" (Heb. 12:10). The claim that divine chastisement is unjust or unreasonable stems from either an implicit denial of the goodness of God or from the despairing belief that God will not help one in distress.

Confrontation with the Pharaoh (Exod. 7:8–13)

7:8–13 "When Pharaoh says to you, 'Prove yourselves by working a miracle,' then you shall say to Aaron, 'Take your rod and cast it down before Pharaoh, that it may become a serpent'" (7:9).

85. *ST* 1–2.87.7.

In this section of Exodus we are meant to witness the confrontation between pagan magic and biblical miracles. The story is told in a dramatic form as the priests of the Pharaoh attempt to intimidate by magical acts or copy the miracles performed by Moses and Aaron. Eventually the priests are shown to be impotent in confrontation with the transcendent power of God. The narrative is meant to depict in miniature the movement of ancient human culture from an era of religious superstition to the era of monotheism.

In the beginning, however, it is difficult to distinguish what is truly miraculous from what is merely magical. Aaron, the priest, acts as an instrument of God to turn a staff into a snake, but this feat is also accomplished by the magicians of Egypt (7:11). Even though Aaron's rod swallows up their rods (7:12), the ambiguity remains. What is it that truly comes from God? Does the sacred author wish to attribute divine power to the Egyptian magicians or their gods? Clearly not, for they are not agents of the Lord. Is one to presuppose that they gain their power from trickery? If so, their religious claims to sacral authority are based on deceit. Do their capacities come from invisible spiritual powers? Exodus is largely taciturn on the subject of angels and especially the issue of demons. Other biblical authors associate the false gods of the Gentiles with demonic spirits, which is a view also found in the New Testament. "I imply that what pagans sacrifice they offer to demons and not to God. I do not want you to be partners with demons" (1 Cor. 10:20).

In modern times many are skeptical about the existence of the demonic, but demonic possession is encountered by Catholic priests with relative frequency—more commonly in the case of persons who have participated in the occult or in parts of the world where tribal societies practice various forms of witchcraft. It is not possible for an angelic spirit to create anything ex nihilo, but it seemingly is possible for them to displace objects, presumably as a tactic of intimidation. Priests who perform exorcisms on a regular basis do sometimes encounter dramatic instances of the physical displacement of objects. One need not necessarily presume that phenomena of this type are being signified by the passage in question, but such passages do invite us to recall the reality of spiritual evil present in the world and its potentially serious effects on human civilization.

First Plague: Blood (Exod. 7:14–24)

7:17–24 "Thus says the LORD, 'By this you shall know that I am the LORD: behold, I will strike the water that is in the Nile with the rod that is in my hand, and it shall be turned to blood'" (7:17).

The Egyptians regarded the Nile River as a manifestation of the god Osiris. Here they are mocked by the creatures they venerate (Wis. 12:24–25). In the first plague, the water of the Nile becomes undrinkable, and the fish in the river die (Exod. 7:21). "All the water that was in the Nile turned to blood" (7:20). Some modern commentators argue that this event can be understood in light of the flooding of the Nile; on rare occasions the Nile source regions would experience extreme floods because of extra-heavy rains that would bring with them masses of *roterde* (red soil) and the bacteria flagellates, which in turn would cause a red coloration of the river and oxygen fluctuation. As a consequence, the fish in the river might have rotted and died, leading to infections in the water.[86] Other instances in ancient Egyptian literature refer to the reddening of the river as "blood."[87] From the perspective of the scriptures, an irony is depicted; while the Nile was used by the Egyptians to put the firstborn of the Hebrews to death, it is now a source of death for the Egyptians.

This miracle is said to occur at the command of God, but it also takes place through Aaron, who holds out his staff (7:20), showing how God works in sacred history through the medium of the priesthood. Interestingly, in this situation the magicians of Egypt are able to do the same, and the Pharaoh is unimpressed; his heart remains hardened (7:22). The Septuagint says that the Egyptian "enchanters" were able to make water undrinkable "with their magical potions" (7:22). According to this interpretation, their power derives from mere artifice (external alteration of natural substances), in contrast to the power of God, who works through the things he has made.

Wisdom 11:6–8 draws a symbolic contrast between this event and the spring of water that is given to the Israelites to drink at Mount Horeb in Exod. 17:5–7. In their idolatry, the Egyptians drink from the waters of death; in their obedience to the Torah, the Israelites drink from the waters of life. This interpretation seems to be the deepest meaning of this passage of scripture. The Israelites will be delivered from the waters of death and will enter into the waters of life as a prefiguration of Christ. In the words of Paul in 1 Cor. 10:4, "For they drank from the supernatural Rock which followed them, and the Rock was Christ."

---

86. See, for example, G. Hort, "The Plagues of Egypt," 2 parts, *Zeitschrift die alttestamentliche Wissenschaft* 69 (1957): 84–103; 70 (1958): 48–59; Kitchen 2003: 251. Roland de Vaux offers a nuanced textual and historical evaluation of this proposal in de Vaux 1978: 1:260–66.

87. Kitchen 2003: 250.

Second Plague: Frogs (Exod. 7:25–8:15)

7:25–8:15 "But if you refuse to let them go, behold, I will plague all your country with frogs" (8:2).

The narrative proceeds by suggesting a sequence of natural catastrophes. After the summer flooding of the Nile receded, frogs began to amass on land. However, due to the poisoning of the water they eventually perished on land in large quantities. "And the LORD did according to the word of Moses; the frogs died out of the houses and courtyards and out of the fields" (8:13).

Hepat, the Egyptian god of prosperity, was depicted symbolically by the head of a frog and was associated with fertility. Wisdom 11:15–16 also indicates here that God made use of physical signs to mock the idolatry of the Egyptians:

> In return for their foolish and wicked thoughts,
> which led them astray to worship irrational serpents and worthless
> animals,
> thou didst send upon them a multitude of irrational creatures to punish
> them,
> that they might learn that one is punished by the very things by which he
> sins.

Due to their desire for control, they who took the lives of innocent children are now subject to a lack of control over their environment.

Wisdom 19:10 contrasts the Israelites crossing the Red Sea with the Egyptians subject to the pollution of the Nile. While the Israelites were able to pass through to safety, the Egyptians were subject to polluted water that sprouted forth frogs and gnats. The religious violence of the Egyptians creates a spiritually polluted world, while the Torah creates a world of spiritual life and health. One body of water leads to death while the other leads to life.

Analogously, the symbol of the frog in Rev. 16:13 represents the "foul spirits" that issue from the mouth of the "false prophet." Here the false prophet seems to represent either heresy within the early Church or more generally the one who leads human beings into error. Those who follow him practice unrecognized submission to unclean spirits. In contrast with the account in Wisdom, it is not God who mocks the idols of Egypt in Revelation. Instead, the demonic spirits seek to mimic the mystery of Christ by distorting divine revelation or seeking to obscure his mystery. According to this interpretation, the "pollution" of the false prophet distorts the true understanding of Christ.

Meanwhile, for the author of Revelation, it is the Passover of Christ the Lamb that frees human beings from this spiritual uncleanliness. It liberates them for the truth.

The magicians are able to multiply frogs, but they cannot cause them to disappear (Exod. 8:7). The Septuagint interprets this power, once again, as deriving not from occult powers but from human artifice. The magicians are like modern chemists, able to rearrange the order of the physical world by acting upon its material parts, but they are not able to act upon it from within, in its very being, to govern its totality. The transcendent power of God that is unique is contrasted with the limited control of human civilization.

In response to the plague of the frogs, the Pharaoh begins to recognize the Lord for the first time: "Entreat the LORD to take away the frogs from me and from my people; and I will let the people go to sacrifice to the LORD" (8:8). When the plague diminishes, however, he hardens his heart (8:15). This sequence is meant to suggest the Pharaoh's culpability. Knowledge of the Lord is itself a gift, stemming from the grace of faith. The Pharaoh can only resist the impulse of the knowledge welling up within him because of an influx of the grace that makes faith possible. In resisting, he is refusing his true capacity to recognize the Lord as God.

Third Plague: Gnats (Exod. 8:16–19)

8:16–19 "Then the LORD said to Moses, 'Say to Aaron, "Stretch out your rod and strike the dust of the earth, that it may become gnats throughout all the land of Egypt"'" (8:16).

Presumably the flooding of the Nile in the summer leaves standing pools of water. In the autumn, the result is the overbreeding of mosquitoes and massive numbers of insects that carry diseases.

The book of Wisdom contrasts the insects that afflict the Egyptians with the quail that the Israelites are later given as food in the desert (Exod. 16:13).

> The enemies of thy people worship even the most hateful animals.
> . . . .
> Therefore those men were deservedly punished through such creatures,
>   and were tormented by a multitude of animals.
> Instead of this punishment thou didst show kindness to thy people,
> and thou didst prepare quails to eat,
> a delicacy to satisfy the desire of appetite. (Wis. 15:18; 16:1–2)

At this point in the story, the magicians attempt to bring forth gnats (Exod. 8:18), adding a peculiar twist to the logic of the story. Why add further insects if insects are the problem? If the story possesses a certain logic, then one must presume that the magicians are meant to be depicted as perverse. They are not seeking to remedy the afflictions of their people but are worried about maintaining their religious power. In this situation, however, they are unable to compete. No matter how much technological prowess and human ingenuity advance, there are forces that transcend the human being. Recourse to God is always more rational, for God possesses incomprehensible power over creation in an infinitely higher and mysterious way, willing our true good.

Fourth Plague: Flies (Exod. 8:20–32)

8:20–32 "There came great swarms of flies into the house of Pharaoh and into his servants' houses, and in all the land of Egypt the land was ruined by reason of the flies" (8:24).

The plague of the flies comes along with that of the gnats or mosquitoes. They seemingly carry diseases dangerous to human beings and thus extend the cycle of miseries. Unlike the previous plagues, this one is predicted in advance to occur on a precise day, in order to show the Pharaoh that it comes from the Lord (8:23). It affects the Egyptians but not the population of the Hebrews living in the region of Goshen (8:22), which is identified in Gen. 45:10 as the Hebrews' place of settlement in Egypt. It may refer to Wadi Tumilat, a region that was often inhabited by foreign tribes during the New Kingdom (between 1500 and 1000 BC).[88]

The book of Wisdom (16:9–10) draws up a contrast here between the plagues of the flies and locusts and the serpents that afflicted the Hebrews in the desert (Num. 21:6; Deut. 32:33). While both peoples experienced chastisements from the Lord, one of them remained impenitent, and the other found healing by recourse to the mercy of God. Behind the deprivations of human existence, even those that are very significant, recourse to the presence of God and the hidden face of divine mercy is always possible. With the grace of God, every human trial can become an occasion for deeper faith and spiritual intimacy with God.

88. Kitchen 2003: 250.

Fifth Plague: Animal Pestilence (Exod. 9:1–7)

9:1–7 "Behold, the hand of the LORD will fall with a very severe plague upon your cattle which are in the field, the horses, the asses, the camels, the herds, and the flocks" (9:3).

The lives of human beings are bound up with those of other animals, which provide human beings with labor, food, and security. The vegetative and animal worlds form part of the "common good" of the larger cosmic environment. Therefore it is not surprising that the power of God, who is the Creator of plants and animals (Gen. 1:11–12, 20–25), should be manifest not only in physical nonliving things but also in plants and animals, especially those of most vital importance to the human community.

The death of the animals here seemingly takes place by plague. Some have conjectured, based on the logic of the narrative, that the death of the frogs and the rotting of their bodies contaminate the soil and plant life (with bacteria from the river). In turn this leads to a widespread sickness among the cattle. According to this theory, the cattle of the Egyptians are in a different region than the cattle of the Hebrews. However, it should be noted that the text portrays the event taking place in a single day, communicating a more supernatural but also spectral vision of the action of God—that is, an image of divine judgment.

Sixth Plague: Boils (Exod. 9:8–12)

9:8–12 "The LORD said to Moses and Aaron, 'Take handfuls of ashes from the kiln, and let Moses throw them toward heaven in the sight of Pharaoh.' . . . So they took ashes from the kiln, and stood before Pharaoh, and Moses threw them toward heaven, and it became boils breaking out in sores on man and beast" (9:8, 10).

The Lord sends boils upon the people of Egypt. The book of Deuteronomy interprets this punishment as in some way symbolic: the external boil is a sign of inner spiritual darkness. "The LORD will smite you with the boils of Egypt, and with the ulcers and the scurvy and the itch, of which you cannot be healed. The LORD will smite you with madness and blindness and confusion of mind; and you shall grope at noonday, as the blind grope in darkness" (Deut. 28:27–29). It should be noted that this Deuteronomic curse is given to the people of Israel, echoing God's former treatment of the Egyptians. From this one can conclude that God will chastise the elect as if they were Gentiles if the elect are not faithful to the law of God. However, an interpretation can also be made in an inverse order. If in Deuteronomy God threatens to chastise the Israelites because he loves them and wishes their conversion, one can conclude that the chastisement of the Egyptians is also ordered toward their conversion and amelioration. It is because the soul has culpably turned away from God that the outward plagues and inward sufferings of God are permitted, so that the soul in its misery may consider a pathway back to God.

Seventh Plague: Hail (Exod. 9:13–35)

9:13–35 "Then Moses stretched forth his rod toward heaven; and the LORD sent thunder and hail, and fire ran down to the earth. And the LORD rained hail upon the land of Egypt" (9:23).

Psalm 78 describes the plague of hail in relatively naturalistic terms. The "fire" mentioned in Exodus is interpreted as lighting; God brings a storm upon the Egyptians.

> He destroyed their vines with hail,
> and their sycamores with frost.
> He gave over their cattle to the hail,
> and their flocks to thunderbolts. (Ps. 78:47–48)

The book of Wisdom, however, understands this fire in what seems to be a miraculous and eschatological sense. The water and fire wondrously coexist.

> For—most incredible of all—in the water, which quenches all things,
> the fire had still greater effect,
> for the universe defends the righteous. (Wis. 16:17)

The universe is not self-moving but is a kind of instrument that becomes transparent to the mystery of God's justice.

> For the ungodly, refusing to know thee,
> were scourged by the strength of thy arm,
> pursued by unusual rains and hail and relentless storms,
> and utterly consumed by fire. (Wis. 16:16)

The Creator works through all things—including the elements of nature—for the sake of his chosen people.

It should be noted that the author of Wisdom perceives in Exodus the revelation of the mysterious power of God even to transform the physical cosmos, rendering it transparent to spiritual purity.

At one time the flame was restrained,

so that it might not consume the creatures sent against the ungodly,

but that seeing this they might know

that they were being pursued by the judgment of God;

and at another time even in the midst of water it burned more intensely

   than fire,

to destroy the crops of the unrighteous land.

. . . .

For creation, serving thee who hast made it,

exerts itself to punish the unrighteous,

and in kindness relaxes on behalf of those who trust in thee. (Wis. 16:18–

   19, 24)

Here the events of the exodus foreshadow a more ultimate revelation of divine judgment in the eschaton. The beginnings of the story of the people of Israel contain the seeds of the final ending. Why is this? Behind the action of God in the plagues lies the mystery of divine omnipotence. The power to work the wonders of Exodus pertains to He Who Is—God who alone creates from nothing in Genesis and is able to re-create the cosmos in eschatological glory. The book of Wisdom, then, comes very close, both historically and conceptually, to the understanding of God's power revealed in the New Testament. Only God can raise the dead. In the resurrection of Jesus Christ from the dead the early Christians recognized the presence and activity of the Creator and Lord, who unveiled to them the mystery of the eschaton and the final judgment.

Eighth Plague: Locusts (Exod. 10:1–20)

10:1–20 "Then the LORD said to Moses, 'Stretch out your hand over the land of Egypt for the locusts, that they may come upon the land of Egypt, and eat every plant in the land, all that the hail has left'" (10:12).

The image of locusts that devour crops appears in many places in the Bible. Locusts create a crisis of famine: "You shall carry much seed into the field, and shall gather little in; for the locust shall consume it" (Deut. 28:38). "He gave their crops to the caterpillar, / and the fruit of their labor to the locust" (Ps. 78:46). "He spoke, and the locusts came, / and young locusts without number" (Ps. 105:34).

The book of Wisdom portrays this outward plague as a sign of inward emptiness. The absence of the knowledge of God is reflected in the barrenness of the land of Egypt. Nevertheless, external signs or events are only secondarily important. What matters most is how a people respond to a given blight. The Egyptians and Israelites both suffer outward afflictions, but the latter are mercifully provided with the inward character to bear with such afflictions in obedience to God. It is not a question of whether all human beings stand in need of God's mercy but whether or not they will accept it (Wis. 16:9–10).

It is significant that in this passage, for the first time, the Pharaoh openly admits moral error before God. "Then Pharaoh called Moses and Aaron in haste, and said, 'I have sinned against the LORD your God, and against you. Now therefore, forgive my sin, I pray you, only this once, and entreat the LORD your God only to remove this death from me'" (Exod. 10:16–17). What is at stake in the deeper underlying drama is the acceptation of dependence upon God, the truth of the moral law, and of one's need for the forgiveness of sins. There is no presupposition that Pharaoh simply lacks moral understanding or monotheistic religious inclinations. On the contrary, the text only makes sense on the presupposition that they are present, however latent they may be. Pharaoh maintains some capacity to recognize the wrong he has done, both in relation to the slaying and oppression of the Israelites and in relation to the true and living God. However, his capacity to recognize these truths seems to have been obscured or ignored, due to a lust for domination and his problematic sense of political and religious self-aggrandizement.

Aquinas notes that there are primary principles of the natural law that pertain only to the most general norms of practical reason.[89] ("The good is to be done, evil is to be avoided." "Man should seek happiness in his rational, practical activity.") Meanwhile, he associates "secondary precepts" of the natural law with basic goods that can be known by a more developed application of natural reason, which many people do arrive at, even in the fallen condition. The precepts of the Ten Commandments, insofar as they reflect essential elements of the natural law, are expressive of such secondary precepts.[90] So, for example, the awareness of the basic goodness of human life and the wrongfulness of taking innocent human life is a "secondary precept" of the natural law.

This raises the question as to what extent the natural law can be blotted out from the human heart. In response to the question, Aquinas answers as follows:

> There belong to the natural law, first, certain most general precepts, that are known to all; and secondly, certain secondary and more detailed precepts, which are, as it

89. *ST* 1–2.92.2, 4.
90. *ST* 1–2.100.1, 3.

were, conclusions following closely from first principles. As to those general principles, the natural law, in the abstract, can nowise be blotted out from men's hearts. But it is blotted out in the case of a particular action, in so far as reason is hindered from applying the general principle to a particular point of practice, on account of concupiscence or some other passion (see *ST* 1–2.77.2). But as to the other, i.e., the secondary precepts, the natural law can be blotted out from the human heart, either by evil persuasions, just as in speculative matters errors occur in respect of necessary conclusions; or by vicious customs and corrupt habits, as among some men, theft, and even unnatural vices, as the Apostle states (Rom. 1:19–32), were not esteemed sinful.[91]

The book of Revelation interprets the "locusts" of Exodus in an apocalyptic and spiritual sense. The spiritual barrenness of humanity is depicted in a post-Christian age, alienated from Christ. The spirits that come up from "the bottomless pit" attempt to turn human beings away from interest in God by way of fear and seduction.

And in those days men will seek death and will not find it; they will long to die, and death will fly from them.
    In appearance the locusts were like horses arrayed for battle; on their heads were what looked like crowns of gold; their faces were like human faces, their hair like women's hair, and their teeth like lions' teeth; they had scales like iron breastplates, and the noise of their wings was like the noise of many chariots with horses rushing into battle. (Rev. 9:6–9)

The battle in question is spiritual and primarily interior, and the victory of the people of God can only come through the power and presence of Christ. A participation in his victory is communicated to the soul by faith. "For whatever is born of God overcomes the world; and this is the victory that overcomes the world, our faith" (1 John 5:4).

Ninth Plague: Darkness (Exod. 10:21–29)

10:21–29 "Then the LORD said to Moses, 'Stretch out your hand toward heaven that there may be darkness over the land of Egypt, a darkness to be felt'" (10:21).
    Darkness is a symbol employed throughout scripture, with a great diversity of significations. In this context the following should be kept in mind: the person who sins blinds himself and in turn is imprisoned in darkness. "You shall grope at

91. *ST* 1–2.94.6 (EDP 1947).

noonday, as the blind grope in darkness, and you shall not prosper in your ways"
(Deut. 28:29). Darkness of mind and heart can stem from human beings who inflict
it upon themselves, but God can also withhold illumination as a form of warning,
perhaps in order to invite repentance: "that thou shouldst have broken us in the
place of jackals, / and covered us with deep darkness" (Ps. 44:19). The symbol of
darkness is also employed to signify the threat of death and nothingness: "Before I
go whence I shall not return, / to the land of gloom and deep darkness" (Job 10:21).

Wisdom 17:2–3 contains an especially profound recollection in this respect.
The Egyptians sought to hide themselves from the light of God, taking their own
counsel as the most ultimate light to guide their behavior. But in doing so, they
darkened their own intellects and lived in separation or alienation from the true
light that saves.

> For when lawless men supposed that they held the holy nation in their
>   power,
> they themselves lay as captives of darkness and prisoners of long night,
> shut in under their roofs, exiles from eternal providence.
> For thinking that in their secret sins they were unobserved
> behind a dark curtain of forgetfulness,
> they were scattered, terribly alarmed,
> and appalled by specters.

Wisdom goes on to contrast this with the light of the Torah that was given
to the Israelites.

> For their enemies deserved to be deprived of light and imprisoned in
>   darkness,
> those who had kept thy sons imprisoned,
> through whom the imperishable light of the law was to be given to the
>   world. (Wis. 18:4)

Precisely because the Egyptians refused the light that was coming into the world
through the Hebrews, their minds were darkened. The sacred author was aware,
of course, that in the narrative of Exodus the law is given only subsequent to the
departure of the Hebrews from Egypt. Consequently, the author sees the truth
already coming into the world through the prophecies and signs of Moses, who
appeals to the inner conscience of the Gentiles and to the law naturally written
on men's hearts.

Of course, the objection may be made that a human being cannot remedy his or her own moral darkness without the help of grace and that, consequently, there is darkness in the mind of a person only as a result of God's neglect of the individual human soul. This interpretation is incorrect, for as Aquinas points out:

> Although one may neither merit in advance nor call forth divine grace by a movement of his free choice, he is able to prevent himself from receiving this grace: Indeed, it is said in Job (21:34): "Who have said to God: Depart from us, we desire not the knowledge of Your ways"; and in Job (24:13): "They have been rebellious to the light." And since this ability to impede or not to impede the reception of divine grace is within the scope of free choice, not undeservedly is responsibility for the fault imputed to him who offers an impediment to the reception of grace. In fact, as far as He is concerned, God is ready to give grace to all; "indeed He wills all men to be saved, and to come to the knowledge of the truth," as is said in 1 Timothy 2:4. But those alone are deprived of grace who offer an obstacle within themselves to grace; just as, while the sun is shining on the world, the man who keeps his eyes closed is held responsible for his fault, if as a result some evil follows, even though he could not see unless he were provided in advance with light from the sun.[92]

Tenth Plague: Death of the Firstborn (Exod. 11:1–10)

11:1–10 "The LORD said to Moses, 'Yet one plague more I will bring upon Pharaoh and upon Egypt; afterwards he will let you go hence; when he lets you go, he will drive you away completely'" (11:1).

The tenth and final plague is announced in Exod. 11, but it transpires in 12:29–32. "At midnight the LORD smote all the first-born in the land of Egypt, from the first-born of Pharaoh who sat on his throne to the first-born of the captive who was in the dungeon, and all the first-born of the cattle" (12:29). In the final redaction of the text, this partition between the announcement and the final action is meant to provide space for the institution of the ritual of the Passover lamb in 12:1–28. It is because the people of God perform this ceremony and cover the lintels of their houses with blood (12:7) that they are spared from the tenth and final plague. As I note in the consideration of Exod. 12, this is theologically significant. The elect people receive mercy and not legitimate punishment because they exist under the protection of the blood of the Passover lamb.

92. *SCG* 3.159 (Bourke 1956).

In their teaching regarding the death of the Egyptian firstborn, the scriptures indicate an ironic form of divine justice. The Egyptians sought to subjugate the Hebrews by means of a strategically planned genocide, but instead they are punished and obliged to liberate the Hebrews due to the death of their own firstborn.

> When they had resolved to kill the babes of thy holy ones,
> and one child had been exposed and rescued,
>   thou [Lord] didst in punishment take away a multitude of their children.
>   (Wis. 18:5)

It is this punishment that seemingly awakens the Pharaoh at last to the truth about the Lord in Exod. 12:31: "And he summoned Moses and Aaron by night, and said, 'Rise up, go forth from among my people, both you and the people of Israel; and go, serve the LORD, as you have said.'"

> For though they had disbelieved everything because of their magic arts,
> yet, when their first-born were destroyed, they acknowledged thy people
>   to be God's son. (Wis. 18:13)

Excursus: The Death of the Firstborn and the Transcendent Justice of God

The death of the firstborn raises an important set of moral questions. The scriptures clearly reveal that Pharaoh does not have the right to take innocent human life, though the God of Israel, the Lord and Creator, does have a transcendent "right" to do so. How are we to understand this? Furthermore, how is this action truly illustrative of the divine justice, goodness, and innocence of God? How are we to understand the role that death plays in the divine economy?

To these concerns we may note three things.

First, due to our fallen condition, human beings do habitually project onto the divine either images of unjust severity or presumptive liberality that are alien to the divinity and that reflect the deformed character of the fallen human creature rather than the Godhead. Consequently, it is reasonable to be concerned about the accuracy or truth of certain portraits of God that have arisen in human history. Human idolatry lurks under the surface of much that people say about God. In addition, we should be aware that the Old Testament contains certain ways of denoting the mystery of divine justice that are quite grave. These denotations are inspired by the Holy Spirit and are instructive as saving truth, but they are also portrayed through the idioms of a culture that was archaic and (at least in some respects) politically brutal. This is not a reason to reject any aspect of the Torah. Rather, its inspired teaching can be more poignant and profound precisely because it is given in an idiom of trenchant severity and even divinely inspired "primitiveness." Furthermore, we are capable of evading truths about the justice of God and our judgment before God by recourse to our own culturally contrived projections upon the deity. By these, we in turn are the idolaters who project onto God a benign indifference to evil or a complacency with the moral outrages of the killing of innocent children. By this delusion, human beings seek to evade a sufficiently realistic sense of the justice of God. The Torah mercifully confronts us with the impermissibility of this strategy and in this way makes room in truth for an ethic of mercy and redemption. There can only be mercy and the forgiveness of sins where the truth about divine justice and the reality of sin are also acknowledged.

Second, it is especially important to see the difference that obtains between human beings and God with respect to human life and human death. Human beings do not have the power to take innocent human life precisely because it is sacred. The human being is made in the image of God (Gen. 1:26), who is the transcendent author of human life. Although this is not made fully explicit in the Torah but only in subsequent scripture, the ultimate foundation for this dignity is the immaterial spiritual soul of the human person, which is the form of the human body.[93] Human beings transmit life biologically by conceiving new human life in the womb, but in doing so, they also cooperate with the transcendent, creative act of God, who creates the spiritual soul of each human being directly and immediately, without the intermediary of the human parents.[94] The human person is one substance (not two), composed of spiritual soul

93. The scriptures affirm the immateriality of the human soul, designating its reality at least implicitly, in Wis. 3:1–9; 2 Macc. 6:30; Matt. 10:28 and 26:38; Luke 16:22–23; John 12:27; Acts 2:41; and Phil. 1:23–24. The scripturally founded notion of the soul as the "form" of the body (such that the human person is one substantial whole, body and soul) was affirmed at the Council of Vienne in 1312.

> Furthermore, with the approval of the holy council We reject as erroneous and contrary to the truth of the Catholic faith any doctrine or opinion that rashly asserts that the substance of the rational and intellectual soul is not truly and of itself the form of the human body or that calls this into doubt. . . . We define that from now on whoever presumes to assert, defend, or obstinately hold that the rational and intellectual soul is not of itself and essentially the form of the human body is to be censured as heretic. (Denzinger 2012: para. 902)

In 1513, the Fifth Lateran Council went on to affirm that the soul that is the form of the body is also of itself immaterial and incorruptible. "The intellectual soul is not only truly, of itself and essentially, the form of the human body, as it is stated in the canon . . . issued by the Council of Vienne, but it is also immortal and, according to the great number of bodies into which it is individually infused, it can be, must be, and is multiplied" (Denzinger 2012: 1440). This truth was reiterated by the Congregation for the Doctrine of Faith in 1979 in the letter to bishops, *Recentiores episcoporum synodi*.

> The Church affirms that a spiritual element survives and subsists after death, an element endowed with consciousness and will, so that the "human self" subsists in the interim but without the complement of its body. To designate this element, the Church uses the word "soul," the accepted term in the usage of Scripture and tradition. Although not unaware that the term has various meanings in the Bible, the Church thinks that there is no valid reason for rejecting it; moreover, she considers that the use of some word as a vehicle is absolutely indispensable in order to support the faith of Christians. (Denzinger 2012: para. 4653)

94. This teaching was already noted above at the Fifth Lateran Council. See, likewise, Pius XII, *Humani generis*: "For these reasons the Teaching Authority of the Church does not forbid that, in conformity with the present state of human sciences and sacred theology, research and discussions, on the part of men experienced in both fields, take place with regard to the doctrine of evolution, in as far as it inquires into the origin of the human body as coming from pre-existent and living matter . . . [However,]

and animal body. This spiritual soul is endowed with immaterial faculties of intellect and free will, which are at the core of human personhood. The human being retains his or her spiritual dignity throughout life as a being who is always sustained in existence directly by God, even as he or she is also dependent for his or her existence upon a great web of physical and social conditions in the larger cosmos. Thus every human life is sacred from conception to natural death because it is spiritual in kind and depends for its very subsistence upon the direct action of God, the author of spiritual personhood.

As pertaining to the inviolability of human life, God is to be understood in differentiation from all human beings. This is not because he is "excused" from respecting the ontological laws of human dignity but because he is their author. There is no shadow of evil in God. He is infinitely good, just, and innocent. But God is also utterly transcendent and the cause of all that exists. Creatures derive their very being from God's wisdom, goodness, and justice and are given existence as an unmerited gift that they can never repay; each human person is a unique expression of God's own eternal dignity. Because God is the total giver of all that exists, including human personhood, there is nothing in the creature that adds to the nobility of God's being, and the creature, in truth, has no rights before God. This does not mean that God is despotic. God is bound to act only in accord with what God is in himself, and God is utterly good and just; God is "faithful to himself." Consequently, God's actions as well as God's permissions are expressive of God's nature.

God is also just and judges human beings by a standard of transcendent justice that is both mysterious and infinite. This justice is never divorced from God's mercy and goodness, but it is nevertheless exacting and real. God has permitted all human beings to die as a consequence of the original sin of the first human couple.[95] While

---

the Catholic faith obliges us to hold that souls are immediately created by God" (Denzinger, 2012: para. 3896). Likewise, see Paul VI, *Solemni Hac Liturgia* [Credo of the People of God], Vatican Website, June 30, 1968, para. 8, http://www.vatican.va/holy_father/paul_vi/motu_proprio/documents/hf_p-vi_motu -proprio_19680630_credo_en.html: "We believe in one only God, Father, Son and Holy Spirit, creator of things visible such as this world in which our transient life passes, of things invisible such as the pure spirits which are also called angels, and creator in each man of his spiritual and immortal soul."

95. *Catechism of the Catholic Church*, para. 390 (Catholic Church 1995): "The account of the fall in Genesis 3 uses figurative language, but affirms a primeval event, a deed that took place at the beginning of the history of man. Revelation gives us the certainty of faith that the whole of human history is marked by the original fault freely committed by our first parents." Paragraphs 402–4 (Catholic Church 1995):

All men are implicated in Adam's sin, as Paul affirms: "By one man's disobedience many (that is, all men) were made sinners": "sin came into the world through one man and death through sin, and so death spread to all men because all men sinned" (Rom. 5:12, 19). The Apostle contrasts the universality of sin and death with the universality of salvation in Christ. "Then as one man's trespass led to condemnation for all men, so one man's act of righteousness leads to acquittal and life for all men" (Rom. 5:18). Following Paul, the Church has always taught that the overwhelming misery which oppresses men and their inclination towards evil and death cannot be understood apart from their connection with Adam's sin and the fact that he has transmitted to us a sin with which we are all born afflicted, a sin which is the "death of the soul" (Council of Trent [Denzinger 2012: para. 1512]). Because of this certainty of faith, the Church baptizes for the remission of sins even tiny infants who have not committed personal sin (Council of Trent [Denzinger 2012: para. 1514]). How did the sin of Adam become the sin of all his descendants? The whole human race

this may seem unfair, it is in fact just and even merciful, for in the face of the offense of the human rejection of God, God has the prerogative for wise reasons to withdraw the privilege of being and life from his creatures. Augustine notes that by making man subject to the first death of Adam, God has given the human being impetus to seek God in the face of his own mortality. Thus the first death is a kind of severe mercy that invites the human being to avoid the punishment of the second, eternal death of everlasting damnation (that is, willfully chosen spiritual separation from God, which endures forever).[96]

That God should make use of the enigmatic event of death to chastise human beings is mysterious and in some real sense terrible or frightening. However, it is not unjust or unwise for God to act in this way. By taking the lives of the firstborn (and in doing so, taking these personal, innocent creatures "back" into God's own eternal mystery), God reveals to pagan humanity that he is the author of life and that his providence alone can safeguard their future. The project of life without God is a project that is futureless. The chastisement of the Pharaoh and the Egyptians is thus meant to open them up to the reality of their dependence upon the transcendent mystery not only of God's sovereign justice but also God's sovereign goodness and mercy.

The hidden, inner side of this mystery is that the Lord God of Israel also intends eventually to "make use" of human death to save the human race. God does so by becoming human and being subject to death in a human body and soul, so as to introduce into human history the mystery of the resurrection from the dead. Through God's own human death, God—who is life without diminishment—communicates to the entire human race the possibility of eternal life. Revealed in Jesus Christ, this mystery has, at least potentially, a universal extension in scope.[97] The death of Christ thus reaches even to those children that God has permitted to die as a consequence of the sins of members of the human race.

In summary, human death is the separation of the body and the spiritual soul. As such, death was not intended by God but entered the world through sin, by which our first parents forsook the graces of original justice (Rom. 5:12). Thus the human race is bound collectively by the reality of death. God makes use of death, however, to

---

is in Adam "as one body of one man" (Aquinas, *De Malo* 4.1). By this "unity of the human race" all men are implicated in Adam's sin, as all are implicated in Christ's justice. Still, the transmission of original sin is a mystery that we cannot fully understand. But we do know by Revelation that Adam had received original holiness and justice not for himself alone, but for all human nature. By yielding to the tempter, Adam and Eve committed a personal sin, but this sin affected the human nature that they would then transmit in a fallen state (Council of Trent, 1546, see Heb. 2:14). It is a sin which will be transmitted by propagation to all mankind, that is, by the transmission of a human nature deprived of original holiness and justice, and that is why original sin is called "sin" only in an analogical sense: it is a sin "contracted" and not "committed"— a state and not an act.

96. Augustine, *City of God* 13.15.

97. Second Vatican Council, *Gaudium et Spes*, para. 22 (Denzinger 2012: para. 4322): "For, since Christ died for all men, and since the ultimate vocation of man is in fact one, and divine, we ought to believe that the Holy Spirit in a manner known to God offers to every man the possibility of being associated with this paschal mystery."

humble and to invite the human race to repentance and eternal salvation. Corporeal suffering can become an occasion for spiritual transformation, even with regard to the death of the firstborn. This particularly severe act of divine judgment is meant to teach the Egyptian civilization its dependence upon God, from whom alone it can receive its future. However, God also united himself to the human race in its collectivity by taking on a human nature like ours and by experiencing death himself. In doing so out of perfect human obedience and charity, the Son of God offers us his grace and makes it possible for all human beings to experience death as a passage toward God. Moreover, God makes it possible for us to hope in the salvation and beatification of children who die prematurely and to confide them to God with confidence in his mercy.

The Passover Lamb (Exod. 12:1–51)

12:1–14

Tell all the congregation of Israel that on the tenth day of this month they shall take every man a lamb according to their fathers' houses, a lamb for a household; and if the household is too small for a lamb, then a man and his neighbor next to his house shall take according to the number of persons; according to what each can eat you shall make your count for the lamb. Your lamb shall be without blemish, a male a year old; you shall take it from the sheep or from the goats; and you shall keep it until the fourteenth day of this month, when the whole assembly of the congregation of Israel shall kill their lambs in the evening. Then they shall take some of the blood, and put it on the two doorposts and the lintel of the houses in which they eat them. They shall eat the flesh that night, roasted; with unleavened bread and bitter herbs they shall eat it. (12:3–8)

The text of Exod. 12 has been subject to an exceptional degree of analysis and debate, both historically and theologically. The chapter contains one version of the institution of the Passover ritual (12:1–14, 21–27), as well as that of the Unleavened Bread (12:15–20). It should be noted that these are two different rituals that have been placed alongside one another in this text. Other accounts of the Passover ritual can be found in Lev. 23:5–8; Num. 28:16–25; and Deut. 16:1–8, but here we are presented with one traditional variant of the rite. According to most commentators, the final version of the text is the product of a complex redaction (perhaps Priestly), though identification of the precise sources that lie behind the text remains controversial.

Most historical commentators note two points of relative theological importance. First, there is a question of the historical origins of these feasts of the Passover and of the Unleavened Bread: Do they have distant origins in non-Israelite religions? Second, there is the question of whether the two rites were originally connected by the early Israelites or whether they were gradually united over time. In addition there is the related issue of whether a third rite, that of the offering of the firstborn (13:1–2, 11–16), was originally connected with these other two.

Regarding the first question, it is customary to conjecture that the Passover ritual derives originally from ancient Semitic religious customs that preceded the age of the exodus. The sacrifice in question is pastoral and domestic rather than sacerdotal. The Hebrews are depicted as requesting permission from the Egyptians to go into the wilderness to offer sacrifice (3:18; 5:3; 7:16, 26; 8:4, 16, 23; 9:1, 13; 10:3, 7, 11, 24, 26). Roland de Vaux speculates that a sacrifice of this kind could have been customary among them at the time, celebrated every spring. "The Passover was ... an annual feast, celebrated during the first full moon in the spring, when the lambs and kids were born and when the flocks and herds were taken to their summer pasture."[98] It is possible that this rite took place during the course of the plague in which the firstborn of the Egyptians perished and that the rite came to be understood theologically in connection with the events of the exodus. However, the joining of the Passover ritual with the rite of the offering of the firstborn of the flock (13:12) seems to be the product of a subsequent practice and textual redaction. (The latter rite is enjoined upon Israelites separately, for example, in 22:28–29.)[99] Likewise, the Feast of Unleavened Bread seems to have a historical precedent in ancient Canaanite forms of religious ritual as an agricultural feast and may not have been observed until the Israelites settled in Canaan (Lev. 23:10 states this rather explicitly).[100] Nevertheless, because the rite is intricately bound up with the observation of the Sabbath (Exod. 12:16; Deut. 16:8; Lev. 23:6–8), the feast may well have taken on a distinctively Israelite meaning from the first era of its adoption.[101]

The celebration of the Passover in a form that combines both the sacrifice of the lamb and the Feast of Unleavened Bread is very ancient. References to it can be found throughout scripture: Num. 9:1–14; Deut. 16:1–6; Josh. 5:10–12; 2 Kgs. 23:21–23; 2 Chr. 30; Ezra 6:19–22. It is clearly meant to serve as a commemoration of the event of the exodus. Presumably, then, the combined ritual

98. De Vaux 1978: 1:367.
99. De Vaux 1978: 1:367–68. See also de Vaux 1997: 484–93.
100. De Vaux 1997: 490–93.
101. De Vaux 1997: 491.

is premonarchical and very ancient. Exodus 12:2 places it in the month of Nisan (March–April), the first month of the calendar. It is possible that King Josiah introduced the practice of celebrating the Passover exclusively in Jerusalem as a means of centralizing sacrifice exclusively around the temple (see 2 Kgs. 23:21–22; 2 Chr. 35:18).[102]

How should we understand the historical complexity of the rituals depicted in Exod. 12 theologically? A principle from Aquinas is helpful here. In the *Summa theologica* 1–2.103.1, he explicitly asks about the presence of pre-Israelite rites in the Torah, "Whether the ceremonies of the Old Law existed before the law?" His answer is affirmative. There are religious rituals in the Bible that did not originate from the Mosaic covenant but that the ancient Israelites themselves had adopted already in the patriarchal age. The most obvious example is ritual circumcision.[103] However, Aquinas also suggests that the Torah's designation of certain animals and foods as clean and unclean had its remote origins in the pre-Israelite religious customs of the ancient Near East.[104] There is a distinction, then, between the external ritual and the signification that it is afforded. According to Aquinas, before the time of Moses the ancient Hebrews did adopt external customs from other peoples. However, these Hebrews were moved by "a heavenly instinct, like a private law, [which] prompted them to worship God in a certain definite way, which would be both in keeping with the interior worship, and a suitable token of Christ's mysteries."[105] In keeping with this view, ancient Near Eastern rites were adopted by the ancient Israelites but were also fundamentally reshaped from within, in and through their experience of the covenant with the Lord. Following from Aquinas, one can simply expand the historical epoch of this process to include not only the era of the patriarchs but also the epoch of the exodus and the early centuries of the Israelite settlement. Explicit legal precepts stemming from the primitive Mosaic movement could coexist with the progressive adoption and "conversion" of ancient Near Eastern rituals. We can see in the larger historical process, then, a kind of phenomenology of the Holy Spirit progressively cleansing and elevating the practices of human religion into the sphere of grace.

In light of this brief historical prolegomena, what is the inspired meaning of Exod. 12?

102. De Vaux 1997: 486.
103. *ST* 1–2.103.1 ad 3.
104. *ST* 1–2.103.1 ad 4.
105. *ST* 1–2.103.1.

In its literal sense, this chapter is concerned with the measuring of human time in light of the eternity of God.[106] Human beings have a natural capacity to measure time and to think about their historical existence in light of eternity.[107] This natural capacity is seemingly one of the causes of the fabrication of seasonal religious rituals in which human beings attempt to depict in religious ways the meaning of the passage of time and of their own particular histories as clans or peoples. The history of religions stands as a testimony to humanity in this regard, and this testimony is inherently ambiguous, both philosophically and morally. Are the myriad of religious festivals and rites of human derivation metaphysically reasonable or unreasonable? Are they morally constructive or destructive? Are they illuminative or illusory? Clearly one could point to examples that seem, from a merely rational point of view, more promising or more condemnable. However, without divine revelation human beings in a fallen state cannot adequately resolve these central questions.[108]

It is to this fundamental human conundrum that Exod. 12 is addressed. Here I would like to note three things. First, in this passage the eternal God, through the inspired author, gives definition to Israel's temporal relationship with God. Time is to be measured for Israelites in relation to their liberation from Egypt. This event of tribulation and deliverance foreshadows all other tribulations that are experienced by the people of God throughout time, including the Babylonian exile.[109]

Second, universal human time can always be measured in reference to the mystery of redemption. Why is this? Because in this event, God has intervened in human history in a definitive, new, and unique way. Consequently, all human time must be understood in relation to the divine election of Israel by God.

Third, in and through the cyclical (annual) remembrance of this event, the Israelite people are mysteriously united with God in his eternity. They become his people anew in time by renewing their contact with divine eternity *in this rite*. Aquinas says that the liturgy of the Passover and the Feast of Unleavened Bread (both commanded in this chapter) are meant to signify an inner grace of election. Those members of the old covenant who celebrated the rites in accordance with supernatural faith in the Lord were sons of God by grace.[110]

---

106. In saying this, I am following the interpretation of Nachmanides, *Commentary on the Torah: Exodus* 12.2.

107. *ST* 1–2.53.3 ad 3: "The intellectual part of the soul, considered in itself, is above time, but the sensitive part is subject to time, and therefore in course of time it undergoes change as to the passions of the sensitive part, and also as to the powers of apprehension."

108. *ST* 1–2.91.3 corp. and ad 1, 1–2.99.3 corp. and ad 2.

109. Nachmanides makes this point explicitly in his *Commentary on the Torah: Exodus* 12.2.

110. *ST* 3.70.4.

In its moral sense, the Passover rite offers an example of the moral virtue of religious sacrifice. As Aquinas notes, sacrifice has two dimensions.[111] The internal act, which is most essential, consists in the prayer of the intellect and in the devotion of the will, by which the mind is turned toward God.[112] The outer act of sacrifice consists in personal adoration (by which the human body is engaged in the act of worship) and the offering to God of external realities, so as to symbolize and intensify the inner act of offering.[113]

Aquinas notes that the offering of sacrifice to God pertains to the virtue of religion, which is a potential part of the natural virtue of justice.[114] To worship God through the medium of ceremonial rites is normal and human. The offering of sacrifices—either due to gratitude or as an action of penitence for moral fault—is something that pertains to the natural law.[115] Nevertheless, Aquinas also notes that in the state of fallen human nature, it is not possible for the human person to effectively love God above all things, even by a natural love of God that would animate authentic human worship. The fallen human being is afflicted by a deep inner turn toward the preferential love of self to the detriment of the love of God and the common good.[116] Consequently, in the fallen order one's religious capacity to offer sacrifice to God, while completely natural, can only be healed and restored by the saving effects of grace.[117]

111. *ST* 1–2.101.2:
    Divine worship is twofold: internal, and external. For since man is composed of soul and body, each of these should be applied to the worship of God; the soul by an interior worship; the body by an outward worship: hence it is written (Ps. 83:3): "My heart and my flesh have rejoiced in the living God." And as the body is ordained to God through the soul, so the outward worship is ordained to the internal worship. Now interior worship consists in the soul being united to God by the intellect and affections. Wherefore according to the various ways in which the intellect and affections of the man who worships God are rightly united to God, his external actions are applied in various ways to the Divine worship.

112. *ST* 2–2.82.1–2.

113. *ST* 2–2.84.2, 2–2.85.1–3.

114. *ST* 2–2.81.5.

115. *ST* 2–2.85.1.

116. *ST* 1–2.109.3.

117. Otherwise, as Aquinas notes, we would fall into the error of Pelagianism. If one compares *ST* 1–2.109.3–4 with *ST* 2–2.85.1, 4, this conclusion becomes apparent. It should be noted that Aquinas here is only restating the dogmatic teaching of the Catholic Church with regard to human natural powers after the fall. It is impossible for human beings in the fallen state to fulfill integrally the natural law, particularly in respect to the commandment of reason to recognize God and to serve and love him above all things. See, for example, Second Vatican Council, *Gaudium et Spes*, paras. 13 and 17 (Denzinger 2012: paras. 4313, 4317):
    What divine revelation makes known to us agrees with experience. Examining his heart, man finds that he has inclinations toward evil too, and is engulfed by manifold ills which cannot come from his good Creator. Often refusing to acknowledge God as his beginning, man has disrupted also

If we consider the moral state of humanity, then, the Passover sacrifice is the sign in the divine economy of the healing effects of grace at work in the ancient Israelite people, who offered true sacrifices to God in charity. It should be noted that this interpretation is consistent with the traditional theological position of the Catholic Church. The grace of God was given to ancient Israel in a particular way so that human nature could be healed, principally through the right worship of God. This reparation of the wounded heart of humanity is at the core of the vocation of Israel. Nevertheless, there is a fundamental difference between the rites of the Old Law and those of the New Law.[118] The sacraments of the New Law are both signs of the presence of grace and also effective instruments of the communication of grace. They cause what they signify.[119] Baptism, for example, imputes a character to the recipient and is the instrumental cause of the infusion of sanctifying grace into the soul of the baptized.[120]

By contrast, the sacraments of the Old Law were true signs of the presence of grace (principally the interior gifts of faith, hope, and charity, which were given to the ancient Israelites). However, they were not instrumental causes of grace as such.[121] Rather they were mere occasions for the actualization or realization of the effects of grace, in and through ceremonies of worship rightly ordered toward God in charity.[122] In short, in the older economy the inward presence of grace causes the outward manifestation of symbolic sacramental worship. In the new economy of Christ the outward application of the sacraments can cause the inward presence of grace (if the recipient is rightly disposed). The reason for this difference is the following: the sacraments of the Old Law did not render human beings just before God. (It is the faith, hope, and love of the ancient Israelites that did this.) However, they did prefigure and indicate in a mysterious way the incarnation and passion of Christ, which is the instrumental cause of all grace

---

his proper relationship to his own ultimate goal as well as his whole relationship toward himself and others and all created things. . . . Since man's freedom has been damaged by sin, only by the aid of God's grace can he bring such a relationship with God into full flower.

118. *ST* 3.70.4, 1–2.103.2, 1–2.101.2.

119. *ST* 3.62.1.

120. *ST* 3.69.1 and 4–5.

121. *ST* 3.62.6.

122. This is my understanding of Aquinas's views in *ST* 3.70.4 and *ST* 1–2.101.1, especially when one reads these arguments in relation to *ST* 1–2.109.3 and *ST* 1–2.103.2. See *ST* 3.62.6 ad 1: "The Fathers of old [i.e., in the old covenant] were justified by faith in Christ's Passion, just as we are. And the sacraments of the Old Law were a kind of protestation of that faith, inasmuch as they signified Christ's Passion and its effects. It is therefore manifest that the sacraments of the Old Law were not endowed with any power by which they conduced to the bestowal of justifying grace: and they merely signified faith by which men were justified."

given to human beings after the fall. Accordingly, the lamb's blood in Exod. 12 saves the people of Israel from destruction, anticipating the notion of a sign that causes what it signifies. The sacraments of the New Law, however, function differently. They are instituted by Christ and come after the time of the incarnation and passion. Consequently, they effectively apply to human beings that which the sacraments of the Old Law could only anticipate: the saving effects of the mystery of the Lord.[123]

What is the typological meaning of the paschal lamb? It should be noted that this typological sign is arguably the most significant given in all of scripture—a symbol that stands at the center of the divine economy and gives unity to the whole. At the dawn of human civilization, after the fall, scripture depicts Abel, the righteous man, offering a firstling from his flock to the Lord (Gen. 4:4). According to Heb. 11:4, he represents the first "holy pagan," that is, the human person made righteous by grace and faith. Accordingly, the Church perceived in this "protosacrifice" of Abel and his subsequent martyrdom by Cain a prefiguration of the lamb of sacrifice, who is Christ. All of the just who offered sacrifices before the time of Christ did so by the power of grace, which was to be merited by his death. Consequently, their sacrifices were conformed in a mysterious way to his own.[124]

The sacrifice of the lamb is also fundamental to the existence of the people of Israel. When Abraham, the father of the covenant, is facing the prospect of offering his own son Isaac, the boy asks, "Where is the lamb for a burnt offering?" to which Abraham answers, "God will provide himself the lamb for a burnt offering, my son" (Gen. 22:7–8). The lamb is provided in Exod. 12. Mystically, then, the answer that Abraham gives in the midst of his dark trial of faith is prophetic and

123. *ST* 3.62.5.

124. The history of this idea in medieval theology is helpfully explained by Yves Congar, in his essay "Ecclesia ab Abel," in *Abhandlungen über theologische Kirche: Festschrift für Karl Adam*, ed. Marcel Reding (Düsseldorf: Patmos-Verlag, 1952), 79–108. The idea is expressed clearly and quite astonishingly by Aquinas in *ST* 2-2.85.1 ad 2:

> Adam, Isaac and other just men offered sacrifice to God in a manner befitting the times in which they lived, according to Gregory the Great, who says (*Moral.* 4.3) that in olden times original sin was remitted through the offering of sacrifices. Nor does Scripture mention all the sacrifices of the just, but only those that have something special connected with them. Perhaps the reason why we read of no sacrifice being offered by Adam may be that, as the origin of sin is ascribed to him, the origin of sanctification ought not to be represented as typified in him. Isaac was a type of Christ, being himself offered in sacrifice; and so there was no need that he should be represented as offering a sacrifice.

For a modern restatement of this idea, see Charles Journet, *The Mass: The Presence of the Sacrifice of the Cross*, trans. V. Szczurek (South Bend, IN: St. Augustine's Press, 2008), 1–27.

signifies the paschal lamb. This sacrifice is offered throughout the history of Israel to signify the presence of the mercy of God, for God has elected Israel not based upon Israel's merits but upon a privilege of grace.

Isaiah 53:7 employs the imagery of a lamb to associate with the sin offering of the Suffering Servant (53:10–11). Here the forgiveness of sins is conveyed by the sacrifice of the Suffering Servant.

> He was oppressed, and he was afflicted,
>   yet he opened not his mouth;
> like a lamb that is led to the slaughter,
>   and like a sheep that before its shearers is dumb,
>   so he opened not his mouth.
> . . . .
> He makes himself an offering for sin.
> . . . .
> By his knowledge shall the righteous one, my servant,
>   make many to be accounted righteous;
>   and he shall bear their iniquities.
> . . . .
> He bore the sin of many,
>   and made intercession for the transgressors. (Isa. 53:7, 10–12)

The "servant" in this passage may be seen to signify the collective people of Israel, who suffer on behalf of the Lord, but may also represent a numinous singular figure in Israelite history. In the New Testament, John the Baptist will designate this figure to be Jesus of Nazareth. "Behold, the Lamb of God, who takes away the sin of the world!" (John 1:29). Similarly, on the night before he died, Jesus seems to have interpreted this imagery in reference to himself. In the narratives that recount the institution of the Eucharist, we see Jesus associating the mystery of the paschal lamb with the sacrifice of the covenant that is found in Exod. 24:8 and with his own death. How is this the case? First of all, Jesus institutes the Eucharist within the context of the Passover meal and in doing so speaks elliptically of his own death as a new "Passover" (Luke 22:15–16). Second, he simultaneously refers to the "blood of the covenant, which is poured out for the many" (Mark 14:24). This language contains an obvious reference to Exod. 24:8 ("the blood of the covenant") and arguably a clear reference to Isa. 53:12 (i.e., because the Suffering Servant gives his life for "many"). Subsequent New Testament interpretation of the meaning of Jesus's death is unambiguous in this regard. In 1 Cor. 5:7 Paul states: "Cleanse out the old leaven that you may be a new lump, as you really are unleavened. For Christ, our paschal lamb, has been sacrificed." First Peter 1:18–20 speaks of Christ as the Lamb "destined before the foundation of the world" to redeem the Christian people.

The anagogical or mystical sense of Exod. 12 is found in Revelation. Imagery of Christ as the Lamb of God is especially important in this book. In the apocalyptic vision, the Lamb of God opens the scroll of the divine government (Rev. 5:6–13). The entire divine government unfolds in light of his sacrifice and his victory over sin, death, and the devil (7:10–14; 12:11; 17:14). His is the "book of life," and all those who are saved are inscribed in it (13:8; 21:27). The consummation of the divine economy occurs in the marriage between the Lamb and his bride the Church (19:7–9; 21:9). His sacrifice illumines the entire city of God, so that "the city has no need of sun or moon to shine upon it, for the glory of God is its light, and its lamp is the Lamb" (21:23). Consequently, he is both the Alpha and the Omega (22:13). In the book of Revelation, then, we see the most ultimate significance of the Passover rite. It signifies the humanity of Christ, both crucified and glorified, and our union with Christ in the beatific vision and in the resurrection from the dead.

If this is true, then it means that every human being who is saved throughout human history is saved by the "Lamb of God," that is to say, by the God-man, through his human self-offering in death and his resurrection from the dead. But how is it possible that Christ, the Lamb of God, might be the genuine cause of the "Passover" of each human being if he has only come to be human somewhere in the midst of a long human history, after ages of human beings who have already lived and died? Note that the grace of God given to humanity subsequent to the fall but prior to the incarnation is *anticipatory and tendential* in nature. This grace is given in view of the merits of Christ, and it also conforms human beings to the mystery of his life, death, and resurrection in a hidden and anticipatory way. It does so in and through the inspired observance of the precepts of the natural law, or the Mosaic law. The work of this christologically inclined grace is achieved or accomplished in the mystery of Holy Saturday, when Christ (in his divinity and his human soul) illumines the world of the dead with the mystery of plenary salvation.

The grace of God that is given to humanity subsequent to the death and resurrection of Christ is *plenary and eschatological* in nature. It is plenary because it derives from the plenitude of holiness that is present in Christ himself and from the radiant charity of his passion. Jesus shares this capital grace (the habitual grace of his own humanity) with his members, the mystical body of the Church. This occurs principally through the medium of the sacraments but can occur also outside of the visible frontiers of the Church. Such grace is *eschatological* in character because it orients man immediately toward perfect conformity to Christ in his death, resurrection, and life in the world to come. The rite of the paschal lamb, then, signifies Christ, but it also signifies the Church in our Passover as we are incorporated mystically by his grace into his death and resurrection.

12:15–20 "Seven days you shall eat unleavened bread; on the first day you shall put away leaven out of your houses, for if any one eats what is leavened, from the first day until the seventh day, that person shall be cut off from Israel" (12:15).

It has been noted above that the Feast of Unleavened Bread may have had its remote origins in a Canaanite festival for the spring harvest. Nevertheless, Israelites reappropriated the ritual in question so as to reinterpret radically its signification. First, there is no pantheism or pantheon of deities. The Torah clearly emphasizes the nonidentification of God and the natural order of the physical world. Israelite celebration of the natural cycle of time is conducted within the framework of monotheistic worship and sacrifice, under the stewardship of the law and its moral commandments. Furthermore, the ceremony is used to designate the passage of time not only in cosmic terms but also in terms of saving history. The historical covenant that was formed with God in the exodus provides the impetus for the celebration and gives to the Israelites the final criteria for the use of all natural goods of the creaturely realm. Broadly speaking one may say that the natural time of man in the cosmos is real, and even sacred, but it is made for the time of grace. The creation is for the covenant. This is why the Old Testament presentation of history is itself punctuated by covenants. These are either anticipatory prefigurations or subsequent renewals of the one supreme historical covenant ratified at Mount Sinai.

Typologically, the Feast of Unleavened Bread is a prefiguration of the sacrament of the Eucharist. As noted above, this is the express teaching of Paul: "Christ, our paschal lamb, has been sacrificed. Let us, therefore, celebrate the festival ... with the unleavened bread of sincerity and truth" (1 Cor. 5:7–8). In commenting upon this verse, Aquinas notes that the sacrament of the Eucharist can be understood in three ways: as a sign only (*sacramentum tantum*), as a sign and reality (*res et sacramentum*), or by the effect it produces (*res tantum*). The bread and wine prior to consecration are the sign only of the body and blood of Christ. After consecration, the Eucharist contains the reality of Christ crucified, his true body and blood, under the signs of bread and wine. This is the *res et sacramentum*. The *res tantum* is the grace of communion in the charity of Christ, which unites the human person to God and the Church. The first of these senses of the Eucharist is prefigured in the Old Testament by Melchizedek, who offered up bread and wine in sacrifice to God (Gen. 14:18). The second is prefigured by multiple typologies in the Old Testament: the unleavened bread, the manna in the desert, and the holocaust sacrifice. The paschal lamb, meanwhile, signifies all three senses.

> First of all, because it was eaten with unleavened loaves, according to Exod. 12:8: "They shall eat flesh . . . and unleavened bread." As to the second because it was immolated by the entire multitude of the children of Israel on the fourteenth day of the moon; and this was a figure of the Passion of Christ, who is called the Lamb on account of His innocence. As to the effect, because by the blood of the Paschal Lamb the children of Israel were preserved from the destroying Angel, and brought from the Egyptian captivity; and in this respect the Paschal Lamb is the chief figure of this sacrament, because it represents it in every respect.[125]

12:21–28 "Take a bunch of hyssop and dip it in the blood which is in the basin, and touch the lintel and the two doorposts with the blood which is in the basin. . . . For the LORD will pass through to slay the Egyptians; and when he sees the blood on the lintel and on the two doorposts, the LORD will pass over the door, and will not allow the destroyer to enter your houses to slay you" (12:22–23). Here we see the remembrance of an ancient, archaic practice. The ancient Semitic peoples may well have placed the blood of sacrifices upon the doorposts of their tents to ward off the presence of evil spirits.[126] Here the Lord tells Moses that the people should perform this ceremony so as to protect them from "the destroyer" and his effects (the plague that will strike the Egyptian firstborn). In 12:24–25 the rite is prescribed after the time of the settlement: "When you come to the land which the LORD will give you, as he has promised, you shall keep this service" (12:25). This version of the rite seems intended for a seminomadic people.

The Gospel of John assigns a typological sense to this text. Jesus Christ is crucified in the course of the Passover (see John 18:28 and 19:31, though whether this indicates the Passover week or the precise day of the Passover meal is debated). Christ is depicted, therefore, as being himself the Lamb of God (1:29, 36). He is touched by the hyssop like the paschal lamb (Exod. 12:22; John 19:29), and no bone of his is broken (Exod. 12:46; John 19:33). The blood that flows from his

125. *ST* 3.73.6.
126. De Vaux 1997: 435–38, 489.

side is a foreshadowing of the Eucharist (John 19:34), a sacrament that makes present the blood of the Lamb, which anoints the bodies and hearts of the Christian people, protecting them from spiritual death. This blood communicates to the Church the life-giving presence of the charity of Christ.

12:29–39 "[Pharaoh] summoned Moses and Aaron by night, and said, 'Rise up, go forth from among my people, both you and the people of Israel; and go, serve the LORD, as you have said'" (12:31).

In 12:29–39 the narrative of the text resumes. The firstborn of the Egyptians die during the night, and the Pharaoh calls Moses and Aaron before him with haste. Concerning this text, three things should be noted. First, the Pharaoh seems to recognize definitively the reality and authority of the Lord. "Go and serve the LORD, as you have said" (12:31). However, an ambiguity in the text could be read to mean, "Go and act according to the terms that you have set for yourself." The Pharaoh recognizes begrudgingly the capacity of the God of Israel to act in the world, but he does not share an internal understanding and voluntary consent to the mystery that is unfolding around him. Here again, he is an example of human refusal of the divine initiative and subsequent divine reprobation, in contrast to Israel's mystery of acceptance of the covenant, which stems from the priority of God's elective choice that precedes Israel's consent.

Second, the text portrays "the spoiling of the Egyptians." "The people of Israel . . . asked of the Egyptians jewelry of silver and of gold, and clothing; and the LORD had given the people favor in the sight of the Egyptians, so that they let them have what they asked. Thus they despoiled the Egyptians" (12:35–36). Morally speaking, this episode is also ambiguous. Perhaps the gesture signifies that the Egyptians held a divided opinion of the Hebrews. Some of them recognized the injustice of the Pharaoh's practices and gave the people goods that would help them on their way. Perhaps some even recognized the reality of Israel's God in the same way that non-Israelites down through time have taken refuge in devotion to the God of the Torah. However, it is also possible to read the gesture as motivated by worldly fear. The Egyptians give gifts to the Hebrews in an attempt to placate the Lord, who remains for them an unknown god. This is a fear that seeks, if possible, to negotiate with the divine by offering just enough to be left alone and not placed under too great a constraint. Read in this way, the "despoiling" stems from the Egyptians' desire to protect their worldly interests. They want to be done with this matter.

Fathers of the Church perceive in this material assimilation of the treasures of Egypt a more general principle: the elect people can and should make use of all truth and spiritual treasures of non-Christian derivation. Origen sees in this passage a typology for the use of philosophy as a "handmaiden" to theology:

> For from the things which the children of Israel took from the Egyptians the vessels in the holy of holies were made—the ark with its lid, and the Cherubim, and the mercy-seat, and the golden coffer, where was the manna, the angels' bread.... I wish to ask you to extract from the philosophy of the Greeks what may serve as a course of study or a preparation for Christianity, and from geometry and astronomy what will serve to explain the sacred scriptures, in order that all that the sons of the philosophers are wont to say about geometry and music, grammar, rhetoric, and astronomy, as *fellow-helpers* to philosophy, *we may say about philosophy itself, in relation to Christianity.*[127]

Third, it should be noted that the text says that six hundred thousand men left Egypt that night, along with women, children, cattle, flocks, and herds (12:37–38). This number should be taken in a figurative sense, as a numerical type. Given the literary genus of the narrative, it is not necessary to suppose that the author intends to communicate a purely empirical representation of events. The number is purposefully meant to be vast and impressive, so as to represent symbolically a material and spiritual plenitude. Israel here represents the presence of the Church, the redeemed, and in a certain sense the whole human race going forth into the mystery of God.

12:40–51 "And at the end of four hundred and thirty years, on that very day, all the hosts of the LORD went out from the land of Egypt" (12:41).

Exodus 12:40–51 is concerned with dating the exact time of the sojourn of the tribes of Jacob in Egypt (12:40–42, 51) and with strict prescriptions regarding the Passover: only Israelites should celebrate the feast. Foreigners may do so if they and their households are circumcised (12:43–50). In both issues we can perceive a Priestly concern that the ancient Israelites preserve a sense of their historical origins and lineage, that they celebrate the rites of their historical tradition, and that they maintain a profound awareness of their unique identity as a chosen people.

With regard to the first issue (the length of the time in Egypt), the point made above can be reiterated. The literary genus of this text is such that one should not seek to find in it a precise empirical measure of the passage of time. Perhaps the number is historically exact. However, the author may not have

127. Origen, *Letter to Gregory* (*ANF* 4:393) (emphasis added).

been able to obtain historical knowledge of this kind. Whatever the literal sense, the number is clearly symbolic. It denotes the longevity of the developments of the plan of God down through time. God is faithful to the choice of the people of Abraham, even in circumstances in which their identity as a people is compromised and their continued survival is threatened. The renewed vitality of the people of Israel down through time and their continued survival throughout history remain a mysterious sign to humanity of the existence and presence of God.

The passage regarding the purity of the celebration of the Passover is also significant spiritually. The people of God are to be held accountable by a kind of communion or excommunication, based upon the practice or nonpractice of circumcision, Passover, and the correct uses of leavened and unleavened bread (12:15, 19, 48). The people of God have both an invisible-spiritual and visible-political integrity throughout the course of time. The Church is both invisible and visible, mystical and political. The unity of Israel and the Church is maintained internally by faith, hope, and charity, but that unity must also be made manifest externally through signs of affiliation to the covenant. The religious life of the human being is a life of devotion not only internally, within the mind, but also externally, in one's emotions, in the body, and in all of one's human life. It is only when Israel is spiritually prepared for a reality of this kind—integral commitment of self—that Israel is truly prepared to leave the "Egypt" of this world and enter the promised land of God's law.

2

WILDERNESS

Exodus 13–18

The tradition of the Church speaks of a *mystagogia* or sacramental pedagogy encoded within the sacred scriptures and the divine liturgy. When Dionysius speaks of this mystagogy he refers to symbols instituted by the prophets that are simultaneously illuminative and numinous,[1] both revealing the presence of the divinity and concealing it at the same time.[2] This concealing is not meant to create a permanent separation between the human person and God but rather acts as a subtle form of invitation toward a progressive discovery of God. As Aquinas notes, the sacred signs of scripture and of the sacraments conceal the mystery from those who would disrespect it, but also invite the faithful to a patient, progressive form of learning, subject to periods of divine instruction.[3]

1. Dionysius, *Ecclesiastical Hierarchy* 1.1.
2. Dionysius, *On the Celestial Hierarchy* 1.2 (Luibhéid and Rorem 1987): "This divine ray can enlighten us only by being upliftingly concealed in a variety of sacred veils which the providence of the Father adapts to our nature as human beings." See also Dionysius, *On the Celestial Hierarchy* 2.2.
3. *ST* 1.1.9 corp. and ad 3:

> As Dionysius says (*On the Celestial Hierarchy* 1), it is more fitting that divine truths should be expounded under the figure of less noble than of nobler bodies, and this for three reasons. Firstly, because thereby men's minds are the better preserved from error. For then it is clear that these things are not literal descriptions of divine truths, which might have been open to doubt had they been expressed under the figure of nobler bodies, especially for those who could think of nothing nobler

I have spoken above of Exod. 4–11 as a kind of pedagogy regarding divine omnipotence. The archaic style of scripture contains profound metaphysical truths regarding God that are communicated in a very direct, intuitive way, associated with real historical events but also encoded within a somewhat symbolic, and at times frloric, literary form. In the following section, Exod. 13–18, we are confronted with a liturgical and sacramental catechesis. These chapters portray the departure from Egypt, but they also prepare us for the formulation of the Israelite people in the context of the covenant with God and the giving of the law. Consequently, they denote symbolically the Israelites' journey out of Egypt and into the mystery of God, God's covenant, and God's law. This is not to deny that there is a basic historical foundation to the wandering of the ancient Israelite people in the wilderness. I will affirm below the necessary inherence of this historical truth within the inner form of biblical faith. Nevertheless, the Israelites' exodus in the wilderness period is portrayed to readers as "our" mystery—as the invitation to belong to the people of God. This belonging occurs principally by means of the symbolic rites that the retelling of these events is meant to depict prefiguratively.

Filial Adoption (Exod. 13:1–16)

13:1–16 "Consecrate to me all the first-born; whatever is the first to open the womb among the people of Israel, both man and beast, is mine" (13:2).

The beginning of Exod. 13 contains a prescription concerning the consecration of the firstborn child and the offering of the firstborn of the flock. In this passage the offering is set within the context of the Passover, but in 22:29 and (arguably) in 34:20b it is depicted as a separate obligation.[4] What does the offering of the firstborn consist of? The consecration of the firstborn child to God and the offering to God of animals from the flock are both acts of religion. They are intended to help the Israelite to recognize that God is the author of existence and life and to give thanks to God for the gifts of being and human flourishing. The animal is offered to God in sacrifice, while the child is "redeemed" (that is to say, purchased back, presumably by animal sacrifice) and marked out in a particular way as a gift from God (13:13; 34:20).

than bodies. Secondly, because this is more befitting the knowledge of God that we have in this life. For what He is not is clearer to us than what He is. Therefore similitudes drawn from things farthest away from God form within us a truer estimate that God is above whatsoever we may say or think of Him. Thirdly, because thereby divine truths are the better hidden from the unworthy.
4. De Vaux 1997: 489.

Some speculate that in ancient Israel some form of this ritual originally entailed human sacrifice of the firstborn. The hypothesis is historically indemonstrable, and one cannot say with certitude one way or another whether such a practice ever existed. Were the case to be made affirmatively, this would be an example of a barbaric superstition that was reprobated, reinterpreted radically, and "converted" through a process of divine inspiration. However, that hypothesis seems unnecessary. The practice of human sacrifice did exist in some cultures in the ancient Near East (particularly among Canaanites), but there is no direct evidence that the ancient Israelites ever embraced the practice.[5] Not only is it categorically condemned in scripture (Lev. 2:2–5; Ezek. 16:20; 20:31), but it is clearly noted that the firstborn child was granted particular privileges in ancient Israelite law (Deut. 21:15–17).

The ceremony in question is placed at the beginning of the historical event of the exodus for profound theological reasons. On one level, this rite of offering signifies Israel's gratitude toward God for the gift of natural life. On a deeper level, however, it is located here in order to signify or demarcate God's choice of Israel and the adoption of Israel as God's son. Note how the idea is framed by the structure of the Torah itself. At the beginning of Moses's mission, he is told to proclaim to the Pharaoh: "Thus says the LORD, Israel is my first-born son" (4:22). Subsequently, the idea is repeated explicitly in Num. 8 and is related to the rite in Exod. 13: "For all the first-born among the people of Israel are mine, both of man and beast; on the day that I slew all the first-born in the land of Egypt I consecrated them for myself" (Num. 8:17). We are beginning to see the emergence in scripture, then, of a very profound theme—the predestination of the people of Israel and its adoption by grace. The notion is taken up again in subsequent prophetic literature. In Second Isaiah (Isa. 44:2), the exiles of Israel are given the promise of the inheritance:

> Thus says the LORD who made you,
>   who formed you from the womb and will help you:
> "Fear not, O Jacob my servant. . . ."

---

5. See de Vaux 1997: 442–44. Genesis 22 is most notably to be contrasted with what ancient Hebrews ascribed to Canaanite custom. Whereas God has the right to ask for the sacrifice of Isaac, he does not require of the Israelites what is or was practiced (presumably) by some Canaanites at the local shrines of the region formerly inhabited by the patriarchs. Ezekiel 20:26 does seem to suppose that there was infant sacrifice in ancient Israel (at least at first glance). However, I think this text raises interpretive questions about Ezekiel's own speculations or presuppositions more than it does the actual practices of Israelites who preceded him in time.

In Jer. 31:9, God speaks through the prophet of the renewal of the covenant by referring to this mystery of filiation.

> With consolations I will lead them back.
> . . . .
> For I am a father to Israel,
> and E'phraim is my first-born.

When reread in a Pauline interpretation of scripture, these passages implicitly denote the presence of grace, by which Israelites are brought into a particular spiritual intimacy with God.

Ultimately the New Testament treats the mystery of filial adoption in the light of Jesus Christ and his eternal generation from God the Father as the Son of God. Because Jesus is the preexistent Son of God, the creation was made through him. "He is the image of the invisible God, the first-born of all creation" (Col. 1:15). "And again, when he brings the first-born into the world, he says, 'Let all God's angels worship him'" (Heb. 1:6). Furthermore, the identity of Christ has been made fully manifest in his resurrection from the dead (Rom. 1:4), wherein he fulfills the mystery of Israel as the "first-born son" of God and opens up the covenant of Israel to the whole of humanity in the Church. "He is the head of the body, the church; he is the beginning, the first-born from the dead, that in everything he might be pre-eminent" (Col. 1:18).

Christ possesses the divine life in himself naturally, as the eternal Son of the Father, but human persons are called to partake of it by participation in his grace. They can receive filial adoption in the Son. Paul perceives here the deepest mystery of God's eternal designs: behind our filial adoption is the mystery of election to eternal life. "For those whom he foreknew he also predestined to be conformed to the image of his Son, in order that he might be the first-born among many brethren" (Rom. 8:29). The mystery of Israel that begins historically with the exodus is ultimately revealed as something founded in the eternal life of the Son, through whom all things were made and in whom both Israel and the Church were elected to divine life.

The Red Sea: What Do the Symbols Mean? (Exod. 13:17–15:21)

13:17–14:31 "Then Moses stretched out his hand over the sea; and the LORD drove the sea back by a strong east wind all night, and made the sea dry land, and the waters were divided" (13:21).

The narrative of the crossing of the Red Sea has raised many questions for modern commentators and archeologists. Is this section of text composed from multiple sources and traditions, or is it not? If so, how many and of what derivation? Is there a historical event that lies behind the various literary texts and traditions? Only one event is recounted, but could there be recollections present from diverse incidents (an exodus of "flight" versus an exodus of "expulsion")? When approximately did the central event recounted take place (if it took place at all)? What would have been the most probable route of passage through the desert and then the waters separating Egypt from the Sinai Peninsula? Does the incident pertain to the Red Sea or to the "Reed Sea" (a body of naturally shallow water)? How should one interpret the claim that a miracle transpired? Are the scriptures reporting merely (at the base of things) a natural event with felicitous political consequences for escaping slaves that was interpreted after the fact to be providential?

Here I will offer a number of theological judgments about what I take to be the literal sense of the scriptures in this section. What is asserted below is compatible with various modern hypotheses about the text, its composition or redaction, and with various archeological theories about the time and place in which this event might have occurred (such as at the Reed Sea, sometime in the mid-thirteenth century BC).[6] However, I also presume that the text of scripture is inspired and is best interpreted in light of the subsequent Catholic tradition. The basic judgments made below, while informed by or taking account of various modern historical and textual hypotheses, are most properly judgments of theological faith not demonstrable per se from natural processes of historical reasoning. Yet they are simultaneously entirely compatible with natural arguments of historical reasoning. In short, the event can be interpreted theologically in faith without being either proven or disproven by merely natural methods of rational argumentation. This does not mean one cannot envisage some convergence between the judgments of supernatural faith and the hypothetical speculations of sound historical and archeological rationality.

Regarding the literal sense, the affirmation of a saving event that took place at the Red Sea is a basic principle affirmed in a myriad of ways in the scriptures.

6. Consider the historical treatment in de Vaux 1978: 1:370–92. Alternative mid-twentieth-century accounts or hypotheses are noted in the course of de Vaux's discussion. See likewise the discussion and references in Durham 1987: 182–87. Brevard Childs (1974: 217–24) gives a plausible interpretation of the textual composition, which is based on the Graf-Wellhausen Documentary Hypothesis, but also notes alternative accounts of the division of the verses.

Diverse but ultimately convergent testimony to the miracle at the Red Sea is found throughout the Torah, the Prophets, and the Writings (for example: Deut. 11:4; Josh. 2:10; 4:23; 2 Sam. 22:16; Isa. 10:26; 51:10; 63:11; Neh. 9:9–11; Pss. 66:6; 78:13, 53; 106:7–9; 136:13–15). The correct way to read these texts (including the traditions present in Exod. 13–14) is not as a diverse set of eyewitness accounts that provide an exact representation of what happened but as a confessional tradition of faith. The event at the Red Sea had a creedal significance in ancient Israel. In a certain sense, it is commemorated as the event in which Israel is "born" (Isa. 43:1–2). Furthermore, as I will show below, the event is seen in subsequent scriptural interpretation to have a cosmic and eschatological significance, ultimately fulfilled in the mystery of the physical resurrection of Christ.

First, I take it that in and through all of the textual ambiguities of this particular passage of scripture a historical event is being presented, one that is believed in by the longstanding faith of the people of Israel and of the universal Church. In the beginning, God saved Israel from Egypt by a mysterious historical intervention that took place during the initial flight out of Egypt of Hebrews gathered around the prophetic figure Moses. This creedal belief is portrayed symbolically in Deut. 6:22: "The LORD showed signs and wonders, great and grievous, against Egypt and against Pharaoh and all his household, before our eyes." One cannot reconstruct with certitude by modern historical methods where and when this event might have taken place (though various plausible hypotheses exist).[7] Nevertheless, knowledge of the precise details of time and place is somewhat nonessential, theologically speaking.

Second, the event is depicted by the use of a plethora of images and narrations. God commands that the people go east toward the mountain at Sinai (13:17–18). The Lord goes out in front of the people in the form of a pillar of cloud by day and a pillar of fire by night (13:21–22). The Lord foretells the destruction of Pharaoh in advance (14:1–2) and hardens his heart for the last time (14:8–9, 17). Moses tells the people the Lord will fight for Israel (14:17–18), and at the command of God he stretches out his rod or his hand to separate the waters and then to close the waters back against the Egyptians (14:15–16, 21, 26–27). The angel of God hides the people in a cloud and under cover of night (14:19–20), and the wind blows back the water by night, creating a way across (14:21). The water is split in the form of walls to the right and left (14:22). The Lord sets the Egyptian army in a panic (14:24); they are caught in the mud (14:25) and covered by the walls

---

7. See de Vaux 1978: 1:376–81, which offers a variety of alternatives.

of water (14:28). In seeing the Egyptian army destroyed, Israel finally comes to
believe in the Lord (14:31).

Ironically, the diversity of images that depict this event creates a kind of representational apophaticism. Like the cloud that surrounds the Israelites, the textual
witnesses to the mystery are so great in number that they render impossible any
"chemically pure" access to the event. This fact is *not* incidental. Rather, it suggests
that the scriptures are inspired in and through a long narrative tradition precisely
to communicate to us retrospectively the theological significance of the event, as
understood subsequently in faith.

Third, it seems to this commentator that the scriptures here communicate
the affirmation of a historical event that is truly miraculous. Certainly there are
symbolic embellishments or signs layered into the text (perhaps, for example, the
Priestly image of the walls of water to the right and the left). However, the primal
confession of faith is that a miracle occurred. One argument for this stems from a
consideration of the hierarchy of miracles reported in scripture. Certainly some
narratives that recount miracles may be purely typological in kind. For example,
the three young men in the furnace in Dan. 1–3 are considered to be primarily
typological rather than historical. One might argue that the men serve principally
to represent the people of Israel who have come through the fire of persecution.
Nevertheless, the mystery of Jesus Christ is a historical reality that gives the ultimate interpretative principle to all biblical narratives and miraculous claims.
One should interpret the centrality and importance of a given miracle narrative
in relation to the physical reality of the incarnation and resurrection of Christ.
These latter mysteries do reveal, among other things, that God has in fact acted
in human history in a real and utterly physical way. "The Word became flesh and
dwelt among us" (John 1:14). Certain miracles of the old covenant especially
prefigure and prepare for that ultimate intervention, and the miracle at the Red
Sea, no matter how difficult it might be to understand as a historical event, is a
distinctive precursor to the mystery of the life, death, and resurrection of Christ.
Just as Israel was saved at the Red Sea by a miraculous intervention, so all of humanity has been offered salvation in the resurrection of Jesus Christ. Based on
this line of thinking, it is possible to see in the crossing of the Red Sea a historical
event of a numinous kind.

The moral and typological significations of this passage are brought out most
especially by the representation of the walls of water, which are separated by
the hand of Moses (14:22, 29). This image is intended to echo that of Gen. 1:6:
"And God said, 'Let there be a firmament in the midst of the waters, and let it

separate the waters from the waters.'" God creates the world by separating out the waters, and Exod. 14:22 depicts a new separation of the waters. In other words, God is now undertaking a "new creation" in the formation of the people of Israel. Israel is a redemptive creation, one in which God brings good out of the evil of mankind.

This typology of the new creation is reiterated in subsequent books of the Bible and applied to the historical life of the people of Israel. In Josh. 3:7–17, the people of Israel make a second crossing, this time over the Jordan River rather than the Red Sea, entering into the promised land. The waters part before the ark of the covenant, which is carried by the priests. The typological significance is clear: in forming the people of Israel, God gives the creation its deepest meaning and fulfillment. The Mosaic law (the precepts of the covenant, the priesthood, the temple) makes possible a new life of friendship with God, by grace.

The prophet Isaiah portrays this mystery in terms of a new creation, claiming that only he who first created the world and gave it being can also re-create or renew the world, acting through the covenant with Israel. Though the people are disseminated in exile, God can gather them together again. This process is portrayed by making use of the imagery of the Red Sea.

> Was it not thou that didst dry up the sea,
>> the waters of the great deep;
> that didst make the depths of the sea a way
>> for the redeemed to pass over? (Isa. 51:10)

(See also 43:1–19; 51:10–11.) Here the scriptures point forward to the eschatological re-creation of the world that is coming to be, in some mysterious way, in and through the life and sufferings of the people of Israel (48:6, 20–21; 53:1–12; 59:19–21; 60:1–22).

The New Testament makes implicit reference to the crossing of the Red Sea. Jesus is baptized by John in the Jordan to signify the re-creation of Israel, a new crossing over into the promised land. Luke portrays this as an eschatological event, one that fulfills the prophecies of Isaiah (Luke 3:3–6, 17). However, this new crossing-over is now the passion of Christ. It is only through the suffering, death, and resurrection of Jesus that the ultimate destiny of the creation is made manifest (24:26–27). All those who would belong to this new covenant must be incorporated into the grace of Christ by passing through baptism. They are conformed by this grace to his passion, death, and resurrection (Rom. 6:3–4; Col.

2:12). Paul speaks of a historical prefiguration of this mystery in the crossing over of the Red Sea in 1 Cor. 10:1–4: "I want you to know, brethren, that our fathers were all under the cloud, and all passed through the sea, and all were baptized into Moses in the cloud and in the sea, and all ate the same supernatural food and all drank the same supernatural drink. For they drank from the supernatural Rock which followed them, and the Rock was Christ."

The cloud that covered the Israelites prefigures the cloud of God's holiness, the presence of the Holy Spirit, who covers over and sanctifies the baptized. In the words of Ambrose:

> Moses held his rod, and led the people of the Hebrews at night in a pillar of light, and in the day in a pillar of cloud. What is the light but truth, since it sheds a full and open brightness? What is the pillar of light but Christ the Lord, who scattered the shadows of unbelief, and poured the light of truth and spiritual grace on human hearts? The pillar of cloud, on the other hand, is the Holy Spirit. The people were in the sea, and the pillar of light went on before; then the pillar of cloud followed, as if the shadowing of the Holy Spirit. You see that by the Holy Spirit and by the water he has shown a type of baptism.[8]

Anagogically the miracle at the Red Sea prefigures the eschatological re-creation of the cosmos. This idea is presented in Rev. 15:3, where the saints in the glory of Christ "sing the song of Moses" and "of the Lamb" (Exod. 15:2–3). The eternal life of the Church in the resurrection stands on the far side of the Red Sea, beyond the "Egypt" of our temporal existence. The anagogical sense is grounded in the literal sense, as Aquinas notes.[9] Based on the interpretation offered above, Rev. 15 makes sense. If the narrative in Exod. 13–14 does denote literally some kind of historical miracle, then it also denotes implicitly that the power of God acts on the very level of the being and essence of things to change them from within. The Lord demonstrates proleptically in this miracle that he can and will remake the world, beginning with the covenant with Israel. This eschatological re-creation is made most perfectly manifest in Jesus. The resurrection of Christ points forward to the end times in which God is able to refashion a fallen creation in a higher and more beautiful way, conforming it perfectly to the glory of the Lamb.

8. Ambrose, *De Sacramentis* 1.6.22, in *On the Mysteries and the Treatise on the Sacraments by an Unknown Author*, trans. and ed. T. Thompson (New York: Macmillan, 1919) (translation slightly modified). For a wealth of reflection on the typological sense of this section of scripture, see Jean Daniélou, *From Shadows to Reality: Studies in the Biblical Typology of the Fathers*, trans. W. Hibberd (Westminster, MD: Newman Press, 1960).
9. *ST* 1.1.10.

15:1–21 "Then Moses and the people of Israel sang this song to the Lord, saying,

> 'I will sing to the Lord, for he has triumphed gloriously;
> the horse and his rider he has thrown into the sea.'" (15:1)

Exodus 15:1–21 is a collective poem or song, composed perhaps of various fragments of Hebrew verse, some of which are very ancient. In the hymn we are told that it is God who has triumphed at the Red Sea. As Exod. 15:3, 8 says:

> The Lord is a man of war.
> . . . .
> At the blast of his nostrils the waters piled up,
> the floods stood up in a heap;
> the deeps congealed in the heart of the sea.

The future conquest of the land of Israel is foretold, and the settlement in Canaan is denoted (15:14–17). After Moses and the people of Israel conclude the song (15:1–19), Miriam the prophetess also sings, foreshadowing typologically the inspired heroines of the Old Testament, such as Judith and Esther (15:20–21).

It should be noted that in this poem the Bible portrays God in almost mythological terms as a warrior in battle with the sea. The idea is present in other texts of scripture as well:

> When the waters saw thee, O God,
> when the waters saw thee, they were afraid,
> yea, the deep trembled. (Ps. 77:16)

> Thou didst trample the sea with thy horses,
> the surging of mighty waters. (Hab. 3:15)

> The sea looked and fled,
> Jordan turned back.
> . . . .
> Tremble, O earth, at the presence of the Lord,
> at the presence of the God of Jacob. (Ps. 114:3, 7)

In this passage, the sea has a symbolic meaning, derived originally from the religious myths of the ancient Near East. Here it seems to represent the cosmic powers of chaos, death, and destruction to which the creation is potentially subject. These powers can destroy man. However, in his action at the Red Sea, God has declared his victory once and for all over the powers of "the deep" that threaten human existence and creation itself. Order has a primacy over chaos; life has a primacy over death. This victory of God and humanity together at the Red Sea foreshadows the final victory of Christ and the Church over the powers of evil and chaos, which risk to destroy the human race. "Then I saw a new heaven and a new earth; for the first heaven and the first earth had passed away, and the sea was no more. . . . And he who sat upon the throne said, 'Behold, I make all things new'" (Rev. 21:1, 5).

Manna and Water: Signs of Salvation (Exod. 15:22–17:7)

15:22–27 "And the people murmured against Moses, saying, 'What shall we drink?' And he cried to the LORD; and the LORD showed him a tree, and he threw it into the water, and the water became sweet" (15:24–25).

The Bible now makes a rather unceremonious transition. Israel is in the desert for the first time, and a crisis arises immediately regarding drinking water; there is a shortage. This is the first trial of Israel in the wilderness, one of many that are depicted in the Torah (Exod. 16:2–3; 17:3; 32:1–4, 25; Num. 11:4–6; 12:1–2; 14:2–3; 16:13–14; 20:2–13; 21:4–5). Understanding the sequence of events is not simple. The event that is portrayed here in Exod. 15:22–27 (at Marah) seems similar to that portrayed in Exod. 17:1–7 (at Massah and Meribah) and in Num. 20:2–13 (at Meribah). The first two events are depicted as occurring prior to arrival at Mount Sinai, while the latter is depicted as having occurred after. Are these diverse accounts of a unique event, recounted in diverse traditions? Are "Marah" and "Massah" in fact identical places? It is impossible to say with certitude.

The moral sense of the trial, however, is fairly clear. The people express a legitimate need for physical nourishment, but they lack any real hope in the ongoing assistance of God. Consequently they murmur against the Lord, as well as Moses, his specially appointed instrument. But their complaint to Moses is heard by God, who mercifully answers them with a miracle of water, a sign of his accompanying presence.

The spiritual danger of murmuring against legitimate authority is a theme in the Torah. It is generally recognized in the Christian tradition as the outward sign of inward vices. Human distrust of the goodness of God frequently stems from despair or religious indifference—defects that can only be remedied by the exercise of the theological virtue of hope. These vices, meanwhile, are closely allied with disobedience of religious precepts and ingratitude toward God. Although it is not immediately evident, the practice of obedience to divine precepts often serves to strengthen greatly one's spiritual hope, while the practice of disobedience almost inevitably isolates the soul and leads to the hardening of the heart. Consequently, it is essential to submit oneself unconditionally in obedience to the precepts of God to grow spiritually in the theological virtue of hope. It is also necessary to participate in concrete acts of worship, repeatedly giving thanks for the gifts of God. The time of Israel in the wilderness is meant to serve as a kind of pedagogy for the development of their hope in God alone. They are tested in the wilderness so as to deepen their sense of sole dependence upon the Lord, and to become inwardly conformed to his commandments even in the midst of outward trials.

Typologically, water serves here as a sign of God's accompanying presence. It is the tree of Moses that causes water to come forth from the ground, foreshadowing the tree of the Cross and the water from the side of Christ (John 19:34). This in turn signifies the grace of eternal life: "Whoever drinks of the water that I shall give him will never thirst; the water that I shall give him will become in him a spring of water welling up to eternal life" (John 4:14). Here the tree of the Cross is the source of the water of life, the baptismal graces that flow out upon the Church. These waters have the power to refresh the soul and to rejuvenate it forever, giving it consolation and removing from it progressively all roots of bitterness and contention with God.

16:1–21 "Then the LORD said to Moses, 'Behold, I will rain bread from heaven for you; and the people shall go out and gather a day's portion every day, that I may prove them, whether they will walk in my law or not'" (16:4).

Exodus 16 describes a miracle of quails and manna that God provides for the people of Israel in the desert. Numbers 11 gives an alternative version of the story (perhaps older) in which the presence of daily manna is already presupposed and the subsequent provision of quails is recounted. There are other references to the tradition in the scriptures. Deuteronomy 8:3 and 8:16 give a spiritual interpretation of the event as one of God's trials: "And he humbled you and let you hunger and fed you with manna, which you did not know, nor did your fathers know; that he might make you know that man does not live by bread alone, but that man lives by everything that proceeds out of the mouth of the LORD" (8:3). Psalm 78:24–25 strikes a very different note, describing the event as an occurrence of communion with God:

He rained down upon them manna to eat,
> and gave them the grain of heaven.
Man ate of the bread of the angels;
> he sent them food in abundance.

Wisdom 16:20–21 (NRSV) seems to build off this latter interpretation:

You supplied them from heaven with bread ready to eat,
> providing every pleasure and suited to every taste.
For your sustenance manifested your sweetness toward your children;
> and the bread, ministering to the desire of the one who took it,
> was changed to suit every one's liking.

Much can be said about this influential passage of scripture.

First, I will simply note the time and location of the event, as recounted in Exod. 16:1: "All the congregation of the people of Israel came to the wilderness of Sin, which is between Elim and Sinai, on the fifteenth day of the second month after they had departed from the land of Egypt." The people are only recently departed from Egypt and are headed into the Sinai Peninsula (eventually toward Mount Sinai). Although they have recently witnessed the miracle at the sea, they are now confronting the physical reality of starvation, and their murmuring begins. "Would that we had died by the hand of the LORD in the land of Egypt, when we sat by the fleshpots and ate bread to the full; for you have brought us out into this wilderness to kill this whole assembly with hunger" (16:3).

The literal sense of the scriptures here is concerned with the authority of Moses and Aaron or with the tradition that they represent. God has liberated the people, but now he is going to prepare them for discipleship. To do so, he places them in an existentially threatening environment in which their dependence upon him will be particularly acute. This invites the people of Israel to develop a deeper sense of their true priorities. They are to learn that the Lord has the power to do whatever is required to sustain them in being but will do so only if they learn to place obedience to God before all else.

The scripture teaches that this discipleship of the people ought to focus upon the commandments of Moses and Aaron. This is one reason that the passage unfolds in such a peculiar order. First, God speaks to Moses about the manna (16:4), and then Moses and Aaron address the people (16:6–9). Next, God manifests his "glory" to the people, alerting them to his accompanying presence (16:10). Then he addresses Moses with a seeming repetition of the promises (16:11–12), and Moses instructs the people concerning how to gather and divide the gift of the manna (16:15–16).

The movement is somewhat elliptical: from God to Moses and Aaron, then to the people, then back again through the same cycle. Even if (hypothetically) this repetition and complexity are effects of an ancient editing process using multiple sources, the basic meaning of the complete passage is still quite clear: Moses and Aaron are the chosen mediators of God's covenant with the people. Fidelity to God in the midst of crisis entails fidelity to their teachings and practices. The event is a parable for the larger history and existence of the people of Israel, who sometimes live amidst threatening circumstances. Israel discovers the possibility of fidelity to God in the midst of trial, through the medium of the law that has been given through Moses and that is ratified through the practices of the Israelite priesthood and worship.

This spiritual interpretation, which is suggested in Deut. 8:3 and 8:16, need not exclude a historical foundation for the events of the manna and quail. Modern interpreters point out that insects that feed off of the tamarisk trees on the Sinai Peninsula emit a natural secretion that is edible. Likewise, flocks of birds from the Mediterranean region sometimes lose their way, far from the sea, and expire in the desert region. It is possible that these phenomena explain the background of the events. However, such naturalistic interpretations do not account for overt characteristics in the text of scripture, particularly the regular abundance of the food, its weekly repetition, and its duration over forty years. If one is to take the biblical revelation as denoting something historical, then it is best to affirm its miraculous nature.

When discussing Jesus Christ's miracle of the multiplication of loaves in John 6 (which seems analogous to the manna of Exod. 16), Aquinas argues that God seemingly does not create the matter of bread from nothing but rather "educes" a greater quantity of substances from already existing natural entities.[10] While real, this kind of miracle is relatively discreet in nature. The activity of God remains hidden and is not intended to overwhelm the human freedom to believe but is meant to sustain regular habits of faith and obedience among a people who depend upon the Lord for their very existence. The "miracle" in question, then, is almost immediately transparent to its typological sense as articulated in Psalm 78: in the wilderness God nourishes the *faith* of the people of Israel, leading them into spiritual communion.

10. See *ST* 3.44.4 ad 4, 1.92.3 ad 1.

This typological sense of the scripture is developed overtly in the New Testament. In Matt. 4:1–11 and Luke 4:1–13 Jesus goes out into the wilderness (at the periphery of Israel) to fast and undergo temptation. Where Israel was sometimes unfaithful, Christ remains obedient. He recapitulates in himself the mystery of the covenant and makes his new life of grace available to the people of Israel. Likewise, in the miracle of the loaves and fishes (Matt. 14:13–21; Mark 6:32–44; Luke 9:10–17; John 6:1–15), Jesus gives to the people food not wholly dissimilar to that which God gave in the wilderness, thus identifying himself implicitly with God, the Lord of Israel.

In John 6, Christ speaks of himself as the "bread of life . . . which comes down from heaven that a man may eat of it and not die" (6:48–50). When pressed by the "murmurs" of the Jewish crowd in the wilderness, he clarifies that "the bread which I shall give for the life of the world is my flesh" (6:51). This prophetic discourse is expressly eucharistic: "He who eats my flesh and drinks my blood has eternal life, and I will raise him up at the last day. For my flesh is true food indeed, and my blood is drink indeed. He who eats my flesh and drinks my blood abides in me, and I in him" (6:54–56).

The eucharistic discourse of the Lord in John 6 recapitulates the typology of Exod. 16. First, Jesus makes clear that it is his eucharistic flesh that gives eternal life, not the sensible rites of the old covenant. "This is the bread which came down from heaven, not such as the fathers ate and died; he who eats this bread will live forever" (John 6:58). The ancient Israelites in the wilderness experienced a conversion, a time of newly formed faith. That faith was saving because it explicitly attained to the living God of the covenant and implicitly attained to the mysteries of the incarnation and the passion.[11] One might say that the rites of the old covenant were saving because they were *occasions* for faith, not because they were *causes* of faith.[12]

In the new covenant this same mystery of salvation is made available to the Church in a more explicit way: through the plenary revelation of Christ and through the sacraments, especially through the presence of Christ in the Eucharist. This presence is real; the Eucharist is the body, blood, soul, and divinity of Christ, present under the sacramental species (or properties) of bread and wine.[13] However, this real presence—which exists independently of the subjective faith

11. *ST* 1–2.98.2 ad 4, 1–2.100.12, 2–2.2.7.
12. *ST* 1–2.103.2.
13. As taught in 1215 at the Fourth Lateran Council, chap. 1, and more explicitly in 1551 by the Council of Trent, Session 13, can. 1 and 3.

of Christians—is only rightly understood and experienced in and through super-natural faith, hope, and love (see John 6:63). Traditionally, Catholic theology understands the Eucharist to be "the sacrament of charity" that nourishes the Church and so sustains her in being daily by communion in the body and blood of Christ. This is her "daily bread" *in via*, spiritual food for those who are on pilgrimage in the wilderness of this world in view of the promised land of the next, that which is found only in the vision of God and in the life of the resurrection.

16:22–36 "The LORD has given you the Sabbath, therefore on the sixth day he gives you bread for two days; remain every man of you in his place, let no man go out of his place on the seventh day" (16:29).

The notion of the Sabbath is introduced in the Torah for the first time explicitly in Exod. 16:22–30. It is not certain when the observation of the Sabbath as a day of rest first originated. It could well stem directly from the early Mosaic movement, or it could derive originally from some other ancient Near Eastern religious culture. Whatever the case, the notion takes on an absolutely unique meaning within the context of the ancient Hebrew faith and the Mosaic law.[14] Here the rite of keeping the Sabbath is prescribed implicitly "before the letter of the law" by the way in which God gives the manna and quails. The people receive a double portion on the sixth day so that they are not obliged to work on the seventh day.

Within the larger context of the Torah, this passage of scripture stands between two others. The creation narrative in Gen. 2:3 portrays God resting on the "seventh day" of creation. In Exod. 20:8–11, the observation of the Sabbath is prescribed as the third of the Ten Commandments, at the heart of the covenant. That passage (20:11) refers explicitly to Gen. 2:3: the observation of the Sabbath entails the imitation of God, who rests on the seventh day of creation. This framing of the issue of the Sabbath points us simultaneously, then, toward the *exitus* and *reditus* of the creation and the covenant. All things that exist come forth from God as a mysterious gift and bear the imprint of God's eternal wisdom. All things are meant to return to God as their ultimate end. The created order is said to "rest" in God because it derives from God's preexistent eternal wisdom. The contemplation of God is eternally immutable and unchanging, simple and perfectly actual. This is the eternal "rest" of divine peace from which the world originates, and this richness and depth of divine contemplation are reflected imperfectly in the order and richness of creatures produced by God. The created order "returns" to

14. On these matters see de Vaux 1997: 475–83.

God particularly through the rational actions of man, who is made in the image of God. The human being finds spiritual rest in the eternal Logos—that is, the reason of God—who is the cause of all things. In this way, the prescription of the Sabbath is at the heart of the covenant, by which man returns to God and enters into the contemplation of He Who Is.

Exodus 16:31–36 speaks of the manna from the perspective of the future. The Torah tells us that God provided the food until the time that the people entered into Canaan. The manna was to be kept in the temple as a sign of the divine care of God afforded to the people of Israel during their sojourn in the desert. "And Moses said to Aaron, 'Take a jar, and put an omer of manna in it, and place it before the LORD, to be kept throughout your generations'" (16:33). Exodus 16:36 states that "an omer is the tenth part of an ephah," suggesting that this passage comes from a much later period. The manna in the wilderness is seen retrospectively as a typological foreshadowing of the temple and of God's accompanying presence with Israel during the course of Israel's historical existence.

17:1–7 "'Behold, I will stand before you there on the rock at Horeb; and you shall strike the rock, and water shall come out of it, that the people may drink.' And Moses did so, in the sight of the elders of Israel. And he called the name of the place Massah and Mer´ibah, because of the faultfinding of the children of Israel, and because they put the LORD to the proof by saying, 'Is the LORD among us or not?'" (17:6–7).

Israel is portrayed moving gradually south on the Sinai Peninsula, through the wilderness of Sin, and toward Mount Horeb or Sinai. They camp at Rephidim, which is said to be near Horeb (similarly, 19:2 claims that it is near Sinai). The narrative portrays a series of revolts among the people that occur in stages against the background of the struggle for survival.

This passage of scripture has, above all, a moral sense that pertains to the mystery of unbelief and the grace of faith. The "testing of God" at Massah and Meribah is a fundamental symbol in the Old Testament of the unbelief of the elect people. In Deut. 6:16–17, Moses commands: "You shall not put the LORD your God to the test, as you tested him at Massah. You shall diligently keep the commandments of the LORD your God, and his testimonies, and his statutes, which he has commanded you." This is said in the context of the giving of the Ten Commandments (in Deut. 5) and the Shema prayer of Deut. 6:4: "Hear, O Israel: The LORD our God is one LORD." The murmur at Massah places in question basic trust in God, who has revealed himself to Israel. Likewise, in Ps. 95:8–11 God gives an imperative to the people of Israel:

> Harden not your hearts, as at Mer′ibah,
>   as on the day at Massah in the wilderness,
> when your fathers tested me,
>   and put me to the proof, though they had seen my work.
> For forty years I loathed that generation
>   and said, "They are a people who err in heart,
>   and they do not regard my ways."
> Therefore I swore in my anger
>   that they should not enter my rest.

Despite the moral gravity of Israel's unbelief, this event in the wilderness is also a symbol of grace. God responds to their unbelief with the kindness of a sign that renews faith—the sign of water—which is often a symbol in the scriptures of the life of grace that comes from God. "He turns a desert into pools of water, / a parched land into springs of water" (Ps. 107:35). "Then he showed me the river of the water of life, bright as crystal, flowing from the throne of God and of the Lamb" (Rev. 22:1).

In 1 Cor. 10:1–4, Paul argues that the ancient Hebrews communed by faith in the mystery of Christ. "I want you to know, brethren, that our fathers were all under the cloud, and all passed through the sea, and all were baptized into Moses in the cloud and in the sea, and all ate the same supernatural food and all drank the same supernatural drink. For they drank from the supernatural Rock which followed them, and the Rock was Christ." He also offers a warning: "Nevertheless with most of them God was not pleased; for they were overthrown in the wilderness" (1 Cor. 10:5). This teaching of Paul suggests that the ancient faith of the Hebrews in the revelation of the Lord made through Moses in the early wilderness setting was itself tendentially ordered toward the fulfillment of the economy given in Christ. Their faith was "explicitly" in the Lord and therefore "implicitly" in Christ.[15] They participated imperfectly and inchoately, but truly, in the grace that was to be merited by Christ, the head of the Church.

Adversity of Gentiles (Exod. 17:8–16)

17:8–16 "Then came Am′alek and fought with Israel at Reph′idim. . . . Whenever Moses held up his hand, Israel prevailed; and whenever he lowered his hand, Am′alek prevailed" (17:8, 11).

15. On this point, see Aquinas, *ST* 2–2.2.5–8.

Here the Torah presents the first armed conflict between Israel and a Gentile people: the Amalekites. The Amalekites were a nomadic tribe. The book of Genesis portrays them as descendants of Esau (Gen. 36:12) who inhabit the Kadesh region, north of Sinai (14:7). Numbers 13:29 refers to them living in the Negeb, and Saul subsequently fights against them during his regency as king of Israel (1 Sam. 14:48). It is because Saul refuses to place the ban upon them (1 Sam. 15) that he is removed by the Lord as the king of Israel (28:18).

Amalek and the Amalekites may seem obscure to the ordinary reader, but they play an important role in scripture. Typologically, they are archetypes that represent a mystery, a repeated sign in scripture of the adversity that Gentile peoples maintain toward the people of Israel throughout the ages (Num. 14:43–45; Deut. 25:17–19; Judg. 3:13; 1 Sam. 15:2).

> They conspire with one accord;
> > against thee they make a covenant—
> . . . .
> Gebal and Ammon and Am´alek,
> > Philistia with the inhabitants of Tyre . . .
> . . . .
> O my God, make them like whirling dust,
> > like chaff before the wind. (Ps. 83:5, 7, 13)

Why do Gentile nations seek to rival the people of Israel? This adversity stems sometimes from the permissive will of God, who allows such aggression on the part of outsiders in order to purify the intentions and spiritual integrity of both Israel and the Church. However, it also stems from a mysterious jealousy on the part of Gentiles and their leaders, of those who would wish to see themselves as the truly elect people in substitution for Israel and eventually for the Church.

The moral sense of the text is significant since it concerns the question of warfare in the service of religious belief. The Amalekites are defeated by Joshua, who makes his first appearance in the Torah here. Reading the text (defensibly) according to a Thomistic anthropological conception, the cooperation of Moses and Joshua represents the interconnection of the speculative and practical components of religious obedience. It is not enough merely to know the law without obeying it, nor is it permissible to act independently of rightly ordered knowledge. But can engagement in armed conflict ever be the form that obedience to God takes? Can engagement in warfare be just and therefore placed authentically at the service of ethical and religious ends? Faustus the Manichean argues against Augustine that this passage demonstrates the noninspired, morally aberrant character of the Old Testament because God here seems to give approbation to war that is fought on behalf of the Israelites.[16] The presupposition is that engagement in armed conflict and obedience to God in God's goodness are always incompatible. Augustine argues against Faustus: some military conflicts are just, and wars can be engaged in by Christians, but only under the conditions of justice.

> A great deal depends on the causes for which men undertake wars, and on the authority they have for doing so; for the natural order which seeks the peace of mankind, ordains that the monarch should have the power of undertaking war if he thinks it advisable, and that the soldiers should perform their military duties on behalf of the peace and safety of the community. When war is undertaken in obedience to God, who would rebuke, or humble, or crush the pride of man, it must be allowed to be a righteous war.
>
> The real evils in war are love of violence, revengeful cruelty, fierce and implacable enmity, wild resistance, and the lust of power, and such like; and it is generally to punish these things, when force is required to inflict the punishment, that, in obedience to God or some lawful authority, good men undertake wars, when they find themselves in such a position as regards the conduct of human affairs, that right conduct requires them to act, or to make others act in this way.[17]

Moses stands above the battle, his arms uplifted. What significance should one ascribe to the fact that Moses's uplifted arms seem to assure victory, while his arms descended invite defeat? In the earlier conflict with the Pharaoh, the Torah made clear that there is a fundamental contrast between the superstitious practices of the Egyptian magicians and the obedience of Moses to the commands of the Lord. Within the context of the larger book, then, this gesture of Moses can only be seen as a derivative occasion of the exercise of God's power and not its cause. God conquers through a sign and makes obedience to the sign in faith the condition for his victory. The spiritual sense of the passage is clear: it is obedience to the law of Moses that will allow Israel to survive throughout the centuries, even amidst the persecutions of the spiritual descendants of Amalek.

Analogically, this passage symbolizes Christ and his grace, which is present in the sacraments of the Church. The arms of Moses uplifted in prayer foretell prophetically the mystery of Christ with his arms outstretched upon the Cross. "Father, forgive them; for they know not what they do" (Luke 23:34). The merits

16. See Augustine, *Contra Faustum* 22.5.
17. Augustine, *Contra Faustum* 22.75, 74 (*NPNF*[1] 4:301).

of Moses, which are a gift of grace, prefigure the uniquely saving merits of Christ crucified, who stands above the plain of the world, saving the people of God from the powers of death. The Church militant survives her many adversaries through the ages of the world and not by trust in her own powers but by the power of the Cross, which is present in the seven sacraments of the Church. That power is active not through any magic (falsely so called) but by means of instrumental causality. How ought we to understand this?

The Holy Trinity is the primary cause of the grace of sacraments.[18] As the unique savior of humanity, Christ in his sacred humanity is the "conjoined" instrumental cause of all grace (including all sacramental grace). The sacraments are "separated" instrumental causes, subordinate to Christ, through which he works.[19] Due to the fidelity of God to his covenant of grace with the Church, the sacraments—when performed properly—always will have an effect *ex opere operato* (through their very working).[20] Christ, then, is the new Moses, "standing" in the glory of the resurrection above the plains of history and interceding on behalf of the Church. He offers grace effectively in and through every valid celebration of a sacrament of the New Law, whether this grace is received properly or not on the part of the recipient.[21] At the heart of the Church's continued existence through the ages is the

---

18. *ST* 3.62.1.

19. *ST* 3.62.5:

> A sacrament in causing grace works after the manner of an instrument. Now an instrument is twofold: the one, separate, as a stick, for instance; the other, united, as a hand. Moreover, the separate instrument is moved by means of the united instrument, as a stick by the hand. Now the principal efficient cause of grace is God himself, in comparison with whom Christ's humanity is as a united instrument, whereas the sacrament is as a separate instrument. Consequently, the saving power must needs be derived by the sacraments from Christ's Godhead through his humanity.
>
> Now sacramental grace seems to be ordained principally to two things: namely, to take away the defects consequent on past sins, in so far as they are transitory in act, but endure in guilt; and, further, to perfect the soul in things pertaining to divine worship in regard to the Christian religion. But it is manifest from what has been stated above (*ST* 3.48.1, 2 and 6, 3.49.1 and 3) that Christ delivered us from our sins principally through his passion, not only by way of efficiency and merit, but also by way of satisfaction. Likewise by his passion he inaugurated the rites of the Christian religion by offering "himself—an oblation and a sacrifice to God" (Eph. 5:2). Wherefore it is manifest that the sacraments of the Church derive their power especially from Christ's passion, the virtue of which is in a manner united to us by our receiving the sacraments. It was in sign of this that from the side of Christ hanging on the Cross there flowed water and blood, the former of which belongs to baptism, the latter to the Eucharist, which are the principal sacraments.

20. See the teaching of the Council of Trent from 1547, Session 7, esp. can. 8 (Denzinger 2012: 1608): "If anyone says that through the sacraments of the New Law grace is not conferred by the performance of the rite itself (*ex opere operato*) but that faith alone in the divine promise is sufficient to obtain grace, let him be anathema." For a positive elaboration of this doctrine, see *ST* 3.62.3, 4, 6.

21. The capacity of the human being to resist grace, at least in certain instances, is underscored by the Council of Trent, Session 6, *Decree on Justification*, especially in chap. 5 and can. 4. The idea

mystery of this sacramental economy of grace. By fidelity to this mystery, the Church eventually overcomes (or outlives) every false messianic ideology and pretense to human self-realization apart from God. As long as the Church remains faithful theologically to the authentic celebration of the seven sacraments, the Church will survive in every age and will eventually triumph in the age of the return of Christ.

Contribution of Gentiles (Exod. 18)

18:1–12 "Jethro, the priest of Mid'ian, Moses' father-in-law, heard of all that God had done for Moses and for Israel his people, how the LORD had brought Israel out of Egypt. . . . And Jethro, Moses' father-in-law, offered a burnt offering and sacrifices to God; and Aaron came with all the elders of Israel to eat bread with Moses' father-in-law before God" (18:1, 12).

If Amalek represents the adversity of the Gentile nations toward the election of Israel, Jethro represents not only the Gentile acceptance of this mystery of the covenant but also a non-Israelite contribution to the covenant. In this way, Israel appears here as a discreet but real centerpiece of human history, around which all other peoples or cultures stand. The claim that God has elected this people is to be transmitted throughout human history, dividing Gentiles on either side but also uniting them in the age of the Messiah. The mystery of Israel will shape the future religious history of the entire human race, throughout all time, in a discreet but remarkable and clear way.

The first part of Exod. 18 presents us with several enigmas. First, some of the events are also recounted in Num. 11:11–17 and Deut. 1:9–18. In those narratives, the events are presumed to take place after the people have sojourned at Mount Sinai. According to the Exodus narrative, they seemingly occur before the people have reached Sinai, and yet the people are referred to as being "encamped at the mountain of God" (Exod. 18:5). Presumably, then, the editors altered the order of an earlier narrative. Traditional Jewish commentators argue that this change was made in order to place Jethro alongside Amalek, presenting a theological diptych of two contrasting icons.[22] Amalek and Jethro are biblical

---

was reiterated by Innocent X in his Constitution *Cum occasione* in 1653, which condemns errors of Cornelius Jansen on grace. See in particular the second of the five famous condemned propositions (Denzinger 2012: 2002): "In the state of fallen nature interior grace is never resisted." Aquinas affirms unequivocally the possibility of resisting grace in numerous places. See, for example, *SCG* 3.159–60; *In Ioan.* 15.5.2055.

22. This is the well-known interpretation of Ibn Ezra, which is discussed critically by Nachmanides, *Commentary on the Torah: Exodus* 18.1. More recently, see Buber 1958: 91–110; Cassuto 2005: 211–12.

archetypes, like the two thieves portrayed alongside Christ crucified in Luke 23:33–43. One rejects the mystery of the covenant while the other accepts it. In opposing fashions, each reacts to the messianic mystery hidden in the people of Israel.

A second enigma of this section is the reappearance of Zipporah, the wife of Moses. She appears here after a long absence (see Exod. 4:24–26) and is depicted with not one but two sons. Her reappearance is meant to be explained by 18:2; Moses had sent her away, back to her father. Does this passage contrast, then, with the story recounted in Exod. 4, where she seems to accompany Moses into Egypt? The text gives no adequate information from which to speculate about the character of Moses's familial relations; nor can one readily pronounce upon the historicity of the passage. The prophet's human family is not brought strongly into light by the divine revelation. Rather, Moses's family is marginalized and eclipsed. In fact, throughout the Old and New Testaments the human families of the prophets are rarely given any particular importance and are typically not even mentioned. The word of God makes an absolute claim upon the human being and renders even the most natural ties of human society peripheral and relative; the prophet is spiritually poor, entirely at the service of the divine revelation.

The final enigma concerns the beliefs of Jethro. After all, the family member of Moses that the Torah deals with most extensively is a Gentile and Midianite priest. Jethro seems to acknowledge the Lord (YHWH) who has revealed himself to Moses in Exod. 3, but at the same time he does not convert to the religion of the Israelites in any overt fashion. This passage tells us (18:12) that Jethro makes burnt offerings to God, but God is designated as "Elohim" and not the "Lord." It is sometimes speculated that this distinction reflects the Elohist division of divine names.[23] God has revealed himself to Israel as the Lord [YHWH] while others know him only by the more universal, natural title of Elohim. And yet clearly the "natural sacrifice" offered by Jethro to God is viewed positively in this context. Aaron, the future priest of the Lord, comes to eat with him.

It should be noted how theologically significant Jethro's act of worship is. Only some chapters later, the Israelites will receive the Ten Commandments of God, the first of which is "I am the LORD your God, who brought you out of the land of Egypt, out of the house of bondage. You shall have no other gods before me" (20:2–3). Furthermore, there is a clear concern in Exodus that the

---

23. See the discussion of Childs 1974: 321–22.

Israelites be faithful to the worship of the Lord alone, which corresponds to the idea that the Gentiles are often subject to idolatry and false worship. The theme is important throughout scripture and is prevalent in the New Testament in the teachings of Paul, who affirms in Rom. 1:18–32 that the Gentile world has fallen culpably into idolatry and related vices. And yet within the larger context of both Exodus and the whole of scripture, one sees the possibility of a "righteous Gentile" whose religious instincts orient him rightly toward God and implicitly toward the Lord, who has revealed himself to Israel. Read within the context of a Pauline anthropology, Jethro's action of worshiping God authentically (as the Torah seems to suggest) demonstrates the presence of grace operating outside the visible boundaries of the covenant and even within some religious actions of noncovenanted peoples. However, this grace is also tangentially oriented toward the explicit recognition of the God of Israel. In Jethro's worship there is the hidden promise of a universalization of the grace of the covenant, a promise that comes to explicit and visible fruition in the New Testament, when Gentiles are incorporated into the covenant by baptism into the Church.

18:13–27

When Moses' father-in-law saw all that he was doing for the people, he said, "What is this that you are doing for the people? Why do you sit alone, and all the people stand about you from morning till evening? . . . Choose able men from all the people, such as fear God, men who are trustworthy and who hate a bribe; and place such men over the people as rulers of thousands, of hundreds, of fifties, and of tens. And let them judge the people at all times; every great matter they shall bring to you, but any small matter they shall decide themselves; so it will be easier for you, and they will bear the burden with you." (18:14, 21–22)

Jethro provides Moses with a system for the division of labor, suggesting to him that a series of judges be appointed to hear cases that arise among the people, while Moses reserves to himself the cases that are particularly difficult (18:22). It is thought by some interpreters that the narrative here serves to justify a subsequent political arrangement in Israel that developed after the settlement. We see King Jehoshaphat enact a similar system in 2 Chr. 19:5–11, though that could itself be a reform conducted according to preexistent legal tradition.[24] Alternately, there could well have existed a system of judges that was established at the beginning

24. See the discussion of de Vaux 1978: 1:337–38.

of the Sinai religious movement, the literary portrayal of which was affected by subsequent, postsettlement traditions.[25]

This same sequence of events (the establishment of a system of judges) is also recounted in Num. 11:11–17 and Deut. 1:9–18. Neither text mentions Jethro. In Num. 11:16 God himself commands Moses to institute the political arrangement. If the passages are read in an overlapping way, should Exodus be contrasted with Numbers? Does the advice of Jethro contrast necessarily with the notion of a divine institution by God? Seemingly there is no necessary contrast for the author of Exod. 18, even if the two ideas remain distinct. Here Jethro is a voice of natural reason or sound political prudence, a non-Israelite through whom God works to organize internally the people of Israel. The author of this portion of the Torah clearly means to underscore that gifts of natural prudential reason, even when they come from outside of the sphere of explicit revelation, are compatible with revelation. In the words of Augustine:

> Did not God talk with Moses, and yet he, with great wisdom and entire absence of jealous pride, accepted the plan of his father-in-law, a man of an alien race, for ruling and administering the affairs of the great nation entrusted to him? For Moses knew that a wise plan, in whatever mind it might originate, was to be ascribed not to the man who devised it, but to him who is the Truth, the unchangeable God.[26]

Moses here is a typological sign of the Church. Although the Church is directly inspired by God and instructed according to the perennial, unchanging principles of divine revelation in Christ, the Church also acquires learning from non-Christian sources, both ancient and new. This is one of the reasons that her theological vision develops down through time. In addition, the Church must continually apply the unchanging principles of the New Law within new historical contexts. Due to this fact, many aspects of the Church's internal life and organization can be subject to alteration across various times and places.

Since the mid-twentieth century, scholars have sometimes hypothesized that the Yahwism of Moses and the primitive Israelite religious movement had its origins in Kenite or Midianite religion on the southern tip of the Sinai Peninsula. The figure of Jethro the Midianite priest, then, might act as a historical symbol of a wider cultural influence upon Moses—that of the preexistent tribal religion of

25. See Childs 1974: 324.
26. Augustine, *On Christian Doctrine*, preface, 7 (*NPNF*[1] 2:520).

the Sinai region, which gave birth progressively to this new religious movement and subsequently migrated into Canaan.

Based on existing evidence, we cannot know with any real certitude if there is something to be said for the "Kenite hypothesis."[27] Theologically, the issue matters only coincidentally. Grace presupposes nature, and human nature only subsists in diverse cultural subconfigurations. Therefore, it is entirely warranted to expect that any gift of divine revelation could only occur within a given cultural and religious context, with its preexistent forms of ritual, language, and belief. Furthermore, the revelation could well be articulated (by Moses and the primitive Israelite movement) by making use of this preexistent "material cause." If modern archeologists were to discover that a large group of Midianites in the southern region of the Sinai Peninsula had a developed theology of the worship of YHWH as a local deity in the era just preceding the time prescribed traditionally to the exodus, this should make very little difference to any sound, traditional theology of revelation. No amount of knowledge of the cultural-linguistic and social conditions of the time and place in which revelation is given can ever be sufficient to explain the giving of the revelation per se, which has a divine object that is known fundamentally only by the divine initiative and through supernatural means of grace. This initiative and this grace can never be confirmed definitively to exist (whether positively or negatively) by empirical study of the external conditions of the act of prophecy. To think that it can be is to fall into some form of rationalism or naturalism. Even if God spoke in and through certain forms of a preexisting tradition (and we have very little evidence of this), it is nevertheless the case (according to Israelite theology) that God spoke in a completely novel and historically unique way, changing human religious history forever.

Likewise, neither can the universal character of the Israelite religion (which appeals to YHWH as the unique God and enshrines God's teachings in a particular law) be denied uniquely by recourse to the study of its original historical setting, in which religion was primarily tribal, provincial, and nonuniversalistic. The capacity for universal thought is simply an inherent dimension of the human mind, made manifest in partial ways by the mere use of language and the employment of any form of common law. Presuming the chronology of a thirteenth- to twelfth-century-BC exodus, these features of culture were already present at the time in which the primitive life of Israel emerged. Consequently, one cannot positively demonstrate the absence or impossibility of a unique historical revelation that

27. See the analysis, still pertinent, of Childs 1974: 321–26; de Vaux 1978: 1:330–38, 424–25.

is, in some sense, explicitly understood as universal in scope by recourse to the study of the historical conditions in which primitive Israelite religion emerged. For the same reason, there is no reason theologically to formulate any opposition to a profound exploration of those same historical conditions. On the contrary, greater knowledge of them can and should, in principle, contribute to a deeper understanding of the mystery of revelation in the life of the people of Israel.

3

COVENANT

Exodus 19–24

Introduction to the Covenant Material

The covenant material in the book of Exodus raises textual, historical, and theological difficulties. What sources are present in the text as we now have it? How was the material arranged historically? What, if anything, should we believe really happened at Sinai? Did the laws of ancient Israel develop historically, and if so, what significance does this have? How is the heart of the law to be interpreted theologically?

Here I will seek only to offer general principles for a right interpretation of the covenant, both historically and theologically, without seeking to make specific claims of a textual and historical kind. In fact, the theological axioms presented here would be compatible, in principle, with diverse interpretations of the textual material, both from a literary and historical point of view.

First, the question of the historical genealogy of the covenant must be distinguished from that of its nature or essential form as such. Asking how something came to be is different from asking what a thing is. The two questions are interrelated but not identical. It is one thing to hypothesize about how Israel came to believe historically and formulate textually its own conviction that a covenant existed between God and Israel. It is another thing to reflect on what the nature of the covenant is and whether such a covenant of grace actually exists.

Genealogy of the Covenant

The first question is difficult to treat due to the fact that the textual material in Exod. 19–24 seems to be heavily edited and to consist of a dense array of texts, stemming perhaps from different ages of the life of the people of Israel. One might think of this section of Exodus as a textual iconostasis: a diversity of icons or images presenting us with what happened at Sinai and giving us a theological account of the significance of this historical event. We cannot easily see behind the iconostasis of scripture, but this is the portrait that the Holy Spirit has given to instruct us.

One should not conclude from this that the question of the historicity of the Sinai event cannot be discussed or that the Sinai event is without historical foundations. True, scholars in modernity have often placed in question the basic delineations of the narrative. Some ask if there was even an original unity of the wilderness traditions, on the one hand, and the Sinai traditions, on the other. Meanwhile, other scholars raise questions of historical reality—of Sinai as a place and of the historical composition of a written covenant document. Nevertheless, as has commonly been pointed out in modern debates, the ancient literature of the Hebrews does exhibit a clear diversity of sources from various historical ages. Amidst this diversity of historical witnesses, there are common themes, including those pertaining to a historical exodus and covenant. Consequently, the Israelite tradition offers a historical genealogy of its own origin, even if this genealogy is in many ways archaic in form. There is no real way to disprove, then, that an original event is being communicated to us effectively through the various sources of tradition that constitute the Hebrew scriptures. On the contrary, the unity of core traditions and historical explanations that are found at the heart of such a historically diverse array of texts and traditions is itself a testimony to the rational likelihood of a primeval event. The references to Sinai in the multiple sources of the Torah and in the early prophets are too prevalent and diverse (both stylistically and at different historical "levels" of textual archeology) for one simply to eradicate them from the primeval history of Israel.[1] Based on this form of reasoning, there is no sound reason to dissociate the historical exodus (and the wilderness traditions) from the subsequent ratification of the covenant at Sinai/Horeb. The two should

---

1. See the arguments of Roland de Vaux (1978: 1:401–19).

be kept together as intrinsically historically related. While some have speculated that the mountain was located on the Arabian Peninsula, where there are active volcanoes and frequent thunderstorms, the majority opinion is that the location is most likely to have been somewhere at the southern end of the Sinai Peninsula.[2]

Analogous things may be said concerning Moses and the primeval giving of a law to the people of the original exodus movement. Admittedly it is difficult to draw up any historically secure "portrait" of the founder of the ancient Israelite religion based on the sources that have come down to us. However, it is possible to perceive something of his personality through his historical effects. In the words of Roland de Vaux:

> It is clear from literary and historical criticism that various developments that were in fact much later than Moses were retrojected, in successive levels, to the period of Moses, but those accretions were added to an already existing nucleus. The whole process cannot be explained without accepting the historical basis of the earliest traditions. In other words, it was during the period of Moses that YHWH was recognized as the God who saved the people at the time of the exodus and who established special relationships between himself and that people at Sinai. There is no doubt, then, that Moses played an essential part in the origins of the religion of Israel.[3]

De Vaux thinks that the essence of the earliest covenant is constituted by the Ten Commandments, given by Moses to the people of Israel as an expression of the will of the Lord.[4] Exodus 20:1–17 and Deut. 5:4–21 offer distinct versions of the Ten Commandments, which both sources posit as the essence or nucleus of the original covenant. Despite the clear differences between the two lists of precepts, the textual traditions are quite similar, suggesting a common tradition that they both depend upon, which is very ancient.

Some scholars have proposed more ambitious theories than that of de Vaux, arguing that the literary form of the covenant portrayed in Exod. 20 and 24:3–8 mirrors a well-known form of ancient vassalage treatise in which a servant gives an oath of allegiance to a king in return for promises of patronage and protection.[5] It is rightly noted that in Exodus this ancient literary motif has been altered in a

2. See de Vaux 1978: 1:426–39.
3. De Vaux 1978: 1:453.
4. De Vaux 1978: 1:441–42, 448–50.
5. See, for example, G. E. Mendenhall, *Law and Covenant in Israel and the Ancient Near East* (Pittsburgh: Biblical Colloquium, 1955) in comparison with de Vaux 1978: 1:439–50.

historically significant way. No longer is the covenant to be understood between human beings and their kings. Instead it is transferred analogically and, in a sense, subverted from within so that it refers to the relation between Israel and God. God is the unique king of Israel. The slaves escaped from Egypt have a covenant of their own, but it is not with a Near Middle Eastern suzerain; it is with the Lord, who has revealed himself to Moses.

This theory rightly notes analogies between the Sinai covenant in the book of Exodus and ancient Hittite covenants from the historical age of the purported exodus, the thirteenth century BC. Consequently, Moses and his original scribes might truly have composed the covenant document at the heart of Exodus. However, analogous texts can be found in Assyrian treatises of a much later period.[6] Therefore, while it is possible to speculate that a covenant treatise was composed by the earliest Israelite movement (derived even from Moses himself), this is not historically demonstrable. Only the following is certain. First, an archeological level of primitive theology cannot be located in Israel in which it is not already understood that Israel is a people uniquely beloved by the Lord and elected by the Lord for a unique form of service. Thus the germ of the covenant idea seems to be primordial.[7] Second, however the genealogical history of ideas unfolded, the ancient Israelites (from the settlement to the age of the monarchy to the postexilic period) progressively formulated in stages a very developed theology of the covenant.

Whatever the history of this development, it is reasonable to see many features of the Exodus narrative at Sinai as historically primeval: the notion of Israel as elect or chosen especially by the Lord, Moses as the mediator of the covenant, the practice of the Sabbath, the giving of the Ten Commandments and perhaps other fundamental laws, prohibition on the use of any images for God, the building of the ark of the covenant and the tent of meeting, some kind of primal system of sacrifices, and some form of organization through the medium of tribal leagues.[8]

When John Henry Newman discusses the notion of a development of doctrine in Catholic thought, he notes seven forms of continuity in the doctrinal development of the life of the Church, stretching from antiquity to modernity: the preservation of type (or inner essence) of the original teaching; continuity

6. See, on this subject, D. J. McCarthy, *Treaty and Covenant: A Study in Form in the Ancient Oriental Documents and in the Old Testament* (Rome: Pontifical Biblical Institute, 1963).

7. See the measured arguments of John Bright, *A History of Israel*, 4th ed. (Louisville: Westminster John Knox, 2000), 148–57.

8. De Vaux 1978: 1:453–72.

of principles across time; the power of assimilation of earlier forms of the religion by later, more developed forms; the logical sequence of the unfolding of ideas from implicit to explicit; the anticipation of a later development in the religious life of the Church in an earlier development; the self-conscious conservation of acquisitions from the past; and the chronic vigor of the identity of doctrines across diverse ages.[9] Newman is identifying a process of development through time that characterizes the theological tradition of the Catholic Church, such that its teaching across time is in some way always identical, even if it undergoes new formulations and clarifications amidst various waves of crisis and expansion.

A process like this one can be envisaged not only in the tradition of the Church that stems from the apostolic deposit of faith, and which seeks to interpret scripture, but also in scripture itself.[10] The life of Israel entails a preservation of types and the unfolding of a logical sequence of ideas based upon original principles, but this unfolding also occurs through a winding historical process, often characterized by intellectual dialectic, religious crises, and fairly innovative new discernments. Most frequently it was the prophets and priestly scribes of ancient Israel who were inspired by God to preserve the essence of the covenant and to interpret and rearticulate it within new circumstances and in the midst of new challenges. This covenant has its remote origins in the patriarchal age and its proximate origins and immediate cause in the new religious movement fashioned at the exodus under the inspired governance of Moses. From this seminal form, it developed vigorously (and at times precariously) into a mature canonical expression, in and through a long history. In its final redacted form, the Torah bears within itself the echoes of the monarchic age, the Deuteronomical reform, and the resettlement following the sixth-century Babylonian exile. It is the subsequent redaction of the Torah and the scriptural canon that gave rise to Judaism in its mature, postexilic form.

Given this genealogical interpretation, how can we understand the character of the divine inspiration given to Moses, subsequent prophets, and inspired authors? Aquinas distinguishes several levels of prophecy and divine inspiration. At the highest level, prophecy entails God giving the prophet infused *species*, a higher form

9. Newman 1989: chaps. 5–12.

10. A theory of this kind has been formulated by Karl Rahner in *Inspiration in the Bible*, trans. C. H. Henkey (New York: Herder and Herder, 1964). I am offering here a somewhat different version with greater emphasis on the inspired character of the text of scripture as such. See the pertinent criticisms of Rahner's construal by Yves Congar in "Inspiration des Écritures canoniques et apostolicité de l'Église," *Revue des sciences philosophiques et théologiques* 45 (1961): 32–42.

of knowledge akin to angelic ideas.[11] This form of knowledge is not to be confused with merely human concepts. It is intuitive and allows the prophet, in faith, to discern with intellectual clarity certain highest truths pertaining to God and the divine economy. A person could explicate these inspired intuitions with the use of lesser, ordinary concepts, words, and representational symbols drawn from his or her own culture and historical epoch.[12] Consequently, one might find a culturally archaic form of writing suffused with a high prophetic awareness and enriched by profound insight into the character of God, expressed in a highly symbolic, textually complex way. On a secondary level, God can infuse ordinary intellectual concepts or sense phantasms that would normally be procured through external experiences.[13] On a third and "lower" level, God can simply give the grace of assistance, enabling authors or editors to use their own natural powers well, assisted by grace, so as to formulate a clear understanding of revelation in their thoughts and writing, expressed in and through a given historical and literary tradition.[14]

Based on this analysis, it is feasible to imagine Moses or Aaron (and other early assistants) as recipients of high inspiration (prophetic *species*). These were received, however, within the context of an archaic cultural context and expressed in a given historical setting through the use of external precepts and practices reflective of that time. This initial Mosaic inspiration gave impetus to the initial religious movement of Israel in the wake of the exodus. Subsequent prophets reactualized, reinterpreted, and expanded this revelation, drawing out what was initially only logically implicit or suggested. High prophets such as Jeremiah, Ezekiel, and the author of Second Isaiah renewed and rearticulated the inner essence of the covenant in subsequent ages. The scribal editors who collated Deuteronomy and the final edition of the Torah were assisted by God to draw into a coherent

---

11. *ST* 2–2.173.1–2. See the interpretation of prophetic inspiration in Aquinas offered by Pierre Benoit in *Aspects of Biblical Inspiration*, trans. J. Murphy-O'Connor and K. Ashe (Chicago: Priory Press, 1965); and Pierre Benoit and P. Synave in *Prophecy and Inspiration: A Commentary on the Summa Theologica II-II, Questions 171–178*, trans. A. Dulles and T. Sheridan (New York: Desclee, 1961).

12. The divine-human complementarity being suggested here is upheld by the teaching of the Second Vatican Council, *Dei Verbum*, paras. 11 and 12 (Denzinger 2012: paras. 4215, 4217):

> In composing the sacred books, God chose men and while employed by Him, they made use of their powers and abilities, so that with Him acting in them and through them, they, as true authors, consigned to writing everything and only those things which He wanted. . . . Since God speaks in Sacred Scripture through men in human fashion, the interpreter of Sacred Scripture, in order to see clearly what God wanted to communicate to us, should carefully investigate what meaning the sacred writers really intended. . . . To search out the intention of the sacred writers, attention should be given, among other things, to "literary forms." For truth is set forth and expressed differently in texts which are variously historical, prophetic, poetic, or of other forms of discourse.

13. *ST* 2–2.173.3.

14. *ST* 2–2.173.4.

unity the textual expression of the covenant, giving an external expression to its internal essence.

Essence of the Covenant

Formally, or essentially, then, what does the covenant consist of? Concretely, the covenant is a kind of spiritual marriage between God and Israel. Its inner essence is the life of grace, exemplified by the theological virtues of faith, hope, and love by which Israel is directed toward union with the living God of Israel. Externally, this spiritual marriage is characterized by the observance of the moral, juridical, and ceremonial precepts of the law.

At the heart of the covenant is the encounter with the living God: He Who Is. This encounter consists in mystical knowledge and in mystical love, initiated by divine revelation and made possible by the grace of God active in the human mind and heart. This experience of encounter with the truth of God's inner essence by grace and in the darkness of faith has its archetypal representation in the example of Moses at the burning bush in Exod. 3:14–15. It is the I AM of the Lord whom Israel comes to know personally in the divine revelation. Exodus clearly gives us to understand that the experience of Sinai is a continuation or expansion of the experience originally given to Moses but now renewed in greater intensity and expanded to the people of Israel collectively.

One cannot prove by any amount of argument or historical analysis that there has come to exist a covenant of grace between God and Israel, nor can one disprove it. It is a truth of supernatural faith that can be known and believed in with unerring certitude only by the acceptance of divine revelation, which by its very character transcends the range of human natural knowledge. At the same time, this belief is in no way contrary to natural reason. There are various signs given to natural reason alerting us to the fact that we ought to take seriously the claim that God chose ancient Israel and revealed to them his law. These include the purity of the monotheism that emerged in the ancient Israelite religion and its nearly universal historical influence, the ethical vision of human behavior that has been bequeathed by the moral law of Israel, and the enduring presence of the Jewish people down through time (remaining in existence despite great adversity) as a sign of the perduring reality of the covenant and the providential protection of God.[15]

Ultimately, the covenant with Israel must be understood as affecting all of humanity in light of the person of Christ, the Son of God made man. In

15. See the arguments of Pascal in *Pensées*, part 1, chaps. 21, 24, 26.

the incarnation, passion, death, and resurrection of Christ, God offers to all nations the possibility of inclusion in the covenant of grace, a covenant that is made available to all through the temporal mission of the Church.[16] The Church, then, is the bride of Christ, wed to him in the covenant of faith, hope, and charity in this world and in the covenant of beatifying vision in the life to come. The knowledge of God that is given at Sinai flowers in the new covenant, through the revelation of the inner life of God as the Holy Trinity. The Lord who is He Who Is is also the Father, Word, and Holy Spirit, a communion of divine persons. Understood in a Christian light, the covenant has a trinitarian horizon from the beginning. It is oriented toward a plenary knowledge and love of the living God.

The letter to the Ephesians offers the most ultimate perspective in this matter, uniting protology and eschatology.

> Blessed be the God and Father of our Lord Jesus Christ, who has blessed us in Christ with every spiritual blessing in the heavenly places, even as he chose us in him before the foundation of the world, that we should be holy and blameless before him. He destined us in love to be his sons through Jesus Christ, according to the purpose of his will, to the praise of his glorious grace which he freely bestowed on us in the Beloved. (Eph. 1:3–6)

God's elective choice of his people stems from before the foundations of the world, from all eternity, and it is meant to guide the elect people—the Church—in and through the historical economy, into the very life of God.

The New Testament confronts us, then, with a subtle point. When God reveals the covenant first to Israel and ultimately to the Church, the central truth of revelation concerns the very inner life of God. The elective covenant of God is an initiative that stems from within the eternal identity and character of God as such. And yet the eternal identity of God does not depend upon the covenant per se. In the language of Aquinas, one must distinguish the eternal processions of the

---

16. Second Vatican Council, *Lumen Gentium*, para. 9 (Denzinger 2012: para. 4122):
It has pleased [God] to bring men together as one people, a people which acknowledges Him in truth and serves Him in holiness. He therefore chose the race of Israel as a people unto Himself. With it He set up a covenant. Step by step He taught and prepared this people, making known in its history both Himself and the decree of His will and making it holy unto Himself. All these things, however, were done by way of preparation and as a figure of that new and perfect covenant, which was to be ratified in Christ, and of that fuller revelation which was to be given through the Word of God Himself made flesh. . . . Christ instituted this new covenant, the New Testament, that is to say, in His Blood, calling together a people made up of Jew and gentile, making them one, not according to the flesh but in the Spirit. This was to be the new People of God.

trinitarian persons from their temporal missions.[17] The missions of the eternal Son and the eternal Sprit, who are "sent" into the world to bring us into communion with God, are the new presence in history of God's eternal processions—of the Word who is eternally generated of the Father and of the Spirit who is eternally spirated from the Father and the Son.[18]

In the heart of the covenant, then, we are given true knowledge of who God is eternally in himself. At the same time, it must also be affirmed that this gift on the part of God includes the revelation that the God of the covenant is a God of transcendent freedom who has created and elected us from all eternity through his own free initiative and decision, stemming from the perfect love that God always has for himself in his eternal goodness.[19] That is to say, God is not required to create or elect us to eternal life, and God is not perfected by electing us. The temporal missions that give us life with God add nothing to the infinite richness of the eternal processions in God. Nor is God constituted in his eternal life by the act of election by which God freely makes himself known to us. However, God does truly reveal to us who he is eternally, in and through his act of election. The gift of the covenant is given in radical freedom, and the gift given is God in himself.

The Archetypal Medium

These two dimensions of the covenant—its genealogical origins and its abiding essence—are both conveyed in an overlapping way in the teaching of Exod. 19–24. On the one hand, the narrative is meant to serve as an account of Israel's historical origins, albeit in a highly symbolic, representational mode. On the other hand, the symbols of Sinai, Moses, and the giving of the law speak of the inner essence of the covenant that endures perennially between God and Israel. Far from being an inherent obstacle to conveying sacred history, this archaic mode of witness is especially powerful. It simultaneously conveys the historical and essential theological features of reality in ways that are both conceptual and iconic. This is why the figure of Moses is so profoundly archetypal throughout the narrative. In him we see the historical mediator of the covenant (denoted by the literal sense, individually embodied in a distant history) and the representation

---

17. *ST* 1.43.1. See the helpful essays by Gilles Emery, "*Theologia* and *Dispensatio*: The Centrality of the Divine Missions in St. Thomas's Trinitarian Theology," *The Thomist* 74 (2010): 515–61, and Bruce D. Marshall, "The Dereliction of Christ and the Impassibility of God," in *Divine Impassibility and the Mystery of Human Suffering*, ed. J. Keating and T. J. White (Grand Rapids: Eerdmans, 2009), 246–98.
18. *ST* 1.43.5.
19. *SCG* 2.23; *ST* 1.19.2–5.

of Israel's living relationship with the transcendent God who is. This relationship is denoted especially by the moral and typological senses. In considering the presentation of the covenant and the law, it is necessary to keep ever in mind this dual intention of the sacred author.

Sinai (Exod. 19)

19:1–2 "And when they set out from Reph′idim and came into the wilderness of Sinai, they encamped in the wilderness; and there Israel encamped before the mountain" (19:2).

I will begin by considering the symbolism of the mountain in the Torah and in scripture more generally. Physically, the mountain of Sinai (or Horeb as it is called in Deuteronomy) represents physical separation. The heights of the mountain are a place that is distant from ordinary life, where one is alone with God in solitude. The mountain creates a natural cloister or spiritual space and denotes a term of pilgrimage. Moses ascends the mountain to be apart, providing an example to Israel of their need to seek intimacy with God in prayer. It is from within this disposition of prayerful receptivity that he is shown receiving the commandments and obeying them.

Spiritually, the mountain represents the ascent of the spirit under the effects of grace.[20] There is a twofold spiritual ascent: the intellectual ascent, which pertains to knowledge, and the ascent of love. The soul ascends to God by knowledge when the mind is carried by the teachings of faith into the darkness and light of God. The soul is thereby purified (in the trial of darkness, with its oblivion to worldly, secondary things) and illumined by the light of the Lord. This illumination is all the more profound when it occurs in the soul of one who is called to be a prophet, to receive the knowledge of God inwardly through infused knowledge, particularly in the form of infused *species*, as distinct from ordinary acquired knowledge. This was the case with Moses, no matter how much he articulated his inspiration in and through the native forms of the culture of his time (and there is theological reason to suppose that he did).[21]

The ascent of love comes by grace through the elevation of the will, which is led to desire God above all things, to do the will of God, and to detest everything

---

20. For an extensive reflection on this symbolism in the Bible, see Aquinas, *In Ioan.*, prologue.

21. Commenting on Deut. 34:10, "There has not arisen a prophet since in Israel like Moses," Aquinas argues that Moses is the greatest of prophets in the Old Testament (*ST* 2–2.174.4). This has to do with his place in the divine economy as both the liberator of the people of Israel and the original founder of the covenant.

other than God insofar as it could pose any obstacle to the right observance of God's law. This love of union with God in grace is most intense in those whom God calls into a particular or special intimacy and obedience, as was especially true in the case of the prophets and apostles. Consequently, Moses ascended outwardly to the mountain, which was employed by God simultaneously as a symbol of God's transcendence and of God's intimate encounter with Israel, undertaken in divine freedom. However, Moses also ascended inwardly above all, in the heights of mystical knowledge and love of God the Lord—a knowledge and a love made possible to him so that he might be the progenitor of the law and be remembered thereafter as the exemplary prophet of the old covenant.

Typologically, the mountain foreshadows Zion. This meaning is perhaps even identical in some way with the literal sense, intended by the sacred author. The temple on Mount Zion is the abiding place of the presence of the transcendent God, the Lord. This is why Exod. 19:1 says that the people arrived "on this day" at Sinai, that is to say, "now, today," which is henceforth the time of the covenant. Likewise, the mountain also refers to Jesus in the new covenant. Christ self-consciously recapitulates this symbolism in his ascent of the mountain of Galilee, where he stands in the place of YHWH, speaking the Beatitudes (Matt. 5:1–12). On Mount Tabor he is transfigured, shining with the effulgence of divine light (Matt. 17:1–19). His human intellect and will are elevated into the closest spiritual union with the deity of God by virtue of his immediate vision of God and due to the fullness of his grace and charity.[22] Consequently, Christ as man is the highest "peak" of prophetic light. "No one has seen the Father except him who is from God; only he has seen the Father" (John 6:46 NIV). From this interior "height," it is Christ who illumines the Church with the teaching of the New Law. This revelation culminates not in the temple on Mount Zion but outside the walls of Jerusalem where Christ—the new temple—is crucified, making manifest the fullness of the revelation of YHWH, who is present among men. "When you have lifted up the Son of man, then you will know that I am" (John 8:28).

19:3b–8 "You have seen what I did to the Egyptians, and how I bore you on eagles' wings and brought you to myself. Now therefore, if you will obey my voice and keep my covenant, you shall be my own possession among all peoples. . . . you shall be to me a kingdom of priests and a holy nation. These are the words which you shall speak to the children of Israel" (19:4–6).

22. For a consideration of this traditional christological teaching, see Thomas Joseph White, "The Voluntary Action of the Earthly Christ and the Necessity of the Beatific Vision," *The Thomist* 69 (2005): 497–534.

The covenant begins with this prologue. The content of 19:3b–8 is quite distinctive from the rest of the chapter, and its language bears some resemblance to Deut. 7:6; 32:11. First God speaks to Moses, promising to make the people his own in a unique way and giving them a covenant (19:5). This is the first mention of the Mosaic covenant in the Torah. Second, God promises to make the people a "kingdom of priests" and a "holy nation." Third, God tells them he bears them up on eagles' wings, that is to say, that he will provide them with a special providential protection because they are God's elect people.

Taking note of the second point, attention should be given to the expression "kingdom" as well as the notion of "priesthood." The expression "kingdom" here is figurative, or metaphorical (though it may refer obliquely to the Davidic monarchy). If God is the "king" of Israel through the treatise of the covenant, then it is the people themselves who are his "spiritual kingdom," constituted as such through their obedience to the law and their worship of God. The "place" of the kingdom is nomadic: God is where his people are, a fact that is symbolized by the tent of meeting in Exodus, which changes places. Spiritually, this denotes that each human being who is consecrated to God and in pilgrimage through this world can become the place where God dwells in the world if that person is united to God in faith and love, in obedience and in holy worship. The soul who lives in Christ is a "tent of meeting" where the Word can descend by grace upon the mind and heart.

The notion of a kingdom of "priests" is difficult to interpret. Clearly the term does not denote the priesthood of Aaron or the Levites. Rather, all of Israel collectively is deemed to be sacerdotal. Why is this? Anthropologically speaking, the priesthood is an office or function that pertains to the mediation between human beings and the sacred. As such it has two general functions: the ascending order and the descending order.[23] In the ascending order, the priest is a person who makes offerings to God on behalf of others. In the descending order, the priest is a person who in some way mediates the presence of God to others, often in a variety of ways (by blessing, teaching, or the administration of sacred rites). Can this broad definition of the priesthood be ascribed, then, to all the chosen people of God? In the ascending order, Israel as a whole is chosen by God in order to stand before God. Israel is meant to represent symbolically all of fallen humanity and is called to pray to God and worship him in truth on behalf of other human beings. Similarly, Israel as a whole mediates the presence of God to all humanity

23. *ST* 3.22.1.

by virtue of the promulgation of the law. The grace of the covenant given to Israel is a sign to the world of God's love for humanity.

In the New Testament, this covenant is universally extended to all human beings in Christ. Consequently, the role of collective priestly mediation falls upon the Church, which worships God sacramentally (ascending mediation) and manifests God's presence to the world by bearing witness to the gospel (descending mediation). As a result of the covenant, then, there is a collective priesthood that pertains to the whole people of God.[24] "Like living stones be yourselves built into a spiritual house, to be a holy priesthood, to offer spiritual sacrifices acceptable to God through Jesus Christ" (1 Pet. 2:5).

19:9–15 "And the LORD said to Moses, 'Go to the people and consecrate them today and tomorrow, and let them wash their garments, and be ready by the third day; for on the third day the LORD will come down upon Mount Sinai in the sight of all the people'" (19:10–11).

The second section of the chapter (19:9–15) is concerned with the preparation of the people for a collective theophany, for which the people are commanded to purify themselves. Two features should be noted concerning this commandment for purification. First, God promises Moses in 19:9 (ESV), "Behold, I am coming to you in a thick cloud, that the people may hear when I speak with you, and may also believe you forever." Here are images of both visual concealment and physical speech. The image of the cloud is present already in 13:21–22, where God leads the people out of Egypt by a pillar of cloud. God covers Israel in a cloud in 14:24 to conceal them from the Egyptian army. In 19:16 God will "descend" upon the mountain in a cloud and continue to manifest his presence over the tabernacle and the tent of meeting in subsequent chapters by this same sign (33:9–10; 40:34–38). The image is particularly interesting because the cloud physically represents the tension between presence and inaccessibility. When God is especially present he gives a sign of himself as one who cannot be perceived or comprehended. Spiritually, this represents the darkness that is given to the human intellect by infused, supernatural faith. This is not referring to merely human faith (for example, reasonable trust in the word of another) but in the supernatural belief in what God has revealed, which is made possible by an illuminative grace—as certain images in Exodus clearly denote. However, it also places the human intellect in proximity

---

24. Second Vatican Council, *Lumen Gentium*, para. 10 (Denzinger 2012: para. 4125): "The baptized, by regeneration and the anointing of the Holy Spirit, are consecrated as a spiritual house and a holy priesthood, in order that through all those works which are those of the Christian man they may offer spiritual sacrifices and proclaim the power of Him who has called them out of darkness into His marvelous light."

to and friendship with a reality that utterly transcends the scope of the mind's natural powers and that may be encountered only by an act of love, a movement of human freedom that embraces the divine communication.

This process of belief in the Lord in the midst of simultaneous clarity and obscurity is not purposeless. The trial of supernatural faith purifies the heart and the motives of the recipient.[25] The heart of the human being is progressively ennobled by entering the cloud of unknowing, by believing in God for God's own sake in an act of free trust. This journey can be sustained habitually over a long duration only through the medium of infused charity (the inward, transformative presence of deifying love). Illumination follows, but it is an illumination that occurs only in charity and that leads to progressive growth in love. Faith thus demands the unity of knowledge of God with love of God and in doing so heals the human person profoundly from within.[26] Knowledge of God is not separated from love of God; the two always advance together.

Second, the cloud is the prelude to God's speaking. The images of theophany that follow are visual and iconic, but they do not supplant the centrality of the word of God and of hearing rather than seeing. "Let me ask you only this: Did you receive the Spirit by works of the law, or by hearing with faith?" (Gal. 3:2). "Now faith is the assurance of things hoped for, the conviction of things not seen" (Heb. 11:1). It is an error to oppose the spiritual senses of seeing and hearing. Faith is a kind of insight into the depths of reality—the presence of God mysteriously revealed to us in the flesh of Christ—and faith is a kind of hearing that trusts in the words of the Lord, who speaks to us, even through the human speech of the Word made flesh. The contemplation of God is both visual and oracular, but when faith is most obscure, there is a primacy of the oracular. The people of God live by God's word, which he speaks to them from out of the cloud of darkness. The soul of the believer is filled with a supernatural cloud of unknowing, which

25. *ST* 2–2.7.2.

26. *ST* 2–2.4.3–4. John of the Cross comments in this way:

[A] basic reason the soul walks securely in darkness is that this light, or obscure wisdom, so absorbs and engulfs the soul in the dark night of contemplation and brings it so near God that it is protected and freed from all that is not God. Since the soul, as it were, is undergoing a cure to regain its health, which is God himself, His Majesty restricts it to a diet, to abstinence from all things, and causes it to lose its appetite for them all. . . . Because of their weakness, individuals feel thick darkness and more profound obscurity the closer they come to God, just as they would feel greater darkness and pain, because of the weakness and impurity of their eyes, the closer they approached the immense brilliance of the sun. The spiritual light is so bright and so transcendent that it blinds and darkens the natural intellect as this latter approaches it. (*The Dark Night* 2.16.10–11, in *The Collected Works of Saint John of the Cross*, rev. ed., trans. K. Kavanaugh and O. Rodriguez [Washington, DC: ICS, 1991], 433–34)

conceals the intimate presence of the Holy Trinity. From within this darkness, the Holy Spirit speaks to the soul by his word, manifesting the hidden presence of the Father and the Son.

The purification that God enjoins upon the people consists of three components: they should cleanse their external garments (Exod. 19:10); they should not approach the mountain (19:12); and they should refrain from sexual relations (19:15). The first purification demonstrates the unity of the human being. Spiritual seriousness should affect one's whole person, including one's external appearance. In this way, the covenant makes claims upon the visible domain of human society. There are human and religious ways to dress, and there are inhuman and irreligious ways to dress.

The second purification is spatial and pertains to the gift-character of divine revelation. God is transcendent and approaches Israel on God's own terms, not those devised by human beings. The community must be purified, then, of the false presupposition of intimacy with God on its own terms.

The third purification shows the profound connection in the Bible between proximity to God and human chastity. Human sexuality is something fundamentally good. "Be fruitful and multiply" (Gen. 1:28). But it is also the source of many forms of moral disintegration and secularizing distance from God. Human moral autonomy divorced from the law of God often allies itself with the indiscriminate pursuit of sexual pleasure. The covenant makes claims upon the sexuality of human persons precisely so that the sacred character of human sexuality can be recovered, ordering human beings toward God in happiness. This reordering is facilitated in the life of each person by the virtue of chastity and by times of abstinence, even in married relationships. Here we see the idea of abstinence as a preparation for the encounter with God so that union with God may be the human person's undivided aim. This notion will undergo a progressive development in ancient Israel, making room for the radical witness of consecrated celibacy on the part of some prophets, like Elijah and Jeremiah. In the New Testament it is perfected by the witness of virginal chastity found in Jesus Christ and the Virgin Mary but also in figures such as John the Baptist and the apostle Paul.

19:16–25 "And the LORD came down upon Mount Sinai, to the top of the mountain; and the LORD called Moses to the top of the mountain, and Moses went up" (19:20).

Exodus now presents us with the great theophany that precedes the giving of the law. The form that it takes is described in terms that are at once majestic and beautiful, cast against the backdrop of the desert solitude. "Mount Sinai was wrapped in smoke, because the LORD descended upon it in fire; and the smoke of it went up like the smoke of a kiln, and the whole mountain quaked greatly" (19:18).

Some have speculated that scripture is referring here to natural forces, such as a massive volcano and a desert storm. Others have posited a kind of collective charismatic miracle—a visible, audible, and tangible manifestation of God given to all the people. What the sacred author intends to denote in fact is not easy to discern.

However, it is not a point of capital importance. Whether the effects are miraculous or natural, the central point is that they stem from God—He Who Is—the author of the very existence of the created realities that God uses to manifest his presence. This manifestation of the Lord refers us implicitly but directly to his divine omnipotence. It also alludes to the gift-character of the presence of God. God freely makes himself known to Israel by divine condescension, a mystery that the sensate phenomena are meant to suggest. This presence is awe-inspiring, and as such it is meant to evoke a sense of transcendent justice: Israel will be held accountable to the terms of the covenant and its law, according to the divine righteousness. At the same time, hidden within this sense of the awful, all-comprehending justice of God is the mysterious suggestion of the "jealousy" of God that stems from divine love. "Take heed to yourselves, lest you forget the covenant of the LORD your God. . . . For the LORD your God is a devouring fire, a jealous God" (Deut. 4:23–24). The signs of the theophany are analogous to sacraments: tangible manifestations of the presence of God that convey knowledge of that which they symbolize. They anticipate a yet more significant gift to come, that of the law.

This section of the text also presents a clear idea of Moses as the mediator of the covenant, which is shown by his rather confusing movements up and down the mountain. In Exod. 19:3 he goes up the mountain, descending to speak to the people in 19:7. Exodus 19:9 and 14 seem to suggest another ascent and descent, followed by another ascent and descent in 19:20 and 25. This seemingly disjointed sequence results from an awkward combination of multiple texts or traditions. Nevertheless, a profound and unified idea is communicated through the final redaction: Moses is the mediator between God and the people of Israel. God has chosen them as a people and has manifested himself to them in the wilderness in an extraordinary way. He does so, however, in view of the gift of the Torah, which comes to them through the inspired mediation of the prophets. Israel is to grow close to God through the mediation of Moses and the priests. Prophecy, law, and the priesthood form the heart of the life of the people in their covenant with God.

Consistent with this idea, the priesthood is brought expressly into theological conjunction with Moses's role as mediator and lawgiver from the start of the covenant, even before narration of any formal institution of the priesthood of Aaron has been mentioned. "Let the priests who come near to the LORD consecrate themselves, lest the LORD break out upon them" (19:22). "Go down, and come up bringing Aaron with you; but do not let the priests and the people break through to come up to the LORD, lest he break out against them" (19:24). Here the Israelite priests are presumed to exist already. Where did they come from? We are not told; furthermore, they are not accorded the same degree of familiarity with God as Moses and Aaron. Here the hierarchical mediations are being envisaged in archetypal and exemplary forms. God gives the revelation through Moses and the inspired prophets of the Israelite religion. As for the priests, they are subordinate to the revelation of the Torah and should observe it from the heart. The law will be explicated and enacted cultically by priests and scribes, and the encounter with God at the mountain of Sinai will be reproduced by the temple liturgy on Mount Zion. In this vision, the priesthood is not opposed to the prophetic office in ancient Israel. According to the Torah, the two offices are related hierarchically and organically. Both stem from God's divine initiative and are integral to the covenant.

The Decalogue: The Heart of the Moral Law (Exod. 20)

The Decalogue stands at the heart of the Torah. It is not by accident that it is portrayed as the central covenantal reality in both Exodus and Deuteronomy. The editors of the Torah want us to see this body of law especially as the core moral reality that binds together God and humanity. Historically speaking, there is no reason that the Ten Commandments cannot go back to Moses himself.

As Bonaventure notes, the Ten Commandments can be understood in either the literal or the spiritual sense.[27] Literally, the Decalogue communicates the most essential moral law of the old covenant (as distinct from what is juridical or ceremonial). In addition, it refers directly to the "natural law" that is written implicitly on the hearts of all human beings and to moral truths that in principle can be attained by the powers of mere natural reason.[28] This law is explicated more

27. Bonaventure's treatment of the commandments is thematically divided into literal and spiritual senses in *Collations on the Ten Commandments* (Spaeth 1995). I take this point of Bonaventure's interpretation to be largely convergent with Aquinas's understanding of the spiritual senses of scripture.
    28. *ST* 1–2.100.1.

fully in the new covenant and in the life of the Church, but the law in question remains essentially that of the Decalogue. In its spiritual sense, the Decalogue must be read in a christocentric fashion. It refers typologically to the mystery of Christ and the Church: to his human perfection under grace and to the New Law of the Holy Spirit written on the hearts of his saints. Before I consider each of the precepts under both of these aspects, it is helpful to state clearly some general theological principles that pertain to the Ten Commandments as a whole.

The Threefold Form of the Law: Moral, Juridical, Ceremonial

First, the Torah is traditionally conceived by Christian tradition as containing three forms of legislation: moral, juridical, and ceremonial.[29] The moral precepts denote human acts, objects, and circumstances that are good and that can be potentially ordered toward God—as distinct from acts, objects, and circumstances that are intrinsically evil or morally problematic.[30] The point of the moral legislation is to lead human beings to happiness by choosing the good and rejecting what is evil.[31]

The juridical precepts pertain to punishments for infractions. They are meant to safeguard the common good: the domestic family, the city-state, and the whole people of Israel.[32] These goods are "common" because they cannot be possessed individually. Human beings participate in them as a unique source of happiness, and in this participation they may order their lives rightly toward God.[33] Ethical transgressions are serious, then, because they can undermine the good and happiness not only of one's self but also of many others and of that which gives happiness to all. Aquinas notes that the juridical punishments of the Torah, which stem from an archaic age of greater human coarseness, are often quite severe or even brutal.[34] The punishments are reflective of their era and were meant to enjoin

---

29. *ST* 1–2.99.2–4.
30. *ST* 1–2.18.
31. *ST* 1–2.99.2:

> The Old Law contained some moral precepts; as is evident from Exod. 20:13–15: "Thou shalt not kill, Thou shalt not steal." This was reasonable: because, just as the principal intention of human law is to create friendship between man and man; so the chief intention of the Divine law is to establish man in friendship with God. Now since likeness is the reason of love, according to Sir. 13:19: "Every beast loveth its like"; there cannot possibly be any friendship of man to God, Who is supremely good, unless man become good: wherefore it is written (Lev. 19:2; 11:45): "You shall be holy, for I am holy." But the goodness of man is virtue, which "makes its possessor good" (*Nicomachean Ethics* 2.6). Therefore it was necessary for the Old Law to include precepts about acts of virtue: and these are the moral precepts of the Law.

32. *ST* 1–2.104.1.
33. *ST* 1–2.113.1, 1–2.105.2.
34. *ST* 1–2.105.2 ad 9–10, 1–2.105.3 ad 1 and 4, 1–2.105.4.

the moral precepts upon human beings in an age not only more sensitive to collective identity than our own but also less sensitive to the politics of individual
dissent or the effects of psychological frailty in moral agents. As Aquinas notes,
the juridical punishments are sometimes harsh not because they are intrinsically
morally problematic (he rightly defends them from this charge) but because they
express a degree of exacting justice that is softened in the subsequent age of the
gospel, itself more prone to the expression of mercy, even in legal and civic forms
of punishment.[35]

The ceremonial precepts denote what can be called the "sacraments" of the
Old Law.[36] These are the religious ceremonies instituted under divine inspiration
throughout the course of the prophetic era of ancient Israel that permit the people
to orient their lives toward God under grace, according to sacred worship and
the virtue of religion.[37] They also prefigure in a hidden way the mystery of Christ
and his salvific death.[38] I will have more to say about this in subsequent chapters.

The Historical Setting and the Christian Claim to Natural Universality

Modern commentators often note that the Decalogue, like many of the moral
and juridical precepts in the Torah, bears striking similarities to many of the ancient law codes of the age in which it was composed. But this does not mean it
has no historical points of uniqueness—quite the contrary. The laws in Exodus are
generally more egalitarian than other contemporary law codes. The punishments
it enjoins are mitigated and more merciful, and it subsumes all legal performances
into a higher religious ethics of obedience to God, the Lord, rereading them from
within, as it were, in light of the covenant.[39]

Nevertheless, this natural similitude with surrounding law codes of the epoch
raises two serious theological questions: First, if the laws of Exodus (including the
Decalogue) seem to be in some sense the product of their surrounding culture, can
the document truly be of divine origin? Second, if these laws originated in a very
particular historical setting in time and place, can the Christian tradition rightly
appeal to the Mosaic law as indicating universal moral precepts applicable to all
human beings? After all, alternative customs and moral claims have predominated
in other cultures, both ancient and modern. Many would claim that these Israelite

35. *ST* 1–2.104.3. *In Ioan.* 8.1.1131.
36. *ST* 1–2.101.1, 4.
37. *ST* 1–2.99.3.
38. *ST* 1–2.101.2.
39. See the analysis of Childs 1974: 462–82.

precepts are not morally normative or that they have been misinterpreted by the Catholic Christian tradition. To claim otherwise could be said to be intellectually anachronistic or morally arbitrary.

I can respond to the first objection simply by noting that the work of God's grace need in no way be opposed to the natural, historical origins of the moral law. Grace presupposes human nature and acts to heal and elevate that nature. As mentioned above, Mosaic inspiration (and high prophecy in general) need not take on an infused conceptual form, as if there need to be concepts involved that are of ahistorical origin and setting. Rather, elevated inspiration may transpire through infused intellectual *species* (effectuating higher intuitions), which are in turn interpreted by the religious prophet in a given historical setting, making use of the language and conceptual habits of his age. At the same time, such grace acts to purify the moral and legal traditions of human culture. The Church claims that this is precisely what transpired in the Mosaic revelation.

The second objection requires a nuanced answer. In what sense is the Decalogue subject to a universalistic interpretation and expressive of normative moral law? It is, after all, reflective of the moral vision of a given religious epoch in an ancient archaic setting. In answer to this query, Aquinas makes a helpful distinction between three degrees of moral knowledge. First, he notes, there are rudimentary spiritual inclinations in the human being that yield fundamental practical knowledge: (1) human beings naturally desire happiness; (2) they seek to do good and avoid evil (however they conceive of the content of what is good or evil); and (3) they admit the general moral worth of human existence, the transmission of life, and goods that follow from reason (the search for truth and human life in community).[40] No matter how artistically or theoretically rudimentary a human civilization is, these features tend to arise. They are also ineradicable in their most generic form, even in the most unethical persons or cultural settings.[41]

Second, there are principles of moral reason that derive closely from these first, ineradicable principles but that do not follow from them by necessity. Aquinas equates this second degree of moral knowledge with the body of natural law implicit in the Ten Commandments.[42] Man can, without too much intellectual application, come to see that it is morally wrong to take innocent human life, that adultery and theft are wrong, and so forth. However, this second degree of moral precepts can be subject to denial or obfuscation, whether by individuals or whole

40. *ST* 1–2.94.2.
41. *ST* 1–2.94.4 and 6.
42. *ST* 1–2.100.3.

civilizations, due to misguided reasoning, the disordered leanings of the passions (which can obscure practical reason), and by vitiated inclinations of the human will that deeply disorient human moral reason.[43]

A third degree of moral rationality stems in turn from the second degree. It is a moral reasoning associated with more subtle cases in which the more general precepts of the natural law (such as that embodied in the commandments) are applied to particular cases, in diverse conditions and circumstances.[44] For example, it is one thing to say that one ought not to steal, but can one take food that another does not need when one's family is starving to death? Can a hospital ever refuse treatment to an indigent patient with a serious medical condition if the cost of the procedure is massive and prohibitive? How are we to understand what justice requires in the context of international laws governing food distribution? How are we rightly to understand prohibitions on insider trading? In questions such as these, the general principles must be applied by those who have a developed moral knowledge, who can arrive at sound and prudent conclusions in difficult cases.

With these distinctions in place, I can attempt a brief but direct answer to the objection. Yes, the Mosaic moral law is given within a particular historical setting, but it presupposes and makes use of the "first degree" of moral perception that is ineradicable in all human cultures, according to which all human beings strive toward the good, however imperfectly. The Decalogue goes further than this "first degree," however, to articulate universal norms of the "second degree" that follow closely from the first. As noted above, even these second-degree precepts can become obscure in human culture because of sin. Consequently, the Decalogue is meant to purify human moral reason and thus restore a sense of man's own calling to human excellence and happiness.[45] It is both like and unlike the laws of its age

43. *ST* 1–2.75.2, 1–2.76.1, 1–2.77.2, 1–2.94.6.
44. *ST* 1–2.94.4, 1–2.100.3.
45. *ST* 1–2.100.3:

> The precepts of the Decalogue differ from the other precepts of the Law, in the fact that God Himself is said to have given the precepts of the Decalogue; whereas He gave the other precepts to the people through Moses. Wherefore the Decalogue includes those precepts the knowledge of which man has immediately from God. Such are those which with but slight reflection can be gathered at once from the first general principles: and those also which become known to man immediately through divinely infused faith. Consequently two kinds of precepts are not reckoned among the precepts of the Decalogue: viz. first general principles, for they need no further promulgation after being once imprinted on the natural reason to which they are self-evident; as, for instance, that one should do evil to no man, and other similar principles: and again those which the careful reflection of wise men shows to be in accord with reason; since the people receive these principles from God, through being taught by wise men. Nevertheless both kinds

for this very reason: it is a recapitulation of something intrinsically natural, but within the context of a supernatural covenant. Grace is restoring nature.

Furthermore, this recapturing of the natural takes place within a long-standing historical economy, from Abraham to Moses to Jesus and the apostolic Church. The moral law is given precisely in view of the "third degree" of understanding—a progressive interpretation of the second-order precepts by which they are applied over time in new circumstances and settings, even as their inner meaning is developed organically so that the fruitfulness of the commandments can be seen more deeply through time. Because they are "only" secondary precepts, the commandments demand by their very nature to be interpreted in more explicit, ornate ways within a tradition (which includes sound debate with the means of gradual resolution, under the guidance of the magisterium). This is precisely what the Catholic intellectual tradition accomplishes gradually, over time. The catholic and apostolic Church, enlightened by Christ, has inherited the "chair of Moses" (Matt. 23:2) and is the perennial *mater et magistra* of the moral law.[46] Down through time the Church continually advances a developing moral wisdom derived explicitly from the light of Sinai, as interpreted universally in the light of Christ.

The Ultimate Purpose of the Moral Law

What are the ultimate origins and final purposes of the law when it is understood within the context of the larger economy of grace? The moral law in the Torah has a divine origin, and so is expressive of eternal law. In the words of Aquinas, "Eternal law is nothing else than the type of divine wisdom, as directing all actions and movements."[47] Consequently, God institutes the moral law as a means to direct the human person toward his or her final end of happiness and to preserve him or

---

of precepts are contained in the precepts of the Decalogue; yet in different ways. For the first general principles are contained in them, as principles in their proximate conclusions; while those which are known through wise men are contained, conversely, as conclusions in their principles.

46. See First Vatican Council, *Pastor Aeternus*, chap. 4; Pope John XXIII, *Mater et Magistra*, para. 42; Second Vatican Council, *Lumen Gentium*, para. 25; *Dignitatis Humanae*, para. 14; *Gaudium et Spes*, para. 89; *Catechism of the Catholic Church*, paras. 2030–51, 2070–71. *Gaudium et Spes*, para. 89: Since, in virtue of her mission received from God, the Church preaches the Gospel to all men and dispenses the treasures of grace, she contributes to the ensuring of peace everywhere on earth and to the placing of the fraternal exchange between men on solid ground by imparting knowledge of the divine and natural law. Therefore, to encourage and stimulate cooperation among men, the Church must be clearly present in the midst of the community of nations both through her official channels and through the full and sincere collaboration of all Christians—a collaboration motivated solely by the desire to be of service to all. (www.vatican.va/archive/hist_councils /ii_vatican_council/documents/vat-ii_const_19651207_gaudium-et-spes_en.html)

47. *ST* 1–2.93.1.

her from sin. In particular, by its prohibitions and prescriptions, the Decalogue points us toward good actions that permit human nature to flourish best.

This does not mean that fallen human beings can successfully observe the moral law of God. In our concrete historical economy, human beings are marked by the wounds of original sin: ignorance in the intellect, malice in the will, weakness in the irascible passions, and lust in the concupiscible passions.[48] In addition, there is the history of personal sin in the life of each human being. Given this context of the reality of human sin and our need for healing grace, one may rightly speak about three uses of the law.

First, the law is given to human beings to act as a moral compass in the midst of ethical confusion. It indicates profound moral truths pertaining to the natural law. Nevertheless, it remains something formally exterior to the human person, indicating the interior principles of moral action as they can best be realized. It does not give the interior healing power to live effectively in accord with the moral truths that it indicates. Even less does it provide the power to elevate human nature beyond its own proportionate ends into the life of grace—the divinizing life of faith, hope, and charity.[49]

In this sense, one can speak of a "second use" of the law by which God demonstrates in the revelation of the Decalogue the moral indigence of the human community in the fallen state. "God sometimes permits certain ones to fall into sin, that they may thereby be humbled. So also did He wish to give such a law as men by their own forces could not fulfill, so that, while presuming on their own powers, they might find themselves to be sinners, and being humbled might have recourse to the help of grace."[50]

The "third use" of the law pertains to its pedagogical role within the sphere of grace. The law itself and its outward observances do not serve to justify the human person (to restore the personal nature of each human being to a state of integral righteousness with God by grace) or sanctify the human being in charity. The Decalogue does indicate, however, a pathway of moral cooperation with the grace of God, especially pertaining to what is best in human nature and its proportionate capacities under grace. Aquinas believes that by having recourse to the mercy of God, especially through the ceremonial sacrifices of the law, the Israelites of the Old Testament participated implicitly by faith in the graces of justification. "Although the Old Law did not suffice to save man, yet another help

48. *ST* 1–2.85.3.
49. *ST* 1–2.100.10 and 12, 1–2.109.4–5.
50. *ST* 1–2.98.2 ad 3.

from God besides the Law was available for man, that is to say, faith in the Mediator, by which the fathers of old were justified even as we were. Accordingly God
did not fail man by giving him insufficient aids to salvation."[51] The faith of the
ancient Israelites was of supernatural origin and was oriented implicitly toward the
mystery of Jesus Christ. This is why Catholic theology traditionally holds that in
ancient Israel God gave inward graces to the members of the covenant that were
meant to accompany the outward gift of the law.

These aids consisted principally in the infused virtues of theological faith, hope,
and charity, as well as infused moral virtues and the gifts of the Holy Spirit. In a
hidden way, the New Law of the grace of the Holy Spirit was already present at
the heart of the older covenant, permitting the Israelites who were in covenant
with God to worship God rightly in charity and to orient their lives toward him
in a progressive process of transformation under grace. This was undergirded by
dependence upon divine mercy and the practices of atonement that were inscribed
in the ceremonial precepts, themselves typologically indicative of the salvific death
of Christ who was to come. The difference between the transformative habits of
grace present in the ancient Israelites and those present in the members of the
Church is only one of degree, not of kind.[52]

Division of the Decalogue

There are different interpretations of the division of the Decalogue. The Catholic tradition customarily treats the whole of Exod. 20:1–6 as one commandment,
thus including the prohibition on the making of graven images within the precept
commanding worship of the Lord alone. It also divides 20:17 into two commandments, distinguishing the prohibitions on covetousness of possessions from that
of persons. Based on these groupings, one can distinguish the first three precepts,

---

51. *ST* 1–2.98.2 ad 4.
52. *ST* 3.70.4:

> Grace was bestowed in circumcision as to all the effects of grace [including that of the power to
> observe the commandments], but not as in Baptism. Because in Baptism grace is bestowed by
> the very power of Baptism itself, which power Baptism has as the instrument of Christ's Passion
> already consummated. Whereas circumcision bestowed grace, inasmuch as it was a sign of faith
> in Christ's future Passion: so that the man who was circumcised, professed to embrace that faith;
> whether, being an adult, he made profession for himself, or, being a child, someone else made
> profession for him. Hence, too, the Apostle says (Rom. 4:11), that Abraham "received the sign of
> circumcision, a seal of the justice of the faith": because, to wit, justice was of faith signified: not
> of circumcision signifying. And since Baptism operates instrumentally by the power of Christ's
> Passion, whereas circumcision does not, therefore Baptism imprints a character that incorporates
> man in Christ, and bestows grace more copiously than does circumcision; since greater is the
> effect of a thing already present, than of the hope thereof.

which direct man to God, from the last seven precepts, which direct man in his behavior toward his neighbor.[53]

Conceived in this way, the internal order of the precepts follows a hierarchical, descending pattern.[54] The first commands the human person to acknowledge God, the Lord, as his or her Creator, providence, and ultimate final end, so as to permit no rival to God into the person's mind and heart. The second prescribes that human beings show due reverence to God in outward actions, forbidding the taking of the name of God in vain. The third incites human beings to offer God service, which is exemplified by the regular observance of the Sabbath. There is a trajectory, then, from what is most interior and essential in religious virtue to what follows from it outwardly. From inner faithfulness of mind stems piety of heart, and from voluntary piety flows forth a regular rhythm of internal and external obedience.

The precepts pertaining to neighbor begin from what is most ethically grievous and move to what is less grave and purely interior. The fourth commandment pertains to the respect of parents, those persons to whom each person is normally most indebted for the gift of life and education. Among the other precepts, sins of action are more grave and irrational than sins by word, and sins by word are worse than those that occur in thought alone.[55] Accordingly, the fifth commandment prohibits murder, which is the taking of life of an innocent human being. The sixth forbids adultery so as to protect the human family and the welfare of the social order. The seventh forbids theft, which regards external goods. The eighth forbids lying, which deals with spoken words. The ninth and tenth forbid inner dispositions of covetousness—jealousy and lust—which pertain to inner states alone.

In what follows I will first consider the three commandments pertaining to God and then the seven commandments pertaining to neighbor. In each case, I will briefly ascertain the literal sense as universal moral teaching and the spiritual sense as pertaining to mystical life in Christ and the inner splendor of charity in the saints.

---

53. Augustine established this division in *Quæstionum in Heptateuchum* 7.2.71. It was subsequently adopted by many medieval theologians and by the Council of Trent, which inscribed it in the universal 1566 *Catechism of the Council of Trent*. It is also found in the majority of Lutheran confessional traditions since it was adopted by Luther in the *Large Catechism*. The alternative division treats the prohibition on graven images as a solitary second commandment and unites the two precepts in Exod. 20:17, treating the prohibitions on covetousness of persons and possessions as one general precept. This division originates with Philo (*De decalogo, De specialibus legibus*) and Origen (*Hom. on Exodus* 8). Traditionally, it has been adopted by the Eastern Orthodox Churches as well as the majority of Reformed ecclesial communities.

54. *ST* 1–2.100.6.

55. *ST* 1–2.100.6.

First Table

FIRST PRECEPT

20:1–6 "You shall have no other gods before me. You shall not make for yourself a graven image, or any likeness of anything that is in heaven above, or that is in the earth beneath, or that is in the water under the earth; you shall not bow down to them or serve them; for I the Lord your God am a jealous God" (20:3–5).

LITERAL SENSE

The traditional historical question that the first precept raises pertains to the nature of "the gods" as distinct from the Lord. Some have claimed that this text in its historical roots presupposes YHWH to be one god among others, perhaps the one who is supreme, but the one alone to whom the Israelites owe their fidelity. In this interpretation, the Decalogue has implicitly polytheistic roots and enjoins some form of monolatry rather than the mature monotheism of later Judaism.

This hypothesis is textually unverifiable and therefore indemonstrable. Nevertheless, it should be said that there is no "archeological level" of textual redaction that one can clearly identify at which the term "gods" is not being employed in a rhetorically ironic way, and in a subtle way at that. Typically, it is not the case that the Bible denies that "the gods" exist. They exist at least in the lives of the other nations, thereby serving as a plausible existential alternative (they can be served). They exist, then, as powerful literary figures who encroach upon Israelite identity in the form of idols. Moreover, they may well exist in reality, in some ontologically real but numinous form. "For all the gods of the peoples are idols; / but the LORD made the heavens" (Ps. 96:6). "They sacrificed to demons which were no gods" (Deut. 32:17). What is clear, however, is that the "gods" are not true gods. To be more exact, they are not the true God, who saved Israel in Egypt by his effective power and mercy and who has created the heavens and the earth (Gen. 1:1). This God who alone is the Creator of the world has revealed himself to Israel under the individual name YHWH as the God who has specially elected Israel to a privileged covenant by grace.[56]

---

56. Such is the inward form of biblical faith in God as Creator. Though the progressive formulation of the scriptural confession of this faith may have a complex prehistory that precedes the text that we are given, that prehistory is not easy to identify. For the sake of argument, it is possible that a prebiblical Yahwist polytheism was illuminated and purified by divine revelation, formed progressively first into an implicit and eventually into an explicit speculative form of monotheism. However, we cannot know definitively from historical study what contours any such historical development took. The speculation remains almost purely hypothetical. Meanwhile, what we are given in the mature, redacted text (which

In its literal sense, the first precept enjoins both a supernatural and a natural fidelity toward God the Creator and Lord. The supernatural fidelity is that which stems from the theological virtues of faith, hope, and charity.[57] The precept enjoins Israel to believe in the Lord by the grace of faith and practices of obedience to divine revelation. Therefore, the believer must reject as contrary to faith all forms of incredulity and voluntary doubt. Heresy (false teaching), apostasy (public refusal of divine teaching), and schism (social division undermining the observance of divine teaching) all undermine in various ways the unity of faith and the holiness of the truth about God.[58] Likewise, the believer is commanded to hope in God and to love God above all things, with the help of God's grace.[59] Despair and presumption are sins against hope in God. Indifference, ingratitude, spiritual laziness, and resentment or hatred of God are sins against charity.[60]

The natural fidelity that the precept enjoins is that which pertains to the natural law. Human persons are inclined by nature to acknowledge the existence of God intellectually, to love God above all things, and to manifest this love through the virtue of religion.[61] In their depths, human beings are meant to lift up their minds to God in prayer, to worship God, and to serve God in their hearts by devotion.[62] This inward demeanor is meant to be expressed outwardly by acts of bodily adoration, sacrifice, tithing, and public promises and oaths, such as religious ceremonies of marriage, priestly ordination, and monastic life.[63]

Contrary to this precept, then, are all practices of idolatry—that is, ascribing what pertains only to God to what is not God, whether in theory or religious practice.[64] Superstition occurs when a person or a community seeks to approach the divinity of God by means that are not in keeping with human dignity (such as human sacrifice or superstitious rituals) or that fail to respect the justice and wisdom of God.[65] Irreligion, atheism, and agnosticism are other forms of culpable transgression. According to the Bible, the godless man is not innocent but is under judgment for his aberrancy, whether he knows it or not.

---

is inspired!) is a stark monotheistic claim regarding the unicity and transcendence of the unique Creator of all things, the God of Israel.

57. *Catechism of the Council of Trent* 3.1.

58. *ST* 2–2.10–12.

59. *Catechism of the Council of Trent* 3.1.

60. *Catechism of the Catholic Church*, para. 2094.

61. A virtue that Aquinas argues is a potential part of justice: *ST* 2–2.81.

62. *ST* 2–2.82–83.

63. *ST* 2–2.84–88.

64. *ST* 2–2.94.

65. *ST* 2–2.92.

The fool says in his heart,
"There is no God."
They are corrupt, doing abominable iniquity. (Ps. 53:1)

SPIRITUAL SENSE

According to its spiritual sense, the first precept must be read christologically, that is to say, denoting the inward inclinations of the grace of Jesus Christ that are at work in the ethical life of his mystical body, the Church. By this grace, which is present in the soul of the believer, the creature can be wed to God by faith, hope, and charity in this life and by vision in the next. [66] Here, then, the precept is meant to counsel inward union with the Holy Trinity. It is this union that is the essence of the New Law, which is hidden at the core of the Old Law. [67]

The basis for the union is the illumination of faith, and it grows daily through the virtue of hope and the immediate (though obscure) union with God through charity. These gifts create a new contemplative closeness of the human soul to the mystery of the Father, Son, and Spirit. Through them the soul touches God. The Holy Trinity lives secretly in the soul of the Christian and prepares the believer for union with God in the life to come. The corresponding ethical stance that is required of believers is total surrender and devotion to the Holy Trinity who indwells within and who commands discipleship through mystical contemplation, worship, and unconditional service. Offering anything less to God constitutes a form of failure in one's relationship to God in Christ, which often stems from inward complicities with unbelief or indifference. However, only this ultimate offering to the truth of the Holy Trinity, by grace, alleviates in the human soul the deepest sources of spiritual agony and human restlessness.

BRIEF EXCURSUS ON THE PROHIBITION OF GRAVEN IMAGES

How should we understand the precept: "You shall not make for yourself a graven image" (20:4)? According to the Decalogue, the Lord cannot be represented visually and cannot be imagined. God is not like the gods of the Gentiles that are cast outwardly in symbolic form or localized by various kinds of sacred totems. Speaking more generally, the Torah teaches that God is not a reality in this world to be grasped like creatures; rather, God is the condition of possibility for the existence of all other realities apart from God. As such, God's essence remains utterly hidden from view and transcendent of any human, conceptual

---

66. *ST* 1–2.106.1: "The New Law is chiefly the grace itself of the Holy Spirit, which is given to those who believe in Christ."
67. *ST* 1–2.107.3.

grasp. God cannot be portrayed in anthropomorphic terms—whether physical or spiritual, imaginary or conceptual. It is true that we can think rightly about God as He Who Is and as one who is subsistent being, goodness, and wisdom. To say all this, however, is to admit that we only grasp something of the transcendent nature of the deity analogically, as perceived imperfectly through God's effects of nature and grace.[68] Consequently, we have no *immediate* grasp of "what" God is in his very essence.[69] God defies every expectation of human conceptual understanding or representation.

Every form of sacral absolutization of human political culture is definitively put to an end with the first commandment. No cosmic process or cultural history (be it evolution, National Socialism, or Hegelian liberalism) can ever be equated with God. The Lord is not identical with human leaders such as Pharaoh, Caesar, or any world leader, and God is not present in any human avatar. No human person, then, may ever become God or be substantively divinized by God. God as Creator remains utterly transcendent of the human creature. For the same reason, however, God—because he is utterly transcendent and thus immanently present at the heart of all created beings—may indeed become human. Needless to say, God becoming human is something utterly different from a creature becoming God.

Likewise, this precept is directly opposed to various forms of religious multiculturalism. According to the Torah, it is a serious intellectual error to think that God (in his transcendence) could have a plurality of incarnate images or forms to represent him in a multiplicity of partial and imperfect ways, across a spectrum of religious cultures and traditions. To affirm that this is the case is not an enrichment of our understanding of God through some form of religious open-mindedness; rather, it is to close our minds in upon themselves, imprisoning them within the merely immanent sphere of human cultural creations. The myriad gods of human religion sometimes do reflect imperfectly some characteristics of the transcendent Creator, but fundamentally they remain all-too-human fabrications, the ingenious products of human creativity that ultimately stem from ignorance, idolatry, and desperation.

This stark, dialectical affirmation of the transcendence of God by the Decalogue is intended to make room for God to reveal himself on God's own terms, over and above all feeble attempts at human portrayal of the gods. This occurs first in the Torah and the temple but ultimately in the human nature of Christ—in the portrayal God gives of himself in the life, death, and resurrection of the Son made

68. *ST* 1.12.12–13, 1.13.5–6.
69. *ST* 1.3 pr., 1.13.12.

man. This "iconic" presence of God in Jesus only makes sense against the backdrop of the transcendence of God that the first commandment underscores. Far from being opposed, the Decalogue and the mystery of the incarnation are deeply interrelated and inseparable. It is because the Creator is so utterly transcendent of all our limited representations and concepts that the presence of God in our human nature is the definitive gift of divine revelation. Christ is the presence of the transcendent God among us, and his gospel—when preached to the Gentile nations—progressively puts an end to the history of human idolatry.

Second and Third Precepts

20:7–11 "You shall not take the name of the LORD your God in vain; for the LORD will not hold him guiltless who takes his name in vain" (20:7).

"Remember the Sabbath day, to keep it holy. . . . for in six days the LORD made heaven and earth, the sea, and all that is in them, and rested the seventh day; therefore the LORD blessed the Sabbath day and hallowed it" (20:8, 11).

Literal Sense

The second and third commandments denote the outward forms of religious observance that stem from the inward acts denoted above. One may think of a river that originates in the mind and heart, from internal knowledge and love. It should flow out into our acts of speech and into our actions, orienting them toward God.[70]

Consequently, the second precept pertains to the holiness of the divine name. The gift of the name "Lord" imposes upon the chosen people both a privilege

70. I have employed a Thomistic interpretation of this order, based on the nature of the human person: the first three precepts speak to diverse dimensions of human behavior, moving from the interior outward. Bonaventure, by contrast, affirms that there is a trinitarian structure in the first table of the law, based on the doctrine of appropriations. Each precept pertains to a person of the Holy Trinity, which is related to human beings as well since the image of God is in man, which is trinitarian in turn. *Collations on the Ten Commandments*, col. 1.22 (Spaeth 1995):

> On the first table are contained the commandments ordering us to God. But God is triune: Father, Son and Holy Spirit. To the Father is attributed majesty; to the Son, truth; and to the Holy Spirit, goodness. In the Father the highest majesty is to be humbly adored; in the Son the highest truth is to be faithfully confessed; in the Holy Spirit the highest goodness is to be sincerely loved. But, if on the basis of the eternal command, we are to do these three things, then it is necessary that on the first table there be three commandments related to these three attributes which are appropriated to the three divine persons. For in the first commandment, humble adoration of the divine majesty is commanded, when it says: "You shall have no strange gods." In the second commandment, faithful confession of divine truth is commanded when it says: "You shall not take the name of your God in vain." In the third commandment, sincere love of the divine goodness is commanded when it says, "Remember to keep holy the Sabbath day." These are the three commandments of the first table.

and a responsibility. Speech about God should not be rendered banal. It reflects the inner dignity of the human person, who is made in God's image and who is called into covenant with God by grace. The human being is meant to speak of God or utter the sacred name of the Lord only in a particular manner: reflecting a spiritual respect for the truth. Interpreted more generally, the precept obliges the human being to bear witness to the truth about God when he or she arrives at it. All human beings, including the inculpably agnostic and the religiously confused, are obliged to seek the truth in religious matters and to investigate questions of the truth regarding monotheism and creation with seriousness and honesty.

Contrary to the second commandment are acts of blasphemy, which pertain to speech not only regarding God himself but also the saints and religious subjects. In the Christian economy, the names of Jesus Christ and the Blessed Virgin Mary are to be venerated, as are the names of the saints. Likewise, this commandment prohibits false oaths made in the name of God—that is, perjury. It forbids any attempt to employ the sacred name of the Lord or of Jesus Christ for magical purposes.

In its literal sense, the third commandment pertains above all to the Sabbath. As has been noted above, the Sabbath may well be of very ancient origins in Israelite history, stemming from the time of the exodus. On the Sabbath, the Israelites are obliged to acknowledge the reality of God in both a public, collective way and also individually. The community is to refrain from unnecessary work. God should be worshiped, and the revelation of God should be studied. It is a day for the cultivation of the life of the mind and devotion to God.

In the Christian economy, the Sabbath is reinterpreted typologically, as pointing toward the death and resurrection of Christ. The paschal mystery fulfills the law and opens the covenant to the Gentile nations, who celebrate the resurrection of the Lord on the day after the Sabbath, the first day of the week. This Sunday celebration has been understood from the earliest times in the Church to take the place of the Sabbath obligation in pre-Christian Judaism. Consequently, the obligation to honor God one day a week remains a divine precept, even in Christianity, but is reoriented around the Sunday commemoration of the resurrection. This takes place especially through the celebration of the Eucharist, itself the real presence of the risen Lord.

SPIRITUAL SENSE

Spiritually, these two commandments denote the purification of the human heart that is effectuated by grace. Each human person is called upon to bear witness to the truth of Christ and to consecrate in a realistic way all temporal activities (both sacred and profane) to the eternity of God, who has revealed himself in historical time.

The second commandment points toward the meeting point between the inner consecration of the mind to divine truth (denoted by the first precept) and the demands of external witness. With the help of God's grace, human beings should speak truthfully about God, who is revealed in Jesus Christ. "Consecrate them in the truth; thy word is truth" (John 17:17). This obligation is meant to affect all the words and gestures of the person. As such, the integration of one's whole person into a pattern of life always devoted to the truth about Christ is a lifelong work for each individual. It is also an exigency incumbent upon every local Church and religious community, which are meant to be a visible communion that witnesses to Christ. This integrity includes the integral confession of the Catholic faith and of the moral teaching of the Church. It also includes the confession of one's own human frailty, brokenness, and sins, and the confession of joyful dependency upon God's mercy. This, too, is part of being in the truth. "The truth will make you free" (John 8:32).

In its spiritual sense, the third commandment indicates the role of Christian prudence in all the works of the spiritual life. Practical wisdom, which is elevated by grace and inspired by charity, should seek to cooperate with the providence of God in all things. The Sabbath is a particular, highest example of this cooperation, which in turn affects our judgment of all lesser examples. In all that he or she does, a person should orient the temporal activities of human existence toward that which is ultimate, the final end. The redactor of Gen. 2:2–3 and Exod. 20:11, who places the Sabbath as the last day of creation, communicates to Israel and the Church a very great mystery. By keeping the Sabbath holy, human beings "return" the creation to God under grace in their minds and hearts. They lead the physical and spiritual creation toward its purpose of beatitude, participating in the eternal life of God himself. The stillness of the last day is the stillness of heaven, of the divine eternity. The civic life of human beings in time is ultimately made to participate (in a derivative and distinctly human way) in this simplicity of the divine life,[71] which occurs above all through the means of religious contemplation and worship. The highest expression of this participation is the eucharistic liturgy, by which we touch God directly in spiritual communion.[72] What is lived eucharistically in the Mass should irradiate the rest of one's lived

71. Philosophical intimations of this idea can be found in Plato's *Laws* (bk. 10) and also in his work *Epinomis*. Aquinas offers his own philosophical version of the argument in *SCG* 3.25–37, 114–21.

72. See Second Vatican Council, *Sacrosanctum Concilium*, para. 10.

existence and external activities at their very root. In this sense, contemplative monastic communities—in which all daily activities are oriented around the Eucharist and the liturgy—are those that fulfill this precept spiritually in the most perfect and exemplary of ways.

Second Table

The first table of precepts moves from the interior to the exterior. The interior worship of God is meant to be exteriorized in what human beings say and do in relation to God. Importantly, the second table moves in the inverse order: from what is exterior to what is interior. The fourth precept denotes the obligation to honor one's parents (and elders more generally), while the fifth prohibits the taking of innocent human life. Adultery and impurity are next prohibited. In this way, the common good is first safeguarded at the most basic level: the ties of political community, the respect of all human life, and the dignity and fidelity of marital relations. Only then do the precepts move toward what is existentially secondary and ultimately more interior: the obligation to respect the place of personal property, the obligation to tell the truth, and the prohibitions on internal covetousness—that is, the vices of lust and avarice.

This inversion is understandable for two reasons. First, our relationship with God is based primarily on the internal ordering of the intellect and only secondarily upon our outward actions and relations. Our relationship to other human beings follows the inverse order. It is based primarily upon our corporeal and spiritual life with others in community, which invites us to a progressive internal development of virtues that purify and refine our way of living with others. Second, then, it is clear that the precepts regarding one's neighbor are meant to safeguard the common good and the conditions for human justice, friendship, and spiritual development. They pass, in a sense, from what is most fundamental to what is most perfect.

Based on this reading, the commandments can be seen to begin and to end in interiority. They originate "from above," in the relationship of the human conscience to God. This relationship is centered around union with God by interior belief and worship. The commandments conclude in the inner sanctum of the human conscience in the face of other human persons. Each human being is called to love and to contribute to the good of others rather than to covet and take egoistically from what others possess. By moving out of ourselves and toward God we are meant eventually to move out of ourselves and toward our neighbor.

In this way, the Decalogue recalls the human being, made in the image of God, to its true self from within to live for the inner essence of the law: the preferential love of God and genuine love of neighbor.

FOURTH PRECEPT

20:12 "Honor your father and your mother, that your days may be long in the land which the LORD your God gives you."

LITERAL SENSE

In commenting on this precept, Aquinas notes that we are commanded by God to love all human beings but that we are not commanded to do good for all; rather, we are to do good to those closest to us, to those whom divine providence places in our path.[73] Above all, our parents are those to whom we owe honor and love, and this for three reasons. First, they are the natural cause of our generation. It is because of them that we have come to be, and no other human being has given us this gift. Second, they usually provide longstanding nourishment and care, whether physical, emotional, or spiritual. Third, parents instruct their children, seeking to lead them by education to a state of adult independence and moral maturity.[74] This is frequently true both in the natural domain and also in the supernatural, as parents transmit the covenantal, supernatural faith to their children and instruct them in it.

Children who receive these gifts from their parents cannot repay them by any proportionate compensation. They remain ontological and moral debtors to their parents for life. Consequently, their appropriate response is to show their parents gratitude, honor, and love. Moreover, they are to be obedient in their youth and care for their parents in their old age or infirmity. These obligations are not one-sided or unqualified in character. The parent has obligations to the child: to provide physically and spiritually for the well-being and education of the child and to communicate the supernatural faith that the parent has received.

One may object that these general observations are subsequent Christian moral teachings projected anachronistically and arbitrarily upon the Decalogue, which is the product of a much more particular line of thinking. Some commentators argue that the precept in its original setting was concerned primarily with the preservation of a Near Middle Eastern patriarchal culture and does not foresee the complexities of universal ethical reflection on the family and society that

73. Aquinas, *Explanation of the Ten Commandments*, a. 4.
74. Aquinas, *Explanation of the Ten Commandments*, a. 4 (Collins 1939).

have developed through subsequent reflection on the fourth commandment by commentators.

It is true that the precepts of the Decalogue were originally exposited within the context of ancient tribes and clans in which father figures were the heads of larger households that were subject to them. Therefore it is possible to envisage the commandment as both identifying an essential concern central to human morality in every age *and* as lending support to a given instantiation of human political culture in a given time and setting. The latter might pass away, but the continuing biblical reflection present both in the Torah and in other books of the Bible (including the New Testament) only gives further testimony to the enduring pertinence of the precept. This biblical process of universalization prepares for the subsequent nuanced interpretations and applications of the precept in the patristic, medieval, and modern epochs. The Ten Commandments are like seeds of wisdom planted in the collective intellect of the people of God that grow progressively into a tree putting out deep roots, high branches, beautiful flowers, and fruits. The roots of the commandments are the metaphysical grounds for moral action, which the Church comes to understand progressively through time. The high branches are the firm certitudes achieved with regard to subtle moral conclusions. The beautiful flowers are the spiritual nobility in souls, produced by the commandments. The fruits are the spiritual love that stems from their observance.

Given this reading of the fourth commandment, it is not an illusion to note in it the perception of a deeper, more general truth about the moral significance of social hierarchies. Not all hierarchies are merely conventional or artifactual. Social hierarchies can reflect something entirely natural to man, especially when they arise in the necessary service of the common good and from diverse degrees of spiritual qualities found in human beings. Here they are indicative of natural human dependency and the need each person has for others, including hierarchs of various kinds. These include not only parents but also educators, employers, and those who govern the community or the state. The virtue of piety should take account of diverse degrees of paternal authority, with respect to diverse instantiations of the common good.[75] There is a measured piety or hierarchical respect that should be given to parents, civic leaders, and cultural and religious leaders.

75. *ST* 2–2.101.1:
 Man becomes a debtor to other men in various ways, according to their various excellence and the various benefits received from them. On both counts God holds first place, for He is supremely excellent, and is for us the first principle of being and government. On the second place, the principles of our being and government are our parents and our country, that have given us birth and nourishment. Consequently man is debtor chiefly to his parents and his country, after God.

In normal instances, the political state to which one naturally belongs is also due a certain natural piety and respect.

Necessarily, mutual rights and responsibilities follow, on behalf of the state, family, and the individual respectively. Children have the right to live within a family, but with that right come various responsibilities of loyalty and love. Citizens have the right to participation in their larger society, but they also have the obligation to promote, protect, and actively contribute to the good of the state or larger community. The state has duties to its citizens, both in the order of distributive justice and social or legal justice.[76] Distributive justice delineates the obligation to give to each one what is necessary to achieve his or her good. Some are in need of more assistance from the collective polity than others, but all are in need of some common services or utilities. Social or "legal" justice is more ultimate since it pertains to each person's right and responsibility to participation in the common good, understood here as a good enjoyed for its own sake. Each genuine member of a community has the opportunity to partake of the common life and the happiness that comes from living in that community, and each person is meant to contribute to the happiness of the others by sharing a common life with them.

The state also has obligations to the family that are expressly signified by the commandment to honor fathers and mothers. The natural family is the foundation and basic cell of every human community. As Gen. 1:26 and 2:18–24 reveal (and as human reason can determine philosophically), the family consists in its essential structure of a heterosexual, spousal union (between man and woman) that is ordered toward the procreation, nurturing, and education of children.[77] God himself is the author of this structure. Accordingly, the state is in no way the ontological author of the family but rather presupposes it, depending directly upon the family for its own subsistence.[78] Consequently, the state is naturally obliged to protect and defend the natural family by legislative means and cannot legitimately pretend to have any right to redefine the essential nature of the family.

Various other obligations follow from the obligation of the state to protect the family and to provide for its basic welfare. People must be free to establish families, have children, and bring them up in accord with their moral and religious

Wherefore just as it belongs to religion to give worship to God, so does it belong to piety, in the second place, to offer devotion to one's parents and one's country.

76. *Catechism of the Catholic Church*, paras. 2234–37; *ST* 1–2.113.1.

77. See the interpretation of these lines by Augustine, *On the Literal Meaning of Genesis* 9.7, as complemented by the analysis in Augustine, *On the Good of Marriage* 24.

78. Pope Leo XIII, *Immortale Dei*, paras. 17 and 27; Pope Pius IX, *Casti connubii*, paras. 5–8.

convictions.[79] Civic protection should be given to the stability of the institution of the family and the marital bond, and divorce should be discouraged. Adequate education should be provided by the community for each member of society, especially children, and special care is to be given for the elderly, the defenseless, or the disabled. Security from various forms of social harm that undermine family life (be it crime, extortion, prostitution, pornography, drug trade, or other social ills) is to be provided. Finally, the state must recognize the right of families to form independent associations, whether educational, civic, or religious.[80]

This developed moral exegesis of the fourth precept is meant to indicate broader features of the natural law that are reflected implicitly in the Decalogue. Read in this light, the Torah gives unequivocal, divine sanction to natural hierarchies that arise in human society. However, it gives only a *qualified* warrant to legitimate authorities in civic and family life. The Torah also offers a sustained critique of the misuse of authority, beginning with Adam's irresponsible blame of God and Eve for his own sin (Gen. 3:12). The moral failures of human authorities are placed under a searing light, which is reflected in the personage of the Pharaoh but also (at times) Moses and Aaron. Plainly, human authority in a fallen world is regularly affected by weakness, error, or moral compromise. The Torah does not divinize human authority or paternity but assigns each a relative value, making them subject to objective norms derived ultimately from God. In this way, the Bible purifies our understanding of authority by a positive but limited assertion of its role, preserving us from the temptation to divinize human hierarchies, however real and necessary they may be.

Spiritual Sense

Read christologically, the fourth commandment refers us to the spiritual father-hood of Christ as the high priest and savior of the human race (Heb. 4:14–16; 9:11–15). From Christ's capital grace as head of the Church, each member of the body of Christ receives the life of grace. "He is the head of the body, the church" (Col. 1:18). "From his fullness have we all received, grace upon grace" (John 1:16). It should be noted that Christ's capital grace accrues to him formally, not insofar as he is God but insofar as he is human.[81] As God, the Word incarnate is the author of our grace, with the Father and the Holy Spirit. As man, Christ is mediator between God and man, the instrumental source of grace for all human

---

79. Second Vatican Council, *Gaudium et Spes*, para. 26.
80. *Catechism of the Catholic Church*, para. 2211.
81. *ST* 3.7.1, 3.8.1.

beings. Consequently, Jesus is the progenitor of our life of grace, even in his human nature. This is a very distinctive form of hierarchy—a supernatural hierarchy in the order of grace—that Christians are alerted to by the *sensus fidei*, which is awakened in them by the gift of faith. In this way, piety takes on a supernatural quality through the infused virtue of charity, and the Christian faithful acquire a special reverence or filial piety ordered toward Christ, his priesthood, and his holiness.

Likewise, the spiritual meaning of the fourth commandment should lead us to honor and love all those closest to Christ in the order of charity: the Mother of God, above all, and the saints, who commend respect as those who are the closest friends of God. It is also fitting to show devotion to the apostolic hierarchy instituted by Christ in order to promote his teaching and perpetuate the presence of his grace sacramentally down through the ages. Despite the limitations and faults of Catholic priests, measured devotion to the priesthood on the part of the Christian laity is appropriate and stems from a right reverence for God and his Church. It shows an awareness of the mysterious presence of Christ, the great high priest, active even in sinful, imperfect human beings.[82]

This higher order of charity does not destroy the natural order of social hierarchies, but it does cast in clear relief their limited character. Christians should love and reverence the Church and the saints (as authentic friends of Christ) more than they do their natural homeland and even more than their natural family. The Church is endowed with a higher authority than the natural family, and the Church's teachings must always be preferred to the opinions of one's family or human society.

The Question of Temporal Rewards

A question traditionally arises about the temporal rewards promised to those who observe the precept, "that your days may be long in the land which the LORD your God gives you" (Exod. 20:12). Aquinas argues that the Old Law is inferior to the New Law because the Old Law announces rewards and punishments of a predominantly temporal character. In this way it offers incentives of a less elevated type and is based more predominantly on fear of the loss of worldly blessings. The New Testament, meanwhile, announces rewards and punishments of an eternal character, speaking more essentially to man's spiritual character and destiny. The human being is invited under grace to pursue the good for the sake of God and

---

82. See the helpful theological consideration of the mystery of the presence of Christ in imperfect human beings in the ecclesial hierarchy by Charles Journet, *L'Église du Verbe Incarné*, vol. 1 of *La hiérarchie apostolique* (Paris: Éditions St. Augustin, 1998), 21–65.

the spiritual welfare of one's neighbor.[83] Aquinas qualifies this claim, however, by noting that the deepest motivations for obedience given in the Old Testament stem from the love of God for God's own sake. Likewise, the New Testament contains some temporal promises and threats as motivations to repentance.[84]

Nachmanides notes that the promise of temporal rewards in the Torah is given by He Who Is, the Eternal One. Consequently, there is a promise of eternal life latent in the precepts regarding temporal things. By obeying God in time, one implicitly approaches God himself. Therefore, temporality and eternity should not be opposed. Israel is given rewards and chastisements in time precisely so that it can live in history with the Eternal One, obeying him with hope for the eternal gift of God himself. Far from being an obstacle, the temporal promises present Israel with an opportunity to approach God in his eternity.[85]

The two viewpoints are convergent if one follows Aquinas's thinking on the unity of the two covenants. One might say that the new covenant is contained at the heart of the old covenant, and the old is preserved in key ways by the new. The two covenants are truly distinct in important ways, but they also contain one essential core (revealed more formally by the new covenant): the promise of eternal life with God by grace.[86] Where they differ, they remain inseparable and dynamically ordered, each being spiritually related to the other. Temporal, external rewards and punishments are ordered toward the internal life of faith, hope, and charity. This internal life in the Holy Spirit is oriented toward the eternal, but if it is authentic, it must also be embodied concretely to encompass all of our temporal and external acts.

Fifth Precept

20:13 "You shall not murder" (NRSV).

Literal Sense

The fifth commandment prohibits murder. Murder is rightly understood as the intentional killing of an innocent human being, whether by direct or indirect means. "Direct means" are those acts by which a human life is taken, while "indirect means" are acts that contribute in adjacent but inevitable and foreseeable ways to the taking of a human life. They could include things like the deliberate privation of nourishment and water or the intentional contribution of resources to someone else in view of taking human life.

83. Aquinas, *Explanation of the Ten Commandments*, prologue.
84. *ST* 1–2.107.1.
85. Nachmanides, *Commentary on the Torah: Exodus* 20.11–12.
86. *ST* 1–2.106.1, 1–2.107.1 and 3.

This prohibition is concerned with human life in particular, not with other forms of animal life. The Torah does not forbid the killing of animals for a just purpose, particularly in view of human nourishment, clothing, or as a form of sacrifice (Gen. 4:4). "It is not a sin to use that which is subordinate to the power of man. It is in the natural order that plants be the nourishment of animals, certain animals nourish others, and all for the nourishment of man."[87]

This precept implies a positive assertion: the human being is made in the image of God and by virtue of that fact possesses an inviolable dignity. Mature theological reflection argues rightly that the human person is in the image of God primarily because he or she possesses a spiritual soul that is the form of the body.[88] The unity of body and soul is substantial, so that the human being is one subsistent being—a rational animal, a spiritual person. To purposefully sunder the unity of body and soul in a man is to destroy the life of a personal being. This being is reflective of the very dignity and nobility of God the Creator, from whom all human beings derive their nature. Murder also interrupts the divine plan for each human person, by which that person is called into communion with God. Only God, who is the author of human life and who has given existence to all things, possesses absolute dominion over human life. The fifth commandment given by the Lord to the Israelites is the logical correlate of the chastisement of the Pharaoh in his presumption to have the authority to take innocent human life.

This does not mean that taking human life is prohibited under any condition. Exodus 23:7 specifies, "Do not slay the innocent and righteous." The protection of innocent human life is a first principle and an exceptionless norm. There are cases, however, in which precisely to defend the innocent from the unjust or to defend society at large, the taking of human life is permissible. Such cases include just acts of self-defense (against an unjust, violent aggressor), the protection of the social order (by capital punishment, in cases where other forms of civic punishment are inadequate to protect the community), and just war (where the criteria for the legitimate defense of a people or a state genuinely obtain).[89]

Sound philosophy and the Catholic moral tradition rightly emphasize that intentional homicide (the killing of an innocent human being) is always an

87. Aquinas, *Explanation of the Ten Commandments*, a. 7 (Collins 1939). See the pertinent reflections of Augustine, *City of God* 1.20.

88. *ST* 1.76.1. This teaching has become a doctrinal teaching of the Catholic Church. See the Council of Vienne (Denzinger 2012: 902); *Catechism of the Catholic Church*, para. 365.

89. Aquinas, *Explanation of the Ten Commandments*, a. 7.

intrinsically evil act. "The deliberate murder of an innocent person is gravely contrary to the dignity of the human being, to the golden rule, and to the holiness of the Creator. The law forbidding it is universally valid: it obliges each and everyone, always and everywhere."[90] As such, the taking of innocent life can never be morally justified as a legitimate means in view of a good end, however legitimate or noble the latter may be. In general, it is always morally wrong to employ an intrinsically evil means in order to attain a good end.[91] By doing so, especially in the case of killing, a human person conspires with evil and, in so doing, gravely offends the justice and wisdom of God.

Each individual human life begins at conception. On one level, this is a fact of scientific and empirical observation. It is also a natural, philosophical truth confirmed by sound human reflection on the nature and origin of human personhood. Simultaneously, it is a truth taught by holy scripture (Ps. 51:5). As a result, the prohibition on intentional homicide extends from conception to natural death for each human being, so it follows that procured abortion is the taking of an innocent human life. Abortion is murder. That procured abortion is prohibited by divine decree is a necessary conclusion of any sound reading of the law of God, revealed at Sinai. It is not somehow accidental that the Catholic Church has perennially insisted on this teaching since the apostolic age. "You shall not kill the embryo by abortion and shall not cause the newborn to perish."[92]

90. *Catechism of the Catholic Church*, para. 2261.
91. Pope John Paul II, *Veritatis Splendor*, para. 80 (emphasis in the original):
   Reason attests that there are objects of the human act which are by their nature "incapable of being ordered" to God, because they radically contradict the good of the person made in his image. These are the acts which, in the Church's moral tradition, have been termed "intrinsically evil" (*intrinsece malum*): they are such *always and per se*, in other words, on account of their very object, and quite apart from the ulterior intentions of the one acting and the circumstances. Consequently, without in the least denying the influence on morality exercised by circumstances and especially by intentions, the Church teaches that there exist acts which *per se* and in themselves, independently of circumstances, are always seriously wrong by reason of their object. The Second Vatican Council itself (*Gaudium et Spes*, para. 27), in discussing the respect due to the human person, gives a number of examples of such acts: "Whatever is hostile to life itself, such as any kind of homicide, genocide, abortion, euthanasia and voluntary suicide; whatever violates the integrity of the human person, such as mutilation, physical and mental torture and attempts to coerce the spirit; whatever is offensive to human dignity, such as subhuman living conditions, arbitrary imprisonment, deportation, slavery, prostitution and trafficking in women and children; degrading conditions of work which treat laborers as mere instruments of profit, and not as free responsible persons: all these and the like are a disgrace, and so long as they infect human civilization they contaminate those who inflict them more than those who suffer injustice, and they are a negation of the honor due to the Creator." (http://w2.vatican.va/content/john-paul-ii/en/encyclicals/documents/hf_jp-ii_enc_06081993_veritatis-splendor.html)
92. *Didache*, para. 2, as cited in the *Catechism of the Catholic Church*, para. 2271.

"Life must be protected with the utmost care from the moment of conception: abortion and infanticide are abominable crimes."[93]

Euthanasia and suicide are also prohibited by the fifth commandment. Sometimes defended as a form of compassionate killing, either of another or of one's self, these acts are said to be undertaken in order to alleviate human suffering. Nevertheless, as Augustine says, "to kill oneself is to kill a human being."[94] The object of these acts, formally speaking, is the direct taking of an innocent human life. However well-intentioned these acts may be, they violate fundamental human dignity and destroy the work of God, which is intrinsically good. In addition, such acts imply grave injustice toward God precisely as irreligious acts: they enter by violence into a sacred domain of divine providence (the time and circumstances of every human death), which is rightly reserved to God alone. Euthanasia and suicide always violate in crucial ways the key virtues of faith, hope, justice, and piety. If they are committed with reflection and deliberate freedom, they stem in some way from unbelief and despair.

Violence, torture, and physical mutilation (of another or one's self) are also forbidden by the fifth commandment. These actions come very close to the act of killing. They do serious harm to the human body and are contrary to the intrinsic dignity of the human person.

In Matt. 5:21–22, Christ recasts the fifth commandment by interiorizing it, identifying one of the principle roots of the sin of murder—the capital vice of anger: "You have heard that it was said to the men of old, 'You shall not kill; and whoever kills shall be liable to judgment.' But I say to you that everyone who is angry with his brother shall be liable to judgment; whoever insults his brother shall be liable to the council, and whoever says, 'You fool!' shall be liable to the hell of fire."

Not all anger is evil or unreasonable. On the contrary, reason can rightly pass judgment on unjust actions, and the emotional passion of anger can rightly participate in such judgments. "Anger is really the impulse to avenge an injury which one has suffered."[95] However, anger becomes sinful when it is excessive or leads to judgments that are unreasonable or unfair. It is especially grave when it develops into personal hatred. "Anyone who hates his brother is a murderer, and you know that no murderer has eternal life abiding in him" (1 John 3:15). The vice of anger

93. Second Vatican Council, *Gaudium et Spes*, para. 51, www.vatican.va/archive/hist_councils /ii_vatican_council/documents/vat-ii_const_19651207_gaudium-et-spes_en.html.

94. Augustine, *City of God* 1.20 (Bettenson 1972).

95. Aquinas, *Explanation of the Ten Commandments*, a. 7 (Collins 1939).

typically stems from inner dispositions of pride and jealousy and is often manifest through calumny, critical speech about others, or gossip. These are various kinds of oracular violence, since they do harm to the reputation of another and stem ultimately from resentment or ill will toward one's neighbor.

Positively speaking, then, the fifth commandment enjoins upon human beings the following virtues: the defense of innocent human life; charity or love of neighbor (which in some fashion is due to every human being); patience, beneficence, and mildness; the forgiveness of injuries; the curbing of undue anger by the virtue of fortitude; charitable and tempered speech about others; the active pursuit of remedies against hatred; and pursuit of the peace of the common good.

SPIRITUAL SENSE

The scriptures alert us to the fact that murder and hatred are sins that have plagued human existence from the dawn of civilization. At the beginning of history, Cain kills his brother Abel (Gen. 4:8). Moses kills the Egyptian, perhaps justly or perhaps not (Exod. 2:12). Even David, a forerunner of the Messiah, conspires unjustly to kill Uriah (2 Sam. 11:15). Human civilization is plagued by the cyclical presence of unjust wars and the string of atrocities that they bring in their wake.

The Bible does not anticipate explicitly the massive taking of life by technological means that has transpired in the twentieth and twenty-first centuries. However, it does treat murder as a serious injustice that extends across human history on a vast scale and is often allied with terrible forms of political injustice. Yet simultaneously the scriptures depict even this reality as ultimately subject to the mystery of God's judgment and mercy. The human decision to take innocent life is not more powerful than the omnipotence and providence of God and his redemptive wisdom.

Understood in this light, the fifth precept can be read in its spiritual sense to mean, "You shall not kill the Son of God." Christ is the Innocent One who identifies in his human life and unjust death with every innocent person unjustly put to death throughout human history. His innocence is superior to any other for three reasons: (1) he is without any form of sin, whether original or actual; (2) a plenitude of grace and charity reside in his human mind and heart; and (3) he possesses in himself as the Lord the infinite innocence of God, who can have no complicity with moral evil of any kind. Jesus, then, is truly the New Abel, who in his death exposes the violence of Cain that inhabits humanity.

This spiritual truth is a great solace for several reasons. It means that God himself is the redeemer of the innocent, of all those who have suffered unjustly, and that he offers in the passion, death, and resurrection of Christ a mysterious response to the existential problem of moral evil that inhabits humanity. God offers human beings the possibility of uniting their sufferings at the hands of others with the merits of Christ, so as to "complete what is lacking in Christ's afflictions for the sake of his body" (Col. 1:24), which is a form of supernatural merit given only by Christ and in him.[96] By the power of Christ, the spiritual trials of the martyrs are the seeds of new life for the Church and the larger human community.

On a deeper level, this teaching points us toward the fact that Christ died for all in order to show us that God can definitively overcome not only the evils of hatred and killing found in others but especially those evils as they are found in ourselves. The *Catechism of the Council of Trent* formulates clearly the New Testament teaching: just as Christ freely accepted death out of love for all human beings, so all human beings by their sins are rightly understood to be in some real sense the authors of the death of Christ.[97] The solace found in this truth can be summarized as follows. The worst moral calamity that could transpire has already happened: human beings have killed God in his human nature. This was not something God willed but only something God allowed. And yet God used the worst moral evil to bring forth the greatest supernatural good—the forgiveness of sins and the elevation of human nature into participation in the divine nature. If God can do this with regard to his own death, then God can act in a similar way with regard to every other unjust human death and every human sin. It pertains to the mores of infinite mercy to make use even of human evils to reveal the ever-greater presence and power of divine goodness. In Christ, God declares the definitive victory of his love over every power of death and sin.

Sixth Precept

20:14 "You shall not commit adultery."

Literal Sense

There is a longstanding discussion about the scope of this commandment. Already in the ancient church there were those who claimed that the precept

---

96. *ST* 1–2.114.1 and 6.
97. See the *Catechism of the Council of Trent* 1.4 (McHugh and Callan 1949), with reference to Heb. 6:6: We must regard as guilty all those who continue to relapse into their sins. Since our sins made the Lord Christ suffer the torment of the cross, those who plunge themselves into disorders and crimes crucify the Son of God anew in their hearts (for he is in them) and hold him up to contempt. And it can be seen that our crime in this case is greater in us than in the Jews. As for them, according to the witness of the Apostle, "None of the rulers of this age understood this; for if they had, they would not have crucified the Lord of glory" (1 Cor. 2:8). We, however, profess to know him. And when we deny him by our deeds, we in some way seem to lay violent hands on him. (57)

pertains only to conjugal fidelity between married persons and offers no overt instruction in any other domain of sexual ethics. Modern interpreters sometimes specify further that the precept is meant to protect only a particular instance of family life: the archaic patriarchal household in which inheritance rights of the children were safeguarded by their genealogical descent from the father. Marital fidelity receives its moral value primarily from the economic and political relations that it seeks to safeguard. This interpretation of the precept makes the mere circumstances of the act of adultery the unique criteria for determining its moral importance and not the formal object of the act as such.[98] In that sense, it evacuates the precept of any essential content and suggests implicitly a merely utilitarian ethics of sexuality based on what is pleasurable and useful.

Over against these views, however, the Torah presents a very unified, highly developed teaching regarding sexual morality. This teaching is further nuanced in homogeneous fashion by subsequent Old and New Testament revelation. Therefore, it is both theologically and historically artificial to remove the interpretation of the sixth commandment from this larger Judaic cultural and intellectual context. Already in Gen. 1:28 the sexual complementarity of man and woman is understood to exist in view of marriage and the fruitfulness of children. Sexuality has its normative place within family life. Adultery, incest, and prostitution are portrayed as immoral (Gen. 38:14–26), and the voluntary sterilization of sexual acts is condemned in Gen. 38:9–10.[99] Leviticus 18:22 and Deut. 23:18 prohibit homosexual acts. Bestiality is condemned in Lev. 18:23, and fornication is prohibited in Deut. 22:22. These teachings are reiterated in subsequent biblical literature (such as Tobit 4:12 and Sir. 23:16–27) and are presented in normative terms in the New Testament. "For out of the heart come evil thoughts, adulteries, fornication" (Matt. 15:19). "For this is the will of God, your sanctification: that you abstain from unchastity" (1 Thess. 4:3–5). "Do not be deceived; neither fornicators, nor idolaters, nor adulterers, nor the effeminate, nor sodomites . . . will possess the kingdom of God" (1 Cor. 6:9–10 NASB). "You have heard that it was said, 'You shall not commit adultery.' But I say to you that everyone who

---

98. On this fundamental distinction for the moral evaluation of human acts, see *ST* 1–2.18. The formal object pertains to the act itself, such as the act of lying, while the circumstances pertain to the surrounding conditions, like the act of lying in order to avoid embarrassment, or to gain the trust of another. The circumstances of a moral act affect the gravity of the act, but they do not specify per se whether the act is wrong or right. The moral object is what determines formally or specifically the good or the evil of an action. If it is always wrong to commit adultery, for example, the moral evil of the act will not be eradicated simply because the adultery is committed in some useful and beneficial circumstance.

99. See the modern interpretations of this passage in the magisterium of Pope Benedict XV, Responses of the Sacred Penitentiary, April 3, 1916, and June 3, 1916 (Denzinger 2012: 3634, 3638–40).

looks at a woman lustfully has already committed adultery with her in his heart"
(Matt. 5:27–28).

The Catholic tradition discerns within this diversity of biblical teachings a
coherent unity based on a profound understanding of the human person and
the teleology of human sexual acts. According to the scriptures, sexual acts attain
their true purpose and authentic moral meaning only when they occur within
the context of a conjugal union between a husband and wife, who are open to
the final end of human sexual acts, namely, reproduction. In the classical Catholic
understanding of the scriptural deposit of faith, there is an indissociable unity
between the unitive dimension of marital love and the procreative dimension.
This unity is willed by God and inscribed within the very nature and purpose of
the human capacity to love sexually.[100]

Sexuality is an important constituent dimension of every human being. It
exerts a powerful influence over human behavior. For this reason, it can contribute profoundly to authentic human flourishing but can also assume forms of
expression that fail to respect the dignity of the human person and the vocation
of each human being to love God and neighbor. Human sexuality needs, then,
to be integrated into a complete human life of virtue and spiritual self-mastery.
This occurs principally through the development of the virtues of chastity, temperance, and charity.

Various kinds of scriptural prohibitions on sexual acts are intelligible and reasonable, insofar as each of these acts derogates in some way from the good of
conjugal married life. Adultery is a moral crime that directly harms the marital
bond of the two spouses and endangers the good of the family in its common life.[101]
Purposeful sterilization of sexual acts (by the use of artificial contraception, for
example) necessarily alters the nature and purpose of the sexual act. It suppresses
voluntarily the ontological openness of the sexual act to God as the Creator of new
human life as well as to divine providence. It acts directly against the acknowledgment of the dignity of the other person as a potential parent and a committed
spouse and alters the moral quality of the gift of self in the act, making the act
inherently self-referential.[102] Fornication suffers from a deficit of justice because
it risks bringing about the conception of a child that either cannot be adequately
cared for by two committed parents or that may well be aborted.[103] This act also

100. Pope Paul VI, *Humanae Vitae*, paras. 11–14.
101. *ST* 2–2.154.8 corp. and ad 2.
102. Pope Paul VI, *Humanae Vitae*, paras. 12–14; Pope John Paul II, *Veritatis Splendor*, para. 80.
103. *ST* 2–2.154.2.

suffers from a lack of ethical responsibility between the partners, whose actions are noncommittal and therefore necessarily selfish on some fundamental level.

Other actions lacking in chastity are unhelpful because they in no way prepare a person for a life of moral maturity and self-giving in marriage (or consecrated celibate life). Instead, they entrap human beings in patterns of egoism and moral immaturity. This is the case with regard to unchaste thoughts, masturbation, or the use of pornography. As Christ himself teaches (Matt. 5:27–28), the voluntary engagement in these acts is always and everywhere wrong. By making this clear, Christ calls each human being to undertake a lifelong struggle for internal purity of conscience and imagination, as well as purity of action. Human sexuality is good, but to be lived rightly in the context of a happily married life it must be purified of the dross of selfish egoism. This personal integration of spiritual love, sensate feeling, and biological instinct is entirely possible with the help of God's grace.

Homosexuality refers to sexual relations between men or between women who are attracted to members of the same sex. Homosexual acts are closed to the transmission of human life and do not originate from a genuine biological and affective complementarity. They cannot participate, therefore, in the basic goods proper to married love. For that reason, the Bible treats them as intrinsically disordered sexual acts. They are unchaste and contrary to the natural law.[104]

The Torah does not ignore the fact that there are many human beings who experience a predominant or exclusive attraction to members of the same sex. Quite frequently people with strong homosexual inclinations do not choose their condition and experience it as a trial. Scripture affirms unequivocally that each human being is created in the image of God and possesses an intrinsic dignity, such that he or she is due respect, affability, and love.[105] This is no less true for people who commit or who are tempted to commit homosexual acts. With regard to the weaknesses that befall human beings in the domain of human sexuality, it is best to recall the saying of Paul: "For God has consigned all men to disobedience, that he may have mercy upon all" (Rom. 11:32). Human beings are frequently morally frail in matters of sexuality and should be looked upon in the light of God's complete truth, which implies his compassion and mercy.

104. *Catechism of the Catholic Church*, para. 2357.
105. See in this respect the *Letter to the Bishops of the Catholic Church on the Pastoral Care of Homosexual Persons*, Congregation of the Doctrine of the Faith, Oct. 1, 1986, www.vatican.va/roman_curia/congregations/cfaith/documents/rc_con_cfaith_doc_19861001_homosexual-persons_en.html.

SPIRITUAL SENSE

Spiritually, the sixth commandment has three distinct significations. First, it refers to the radiant purity of Jesus as the Messiah. It is Christ alone who in his human perfection of charity and virtue utterly fulfills the internal and external demands of the Torah. Christ is the model of perfect human chastity in the service of love. Accordingly he is also the chaste bridegroom of the Church. By offering his life for the human race in the purity of love, he has made it possible for the Church to give herself to him, purified internally by the gift of the Holy Spirit.

Second, then, this commandment refers to the spiritual marriage of Christ and the Church. "Christ loved the church and gave himself up for her, that he might sanctify her, having cleansed her by the washing of water with the word, that he might present the church to himself in splendor, without spot or wrinkle or any such thing, that she might be holy and without blemish" (Eph. 5:25–27). Revelation 17:2–4 and 19:2 speak of "fidelity" and "fornication" in a primarily spiritual sense. The Church is called to reject idolatry and to cling to Christ in the marital fidelity of faith. Grace provides Christians with the capacity to remain within the Church and to love the doctrine of Christ, based upon a sense of spiritual chastity. This inward fidelity is at the heart of the union between Christ and the Church.

Third, this verse refers spiritually to the particular states of life of persons in the Church who are sanctified by the grace of Christ in distinct ways. Persons consecrated to Christ by vows of virginity or celibacy are given the grace to be conformed inwardly to the life of Christ, to his purity and charity, for the sake of the kingdom of God (Matt. 19:29; 1 Cor. 7:25–35). Accordingly, the exigency of spiritual and corporeal purity of heart is most elevated in their cases. Married Christian laypersons, meanwhile, are invited to sanctification by the sacrament of marriage so that their friendship may reflect the mutual love between Christ and the Church (Eph. 5:31–32). The commandment to spiritual and physical chastity also takes on a particular exigency in the context of the sacrament of marriage, in which the spouses have been granted together the interior grace to dwell mutually in Christ.

SEVENTH PRECEPT

20:15 "You shall not steal."

LITERAL SENSE

The fourth, fifth, and sixth commandments protect the substance of the human being in his or her own person or family relations. The seventh commandment moves from persons to possessions, which are of immediate proximate importance to human well-being. The Hebrew word for stealing here (*ganab*) is traditionally interpreted to pertain to kidnapping or human trafficking (Gen. 40:15; Exod. 21:16), but it also clearly refers to the unjust theft of external things (Gen. 44:8; Exod. 22:1). In this way, the commandment seeks to safeguard the good of persons with reference to issues of ownership and possession.

Exodus seems simply to presuppose that there is a human right to private property, which is granted by God through the medium of the created order. The question is never raised explicitly as to whether this might be a false assumption, and the immorality of theft is affirmed repeatedly throughout the course of scripture. The teaching is constant and also has different applications in a diversity of circumstances.

At the same time, these assertions have to be read against the backdrop of a larger theme: the universal destination of goods. When God first makes the man and the woman in Genesis, God gives dominion over the visible creation to them and their progeny (Gen. 1:28). There is no reference at this point to a division of property. Most importantly, the fundamental gift is understood inclusively: all of the descendants of the first couple are meant to partake of a just share of the goods of creation.

We see something analogous in the exodus narrative. On the one hand, the enslavement and exploitation of the Hebrews are depicted as something radically unjust. They have a right to self-determination and to some form of private ownership. On the other hand, the Israelites who are fleeing Egypt receive the gift of manna and quails, goods intended for the use of all. There is no question of private property concerning goods that are required merely to sustain a person in existence. The prohibition on stealing is not meant, then, to be read in an unqualified way. Rather, the right to private property is a relative right that should be understood over against the backdrop of extremes—whether of state collectivism (which denies citizens the freedom to acquire personal property) or extreme libertarianism (which denies the obligation of those with possessions to care for the disenfranchised).

Theft can occur in many ways: by stealth and deceit, violent acquisition of another's goods, the refusal to pay just wages, or fraud in buying and selling. It can also occur by those who purchase positions of honor unjustly, whether this honor is temporal or ecclesiastical.[106] The transgression can be understood in more

106. Aquinas, *Explanation of the Ten Commandments*, a. 9.

collective terms when whole population groups are denied basic human rights, such as food and clean water, basic educational opportunities, the possibility of dignified work, just compensation, freedom of movement, and self-expression.[107] Respect for the universal destination of goods is also violated when the natural resources of human well-being are not adequately respected. The destruction of the visible creation through pollution or wasteful consumption is a kind of theft because it deprives the larger human community of a long-term, sustainable environment of life.[108]

The positive precepts that stem from this commandment pertain to the just distribution of goods. Generosity and liberality are virtues that help cultivate a just and humane attitude toward the needs of others.[109] Almsgiving is the biblically mandated practice for serving the needs of the poor and economically disenfranchised.[110] In cases where the sin of theft has occurred, there is an obligation to make just restitution by restoring stolen goods to their owner (if possible) or at least by making some kind of proportionate contribution of temporal resources to the larger common good.[111]

SPIRITUAL SENSE

In its spiritual sense, the seventh commandment must be read in light of the mystery of the poverty of Christ. Poverty and simplicity of life have a distinctly christological form in the New Testament. Here it is not a question of involuntary poverty but of voluntary renunciation of temporal goods for the sake of God and the kingdom of heaven. While the Lord is born into a poor family of manual laborers, his way of life is one of voluntary poverty, and he promises beatitude to the "poor in spirit" (Matt. 5:3). The early Christian community is marked by the renunciation of temporal goods, generous sharing of resources, and even certain instances of collective ownership. "Now the company of those who believed were of one heart and soul, and no one said that any of the things which he possessed was his own, but they had everything in common" (Acts 4:32).

In addition, however, Christ mysteriously identifies himself with the involuntarily poor. Human beings will be judged eschatologically based on their treatment of Christ himself in the materially and spiritually poor of this world. "For I was hungry and you gave me food, I was thirsty and you gave me drink, I was a

107. *Catechism of the Catholic Church*, paras. 2426–42.
108. Pope John Paul II, *Centesimus Annus*, paras. 37–40.
109. *ST* 2–2.117.
110. *ST* 2–2.32.
111. *Catechism of the Council of Trent* 3.7.

stranger and you welcomed me, I was naked and you clothed me, I was sick and you visited me, I was in prison and you came to me" (Matt. 25:35–36).

Three principles stand at the origin of these teachings. First, the New Testament is concerned above all with the promise of eternal life; consequently it teaches us to regard the passing things of this world with a healthy degree of detachment and indifference. Particularly in light of voluntary celibacy for the sake of the kingdom of God, temporal goods are primarily a means for the works of mercy and charity, as well as an opportunity to give oneself to others. Second, Christ himself "became poor, so that by his poverty [we] might become rich" (2 Cor. 8:9). The poverty of Christ is mysterious on one level because it shows us the mystery of charity, which is indifferent to temporal goods and tends toward eternal life. On an even deeper level, however, it is expressive of the condescension of divine love. God who possesses all things in himself emptied himself by taking on a human nature like ours, deprived of any special human privileges, in order to show us how to live in this world in view of the world to come but also to show us who God is in himself, in the freedom of his omnipotent love. God has the power and freedom to become poor as man, precisely to enrich us with the life of God himself. Third, by voluntarily becoming poor, God establishes a mysterious relation to the socially and spiritually disenfranchised. The identification of Christ with the poor is ontological, not in the sense that they are the incarnate Lord (which is not the case) but in the sense that his grace is most readily available to those who, through no fault of their own, are most subject to the effects of evil in this world. This identification of Christ with the poor as the privileged locus of his mystical body partially reveals (but also partially hides) a mystery of Christ's victory of charity over all of the effects of sin. Belief in this victory is the source of a desire to alleviate involuntary poverty, not a reason to remain indifferent to it. In its deepest dimension, "You shall not steal" refers to the prohibition against taking from Christ what belongs to him. His love for the poor commends the Christian to venture out toward those who are most spiritually and temporally marginalized or suffering.

Eighth Precept

20:16 "You shall not bear false witness against your neighbor."

Literal Sense

The eighth precept concerns the matter of truths spoken to another or about another. As such, its subject matter is further removed from the substantial well-being of persons than the previous precepts. However, it touches more immediately upon the interior dispositions of those who obey the commandment. The positive corollary to the commandment is the injunction to cultivate the virtue of truthfulness. Human beings have a moral obligation to tell one another the truth and not to deceive each other.

Truthfulness, as Aquinas notes, is a dimension of the virtue of justice.[112] It is grounded in a recognition of the authentic dignity of persons and seeks to offer each person what he or she is owed. As such, telling the truth to others contributes to the authentic love of neighbor, social unity, and human friendliness. Truthfulness also profoundly affects the integrity of the person who speaks. By fostering the virtue of truthfulness, a human being attains to a profound unity of thought, word, and action, in correspondence to one's internal dispositions. This integrity breaks down in cases of lying; not only does lying fracture and undermine social bonds, but it also fractures and disintegrates the inward moral unity of the human person who deceives.[113] However, it is not necessarily the case that every truth one knows should be spoken. Often it is prudent to refrain from communicating a given truth; not everyone has an equal right to the full measure of the truth in every instance. Nevertheless, no one should be subject to deceit either. The telling of lies is always and everywhere wrong.

Aquinas notes that there are various forms of deception as well as very subtle forms of "false witness."[114] The most evident form of transgression is the outright lie—the gravity of which is subject to degrees based on the "matter" of the lie (what the lie is about) or the circumstances in which it takes place.[115] Not all lies entail what the Catholic tradition calls mortal sin, that is, sins that extinguish the grace of charity in the human heart.[116] However, there are serious sins of lying that are morally grave in kind.

In addition to lying as such, there is the act of detraction or the related sin of listening to detraction.[117] These are sins in which a person's good reputation is

112. *ST* 2–2.109.3.
113. *ST* 2–2.109.2–3, 2–2.110.1.
114. Aquinas, *Explanation of the Ten Commandments*, a. 10.
115. *ST* 2–2.110.2. In obj. 2 of this article, Aquinas notes the eightfold division of lies given by Augustine in the *Contra Mendacium* 14:
   The first is "in religious doctrine"; the second is "a lie that profits no one and injures someone"; the third "profits one party so as to injure another"; the fourth "told out of mere lust of lying and deceiving"; the fifth "told out of the desire to please"; the sixth "injures no one, and profits someone in saving his money"; the seventh "injures no one and profits someone in saving him from death"; the eighth "injures no one, and profits someone in saving him from defilement of the body."
116. *ST* 2–2.110.4.
117. Aquinas, *Explanation of the Ten Commandments*, a. 10.

undermined or diminished through the gratuitous communication of criticism of character, often motivated by jealousy, resentment, or ambition. Other vices that undercut the virtue of truthfulness include gossip, boasting, exaggeration, flattery of others, and the habit of undue complaining. Actions can also become lies when they are forms of social dissimulation or hypocrisy.[118]

Sins of lying are frequently allied with insecurity or false love of self, lax convenience, evasion of responsibility, ambition, or cowardice. In lying, especially in grave matters, a human being unwittingly imitates the devil, who is "a liar and the father of lies" (John 8:44). This is in contrast to God, who is subsistent Truth and can neither deceive nor be deceived. Sins of lying corrupt human society, especially when they become systemic within families, corporations, governments, economies, or religious organizations. In lying a person progressively undermines his or her own reputation and puts himself or herself to death spiritually, especially in grave matters pertaining to faith, where public commitment to the truth is of the upmost importance.

Scripture teaches that "all men are liars" (Ps. 116:11 NASB), meaning that all fallen human beings fail in myriad ways to be truthful in speech or in act. This teaching points us toward a fundamental soteriological principle: God alone, who is the Truth (or the truth of God himself), can save human beings from the throes of human deceit. The activity of grace and the gift of truth are deeply aligned within the one saving economy. Salvation for human persons consists necessarily in deliverance from falsehood and conversion to the truth about God and God's creation.

SPIRITUAL SENSE

The eighth commandment convicts the hearts of human persons universally because each human being is radically threatened by intellectual and moral falsehood. However, this precept also points toward a christological resolution. Christ is the New Adam, the man in whom there is no lie, who does not succumb to the deceit of the tempter and whose truthful life redeems the human race from sin. In the Gospel of John, the theme of the truth of Christ's word is central. Jesus's public life unfolds as a mission to bring the truth about the Father into the world. "If you continue in my word, you are truly my disciples, and you will know the truth, and the truth will make you free" (John 8:31–32). The night before his death, he institutes the apostolic hierarchy, sanctifying them in view of the communication of his word. "Sanctify them in the truth; thy word is truth" (17:17). On a deeper

---

118. *ST* 2–2.111.

level, this human truthfulness of Christ is expressive of a more fundamental reality: Christ as God is himself Truth, by virtue of his divinity. "I am the way, and the truth, and the life; no one comes to the Father, but by me" (14:6). It is he who sends the "Spirit of truth," the Paraclete, upon the Church, so that the college of apostles might be led into the "all the truth" (16:13). Behind the many words of truth that Christ speaks, then, is his deeper identity as the eternal Logos, the Word of the Father, who communicates divine life and truth (1:1–3).

The Christian revelation teaches that faith is a spiritual illumination of the intellect. In Christ, God reveals a truth about God that redeems the human mind. Implicit in this theological teaching are various positive moral injunctions: human beings are bound to seek the truth about God and to adhere to it once they discover it.[119] Disciples of Christ are called to become persons of the truth in every facet of their lives. When Paul describes those who forfeit their salvation, he says that they "refused to love the truth and so be saved" (2 Thess. 2:10). For the Christian, the precept "you shall not lie" contains an inward spiritual imperative: "you shall confess the truth about Christ." Witness in the public square forms an integral part of the Christian life. "How are they to believe in him of whom they have never heard? And how are they to hear without a preacher?" (Rom. 10:14). "For whoever is ashamed of me and of my words, of him will the Son of Man be ashamed when he comes in his glory and the glory of the Father and of the holy angels" (Luke 9:26). "Woe to me if I do not preach the gospel!" (1 Cor. 9:16).

NINTH AND TENTH PRECEPTS

20:17 "You shall not covet your neighbor's house; you shall not covet your neighbor's wife, or his manservant, or his maidservant, or his ox, or his ass, or anything that is your neighbor's."

LITERAL SENSE

Aquinas notes that human law pertains principally to deeds, while divine law pertains both to deeds and to thoughts.[120] As noted above, these last two commandments are, of all those pertaining to the love of neighbor, the most interior. By prohibiting the inner covetousness of lust and of possessions, they rejoin in their own way the first precept. In the inner dispositions of the soul, a profound love

119. Second Vatican Council, *Dignitatis Humanae*, para. 2 (Denzinger 2012: para. 4240): "It is in accordance with their dignity as persons . . . all men should be at once impelled by nature and also bound by a moral obligation to seek the truth, especially religious truth. They are also bound to adhere to the truth, once it is known, and to order their whole lives in accord with the demands of truth."
120. Aquinas, *Explanation of the Ten Commandments*, a. 11.

of God is integrally related to a realistic love of self and a genuine love of others. Authentic love of God purifies the heart, opening the path toward a realistic and humble love of self (for we cannot love ourselves truly when we prefer ourselves to God). A true love of God and self, in turn, helps purify and strengthen the genuine love of others. These three commandments (the first, ninth, and tenth) attain to the roots of virtue in the human person.

Why is covetousness dangerous to the human heart? As Aquinas notes, it is because human desire has no limits. Precisely because the human heart is *capax Dei*, capable of desiring God who is infinite, it can readily become a kind of perverse mirror of God, willing a "substitute infinity" that is not God.[121] The human being can become lost in the indeterminate desire for temporal things, wandering indefinitely in the love of a multiplicity of creatures incapable of satisfying the heart's deepest native desire. Covetousness destroys peace of heart, undermines love of neighbor as one's self, obscures justice, and frequently produces wickedness; it is useless to man's true flourishing.[122] Consequently, there is a need to curb our human desires by a knowing asceticism, precisely so as to maintain our human dignity and orient our desires and acts toward authentic human ends.

In matters of human sexuality, the human being is subject to a particularly tangible form of lust or "concupiscence." Sexual passions and instinctual appetites are not intrinsically bad, but they can readily enslave human desires and mar human decision making. As an effect of original sin, fallen human beings frequently experience moral instabilities and failings in this domain (whether in thought, word, or action). This occurs when sexual desires have a negative effect upon the human mind and heart, becoming the occasion for disordered reasoning and action. As noted above, Christ is unambiguous on this point, linking together the sixth and the tenth precepts: "You have heard that it was said, 'You shall not commit adultery.' But I say to you that everyone who looks at a woman lustfully has already committed adultery with her in his heart" (Matt. 5:27–28).

The virtues that allow a person to observe these two final precepts of the law are multiple. Covetousness is best avoided by the measured practice of detachment from temporal things, coupled with attachment to spiritual things. Humility and poverty of heart are essential to the life of a person who wishes to remain firmly attached to God as his or her final end, in the face of competing attractions. Temperance is the virtue by which one governs well the use of sensible goods and inward desires, especially in the domains of food, drink, and sexuality. Chastity

---

121. Aquinas, *Explanation of the Ten Commandments*, a. 11.
122. Aquinas, *Explanation of the Ten Commandments*, a. 11.

is the virtue by which a person seeks to integrate his or her sexuality into a larger moral pattern of existence, governing the passions and instincts judiciously in the light of reason and the vocation to love others personally and spiritually. Chastity (whether in the married state or an unmarried celibate state) gives peace to the soul, allows for the development of genuine self-respect and love of others, brings the soul closer to God, and helps create peaceful relationships between persons and families.

In our fallen human state, the inward battle to maintain interior purity of heart is often difficult and remains a challenge to most people through the entire course of their lives. Ultimately, profound inward purification and stability in virtue are possible only by grace. This grace is the sign of the inward presence and activity of Christ and the Holy Spirit, acting upon the soul. "For God has done what the law, weakened by the flesh, could not do: sending his own Son in the likeness of sinful flesh and for sin, he condemned sin in the flesh, in order that the just requirement of the law might be fulfilled in us, who walk not according to the flesh but according to the Spirit" (Rom. 8:3–4).

Though the virtue of chastity is often only made possible by grace, it is also acquired through genuine human cooperation with God. This entails a set of prudent behavior patterns designed to help the soul enjoy moral stability: habitual avoidance of external temptations, as well as impure internal thoughts and images; regular prayer; and the practice of remaining peacefully occupied with meaningful concerns.[123]

SPIRITUAL SENSE

The spiritual sense of the ninth and tenth precepts is christological, pointing us implicitly toward the inward purity and the radiant charity of the heart of Christ. Christ has a heart entirely free from covetousness or disordered desire. "Come to me, all who labor and are heavy laden, and I will give you rest. Take my yoke upon you, and learn from me; for I am gentle and lowly in heart, and you will find rest for your souls" (Matt. 11:28–29). The human being is frequently tormented or at least bewildered by internal moral instability that stems from the unstable desires of the human heart. The "second use" of the law (by which God demonstrates the moral poverty of the human community in the fallen state) serves only to expose more profoundly the internal fractures and weaknesses that riddle the human person (Rom. 5:20). However, the "third use" of the law (that is, its pedagogical role within the sphere of grace) teaches the soul

123. Aquinas, *Explanation of the Ten Commandments*, a. 12.

to place its absolute confidence in the grace and charity of the heart of Christ, who is merciful and whose mercy gives peace and rest to the human being in his or her frailty. In this way, the ninth and tenth commandments, precisely because of their interiority, operate in the human being by a kind of "dialectic" between conviction and inward transformation, pointing always toward the righteousness of Christ—by which he saves us and that he effectively communicates to us. As the Council of Trent rightly underscored, this righteousness is indeed communicable and can be transformative even of our most interior acts and habitual dispositions.[124] "God's love has been poured into our hearts through the Holy Spirit which has been given to us" (Rom. 5:5). "For in Christ Jesus neither circumcision nor uncircumcision is of any avail, but faith working through love" (Gal. 5:6). "Do not yield your members to sin as instruments of wickedness, but yield yourselves to God as men who have been brought from death to life, and your members to God as instruments of righteousness" (Rom. 6:13). In their spiritual sense, then, the ninth and tenth precepts, like the first, point us toward the inward meaning of the Ten Commandments as a whole. They are meant to call us to a life of transformation in the grace of Christ.

Juridical Law: The Book of the Covenant (Exod. 20:22–23:33)

This section of Exodus contains a code of law that is traditionally termed the "Book of the Covenant." The title comes from Exod. 24:7, where Moses reads the book to the people, communicating the terms of the covenant that they are about to seal with the Lord. "Then he took the book of the covenant, and read it in the hearing of the people; and they said, 'All that the LORD has spoken we will do, and we will be obedient.'" Significantly, in 24:3, we are told that "Moses told the people all the *words* of the LORD and all the *ordinances*" (emphasis added). Traditionally it is thought that the "words" (*debarim*) here denote the Decalogue (the words of God) while the "ordinances" (*mishpatim*) denote the laws present in this section of the text.

The Book of the Covenant is generally thought to be one of the oldest bodies of law in the Bible, predating the Deuteronomical reform but not necessarily the settlement. It may well have laws within it dating back to the time of the wilderness. Much of it seems to presuppose an agricultural society and a stable domestic settlement, most likely dating from a period just after the occupation

---

124. Council of Trent, Session 6, *Decree on Justification*, chap. 7 and can. 11–12.

of the land of Israel, perhaps with some expansion from the monarchic period.[125] The inner structure of the book seems to reflect an internal history of development, based upon ongoing cases that arose after settlement in Israel. In its edited form, the Book of the Covenant interrupts the Sinai narrative. A closing phrase of the Book of the Covenant in 24:3 refers to "all the words" Moses read. This may have originally referred to the ten "words" of the Decalogue, but the verse has been situated by the redactor to refer to the Book of the Covenant as well.[126]

The Theological Significance of the Juridical Laws

Various theological issues arise at this juncture. One may begin by asking about the relationship between the Decalogue and the Book of the Covenant. In 20:18–22, the Torah refers again to Moses as the mediator between the Lord and Israel, prior to the giving of the ordinances of the covenant. It is Moses who stands in thick darkness and receives the divine revelation, while the people tremble with fear before the epiphany. He is the archetypal prophet and mediator between God and humanity. The teachings that are then given in 20:23–23:33 are placed under his auspices as divinely revealed teachings. Why, then, are they separated intentionally from the Decalogue? According to the sacred text, do they have a subordinate status of some kind to the Ten Commandments?

I have noted above that the Decalogue has a universal moral character that has been understood more and more perfectly through time, in the light of the New Testament revelation. By contrast, the Christian tradition rightly emphasizes the temporal and historical setting of much that is found in the Book of the Covenant. This law is primarily "juridical." It is not concerned most of all with universal moral truth claims but with their applications in particular circumstances of governance. As has been commonly noted, the book is composed primarily of apodictic laws stipulating moral acts that should obtain in particular cases, as well as penal laws applicable to civic and familial situations in the epoch of Israel's first settlement.

Based on this reading, one can maintain two important theological truths. First, there is an organic continuity between the Decalogue and these laws, as the ancient Jewish tradition has rightly maintained. These laws are a kind of application of the Mosaic Decalogue, tailored to various concrete civic circumstances of life. The Torah demands to be embodied in time and history, in the life of the Israelite people.

125. See on this matter Childs 1974: 456.
126. Childs 1974: 454.

Second, however, it is essential to the right interpretation of the Torah to maintain the medieval Catholic distinction between moral law and its judicial prescriptions or applications. Aquinas insists that the Ten Commandments are the essence of the moral law and cannot be abrogated, while the juridical precepts were intended to govern the people of Israel in particular historical circumstances. As such, they may contain universal moral norms applicable to particular circumstances. However, they may also contain contingent applications of the moral law within a particular social and historical context. They are expressions of the moral law as applied in a particular epoch, primarily to the regulations of human beings in civic life with one another.[127] This means that the Book of the Covenant is not simply identical with the universal moral law but is a law conditioned in its development and application by a given context of human and sacred history. Civic laws are meant to protect and promote civil institutions. Culturally specific and case-specific laws are not identical with the natural law as such.

This does not mean that the Book of the Covenant is unimportant to Christian understandings of the covenant. These laws can contain and embody notions of prescription or prohibition that are valid to every civilization and age, which is a matter of discernment for the Church as she reads the scriptures (inspired by the Holy Spirit) down through the ages. In addition, these laws are prefigurative of the Church, even in their historical contingency. As Aquinas notes: "They were not instituted for the purpose of being figurative, but in order that they might regulate the state of that people according to justice and equity. Nevertheless they did foreshadow something consequent, since the entire state of that people who were directed by these precepts, was figurative."[128] That is to say, just because these laws were meant to aid the people to live together in civic harmony, they foreshadow the particular laws of the Christian people, lived out in accordance with the gospel and the moral law through various ages and places. In the words of Augustine:

> Not only the speech of these men, but their life also, was prophetic; and the whole kingdom of the Hebrews was like a great prophet, corresponding to the greatness of the Person prophesied. So, as regards those Hebrews who were made wise in heart by divine instruction, we may discover a prophecy of the coming of Christ and of the church, both in what they said and in what they did; and the same is true as regards the divine procedure towards the whole nation as a body.[129]

127. *ST* 1–2.104.1.
128. *ST* 1–2.104.2.
129. *Reply to Faustus the Manichean* 22.24 (*NPNF*[1] 4:282).

Ancient Laws and Divine Inspiration: Inspired Development of Teaching in an Ancient Cultural Context

Given the interpretation I am offering, the Book of the Covenant is a collection of early Israelite legislation. Some of it may well stem from the wilderness era, but much of it was developed after the settlement by keepers of the Mosaic tradition (quite possibly Israelite priests). It may have undergone subsequent redaction in the monarchical era, and it was integrated into the edited Torah in the postexilic phase by priest-scribes. Does a hypothesis like this contradict a traditional Catholic theory of biblical inspiration?

It need not. I have noted above the symbolic and archetypal character of the portrayal of Moses in the Torah. Exodus 20:18 provides a key instance: Moses is the archetypal mediator, standing in thick darkness and receiving divine revelation. This image joins together the Decalogue and the Book of the Covenant, suggesting that the latter stems organically from the former. If one understands this connection not only logically (as jurisdictional law that is an application of moral law) but also historically, then the image of Moses in its literal sense represents the development of doctrine in Israelite tradition. In visual form, it spells out the notion of an organic continuity of the tradition from Moses to postexilic Judaism—that is, a historical unity of Israelite life within the covenant.

In What Ways Laws Are and Are Not Applicable in a Given Historical and Cultural Situation

It is often said that laws differ in various times and places principally due to the general relativity of all moral norms. Because there are no universal moral principles, the legal norms of various cultures are subject to significant variation. This idea is erroneous, however, because moral principles, both positive and negative, do obtain in every culture based on the essence of human nature and its perennial qualities. It is always good, for example, that human beings seek to advance in knowledge through true understanding of created reality. It is always wrong to intentionally take innocent human life.

However, Aquinas allows at least five ways to understand the historical and cultural "relativity" of legal texts in diverse contexts. (1) Moral laws can be clarifications of more universal precepts in more precise cases. Here it is not a question of changing moral norms but of drawing more precise conclusions from implicit principles. This is what Aquinas (following Gaius) calls the *jus gentium*, or "law of nations."[130] One civilization can have a more advanced moral awareness than another, at least in a given domain. Such a process of moral discovery can occur more or less perfectly across a diversity of ages and cultures. Moral teachings can also be forgotten or progressively obscured; sometimes they simply remain undiscovered or become the subject of new discovery. (2) The moral law can be given diverse civic applications in diverse historical and cultural circumstances. Aquinas calls this the "civil law."[131] It is distinct from the natural law and is the appropriation of moral teaching to a particular set of legal norms for a given people, based upon their current limitations, needs, moral capacities, or customs. Juridical rewards and punishments and relative prohibitions or stigmas differ according to time and place, and penalties differ greatly according to the moral and psychological sensibilities of a given epoch and culture. For example, murder can be punished in one culture by capital punishment and in another culture by temporary imprisonment, while theft of oxen was a more serious crime in antiquity than it is in modernity. Civic and legal norms differ widely for a variety of reasons.[132] (3) Cultural customs are not entirely identical with moral norms, but cultural customs often enshrine morality and are "codes" of etiquette in which moral practices are embedded. They have subtle forms of moral connotation and differ widely according to time and place.[133] For example, one might consider the

130. *ST* 1–2.95.2 and 4. On the *jus gentium* in Aquinas, see Jacques Maritain, *Man and the State* (Chicago: University of Chicago Press, 1951), chap. 4.

131. *ST* 1–2.95.4.

132. *ST* 2–2.87.1. See also International Theological Commission, *In Search of a Universal Ethic: A New Look at the Natural Law*, Vatican Website, 2009, n. 33, http://www.vatican.va/roman_curia /congregations/cfaith/cti_documents/rc_con_cfaith_doc_20090520_legge-naturale_en.html:

> The modern rationalist model of natural law is characterized: 1) by the essentialist belief in an immutable and ahistorical human nature, of which reason can perfectly grasp the definition and essential properties; 2) by putting into parentheses the concrete situation of human persons in the history of salvation, marked by sin and grace, which however have a decisive influence on the knowledge and practice of the natural law; 3) by the idea that it is possible for reason to deduce a priori the precepts of the natural law, beginning from the definition of the essence of the human being; 4) by the maximal extension thus given to those deduced precepts, so that natural law appears as a code of pre-made laws regulating almost the entire range of behavior. This tendency to extend the field of the determinations of natural law was at the origin of a grave crisis when, particularly with the rapid development of the human sciences, Western thought became more aware of the historicity of human institutions and of the cultural relativity of many ways of acting that at times had been justified by appeal to the evidence of natural law. The gap between an abstract maximalist theory and the complexity of the empirical data explains in part the disaffection for the very idea of natural law. In order that the notion of natural law can be of use in the elaboration of a universal ethic in a secularized and pluralistic society such as our own, it is therefore necessary to avoid presenting it in the rigid form that it assumed, particularly in modern rationalism.

133. *ST* 1–2.94.6.

difference of dress between men and women as something culturally conventional, at least in part, yet the distinction of dress might serve to uphold a set of
moral aims. Diverse courtship rituals, as related to the institution of marriage,
are another example. (4) As noted above, a given culture may have an imperfect
understanding of the moral law due to a kind of collective moral ignorance. Because Christian theology holds that there are progressive stages of revelation, this
natural phenomenon of cultural ignorance can be taken up into the mystery of
revelation itself.[134] Jesus Christ teaches explicitly (Matt. 19:8) that the permission
of divorce in the Torah was granted for the sake of human moral imperfection
but that he is revealing a higher and more noble teaching, which is implicitly
present in Gen. 1:27 and 2:20–24. The Second Vatican Council teaches that the
New Testament revelation is in many respects more perfect than that of the Old
Testament; the moral teachings of the New Testament perfect the revelation of
the Torah.[135] (5) Finally, Aquinas affirms that a culture can come to believe that
actions that are contrary to human dignity and intrinsically evil are morally licit.
A culture may even go so far as to legalize these practices.[136] In these cases, serious
misunderstanding of the moral law ensues. Because the Torah is inspired by God,
theologians traditionally hold that its moral teachings are free from errors of this
kind. It is problematic to claim that the Torah, due to the time in which it was
written, contains prescriptions that are inherently unethical.

The differences between point (4) and point (5) may seem obscure in some
cases. For example, the Torah simply presupposes a world in which slavery exists
and legislates behavior for the moral treatment of persons who are in servitude
within the archaic economic and social context in which the ancient Israelites
lived. However, the Torah also explicitly promotes the recognition of the human
dignity of each person, including those who are slaves. I am interpreting cases like
this under points (1) through (4) but not under point (5). This reading treats the
mystery of revelation as an authentically divine communication that has occurred
in an authentically human context. Because it is divine, it accords a purification of
human understanding and relates all human behavior to God, including all moral

134. *ST* 1–2.104.3 corp. and ad 1.
135. Second Vatican Council, *Dei Verbum*, para. 15 (Denzinger 2012: para. 4222): "Now the books
of the Old Testament, in accordance with the state of mankind before the time of salvation established
by Christ, reveal to all men the knowledge of God and of man and the ways in which God, just and
merciful, deals with men. These books, though they also contain some things which are incomplete and
temporary, nevertheless show us true divine pedagogy." The document makes reference to Augustine,
De catechizandis rudibus 4.8, for a similar argument.
136. *ST* 1–2.93.3 ad 2, 1–2.94.6, 1–2.95.2.

and legal activity. Because it is human, it is given in a particular time in which human beings were subject to constraints of understanding and moral intuition that were characteristic of their epoch. However, the universal ethical principles elaborated by the Torah do effectively open up human history from within to a new dynamic of progressive moral insight and transformation.[137]

Divisions of the Book of the Covenant

How should the laws in the Book of the Covenant be divided? Below, I adopt divisions that are commonly found in modern commentaries on Exodus and will treat each of these sections briefly:[138]

1. Altar law (20:22–26)
2. Slave law (21:1–11)
3. Capital offenses (21:12–17)
4. Laws regulating bodily injuries (21:18–36)
5. Damage to property (22:1–17)
6. Offenses against covenant holiness (22:18–20)
7. Treatment of dependents (22:21–27)
8. Treatment of superiors (22:28–30)
9. Laws regulating court procedures (23:1–9)
10. Laws regarding the Sabbath and festivals (23:10–19)
11. Epilogue with divine promises (23:20–33)

I should note that this order, while entirely reasonable, groups laws according to the topics with which they deal. Aquinas, meanwhile, offers a very different, though not incompatible, division. His is more analytical and overarching and considers the whole purpose of such juridical laws in keeping with the nature of the human person and human society: "Now in every people a fourfold order is to be found: one, of the people's sovereign to his subjects; a second of the subjects among themselves; a third, of the citizens to foreigners; a fourth, of members of the same household, such as the order of the father to his son; of the wife to her husband; of the master to his servant."[139]

137. See also the helpful comments on this matter by Childs 1974: 496.
138. These divisions are based in great part upon the analysis of Childs 1974: 460, with some alterations.
139. *ST* 1–2.104.4.

Based upon this fourfold distinction, the juridical order consists primarily of civic legislation. It seeks to order human beings to their governmental superiors as licit subjects protected by law. It orders Israelites to the care and respect of one another through just practices regarding the respect of human life, spouses, and property. It orders the polity of Israel toward the stranger who is subject to religious and natural protections. It orders the personages of family to one another in justice—husband to wife, child to parent, and so forth. None of this eclipses the fact that the jurisdictional law is above all a religious law set within the context of the covenant. On the contrary, this law contains clear denotations of religious obligations, and I point out below that ceremonial laws are part of the earliest civic law of Israel. The jurisdictional principles allow all of civic life to be ordered "from within" by the demands of the covenant, even in the most ordinary fabric of daily existence. This is true even of those domains of society where grace and virtue are refused and where the human person must come under judgment and civic punishment. The transgressor is also judged in the light of the mercy and justice of the law of the covenant. Such judgments presuppose the intrinsic dignity of the person, who is made for God and thus cannot evade responsibility for his or her crimes. Nor can the person who is a criminal be treated as something less than a human being by the larger community. Ultimately the underlying spiritual sense of this dimension of the jurisdictional law should confront each of us: every human being is in some way a sinner subject to judgment under the law, in need of a Redeemer.

Altar Law (20:22–26)

20:22–26 This first section is very ancient and certainly predates the Deuteronomical reform. It presupposes multiple altars and the practice of both holocaust and peace offerings. It may refer to places such as Megiddo, Jericho, and Shechem after the time of the settlement, in which case the prohibitions could be intended to exclude Canaanite altars of stone. However, as Brevard Childs notes, "the original law seems to reflect a semi-nomadic form of life and could even predate the settlement."[140] In keeping with this idea, it is significant to note that the text suggests a nonlocative notion of the presence of the Lord (YHWH). God can render himself present to his people wherever he wants to be. Equally significant is the presupposition that Israelites may worship the Lord (YHWH) alone.

Following Aquinas's analytic order of the jurisdictional law, a significant theme can be detected here. The precepts governing the common life of Israelite society

140. Childs 1974: 466.

begin with the consideration of altars. In its moral sense, this denotes that the virtue of religion is the linchpin of civic society. If the people must relate as subject to their superior, the first superior they must relate to is God, who is to be worshiped according to the terms of the covenant.

Slave Law (21:1-11)

21:1-11 Ancient society made use of slaves, and Israelite society was no exception to this widespread economic practice. Persons who were debtors could sell a child or other family member into slavery to pay off the debt (Neh. 5:1-5). A creditor who was not being paid could seize a family member of the debtor either to serve as a slave or to sell off as a slave (2 Kgs. 4:1). This arrangement was temporary and could not last for more than seven years.

In the redacted version of Exodus the context is significant. Laws about slaves are given to people recently liberated from slavery, which means that the law for proper treatment of slaves has to be interpreted theologically within a broader presumption of equality-under-judgment. Just as the Egyptians have come under judgment for their treatment of slaves, so may the Israelites. Just as the Israelites were slaves who have been saved by God, so may the Israelites' slaves be. According to the Torah, all human beings are made in the image of God.

Every seven years a sabbatical is given for slaves, and they are set free. The number reflects a logical parallel to that of the Sabbath rest and the notion of God's contemplative "rest" on the seventh day. This parallelism here is significant. Like the original creation, the slave is part of God's created order and ultimately must be referred back to God. He or she is a person who belongs to God and is therefore not reducible to the designs of the household owner. Here the law is applied to Hebrew slaves, but this teaching plants a seed of universality that Paul will apply to all human persons in Philemon. Every human being is on some fundamental level equal because every human being is a spiritual creature made in God's image, that is, derived from God.

Exodus 21:4 situates the household of the owner and the marriage of slaves in relative importance to one another. Any male slave should be set free after seven years. If he accepted the contract as one already married, his wife departs with him, but if he has married a fellow female slave, she and her children may not be set free. Presumably the law is meant to prevent slaves from making use of marriage as a way to make void the contract with the household owner. This law is intelligible within the context of a society in which contractual servitude is normal, but humanly speaking, it is quite harsh. Likewise, Exod. 21:7-11 seems designed to protect the female slave who has become a concubine. She cannot be discarded by the owner at his discretion but must be cared for and given inheritance rights. In this way she becomes a stipulated member of the family. While these laws seek to mandate and safeguard material care for women within the context of ancient household economies, they are very imperfect, presupposing a high degree of human selfishness and callousness of heart.

An important relativization of the practice of slavery takes place progressively in the Old and New Testaments. Exodus, which is the metanarrative of Israel, is already a tale of mistreated slaves. In the New Testament the dignity of each baptized person as a child of God is employed paradoxically by Paul with regard to slavery. On the one hand, the slave of Philemon, Onesimus, is "no longer a slave, but more than a slave, as a beloved brother, especially to me but how much more to you, both in the flesh and in the Lord" (Phlm. 16). "There is neither Jew nor Greek, there is neither slave nor free, there is neither male nor female; for you are all one in Christ Jesus" (Gal. 3:28). On the other hand, Paul does not hesitate to characterize all Christians as "slaves" of others in the service of charity. "For though I am free from all men, I have made myself a slave to all, that I might win more" (1 Cor. 9:19). The principle is not inconsistent. Just as God has implicitly liberated the slave from subordination to his master by the new law of charity, so he has also "enslaved" the Christian to the service of his neighbor through that same law. This new "slavery" must cast out the old, for it is a service undertaken freely out of faith in the mystery of Christ crucified and resurrected. "Here there cannot be Greek and Jew, circumcised and uncircumcised, barbarian, Scyth'ian, slave, free man, but Christ is all, and in all" (Col. 3:11).

Capital Offenses (21:12–17)

21:12–17 There are no absolute distinctions in the Torah between religious and civil laws or moral and civil laws. Providing for governance over seriously sinful actions is a necessary part of civic life, and this form of governance is provided for in the Torah; fallen humanity still needs general governance from God, even in its sinfulness. There are descending cases of severity in this section that move from the most grave cases to the least grave. Four grades are listed, each of which is punishable by death: homicide, violence toward parents, kidnapping, and the cursing of parents. Cursing is punished severely because this "curse" may entail abandonment of the parents. The passage notes that the perpetrator may seek the right of asylum and in doing so seems to grant a special status to manslaughter as distinct from intentional homicide. "The law of asylum was the first attempt to check the custom of blood vengeance."[141] Presumably this was vengeance enacted by one's clan or extended family, and the law is intended to check vigilantism and unending cycles of retributive killing. For more on asylum, see also Deut. 4:41–43; 19:11–13; and Num. 35.

LAWS REGULATING BODILY INJURIES (21:18–36)

21:18–36 Adequate compensation for injury is the normative principle here, and a kind of commutative justice is presupposed. Equal measure should be returned for the offense given. As such, the important teaching, "life for life, eye for eye, tooth for tooth, hand for hand, foot for foot" (Exod. 21:23–24), is not hypocritical or resentful but based on an egalitarian sense of universal justice. It serves to limit or regulate justice so that it is not excessively vindictive and so that the rich are not able to exploit the poor under the pretext of punishment, taking more than is truly owed to them. It is important to note that this teaching can be transcended in obedience to Christ's counsels, but its justice and reasonableness should not be denied. "You have heard that it was said, 'an eye for an eye and a tooth for a tooth,' but I say to you, Do not resist one who is evil. But if anyone strikes you on the right cheek, turn to him the other also" (Matt. 5:38–39). Augustine comments:

> It is the lesser righteousness . . . not to go beyond measure in revenge, that no one should give back more than he has received: and this is a great step. For it is not easy to find anyone who, when he has received a blow, wishes merely to return the blow; and who, on hearing one word from a man who reviles him, is content to return only one, and that just an equivalent. . . . And this is the beginning of peace: but perfect peace is to have no wish at all for such vengeance.[142]

Furthermore, the Torah distinguishes homicide from unintentional killing (Exod. 21:18–19). The killing of a slave is to be punished because the slave is a subject who has dignity and rights. In the Jewish tradition, many interpret this call for the owner's punishment to imply the death penalty (21:20). In other words, the killing of a slave is not punished less severely than the killing of any other person. This reading of the commandment is permissible, but it is also not obligatory. Exodus 21:22 considers the miscarriage of an unborn child through harm inflicted unintentionally upon the mother. The death of the unborn is not

---

141. Childs 1974: 470.
142. Augustine, *Our Lord's Sermon on the Mount* 1.19.56 (*NPNF*[1] 6:24).

counted as voluntary homicide in this section of the law because the death is unintentional. To claim that this passage allows for licit forms of the taking of human life in the womb, as some rabbinic sources do, is to invoke scripture in order to permit the intentional killing of innocent human life, which constitutes a profound betrayal of the teaching of the Torah and a kind of sacrilege.

The treatment of the ox that gores a human being (21:28–36) is a standard case in Mesopotamian law. Why is the ox killed if it kills a man? Why is it stoned to death? The ox that takes human life has inadvertently transgressed its proper religious context within the universe. Human life is sacred in a higher and different sense than animal life. The point is not to punish the animal (which is not a subject of moral transgression) but to frame the tragedy in religious terms, recalling thereby the dignity of human beings. It would not be adequate to treat the animal as if nothing had happened. In fact, an analogous practice is undertaken even in secular societies by a kind of residual religious instinct. When animals on farms or in zoos kill their keepers, they are typically put to death.

DAMAGE TO PROPERTY (22:1–17)

22:1–17 The laws on the restoration of property that is stolen or damaged presuppose the principle of commutative justice. A person owes to another in equal measure that which he has taken away. As such, restitution is a general principle stemming from the seventh commandment. One has an obligation to restore goods to those who justly deserve them, in proportionate measure to what was taken. At the same time, the laws include a measured penalty as a just form of punishment for malfeasance. These in turn act as dissuasions to those who might be tempted toward acts of theft. The degrees of restitution and punishment differ according to cases, making graver injustices against property more prohibitive to the perpetrator. For example, an ox is of more value than a sheep because it sustains a household's agricultural good. Consequently, the theft of the ox is punished slightly more severely than that of the sheep (22:1), which also serves to dissuade the theft of the ox.

The thief can be killed in the night if there is a legitimate reason for self-defense. However, the thief is protected from blood vengeance in case the one who has been robbed seeks to take his life merely for theft (22:2–3). Possessions are important, but they do not have the same importance as human life, which is sacred.

Seduction of a maiden was traditionally treated in the property section of the laws of this epoch, and the same practice is evident in 22:16–17. This seems morally ambiguous since it suggests that the young woman is the property of her father.

However, against this presupposition, the Torah insists upon the universal rights of the woman in significant ways. It does not matter if she is free or a slave; she is a subject with rights under the law. The seducer is obliged to marry her, which is a recognition that she is not property but must be cared for as a spouse and not abandoned.[143] Fornication is condemned because of the public irresponsibility it implies—that is, the potential harm to the unwed woman and to the child born without familial stability and legal protections.

Gregory the Great points out that these property laws foreshadow by antetype the generosity prescribed by the New Testament. "Some people consider the commandments of the Old Testament stricter than those of the New, but they are deceived by a shortsighted interpretation. In the Old Testament... wrongful taking of property is punished by restitution. In the New Testament the rich man is not censured for having taken away someone else's property but for not having given away his own."[144]

OFFENSES AGAINST COVENANT HOLINESS (22:18–20)

22:18–20 Exodus 22:18 states, "You shall not allow a sorceress to live" (NASB). The ban is clearly indicated here, as in Num. 31:15; Deut. 20:16; and 1 Sam. 27:9–11. This law justly underscores the gravity of human superstition and idolatry. By failing to worship God and by seeking recourse to spiritual forces that are not God, a human being does grave injustice to God and the human community.

Just laws, however, are not always enforceable or enforced. Aquinas notes that laws calling for capital punishment serve in theory to reconcile a penitent to God if the person accepts the punishment as just chastisement and as a preparation to embrace the mercy of God in the life to come. In that case, the death of the body can coexist with the eternal life of the personal soul. However, it is often the case that external chastisement does not lead to internal repentance. In fact, the opposite effect can transpire. In the face of harsh punishments, human hearts can harden more severely in response. External death of the body is not to be feared so much as the spiritual death of the soul.[145] Consequently, laws such as this can rightly serve as symbols or reminders of the gravity of human idolatry, though this does not necessarily mean that they ought to be enforced. Moreover, Aquinas's interpretation is the very teaching of Christ in John 8:1–11, with regard to the woman caught in the

143. See Childs 1974: 476.
144. Gregory the Great, "Homily 40" (Lienhard 2001: 114).
145. Aquinas, *Explanation of the Ten Commandments*, aa. 2 and 8.

act of adultery. She is offered mercy not because she does not deserve stoning but to teach us something about ourselves in light of the justice and mercy of God. The woman represents all of humanity. Each of us deserves to be stoned with her, and so the mercy offered to her is a sign of the mercy offered to each human being by God.[146] Justice and mercy are never opposed. Divine mercy acknowledges the objective demands of justice but acts out of the mysterious depths of divine charity and goodness, so as to take account of the misery and weakness of human persons.

Bestiality (Exod. 22:19) is prohibited in part because of its practice in the context of magic ceremonies or alternative religious rituals. However, the prohibition also has a meaning within the larger context of the sexual ethics of scripture: the act falls outside the reproductive covenant between man and woman. It is specifically contrary to the natural law and is objectively disordered.

TREATMENT OF DEPENDENTS (22:21–27)

22:21–27 The defense of the poor is a profound theme throughout the Old and New Testaments. God is above the rich and poor alike and will judge the former for their treatment of the latter. Due to their history and humble origins, Israelites should recall what it is like to be a stranger or an immigrant. The privilege of the covenant that is given to Israel alone does not rule out the universal inclusivity of ethical responsibility toward those who are outsiders and Gentiles. Widows and orphans are vulnerable without a familial protector or benefactor, and poor families must be assisted by members of the larger society.

TREATMENT OF SUPERIORS (22:28–30)

22:28–30 These verses stress the importance of public duties toward God. "You shall not revile God, nor curse a ruler of your people" (22:28). God should not be reviled in public speech acts, and human superiors should be treated with public respect. One should consecrate the firstborn son to the Lord and offer to him the firstfruits of the harvest and the flock (22:29–30).

Exodus 22:31 contains a curious prohibition on the eating of strangled meat. "You shall be men consecrated to me; therefore you shall not eat any flesh that is torn by beasts in the field." A common interpretation claims that this is meant

---

146. See, for example, Augustine, *City of God* 19.21, where he quotes this verse to underscore the errors of Greco-Roman paganism. It is clear that Augustine thinks the verse should be read as a reminder of the gravity of human sin (precisely because it is so universal) and not as a mandate for action. This seems to be a right interpretation of the original literal sense of Exod. 22:18.

to prevent inhumane forms of nourishment in an economy of scarcity. Human beings who go hungry retain their dignity and must avoid the temptation to descend into dehumanizing practices out of desperation.

Laws Regulating Court Procedures (23:1–9)

23:1–9 This section of the law insists upon uniform fairness of judges and witnesses acting under the law. Exodus 23:3 oddly states, "nor shall you be partial to a poor man in his suit." Here, "the poor" is commonly taken to be a textual error that should read "the great." Judges should not afford special privileges to the wealthy. But as John Chrysostom notes, if it really is the "poor," the text has an even stronger signification.[147] For if one cannot show any morally compromised partiality to the poor in legal matters (even in cases stemming from compelling circumstances of poverty), then making exceptions for the wealthy for any reason whatsoever is unthinkable.

Exodus 23:4–5 pertains to the treatment of the ox and ass of one's enemy. These animals are to be cared for and returned to him when lost or hurt. Here we find an implicit command to love one's enemy, a teaching made explicit by Christ in Matt. 5:44. Love is not an emotional attitude but the desire for the good of the other. This desire takes account of the order of justice but also transcends it. We are to acknowledge in our enemies their human dignity and their capacity to love, even when they perpetuate injustice. Not only should we be just to our enemies, but we should also will their good and desire their conversion and repentance. When love and mercy are absent from the relations that govern human justice, justice often degrades quickly into resentment and vengeance.[148]

Laws Regarding the Sabbath and Festivals (23:10–19)

23:10–19 These verses contain laws about the sabbatical year (in which fields are to lie fallow) and the Sabbath day. A symbolic parallel is at work here that divides up the passage of time. Every seven days and every seven years civic life is to be punctuated by vivid forms of the ceremonial remembrance of God. Martin Buber notes that this idea could readily derive from the original age of the exodus

---

147. John Chrysostom, *Homilies on the Gospel of John* 49, as noted by Lienhard 2001: 117.

148. See Clement of Alexandria, *Stromateis* 2.18.90 (Lienhard 2001: 117–18): "The Lord tells us to relieve and lighten the burden of beasts of burden, even when they belong to our enemies. He is teaching us at a distance not to take pleasure in the misfortunes of others and not to laugh at our enemies. He wants to teach those who have exercised themselves in these disciplines to pray for their enemies."

and from Moses himself.[149] Human time should be punctuated so as to remember the Lord. It should also be noted that an ethical responsibility toward the broader environment of creation is implied by this passage. Human beings are dependent upon animals and agriculture, which are to be left to rest periodically and allowed to act in accord with their own natural principles. Not everything is subject to human dominion, and a kind of cosmic distributive justice is implied: one must grant that which is due to each thing, according to the natures of organisms and the deeper order of the creation given by the Lord.

Exodus 23:14–19a prescribes an annual cycle of religious ceremonies and may represent the oldest cultic calendar in the Torah, preceding the calendars found in Deut. 16; Lev. 23; and Num. 28.[150] The three annual festivals that are prescribed are related to an annual agricultural calendar. The Festival of Unleavened Bread (associated with the exodus, as Passover) takes place in the spring. The Festival of Harvest or Festival of Weeks (Pentecost) marks the first completion of the grain harvest (Lev. 23:15–21; Deut. 16:9–12). The Festival of Ingathering takes place in autumn, the end of the calendar year, marking the first completion of the fruit harvest. This is the Festival of Tabernacles or Booths, which is associated with the time of the wilderness (see Lev. 23:33–36; Deut. 16:13–15).

The final prohibition of this section is well known. "You shall not boil a kid in its mother's milk" (Exod. 23:19). The verse is most likely meant to prohibit the practice of a Canaanite ceremony.

Epilogue with Divine Promises (23:20–33)

23:20–33 The epilogue to the Book of the Covenant terminates with a series of divine promises. The Lord will send his "angel" before the people to instruct and lead them into the place God has prepared for them. If they abide by this messenger, then God will settle them in the land of Israel as their own land, driving out their enemies.

Who is the angel? The angel might represent the presence of God among the people and thus refer symbolically to God as he is known through his prophets.

---

149. Buber 1958: 145:
> The basic feeling [of the Book of the Covenant], to which it is impossible to find [an exact] parallel within the old Oriental cycle, is [the] spirit of Moses' spirit, no matter when the presumably archaic law might have found its actual formulation. And so we are presumably justified in ascribing to the man by whom the Sabbath was inaugurated the initiative for extending the Sabbatical manner of thought into the cycle of the years; in which, as in the days, six units of work and dependence have to be followed by one unit of liberation.

150. Childs 1974: 483.

It may refer, however, to a mediating figure and angelic guide. This seems most likely since God speaks of this angel again in Exod. 33:2, where God claims the angel will lead the people but intimates that he will not dwell with them himself, due to their sinfulness. However, Moses and the people do successfully implore God to have mercy, and God remains with them (33:13–14).

How then is the promise in this prophecy true? A traditional answer is to claim that it denotes Moses (as the giver of the law) or Joshua (who will lead the people into the land that has been promised). Christian commentary tends to see here a literal signification for Joshua, who leads the people into the land, but also a typological signification of Jesus, the new Joshua, who is the ultimate mediator of salvation. As Augustine writes:

> Let the Jew, not to speak of the Manichean, say what other angel he can find in Scripture to whom these words apply, but this leader who was to bring the people into the land of promise. Then let him inquire who it was that succeeded Moses, and brought in the people. He will find that it was Jesus [i.e., Joshua] . . . the leader who brings His people into the inheritance of eternal life, according to the New Testament, of which the Old was a figure. No event or action could have a more distinctly prophetical character than this, where the very name is a prediction.[151]

Exodus 23:29–30 suggests that God will drive out the enemies of the Israelites (the Hivites, Canaanites, and Hittites) only gradually and not immediately during the initial conquest. The extent of the land promised in 23:31 is cast in ideal terms: "I will set your bounds from the Red Sea to the sea of the Philistines, and from the wilderness to the Euphrates," an ideal that may be associated with the epoch of Solomon (see 1 Kgs. 4:21; 9:26). However, it is not an ideal that was ever historically achieved, though one may interpret this notion literally, in a spiritual way. Over and above every temporal realization of sovereign power, Israel remains an ever-greater ideal to which no historical instantiation has ever attained. There is a messianic or eschatological dynamism built into the very fabric of the Torah promises. Even in the land of Israel, the people will remain in permanent pilgrimage or in spiritual exodus toward a more perfect realization of the observance of the Torah.

What should a Christian make of the promise of the land to Israel after the coming of Christ? Christian understandings are multiple. Some have said that the Jews remain an elect people, as Paul stipulates in Rom. 9–11, though they

151. Augustine, *Reply to Faustus the Manichean* 16.19 (*NPNF*[1] 4:226).

have lost all rights or privileges to the land of Israel and live in a kind of diaspora (real or spiritual) until the time of the definitive coming of Christ in glory. Others have said that the promises regarding the land have not been abrogated and are retained until the end of the world. A third position, which I favor, is that the Jewish people remain elect by God and so have a divine right, as well as a human right, to a collective life together in relative safety and political integrity. It is fitting, therefore, for both theological and humanitarian reasons, that they live together on the land historically promised to their forefathers by God. This does not mean that they retain a strict, divine right to the land, but it does mean that Christians have theological as well as humanitarian reasons to support the existence of the modern state of Israel, even after the time of the coming of Christ. Evidently, this does not mean that any unjust actions of the modern Israeli government should escape warranted criticism or moral scrutiny. Modern Israelis are bound by natural-law principles of universal justice with respect not only to the non-Jews living among them but also in their relations with other nations.

Nevertheless, the resurrection of Christ represents the final culmination of this promise made in the book of Exodus. The promised land of salvation is ultimately eschatological, inaugurated in the glorified physical body of Christ risen from the dead. The eschatological mystery of Israel will coincide ultimately with the eschatological mystery of the Church, because all human beings will be subject in time to the mystery of Christ crucified and resurrected. Israel's pilgrimage down through time, like that of the Church, culminates in eventual conformity to the mystery of the Cross and resurrection, and in the life of the world to come.

Ratification of the Covenant by Sacrifice (Exod. 24:1–11)

24:1–11 "And Moses took the blood and threw it upon the people, and said, 'Behold the blood of the covenant which the LORD has made with you in accordance with these words'" (24:8).

The textual unity of Exod. 24 is infamously puzzling due to the fragmentary and edited character of the chapter, which has been a source of discussion even among classical and medieval commentators. Exodus 24:1–2 is clearly connected to 24:9–11 and can be read sequentially. However, 24:3–8 has been interjected between them and suggests a separate strand of tradition. These verses may themselves be composed of diverse sources, since 24:3 and 7 seem artificially repetitive. Exodus 24:12–18 is yet another unit of text that seems to contain diverse traditions (for example, 24:14–15 reiterates things said in 24:13). In saying this, I do not mean to imply that there is nothing ancient in Exod. 24 or that the traditions presented there could not originate from the earliest strata of Israelite history. On the contrary, the latter is entirely possible.

Despite all of this textual complexity, the chapter is quite unified in theme, due to the theological vision of the final redactors. The first half recounts the ratification of the covenant between the Lord and his people, after which Moses and the elders of Israel go up and "see" God on Mount Sinai (24:1–11). The second half (24:12–18) recounts Moses entering into the glory of God for forty days and forty nights as a preparation for the revelation of the tabernacle, which will take place in the subsequent chapters. Clearly, the text has been edited by the sacred author—or inspired final editor—to communicate a number of profound theological ideas.

First, we see in 24:1–2 that having received the commandments and the Book of the Covenant, Moses is called again up to Mount Sinai. (Did he ever come down?) He is to bring with him "Aaron, Nadab, and Abi´hu, and seventy of the elders of Israel" who worship God on the mountain from afar. The seventy prostrate themselves before God not unlike vassals before a suzerain or overlord in an ancient oriental court. God, the Lord, is the true King of Israel. The covenant binds this people not to a human leader but to the Almighty, who made heaven and earth, as his particular people.

This order of events clearly serves to designate a hierarchy: Moses the prophet is intimately associated with God; the Israelite priesthood and government (represented by Aaron and the elders) are subject to the revelation given by Moses; and the people who remain at the base of the mountain are subject to God through both Moses and the priests and elders. In the descending order of this revelation, God multiplies the instruments of his teaching, including a greater number of ministers the more he wishes his law to be widely known. Why does God work through fallible human beings of this kind? At least two reasons can readily be identified. First, this practice is in keeping with the social nature of the human being, who is generally taught and governed in and through common life in society with others. God sanctifies Israel in a way that is not alien to human nature, acting in and through Israel's social life by the instrumental agency of her priests and leaders. Second, God does this as a mercy to the ministers themselves. By incorporating the meager human efforts of fallible human beings into his own service, God manifests more clearly his mercy and goodness toward those who serve him and those who receive their ministrations.

While the Torah clearly affirms these principles in symbolic fashion, the teaching is also qualified. Even as we read about Aaron and his sons Nadab and Abihu in Exod. 24, we know that Aaron will be responsible for the construction of the golden calf in Exod. 32 and that Nadab and Abihu will be disobedient to God and to the teachings of Moses in Lev. 10:1–2. The moral sense of scripture here is clear. The priesthood is something instituted by God for the good of the people of God; it is not an arbitrary or dispensable institution. And yet it can be betrayed in very serious ways by its occupants, to their own destruction and to the harm of the people of God. Why does God permit some priests to fail so utterly in their service of God? Perhaps it is so that we remember that God alone is God. Although God is merciful to human beings by employing them to communicate his grace and teaching to others, God has no need of them, and they, even as priests, remain utterly relative to God both in their being and in the gifts of holiness they receive from him.

The heart of Exod. 24 is found in 24:3–8, where we are confronted with the ceremony that ratifies the covenant. As presented here, it is the foundational sacrifice of the covenant.[152] Exod. 24:3 tells us that Moses repeats to the people all the "words and ordinances" of the Lord—in other words, the Decalogue and the Book of the Covenant. The moral and juridical laws together are being presented as the "matter" of the covenant of grace that is being formed with God. The consent of the people is universal: "All the people answered with one voice, and said, 'All the words which the LORD has spoken we will do.'" This verse echoes the similar acclamation of the people in Exod. 19:8, where the people consented to the revelation that God would make them "a kingdom of priests." Here, then, we see *how* they are to be a people of "priests" who teach the nations and intercede for the universal good of humanity; they are to do so by teaching and observing the law of God.

From a Christian point of view, this consent of the people must be seen as a profound and mysterious work of divine grace in human history. By a special initiative of God working inwardly in the hearts and minds of the ancient Hebrews, they consented in faith, hope, and charity to live in communion with God, in and through the observance of the sacred law. At the same time, there is an irony in their response, for they will not find it so easy to accomplish what

152. Modern commentators sometimes speculate that this biblically unique ceremony is the portrayal of an ancient "covenant renewal" ritual from the epoch of early Israel during the wilderness period or after the settlement. See the discussion in Ernest W. Nicholson, *God and His People: Covenant Theology in the Old Testament* (Oxford: Clarendon, 1986), 164–78.

they have promised. The promise they make will have to be fulfilled by another, who is himself the Lord.

At the heart of this communion is sacrifice. Moses officiates at the sacrifice that ratifies the covenant, along with young men chosen from the people (according to the logic of the Torah, the priesthood is not yet instituted, even if it is symbolically prefigured by the presence of Aaron). Twelve altars are erected, symbolizing the twelve tribes of Israel.[153] Moses takes half of the blood and puts it in basins, and half of the blood he throws against the altar (24:6). Why is blood such a powerful symbol of sacrifice? Because it naturally represents the gift of life and the real possibility of life or death. The symbolism of the blood here seems to be twofold. One element is representative and signifies atonement; the animals stand for the people and are offered symbolically to God in the people's place as a sign of their moral dedication to God. The second element is found in 24:8 where Moses sprinkles "the blood of the covenant" on the people as the sign of their shared life of communion in covenant with God. They are the elect people or "bloodline" of God in the world.

One might ask how animals that are sacrificed physically symbolize the inward moral offering of human beings. Is this a morally reasonable idea? Sacrifice, Aquinas teaches, has both internal and external components.[154] The internal act of sacrifice is grounded in the virtue of religion, itself consisting of prayer and devotion. Prayer is the act of the mind or intellect, lifted up to God through meditation upon the mystery of God who has revealed himself.[155] Devotion is the act of the will or of the spiritual heart of man, which is prompted by charity to submit to God.[156] Devotion recognizes God in his transcendence, goodness, and beauty, placing the human being in an inward relationship of justice toward his or her Creator. This is why Aquinas rightly classes the virtue of religion as a potential part of the virtue of justice.[157]

Sacrifice first occurs externally through the body, which pertains to the very substance of the human person. The person offers himself to God inwardly in mind and heart by prayer and devotion, but because the person offers his whole

---

153. If we take this numerical symbolism as pertaining to the early history of Israel, it seems to imply the reality of a tribal league present in the early era of Israel, a hypothesis that has been subject to much discussion in modern literature. See the historically influential arguments of Martin Noth, *Das System der zwölf Stämme Israels* (Stuttgart: Kohlhammer, 1930), and the very balanced discussion of John Bright, *A History of Israel*, 4th ed. (Louisville: Westminster John Knox, 2000), 162–73.

154. *ST* 2–2.81–88.

155. *ST* 2–2.83.1.

156. *ST* 2–2.82.1–2.

157. *ST* 2–2.81.1 and 5.

self, he also offers the human body to God in acts of adoration, prostration, and so forth. This act of self-offering is concretized in a liturgical, corporate way by common worship, a natural religious activity of human society. It is also concretized in the offering of external realities by way of sacrifices, tithes, and the like. In sacrifice the human community recognizes in a public and corporate way that all that it possesses comes from God the Creator: our human life and bodies, physical possessions, all living things, and the entire physical creation. Because animals are physical creatures, living beings, and possessions of human beings central to the well-being of the whole community, the offering of their lives to God is a symbol of this utter dependence. The sacrifice and consumption of them in a meal of thanksgiving are not meant to debase or devalue animal life. On the contrary, this usage amounts to a theocentric (rather than anthropocentric) use of animals. Far from being disrespectful of the body or animal life, the sacrificial offerings of animals in the Torah serve as a profound sign of the sacred character of the physical creation. They mark the fact that life is a particularly great gift from God, which is being offered in turn back to God through inward devotion and external gestures of the sacred liturgy.

In its typological sense, this passage has a very profound christological orientation. In this passage the original covenant is ratified by an authentic sacrifice of Israel, offered to God in spiritual devotion. At the same time, the prophetic tradition of Israel is replete with a series of revelations concerning the deep imperfection of all human self-offering and with multiple warnings concerning the all-too-external or mechanistic character of Israelite religious actions and devotions ("For I desire steadfast love and not sacrifice, / the knowledge of God, rather than burnt offerings" [Hos. 6:6]). All too often the actions of Israel's priests and people are divorced from the "second table" of the law, which regards genuine justice and mercy toward one's neighbor (for a pivotal example, see Mal. 1:6–12).

Therefore, the revelation of Israel's moral obligation to sacrifice that stands at the heart of the covenant brings with it a corresponding revelation of the fallen and wounded character of human religious actions, even under grace and in the midst of the life of the covenant. Typologically, this moral syndrome calls forth the perfect sacrifice of Christ. The night before he died, Jesus made explicit reference to this sacrifice (Exod. 24:8) in his institution of the Eucharist. "Now as they were eating, Jesus took bread, and blessed, and broke it, and gave it to the disciples and said, 'Take, eat; this is my body.' And he took a cup, and when he had given thanks he gave it to them, saying, 'Drink of it, all of you; *for this is my blood of the covenant*, which is poured out for many for the forgiveness of sins'" (Matt. 26:26–28, emphasis added).

I mentioned above that the sacrifice of Exod. 24:3–8 contains two elements: the substitution of the sacrificed victim, which represents the offering of the people, and the blood sprinkled upon the people as a sign of communion with God. In the Last Supper, Jesus purposefully reappropriates these two elements of the foundational sacrifice. Instead of the twelve altars for the twelve tribes, there are twelve apostles. Rather than an animal representing the people, the sacrifice is the Lord himself, offering his human life and body on behalf of the people ("His blood be on us and on our children!" [Matt. 27:25]). The inward sacrifice is no longer the broken humanity of Israel (wounded by sin throughout its history) but the perfect humanity of Jesus, the Christ of Israel, who is without sin. The blood of communion is no longer the symbolic blood of animals (a mere sign of grace) but the blood of Christ crucified—a true cause of grace, given to the apostles to eat and drink in the mystery of the Holy Eucharist.

In Jesus, then, the two elements of the foundational covenant sacrifice attain their own inner apex. Atonement-substitution and covenantal unity are both recapitulated in the blood of Christ. He atones for our sins by offering a sacrifice of love and obedience on our behalf, making satisfaction for human sin.[158] Instead of becoming subject to the divine wrath on our behalf (which makes little sense, due to his innocence), he offers the love of charity to God where we have failed to love.[159] The blood of Christ shed in sacrifice for all peoples is in turn the ground of covenantal unity. In the passion of Christ, the covenant of God with Israel is opened to the Gentiles. Admittance to the covenant is no longer achieved through genealogical lineage and circumcision but through baptism and communion in the Eucharist. This new sacramental economy is intrinsically open to all in a way that the economy of the Old Law was not. However, the first covenantal sacrifice of Exod. 24 should be seen in light of Christ as foundational and instituted by God in view of the universal mission of Christ and the Church. Israel and the Church do not share two distinct covenants but one covenant of grace, present in two distinct stages of history. Israel and the Church together are the one people of God, united in the person of Christ. But this unity exists in a complex way. The Church recognizes it "openly" in the light of faith, but Israel's sight is still covered by a veil (2 Cor. 3:13–14). And yet the two are

158. *ST* 3.48.2.
159. See the argument regarding this topic in Thomas Joseph White, "Jesus' Cry on the Cross and His Beatific Vision," *Nova et Vetera* 5 (2007): 555–82.

bound together in this complex relation to Christ until the end of history and the advent of the eschaton.

A communion meal follows the sacrifice. "Then Moses and Aaron, Nadab, and Abi´hu, and seventy of the elders of Israel went up, and they saw the God of Israel; and there was under his feet as it were a pavement of sapphire stone, like the very heaven for clearness. And he did not lay his hand on the chief men of the people of Israel; they beheld God, and ate and drank" (Exod. 24:9–11). What does it mean to say that the elders of Israel saw the God of Israel? How should this be interpreted? Is the vision intellectual, or is it sensible? If it is intellectual, is the vision immediate (a momentary experience of the beatific vision), or is it indirect (a kind of prophetic insight)? If the vision is sensible, does the text mean to indicate a physical presence of God? Is the presentation of God here anthropomorphic? How should one interpret the idea that the elders eat with God? Does the text mean to signify that the Lord literally shared a meal with the people?

In answer to these questions I should first say that the vision in Exod. 24 seems to be both spiritual and physical. It is holistic, affecting both soul and body, but this holism is clearly mystical and spiritual in nature. It cannot be reduced to a physical experience. The same can be seen in Isa. 6:1 and Ezek. 1:26, where the Hebrew prophets see God seated upon a throne. The sapphire stone in Exod. 24:10 and Ezek. 1:26 clearly represents the vault of heaven: the "ceiling" of creation and the beginning of the uncreated. God is depicted as the king of Israel because God governs all created reality. God appears like a man to denote by a physical sign that God is personal, and God appears in a human form because the human being who is personal is made in the image of God, principally by powers of intellectual knowledge and deliberative free will.

Maimonides insists that passages like these be read as having a figurative sense— that is, indicating a specifically intellectual form of vision.

> Every mention of seeing, when referring to God, may he be exalted, has this figurative meaning—as when Scripture says, "I saw the Lord" (1 Kgs. 22:19); "And the Lord was seen by him" (Gen. 18:1); "And God saw that it was good" (Gen. 1:10); "I beseech thee, let me see thy glory" (Exod. 33:18); "and they saw the God of Israel" (Exod. 24:10). All this refers to intellectual apprehension and in no way to the eye's seeing.[160]

Aquinas makes a similar argument:

160. Maimonides, *Guide of the Perplexed* 1.4 (Pines 1963).

It is impossible for God to be seen by the sense of sight, or by any other sense, or faculty of the sensitive power. For every such kind of power is the act of a corporeal organ. . . . Now act is proportional to the nature which possesses it. Hence no power of that kind can go beyond corporeal things. For God is incorporeal. Hence He cannot be seen by the sense or the imagination, but only by the intellect.[161]

Pursuing this line of inquiry, one may ask, is the intellectual "sight" direct or indirect? Does the symbolism of Exodus connote the beatific vision (the immediate vision of God) or a mediated, infused vision received in faith, that is to say, a vision of a "merely" prophetic kind by which God is perceived through his spiritual effects? This may seem like an anachronistic question that imposes later medieval and modern Christian categories upon a very ancient Israelite text. To be sure, the form in which the question is expressed is not employed by the Torah. However, the question is asked by the text of scripture fairly directly. Augustine recognized this in his *Literal Commentary on Genesis* 12.27, where he notes that in Exod. 24:10 the elders "see God," and God does not take their lives (24:11). That is to say, they see God and live. And yet in 33:18 Moses later says, "Show me thy glory," a request that might suggest that Moses has not yet truly seen God directly and that he is still seeking to do so. God responds, "You cannot see my face; for man shall not see me and live" (33:20), but then allows Moses to see "his back" (33:23), which may suggest a brief, immediate vision of God's essence.

Modern interpreters may wish to argue that the passage in Exod. 24 is from a different author or tradition than that found in Exod. 33 (for example, the Yahwist source as distinct from the Priestly source). Such may well be the case. However, the final editor of the text has clearly wished to maintain the tension of two distinct vantage points, placing them in chronological succession and maintaining a theological tension. Moses and the elders in Exod. 24 do see God and live; yet in Exod. 33 we are told that no man can see God's face and live, and yet Moses sees God "pass by" in his glory, if fleetingly. Furthermore, we are told, "Thus the LORD used to speak to Moses face to face, as a man speaks to his friend" (33:11). This clear diversity of affirmations is almost playful and evasive. Although written in an ancient form, it invites theological speculation of the kind I am undertaking here. The *form* of expression is symbolic. The *content* of the reflection is deeply theological and mystical.

In light of these reflections, Aquinas follows Augustine in positing that the revelation made to the Israelites in Exod. 24 is indirect—that God is known

161. *ST* 1.12.3.

spiritually in his glory by means of infused prophetic insight but that this insight occurs in the darkness of faith and not in the immediacy of vision.

> As Augustine says (*Literal Comm. on Genesis* 12.27), it is stated in *Exodus* that "the Lord spoke to Moses face to face"; and shortly afterwards we read, "Show me thy glory. Therefore he perceived what he saw and he desired what he saw not." Hence he did not see the very essence of God; and consequently he was not taught by Him immediately. Accordingly when Scripture states that "He spoke to him face to face," this is to be understood as expressing the opinion of the people, who thought that Moses was speaking with God mouth to mouth, when God spoke and appeared to him, by means of a subordinate creature, i.e., an angel and a cloud. Again we may say that this vision "face to face" means some kind of sublime and familiar contemplation [*eminens contemplatio et familiaris*], inferior to the vision of the divine essence.[162]

What should be said then about the vision of God's back in Exod. 33? Let us presuppose, rightfully, that there is a theological unity to the whole of the Torah and to the entirety of the book of Exodus. In this case, the text should be interpreted in the final edited form as denoting an ultimate request from Moses. He wishes to have a yet-more-perfect vision of God than has been granted in previous visions. Here, Aquinas speculates, the vision of the essence of God is direct but is also transient.[163] The symbol of the "back" of God signifies a vision of God's very essence (the beatific vision) but not a vision of stable, perennial possession. This is an experience analogous to prophetic inspiration.[164] It is given to Moses in particular, Aquinas states, so as to strengthen him in view of the universal mission he bears in responsibility to all the Jewish people, and through them, to all humanity.[165] His especially elevated knowledge of God, and intimacy with God, prepare him to initiate a new religious movement that will henceforth definitively alter human history.

All this being said, one may still ask whether the elders' vision of the Lord described on Mount Sinai is also meant to connote a sensible vision. If so, is the image of God that is communicated there not patently anthropomorphic? This can be answered in two ways. First, the supposed anthropomorphism of the account should be denied. The text of Exodus is latent with many subtle forms

162. *ST* 1–2.98.3 ad 2.
163. On Exod. 33:11 and Deut. 34:10–11, see *ST* 2–2.175.3 corp., 2–2.174.4 corp. and ad 1.
164. *ST* 2–2.175.3 ad 2 and 3.
165. *ST* 2–2.175.3 corp.

of symbolism, and the use of such symbols is clearly at play here. God's spiritual presence and hiddenness are frequently denoted by physical symbols of cloud or darkness, while his personal address can be denoted by anthropomorphic signs. In their literal sense such signs are symbolic and not intended to be taken in a simplistically material way. As such they both reveal and conceal the mystery of God and invite reflection and (one might even say) scholastic or rabbinic theological debate about the meaning of the Torah.

Second, however, one might consider the sensible character of the vision as it pertains to our human nature; here there is a greater reason to consider the possibility of a physical or sensible experience. Human beings are animals that normally learn intellectually in and through the senses. It is fitting, then, that they might perceive something of God in and through a sensible theophany. In addition, a sensible experience of God need not work to the exclusion of an intellectual illumination of human understanding. On the contrary, the two might happen together in keeping with our human constitution as spiritual animals.

If one takes the vision as connoting something sensible as well as spiritual, then how should this theophany be understood? The divine condescension of a sensate vision has two meanings in this text. First, it is meant to teach Israel that human beings are made in the image and likeness of God. God, one might say, is the most human of all. This is not due to an eternal, preexistent humanity in God (since God in his divine essence has no body) but because God is the source of all our humanity. He is the exemplary and efficient cause of all that we are. Here the text of scripture is not composed without irony. As Exod. 20:4 states, God cannot be depicted under any images, unlike the false gods of the Gentile peoples. The theophany has to be understood paradoxically against the background of that prohibition. God is too transcendent to be known corporeally. Yet God's transcendence is mysteriously breached by intimacy in the divine revelation. The people who alone do not accept idolatry are the same people who alone are truly given to know God. In revealing his eternal "humanity" God reveals his eternal kindness and love for Israel.

In its second sense, the sensible character of the theophany is clearly meant to prefigure the incarnation. Christ in his Last Supper purposefully sought to recapitulate the events and imagery of Exod. 24. He instituted the sacrifice of the covenant (Matt. 26:28; Mark 14:24; 1 Cor. 11:25), and he ate with the twelve, the founding elders of the new and restored Israel. This is the fulfillment of the ancient image from Mount Sinai: God in the flesh, eating with the Church. The

Church receives communion with God from God's own hand, taking Christ's body and blood as nourishment so that it can live in the grace of his covenant.

Divine Glory (Exod. 24:12–18)

24:12–18 "The glory of the LORD settled on Mount Sinai, and the cloud covered it six days; and on the seventh day he called to Moses out of the midst of the cloud. Now the appearance of the glory of the LORD was like a devouring fire on the top of the mountain in the sight of the people of Israel. And Moses entered the cloud, and went up on the mountain. And Moses was on the mountain forty days and forty nights" (24:16–18).

In 24:12 Moses makes yet another ascent up Mount Sinai, this time with Joshua. It is reasonable to infer that Joshua remains present with Moses for the forty days that he is on the mountain, while Aaron is below (see 24:14; 32:17). Consequently, Joshua does not participate in the golden calf incident (32:1–6). Is it for this fitting reason that he is designated to lead the people into the land of Israel? In any event, Joshua typologically prefigures Jesus, who is with Moses in the cloud of divine glory on Mount Sinai. He is a shadowy figure, discreetly present in the background and not unlike the fourth man who is present in the fire with Shadrach, Meshach, and Abednego in Dan. 3:13–30. Why is Christ hidden among the Old Testament prophets? All the prophets of God who approach God are somehow imperfect manifestations of Christ; they are prefigurations of him, but at the same time he remains at a significant remove from them, due to his unique, transcendent origin. Consequently, in the Old Testament the God-man remains hidden among the prophets in the darkness of God's glory. The prophets are human beings inspired to approach God, but Christ is God's advent in human flesh, God's own "approach" to humanity, hidden among us as an ordinary human being.

Moses goes up the mountain to receive the revelation of the ark and the tabernacle, which takes place in Exod. 25–31. What does Moses see in the vision he is given over the next forty days and nights? The literal sense of the text is unambiguous. Moses is given a vision of *how* God will dwell with Israel and therefore with all humanity. God will dwell with them in the ark and the tabernacle, which will also contain the law that Moses writes down for the people (24:12). The final vision on Sinai is of ultimate importance: it is about the future of God dwelling with Israel through the covenantal law and the liturgical cult.

At the same time, the sacred author seems to be aware of the vision's typological sense as well. It does not end with the ark and the tabernacle alone; it looks forward to the temple, where God will dwell with humanity in Israel. When read in light of the New Testament revelation, this vision also looks forward to the incarnation. "In the beginning was the Word . . . and the Word became flesh, and tabernacled among us" (John 1:1, 14, my translation). As Gregory of Nyssa comments:

> Taking a hint from what has been said by Paul, who partially uncovered the mystery of these things, we say that Moses was earlier instructed by a type in the mystery of the tabernacle which encompasses the universe. This tabernacle would be *Christ who is the power and the wisdom of God* [1 Cor. 1:24], who in his own nature was not made with hands, yet capable of being made when it became necessary for this tabernacle to be erected among us. Thus, the same tabernacle is in a way both unfashioned and fashioned, uncreated in preexistence but created in having received this material composition.[166]

How realistic is this interpretation of the prophetic knowledge of Moses? Aquinas thinks that many Old Testament prophets received explicit prophetic insight into the mystery of the incarnation hundreds of years prior to that event.[167] This was an intuitive form of knowledge, made possible by infused *species*, or conceptual forms (as I mentioned earlier), similar to angelic knowledge.[168] Such knowledge could coexist with images and human language drawn from the surrounding cultures. It could be more or less vague or numinous (or more or less clear). Yet the prophets knew that more was coming. Aquinas believes that the high prophets, in particular, were given this numinous knowledge explicitly (Moses, David, Isaiah, etc.). He denotes them as *maiores*, distinguishing them from the "ordinary" believers of the Old Testament, the *minores*. The *minores* partake implicitly of the knowledge of the *maiores* by adhering to their teachings. In this way they are prepared collectively, in a numinous and mysterious way, for ulterior revelation.

One should keep in mind that Jesus himself teaches something like this in the New Testament. In John 8:56 he tells his interlocutors that "Abraham rejoiced that he was to see my day; he saw it and was glad," and says in 5:46, "If you believed Moses, you would believe me, for he wrote of me." In Mark 12:36–37 he quotes a

---

166. Gregory of Nyssa, *Life of Moses* 2.174 (Malherbe and Ferguson 1978).
167. *ST* 2–2.2.7.
168. *ST* 2–2.173.2.

Davidic psalm as a prophecy of his lordship and kingship. Peter, meanwhile, speaks in Acts 3:22 of Deut. 18:15 as a prophecy of the Torah that alludes numinously to Christ. These verses and others suggest a theology of the explicit revelation of the incarnation that was given even in the Old Testament period.

Here, however, modern historians and biblical scholars can pose a series of reasonable objections. First, is this theology not intrinsically allied to a premodern theory of biblical sources, which considers the Psalter as the unique work of David or Moses as the unique author of the Torah? Once one admits to sources that are employed to compose biblical books, with their own complex internal history and redaction, is one not obliged to abandon the classical idea of prophecies of this kind? Should the attempt be made instead to understand the prophetic books primarily and even exclusively through the study of their historical contexts and linguistic and conceptual resources, as products of their times? If there was genuine knowledge of the incarnation at an early stage, why would it be kept secret, and if it could be, could one not also ascribe to the prophets of that epoch any number of secret and fantastic theories that are not in fact biblical in origin?

These are intellectually responsible objections. And yet they are not determinative theologically, nor can they be. Yes, it is true that modern reflections on the origins, sources, and redaction of the biblical texts are quite complex and that some of these texts cannot reasonably be ascribed to their traditionally assigned authors, either in part or in whole. (And yes, the whole enterprise of hypothetical reasoning about ancient history in this regard is speculative and precarious, and yet it also cannot be evaded for supposedly "pious" reasons.) However, it is fitting to ascribe to the ancient prophets a hierarchically higher degree of insight than those around them, and the New Testament unambiguously ascribes to them some degree of explicit awareness of the mystery of Christ. Furthermore, the Bible is in fact full of concepts and symbols that are meant simultaneously to reveal and to conceal and that are often only understood after the fact. Pedagogical reasons exist for this form of communication, as Dionysius notes.[169] It invites the reverent and fervent to deeper study, and it prohibits the spiritually crass or intellectually callous from reacting with irreverence in the face of the mysteries of God. A complex history of textual redaction of the traditional prophetic texts can be acknowledged while also affirming the fitting belief that both the foundational prophets (Abraham, Moses, Isaiah, etc.) and the final redactors might have had some awareness (however dim, however radiant) of the Son of Man.

169. Dionysius, *On the Celestial Hierarchy* 1.2.

In concluding this consideration of the Book of the Covenant, I would like to consider the mystery of the "glory" [*kabod*] of the Lord. The glory of God rests upon Mount Sinai in Exod. 24:16; Moses remains outside the theophany for six days and is called into it on the seventh. While the presence of God is described as a "devouring fire" in the face of the people (24:17), this "glory" is a kind of darkness, a dark cloud in which Moses spends forty days and nights. In this symbolism, the mystery of the transcendence of God is reaffirmed (1) even after the immanence of seeing God/communion with God, and (2) in view of the immanence of God's dwelling with Israel in the tabernacle. This is how God works with the individual soul and with the whole people of God, through various epochs and cycles of time. There are periods of purification by darkness and times of elevation by light.

As many commentators point out, this depiction of the manifestation of the glory of God bears likenesses to other moments in Old Testament scripture (see 1 Kgs. 8:11, which is a very similar passage about the temple as a new Sinai; Isa. 6:3, which portrays Isaiah as a kind of new Moses, seeing God on his throne; and Ezek. 1:28; 10:19b; 43:2). In each case, the symbolism of the theophany signifies, among other things, that the immanent presence of God with Israel, while utterly real, is also incomprehensible. The glory of God is like an iconostasis behind which God is enthroned in divine mystery.

But what is divine glory? How should we to understand the "glory of the Lord"? At the heart of God's glory is God's beauty, and beauty in creatures consists of three things. First is the *integrity* of a given form (be it a natural form, like a tree, or an artificial form, like a painting). There is an integrity to the whole from which the beauty shines through, as in the case of a tree that is integral in its wholeness, as distinct from a tree that has been mutilated by a storm or a human agent. Second, there is *proportion* to the form. The diversity of elements in a given form (such as a painting) has a certain proportion, be it a proportion of quantities arranged in beauty or a proportion of qualities (like colors or symbols). Third, there is the *splendor* of the form. A given form shines forth with perceptible glory when it has a holistic integrity and internal proportion of elements. A ballet, for example, can manifest a unity of bodily movements and proportion of gestures that, when set to music, shines forth with beauty, revealing the spiritual nobility and sensible finesse of the human body.

Taking these three elements together (integrity, proportion, and splendor), it can be said that beauty is understood most essentially as the splendor of the truth. The truth of a given form shines forth in its beauty. Put another way, beauty is the herald of truth, touching the intellect and calling it to recognize the goodness of the truth.

Now if this definition is transposed analogically to speak of the beauty and splendor of the divine mystery of God, then it must be carefully qualified. The integrity of God is not holistic, if by this one means that God is composed of material or spiritual parts and that God's being consists of a complexity of elements. Nor can it be said that there is a proportion among the various elements within God, such as the proportion of diverse colors in a painting or diverse branches that are all part of one beautiful tree. God is simple, and God's essence, which is incomprehensible to us, is not composed of any complexity, whether spiritual or material.

All this being said, God *is* the author of all created forms, and all that exists, insofar as it exists, possesses a certain beauty or intellectual goodness. There is integrity, proportion, and splendor in all things, insofar as they exist. Consequently, in analogical terms the author of all things that exist is himself beautiful. God's incomprehensible essence as God is simple and incomposite, but it is also perfect and infinite. Therefore the essence of God, as pure actuality without blemish or limitation of any kind, is infinite in its integrality. There is no proportion of elements in God, but God's perfection contains supereminently within itself the creative power of making any and all proportionate perfections that are found in creatures. The splendor of God's perfect beauty, then, is infinite in nature and utterly transcends the comprehension of the human intellect, even as the simplicity and pure actuality of God in his truth and goodness utterly transcend our immediate understanding. And yet God's beauty is perceived in God's effects, both of nature and grace. The splendor or glory of God revealed on Mount Sinai represents through God's effects (be they physical or spiritual) the unseen cause and hidden source of beauty: the uncreated essence of God. This is the deepest and most profound beauty at the heart of all things, hidden within all things, unknown to all things. It is the beauty and splendor of God himself that is eternal.

Is the notion of glory merely equivalent to the notion of divine beauty? Perhaps one should say that the notion of "glory" implies the notion of "beauty," with an addition: the accompanying properties of power and goodness. The glory of the Lord manifests the beauty of God, but it does so in and through God's power, and that power is placed at the service of God's goodness or mercy. This explains why the various epiphanies of the glory of God in the Old Testament (as in Exod. 24) produce sacred fear in their recipients. The epiphany of God in his glory entails a manifestation of God's transcendent power, which produces a sense of awe at the incomprehensible grandeur of God. Meanwhile, the epiphany of God is also oriented toward God's compassionate mercy, springing from the mysterious, alien depths of divine goodness. God teaches Israel a sense of awe and reverence not in order to inspire alienation in them but to prepare them to receive rightly his mercy and the favor of his election.

My treatment of the covenant in Exod. 19 began with the desire of God to share with humanity a participation in God's own life of grace. That life in its very essence is trinitarian, the eternal communion of the Father, Son, and Holy Spirit. The revelation of Exod. 24 demonstrates the final end of revelation: that humanity might enter into the dark cloud of the knowledge of God in order to be ultimately enlightened by the clear day of the vision of God's essence, the knowledge of the Holy Trinity. It is the beatific vision that forms the final end or goal of the life of the covenant of grace. At the same time, the revelation of Exod. 24 is concerned with how humanity might venture forth in view of this goal, the supreme means of which are given to Israel: the liturgical cult of ark and tabernacle, which are prefigurations of the temple. All of these (the ark, tabernacle, and temple) foreshadow the mystery of the incarnation, by which we are enabled to approach the ultimate knowledge of God in the presence of the God-man among us: "I am the way, and the truth, and the life; no one comes to the Father, but by me" (John 14:6). There is a correlation, then, between the two visions of Moses on the mountain in Exod. 24 and the two deepest mysteries of revelation. Moses is invited to peer into the mystery of God, and he is instructed concerning the mystery of the ark and tabernacle. These two visions correspond to the mysteries of the Holy Trinity and the incarnation, respectively. These are the two central mysteries of Christianity, to which all others can be traced back in some way.

4

CULTIC RITUALS

Exodus 25–31

Ceremonial Law: Aquinas on the Sacraments of the Old Law

The last third of Exodus is concerned with the institution of the tabernacle, the priesthood, and liturgical cult of Israel. In Exod. 25–31 the Lord gives detailed instructions for the construction of the tabernacle. Exodus 32–34 treats the incident of the golden calf and its aftermath as it threatens to undermine the covenant between Israel and God. Exodus 35–40 recounts the actual construction of the tabernacle, recapitulating, as it were, what is written in Exod. 25–31.

Christian theology must determine how to treat this material rightly. As such, I will propose some general principles to guide our interpretation, beginning with the following questions: What historicity should one accord to this material, if any? What is the relation between the literal and typological senses of the scripture in this section of the Torah? How should Christians understand the deeper purpose of the ceremonial observances in the Old Law? And how does the mystery of Christ fulfill the ceremonial law in such a way so as to preserve its inner essence?

Historicity of the Tabernacle: Ark and Tent of Meeting

Modern scholars debate the question of the historicity of the cultic material in Exodus. Julius Wellhausen famously claimed that the material is almost entirely the literary production of a subsequent age, composed by the P source, or priestly tradition, and that the material is meant to reflect an idealized presentation of the temple cult during the monarchic age.[1] Others argue that the entire presentation could be postexilic in origin: the Mosaic era is being presented as a prefiguration of the reconstructed temple that was built after the return from Babylon of Israel's religious leadership. However, mainstream scholarship in the twentieth century rightly pushed back against this viewpoint as an extreme.[2] Modern archeology attests to the existence of ancient Near Eastern liturgical worship that resembles elements of the tabernacle cult at the purported time of the exodus.[3] There is ancient, textually diverse testimony in scripture to the historical existence of the tent of meeting (see Exod. 33:7–11) and tabernacle (Num. 10:33–36; 14:44) from the time of the wilderness and settlement through to the exilic period. These objects are not present in the period of Second Temple Judaism. Within the historical context of the time, it is entirely possible to conceive of the nomadic tribes of primitive Israel carrying with them a small ark and a tent, around which was centered a liturgical system of sacrifices.[4] Some modern scholars argue that in the age of the conquest and settlement in Israel the ark was initially deposited at a shrine at Shiloh (see Josh. 18:1; 19:51; 1 Sam. 1:7, 24; 3:3, 15) before being taken eventually to Jerusalem during the emergence of the Davidic monarchy.[5]

At the same time, it is clear that the presentation of Exod. 25–31 is meant to portray in great detail the inner workings of the temple cult from a subsequent age of Israel. The tabernacle and tent of meeting serve as a foreshadowing of the temple, and the instructions given in great detail in Exodus are intended for observance in the context of the monarchic and ultimately the postexilic age.[6] This section of the document is Priestly, or sacerdotal, through and through. The details of the text, which often bewilder the uninitiated reader, are meant to safeguard a detailed presentation of how the temple cult should operate. The reader should also remember that the majority of Israelites were not permitted in the inner sanctuary of the temple, or into the Holy of Holies. For that reason,

1. Julius Wellhausen, *Prolegomena to the History of Israel*, trans. J. S. Black and A. Menzies (Edinburgh: Adam & Charles Black, 1885), 38–51.

2. See, for example, Gerhard von Rad, "The Tent and the Ark," in *The Problem of the Hexateuch and Other Essays*, trans. E. Dicken (London: SCM, 1984), 103–24; Childs 1974: 530–32; de Vaux 1997: 297–302.

3. See F. M. Cross, "The Tabernacle: A Study from an Archaeological and Historical Approach," *Biblical Archeologist* 10 (1947): 45–68; de Vaux 1997: 297–302; Cassuto 2005: 319–24.

4. De Vaux 1997: 294–302.

5. De Vaux 1997: 302–11.

6. In this respect, see the pertinent study of Jon Levenson, *Sinai and Zion* (Minneapolis: Seabury, 1985).

the Torah offers a detailed pictorial representation of all that is within. The worship of Israel is not esoteric, even if it is hierarchically stratified. The whole of the people can "see" the inner working of the sanctuary and understand its meaning, not directly in a visual way but through the depiction that is given in the Torah.[7]

What should be said then about the continuity between the Mosaic tent of meeting and the cult of the temple, from Solomon to Ezra and Nehemiah? The biblical hermeneutic of Catholic theology is fundamentally incarnational. The spiritual mystery of God is mediated to us in and through history through real and visible figures of the Old Testament, culminating in the incarnation of the Lord in the person of Christ. Theologically speaking (as a matter of supernatural faith independent of the evidential demonstrability of the fact from our vantage point in history), one should posit some form of historical continuity between the cultic apparatus of the Mosaic age and the establishment of the liturgical cult in Jerusalem during the epoch of the monarchy. Notice that this biblically conservative claim is a moderate one and could be affirmed licitly in a diversity of ways. A more material or "Antiochene" reading of scripture might argue in favor of a continuity of details between the inspiration received by Moses and the ancient Israelites and the subsequent temple practices, based on the scribal preservation (and reediting) of ancient texts. A more allegorical or "Alexandrian" reading might see in this section of scripture an idealized portrait of a past liturgy that may in reality have been quite different. However, the idealized portrait serves to underscore the spiritual continuity willed by God between the time of Israel in exodus and Israel in exile. God always remains with the people of Israel, even as they peregrinate through time.

My own point of view lies somewhere between these two extreme points of reference. The text of Exod. 25–31 is clearly stylized. It disrupts the narrative flow of the Torah with an almost timeless account of liturgical observances.[8] The text also bears important analogies to the opening chapter of the Bible in which God creates in seven days.[9] First God speaks, and then the world is made (Gen 1:6; see the comments under Exod. 1:1–7). First God speaks, and then the tabernacle is constructed (Exod. 25:15–16; see the comments under Exod. 35:1–40:38). Exodus 40 notes that the final completion of the tabernacle takes place in seven

7. See G. Anderson 2002.
8. See G. Anderson 2002: 56–57.
9. On the sevenfold construction of creation and temple, see P. Kearney, "Creation and Liturgy: The P Redaction of Exodus 25–40," *Zeitschrift für die alttestamentliche Wissenschaft* 89 (1977): 375–87; G. Anderson 2002: 55–56.

stages, each of which effectuates a commandment of God, not unlike the beginning of Genesis.[10] Thus, the worship of Israel recapitulates the opening chapter of the Torah and represents the ultimate purpose of creation. The temple is the center of the universe; the ark and the tent of meeting are the seed of the life of worship that will subsequently take place in the temple in Jerusalem.

At the same time, however symbolic and theological the presentation of the tabernacle is, it also seeks to present a kind of ancient or archaic form of history. The symbols are intended to present us with a historical truth: God liberated Israel from Egypt and instituted a cultic liturgy for honoring the Lord by which God could remain present among the people of Israel for all time. This material need not be treated as merely ahistorical. The ark, tent of meeting, sacrifices, and elements of the sacerdotal institution could well go back to Moses and the most primitive Israelite epoch. There is no way to demonstrate anything to the contrary, and the texts (which serve as our unique historical evidence) do suggest to mere natural reason the possible historical antiquity of much of the Israelite cult. Furthermore, there is the real possibility that much of the Priestly material in these chapters originates not from the postexilic era but from ancient sacerdotal traditions of the First Temple epoch during the time of the monarchy. In that sense, it is possible to conjecture reasonably that some of the liturgical law included in the text is very ancient, dating back to the Mosaic period.

Resorting again to the thought of John Henry Newman, we might say that the Torah presents us with a complex textual "archeology" of laws that derive not only from a variety of eras (including that of the later editors) but also from ancient material that has been preserved, re-sorted, and reorganized. Amidst the jagged edges and diversity of this historical layering, one can discern the possibility of an organic development of tradition. This cultic development took place in and through various stages of prophetic inspiration, cultic formalization, religious crisis, and reformulation throughout the long span of ancient Israelite history. Not every detail of this history must be known (indeed, it cannot be!) in order to affirm its basic intelligibility across time and to decipher its profound inner theological meaning. Just as with a living organism, embryonic processes are best understood in light of subsequent mature developments, so the same can be said of the liturgical life of the people of Israel. The significance of the earliest cultic life of Israel is best understood in the light of the cultic life of the temple. Is it not a theological idea of this kind that the final redactors of the Mosaic law wished

10. G. Anderson 2002: 55. See Exod. 40:19, 21, 23, 25, 27, 29, 32.

to present by the very way in which they arranged the Torah? The fact that the tabernacle functions as a symbol of the temple was intended precisely to suggest the developmental continuity of one from the other.

Literal Sense and Typological Sense

Given what has just been stated, it follows that the literal and the typological senses of this section of the Torah align very closely. One might say that they are at times virtually indistinguishable—or distinguishable in principle but difficult to distinguish in practice. Here it is helpful to recall my explanation in the introduction of this volume concerning the literal sense according to Thomas Aquinas: it has a primacy and is the foundation for the other senses. The literal sense denotes realities themselves, and these in turn bear within them the typological, moral, and anagogical significations of the Word of God. God denotes the meaning of revelation in the works and events of sacred history that are his effects.

If that principle is applied here, the literal purpose of the text is to prescribe the structure of liturgical worship in Israel. However, the earliest historical manifestation of this worship (the ark, the tent of meeting, the priesthood, etc.) is seen by the sacred author *as itself from the beginning* signifying the later life of the temple typologically. In a sense, everything historical is typological, or inversely, everything in the text is primarily symbolic of the later liturgical life of Israel (as Wellhausen reasonably posits). And yet this liturgy is also seen as having profound roots in history and Mosaic prophecy.

The symbolic depth does not merely move "backward" from the priestly scribes in the time of the temple to depict the tent of meeting in the wilderness. It also has other significations. The ritual purity of the temple practice is seen by the sacred authors as symbolic of the inner purity of the spiritual life of Israel (the moral sense). The temple itself is idealized in Israelite spiritual life as an eschatological symbol of the creation: here the world achieves its final purpose as the place that God has come to dwell. In this way, the symbolism of Israel in the wilderness and Israel traveling homeward (from Egypt, from Babylon) also "presses forward" toward a restored Israel and even an "everlasting covenant" in which God ultimately comes to dwell with man (Ezek. 16:60; 37:26; Isa. 55:3; 60:19). This symbolism opens the door to the mystery of Christ: the incarnation, death, and resurrection of the Lord and his inauguration of a "new heaven and a new earth" (Isa. 65:17; Rev. 21:1). If all of this is true, then there are several strands of typological meaning in this section of Exodus, which I will briefly clarify in a more formal way.

HEAVEN

The first typological signification of the tabernacle in Exod. 25–31 is not concerned with the temple but with heaven, or with the eternal dwelling place of the Lord. This is quite possibly the earliest historical "stratum" of Israelite cultic life that was centered around the ark. It has been shown by modern historiography that Near Middle Eastern religions at the purported time of the exodus frequently constructed the inner sanctum of temples as dwelling places of the gods, providing food, couches, thrones, and other tributes of honor in accordance with various anthropomorphic conceptions of the deity. The throne room of the sanctuary is an image on earth of the life of the god in heaven.[11]

This apparatus is present in the liturgy of the ark but is reappropriated critically and recast in iconoclastic terms. God is not in a place—not even Mount Sinai—but is present with his people because God freely chooses to be. God alone is the king of Israel; no human avatar embodies or represents him. God can be worshiped and encountered at the tent of meeting, but God is not subject to any representation and has no physical or anthropomorphic features.[12] The mercy seat of the ark depicts the real presence of God (who chooses to be present to Israel in his mercy), but it simultaneously connotes God's hiddenness (because the Lord is incomprehensible and unenvisagable).

CREATION

As mentioned above, there is a parallelism in the Torah between the construction of the creation of the world in Genesis and the construction of the tabernacle and tent of meeting in Exodus. There are seven days in the Priestly account of the creation, and there are seven distinct moments in the construction of the tabernacle in Exod. 40. This Priestly imagery is symbolic: God creates man in his image in order to live in a community dedicated to the worship of God. After the fall, God redeems the human being for worship by establishing a covenant with Israel. Here the first causes of creation and its final ends are correlated by the final redactors of the Torah. The tabernacle recapitulates creation and symbolizes why God created in the first place: that he might dwell with man. Relating this idea to the symbolism just noted concerning heaven, the tabernacle represents both the Lord of Hosts in heaven and the Lord present on earth. It is a meeting point or bridge between God and man, between the eternal dwelling of God and the temporal dwelling of man. The tabernacle depicts the living presence of God with human beings.

11. See the helpful examples in Cassuto 2005: 322–23.
12. Cassuto 2005: 323.

Temple

It is clear that the tabernacle is meant to prefigure the temple in Jerusalem. With respect to the architecture of both, the presence of God passes from the inside outward. At the heart of the tabernacle is the ark in the Holy of Holies, where God by grace is truly present in a mysterious and special way. Only Aaron and his descendants can enter here (Exod. 27:21; Lev. 16:2–24). The Holy Place that adjoins the Holy of Holies is also reserved for the priesthood and contains the altar of incense, the menorah (or lampstand), and the table for the showbread. Moving outward, we come to the inner court of the tent of meeting, which represents the inner court of the temple. This is where sacrifices are offered, and the altar for burnt offering and the bronze laver are located here. The people encounter God's real presence in the sanctuary, but they do so through the "veil" of the Holy of Holies. Their own intimacy with God is symbolically enacted externally by the ritual actions of priests, through the mediation of the sacrifices that take place in the outer court. God is truly present here in a special way, but he is only encountered on the terms that he has designated by instituting the sacrifices of the law and the office of the priesthood.

Through this description, the sacred author depicts the practices of the temple, showing that they are already prefigured historically in the institution of the tabernacle. The temple thus signifies the presence of God with the people of Israel, leaving one mountain (Sinai in Egypt) and moving to another (Zion in Jerusalem). Of course this typology recapitulates the two symbolisms mentioned above. The inner sanctuary of the temple represents heaven, the eternal dwelling place of the Lord, and the temple in Jerusalem represents the final purpose of creation. The temple is the meeting place of God and man on earth, a place designated by God in his covenant of grace. Consequently, the temple is the center of the created cosmos. This theology of God's presence with Israel raises the issue of the deeper moral sense of scripture, which I will return to below: the indwelling of God with and in the people by grace.

Exile and New Creation

The tabernacle and tent of meeting also prefigure Israel in exile from Jerusalem. Just as the descent of Israel into Egypt in the Torah prefigures the Babylonian captivity, so the wandering in the wilderness prefigures the worship of Israel after the destruction of the First Temple of Solomon. The "blueprint" of the temple sacrifices remains with the people in the Torah even when the temple is destroyed. The presence of God is not primarily at Sinai or Jerusalem but with the people in their exilic wanderings. Israel in exile is bound to the Torah, waiting for the restoration of the temple in a time that is yet to come.

As we know from the major prophets of the Old Testament, this dynamic hope and expectation of temple restoration acquired an explicitly eschatological dimension in the age of the exile. In Babylon, Ezekiel has visions of the rebuilding of a new temple that restores the living presence of the Lord to Israel. This new temple is symbolic of an everlasting covenant with Israel and of God's final judgment of Israel and the nations. "I will make a covenant of peace with them; it shall be an everlasting covenant with them; and I will bless them and multiply them, and will set my sanctuary in the midst of them for evermore. My dwelling place shall be with them; and I will be their God, and they shall be my people" (Ezek. 37:26–27; see also 36:33–36). Meanwhile, Isaiah depicts the creation of a new heaven and a new earth in the eschaton, in which Israel will be vindicated and all humanity will come to recognize the Lord.

> For as the new heavens and the new earth
>   which I will make
> shall remain before me, says the LORD;
>   so shall your descendants and your name remain.
> From new moon to new moon,
>   and from sabbath to sabbath,
> all flesh shall come to worship before me,
> says the Lord. (Isa. 66:22–23)

(See also Isa. 65:17–25 and 66:6, which refer explicitly to the temple.)

Such ideas produce an eschatological dynamism in postexilic Judaism in which the earthly temple is seen as a prefiguration of a yet-more-ultimate state that is to come. The presence of God with human beings that the temple represents or embodies is emblematic of the mission of Israel to be a "light to the nations" (Isa. 42:6; 49:6; 60:3).

> These I will bring to my holy mountain,
>   and make them joyful in my house of prayer;
> their burnt offerings and their sacrifices
>   will be accepted on my altar;
> for my house shall be called a house of prayer
>   for all people. (Isa. 56:7; see Mark 11:17)

Malachi speaks of every Gentile nation offering sacrifice to the Lord (Mal. 1:11), and Isaiah speaks of "every knee [bending] / and every tongue [confessing]" the name of the Lord (Isa. 45:23; Phil. 2:10). That is to say, all nations will come to recognize the sacred name of the God of Israel and will offer him true worship, such as what is offered in the temple of Jerusalem. If the worship of Israel is meant to be the center of the cosmos, then that center will be expanded eschatologically to shine out among all the nations and to draw all of them into the worship of the God of Israel. Ultimately this process initiates the final age, where the glory of God will shine throughout all creation. God will judge the living and the dead, beatifying those who are righteous by grace in the age of the life to come, which is the age of the resurrection. "And many of those who sleep in the dust of the earth shall awake, some to everlasting life, and some to everlasting contempt. And those who are wise shall shine like the brightness of the firmament; and those who turn many to righteousness, like the stars forever and ever" (Dan. 12:2–3). This, too, is prefigured by the tabernacle and the temple, since these "places" of the privileged presence of the Lord with humanity are indicative of the eschatological glory that is to come.

Israelite Ceremonial Law according to Aquinas

These reflections lead us to the question of the spiritual or inner moral meaning of the liturgical life of Israel. If the covenant with God is a covenant by grace, why did God institute the outward observances of the ceremonial law of ancient Israel? How should we understand there to be any fundamental continuity between the older covenant of the Torah and the covenant of grace in the New Testament? Aquinas offers a twofold answer to this question.

LITERAL SENSE

Aquinas sees the ceremonial law as having primarily a literal meaning that is moral in kind; the law is meant to teach Israel the practice of monotheistic worship and to prevent the practice of idolatry.[13] Authentic worship of God is not primarily ceremonial. First and foremost it is interior and pertains to the spiritual faculties of the intellect and will. As noted above, the virtue of religion consists in the intellectual act of prayer—by which the mind is raised to God in thought, contemplation, and petition—and devotion, by which the heart is subordinated to God and placed by love under the radiant attraction of God's mysterious and

13. *ST* 1–2.101.1–2, 1–2.102.2.

ineffable goodness.[14] However, profound inward acts of prayer and devotion naturally express themselves through outward acts of the body: bodily adoration, sacrifice, oaths, tithes, and so forth.[15] In this context it is normal that the human community should make use of symbolic rites and ceremonies to signify externally the inward worship of God. The gestures of religious cult are expressions of this kind and are typically derived from diverse human communities and religious traditions. In the case of the Mosaic ceremonial law, however, God himself has inspired a particular human community to offer right worship to him in a purified and elevated way, by which they are progressively freed by grace from the errors of polytheism and superstitious practices.

At the heart of the ceremonial law is the practice of sacrifice, which is the outward act of religion that most closely grafts onto or flowers out from the inward acts of prayer and devotion.[16] Sacrifices are outward offerings of physical goods that represent and instantiate the inward offering of the mind and heart to God as the human spirit is consecrated to God in truth and love.

Consequently, Aquinas sees the tabernacle and the temple as being instituted primarily for the purpose of sacrificial worship.[17] This practice or set of practices embodies the fulfillment of the first commandment of the Decalogue. The cultic worship of Israel is a central point of contact between the natural law, which enjoins the worship of the Creator, and the covenant of grace, which enjoins Israel to acknowledge God in faith, hope, and charity. If God is particularly present in the ark, tabernacle, and temple by a special effect of his grace, it is in view of God's mysterious presence in the minds and hearts of the chosen people, by the theological virtues of faith, hope, and love. These theological virtues flower in the human heart most especially through acts of religion: prayer, devotion, and sacrifice.

The other features of the ceremonial law (food laws, purity laws, clothing prohibitions, etc.) are depicted by Aquinas as a complex cultural web of observances surrounding the act of sacrificial worship and ordained toward it.[18] In other words, all the observances of the ceremonial law are meant to prohibit idolatry and to remind Israel of the covenant to which they are committed. This system of cultic observances finds its source and summit in the practices of sacrificial worship. In

14. *ST* 2–2.82–83.
15. *ST* 2–2.84–88.
16. *ST* 2–2.85.1–2, 1–2.82.3.
17. *ST* 1–2.102.3–5.
18. *ST* 1–2.101.3–4, 1–2.102.5.

keeping with Peter's speech in Acts 15:10, Aquinas notes that the ceremonial law is in fact burdensome.[19] In this way it has both a penal and a dispositive character. It is penal for those who resist religious observances and is meant to continually dissuade against idolatry. It is dispositive for those who seek to love and serve God more fully since it invites them to consecrate every feature of civic and family life to the worship of God. In this latter way the observances of the Torah foreshadow the grace of the New Testament.[20]

Here one might pose an objection. Christian theology rightly insists that in our fallen condition we cannot effectively love God above all things, even naturally, without the healing effects of grace.[21] Furthermore, the observances of the ceremonial law do not communicate grace in and of themselves, as do the sacraments of the New Law, which were instituted by Christ.[22] Consequently, the sacraments of the Old Law (i.e., the ceremonial laws of the Torah) might signify right worship of God, but they do not grant their adherents the effective power to observe what they signify. This is all true.

Should one conclude, then, that the grace of true worship was in fact absent in the practices of the ancient Israelites? No. This would be unfitting for two reasons. First, the covenant of ancient Israel was in some real sense already a saving covenant of grace, and it is traditional for Catholic Christians to confess that many of the Old Testament's patriarchs and prophets are saints, saved by grace. Second, this covenant with Israel was a proximate preparation for the mystery of Christ the Savior and the opening of the covenant to all of humanity through

19. *ST* 1–2.101.3 obj. 2, 1–2.107.4.
20. *ST* 1–2.101.3 corp.:

> Now a people contains two kinds of men: some, prone to evil, who have to be coerced by the precepts of the law; some, inclined to good, either from nature or from custom, or rather from grace; and the like have to be taught and improved by means of the precepts of the law. . . . Accordingly, with regard to both kinds of men it was expedient that the Old Law should contain many ceremonial precepts. For in that people there were many prone to idolatry; wherefore it was necessary to recall them by means of ceremonial precepts from the worship of idols to the worship of God. And since men served idols in many ways, it was necessary on the other hand to devise many means of repressing every single one: and again, to lay many obligations on such like men, in order that being burdened, as it were, by their duties to the Divine worship, they might have no time for the service of idols. As to those who were inclined to good, it was again necessary that there should be many ceremonial precepts; both because thus their mind turned to God in many ways, and more continually; and because the mystery of Christ, which was foreshadowed by these ceremonial precepts, brought many boons to the world, and afforded men many considerations, which needed to be signified by various ceremonies.

See likewise *ST* 1–2.102.6.
21. *ST* 1–2.109.3.
22. *ST* 1–2.103.2.

baptism.[23] It is a traditional claim of Catholic theology, then, that the very grace of the new covenant was present in a hidden, inward way even in the practices of the old covenant.[24] How is this the case? Aquinas argues that the ceremonial observances, in the time before the coming of Christ, were not causes of grace but acted as divinely instituted dispositions toward and occasions for the infusion of the grace of the theological virtues. They also could be (but might not be in each instance) expressions of that grace.[25] This means that God was committed in his covenant with ancient Israel to offer graces of justification and sanctification to the people when they observed the cultic worship of the Torah in true faith, hope, and charity directed toward the Lord, the God of revelation. These observances could in turn also be themselves expressions of this life of grace, inwardly sanctifying the hearts of ancient Israelites. The law is not a cause of grace, but the law (when rightly lived) is an effect of grace. Inspired observance of the law by faithful Israelites was meant to dispose them to habitual acts of the theological virtues.

Seen in this light, the ancient religion of Israel is at its deepest level a mystery of grace meant to prepare the way for Christ and the Church. Just as Abraham was justified by faith before the time of the Mosaic law (Rom. 4:1–25), so the adherents of the law are justified by faith in the Lord before the time of Christ, and their observances of the Torah, when authentic, are manifestations of grace. "By grace you have been saved" (Eph. 2:8).

FIGURATIVE OR TYPOLOGICAL SENSE

The second meaning of the ceremonial precepts is figurative.[26] The sacrificial practice of the Torah prefigures the sacrifice of Christ for three reasons. The first comes from the final end of the law. The law is meant ultimately to lead human beings to union with God by grace, culminating in the vision of God and the glorification of the creation (the resurrection life). But the supreme means by which we attain to this beatitude and eternal life is Christ. "I am the way, and the truth, and the life" (John 14:6). The ceremonial sacrifices, then, are not the primary way by which we are united to God: Christ is the Way, through his incarnation, life, death, and resurrection. He is the source of grace and salvation for all human beings. However, the ceremonial precepts do prefigure Christ in sign and are the historical precedents, as it were, of his own self-offering. In this

---

23. *ST* 3.70.1 and 4.
24. *ST* 1–2.107.1–3.
25. *ST* 1–2.103.3, 3.70.4.
26. *ST* 1–2.101.2.

sense, they indicate obliquely in figure not only the final end of man (beatitude) but also the supreme means by which we might arrive at this end (the passion of the Lord).[27] The ancient Israelites were justified by faith and hope in the God of the covenant and by love for him. However, precisely because they believed in *this* Lord, and in his revelation of the Torah with its ceremonies and sacrifices, they also believed implicitly in the mystery of Christ who was to come, who was signified obliquely and indirectly in the ceremonies of the law itself.[28]

Second, the sacraments of the Old Law are not the causes of grace but rather the signs of a covenant of saving grace. This grace is given in view of the merits of Christ, whose unique sacrifice has procured the salvation of the human race once and for all. "He entered once for all into the Holy Place, taking not the blood of goats and calves but his own blood, thus securing an eternal redemption" (Heb. 9:12). "For by a single offering he has perfected for all time those who are sanctified" (Heb. 10:14). Insofar as the cultic life of Israel is an effect of grace, it is indicative of the Redeemer who is to come. Christ exemplifies perfectly once and for all what it means truly to live in the grace of the covenant. The dynamic of grace that is present throughout the history of ancient Israel attains its archetypal summit in his person.

Third, the worship of ancient Israel is imperfect—most especially because it coexists with the serious sins and faults of the human adherents of the religion in question. Christ as man, however, is sinless. His human prayer and devotion stem from a uniquely perfect degree of charity and are without moral blemish. The high priesthood of Christ, then, is the perfect fulfillment of the inward dynamic of the ceremonial law established in the covenant, even as Christ also transcends

27. *ST* 1–2.101.2:
> For in the state of future bliss, the human intellect will gaze on the divine truth in itself. Wherefore the external worship will not consist in anything figurative, but solely in the praise of God, proceeding from the inward knowledge and affection. . . . but in the present state of life, we are unable to gaze on the divine truth in itself, and we need the ray of divine light to shine upon us under the form of certain sensible figures; in various ways, however, according to the various states of human knowledge. For under the Old Law, neither was the divine truth manifest in itself, nor was the way leading to that manifestation as yet opened out, as the apostle declares (Heb. 9:8). Hence the external worship of the Old Law needed to be figurative not only of the future truth to be manifested in our heavenly country, but also of Christ, who is the way leading to that heavenly manifestation. But under the New Law this way is already revealed: and therefore it needs no longer to be foreshadowed as something future, but to be brought to our minds as something past or present: and the truth of the glory to come, which is not yet revealed, alone needs to be foreshadowed. This is what the apostle says (Heb. 11:1): "The Law has a shadow of the good things to come, not the very image of the things": for a shadow is less than an image; so that the image belongs to the New Law, but the shadow to the Old.

28. *ST* 2–2.2.6–7.

the Levitical priesthood in its entirety. "Every priest stands daily at his service, offering repeatedly the same sacrifices, which can never take away sins. But when Christ had offered for all time a single sacrifice for sins, he sat down at the right hand of God, then to wait until his enemies should be made a stool for his feet" (Heb. 10:11–13; Ps. 104).

Christological Fulfillment

Christ, then, is the fulfillment of the ceremonial law of the Old Testament. This fulfillment takes place in and through the whole of the life of Christ, as his interior and exterior "sacrifices" of perfect obedience are offered to God, culminating in his passion and death, which he freely accepted out of love for the Father and for the human race, for the salvation of the world. His self-offering in charity is the supremely meritorious cause of our salvation.

But why is his sacrifice definitive while others are only prefigurative? In essence there are three reasons.[29] The most fundamental of these pertains to Christ's divinity: he is the *dabar* or *logos* made flesh, the eternal Word of the Father existing as a human being. Because of the hypostatic union, there is an infinite dignity to all that Christ does and all that he suffers as man. The shedding of his blood in the free self-offering of the Cross is of infinite worth, by virtue of the person whose blood is shed—the person of the Word.

The second reason is more formal or essential. Christ as man possesses the highest degree of perfection of grace in his human mind and heart; therefore, in the crucifixion he is able to offer himself to God on our behalf as our brother in a unique plenitude of charity. Christ as man is able to love where the human race has failed to love and to obey where the human race has failed to obey. His plenitude of charity is without any shadow of imperfection or sin and casts a unique light upon the whole of the human condition. Christ's sacrificial offering makes atonement for the lovelessness and sin of the entire human race.

Third, the self-offering of Christ takes place in and through a most intensive form of human suffering, which qualifies the character of his sacrifice, making its moral worth more profound and more evident. He suffers in his soul (his intellect and will) most especially because he experiences a unique intensity of spiritual grief or "contrition" of mourning on behalf of all human sins precisely because of the perfection of knowledge and love that he possesses as man, in the plenitude of his grace. Jesus possesses a unique insight into the darkness of

29. See *ST* 3.48.2.

the hearts of all human beings and a unique degree of love for sinners, which is the source of his inner agony. "My God, my God, why have you forsaken me?" (Mark 15:34; Ps. 22:1). He also suffers from the knowledge of his own rejection by the leaders of his people and because of the abandonment and betrayal by his disciples (Matt. 26:37–39). Emotionally, then, Christ experiences intensively the depths of human suffering with a spiritual pathos or sensitivity that is unique. This sensitivity is also present in his physical suffering. Due to his perfection as man, Christ possesses a beautiful internal balance and a most profound integration of sensation and spiritual life. He is the most human of men. Consequently, he can suffer more deeply. The suffering of his senses by way of torture, crucifixion, and mockery affects him intensively in sensible ways but also contributes to the intensive suffering of his spiritual faculties.

The atonement of Christ, then, is grounded in the dignity of his person and the perfection of his charity and is expressed even in the midst of the most intensive human suffering. The priesthood of Christ pertains to his person and is above all interior and spiritual, exemplified in his human obedience and love. This internal mystery of self-offering extends to all his outward actions and sufferings, culminating in the mystery of the passion.

How, then, might we understand this mystery of the priesthood of Christ in the New Testament in relation to the cultic life and priesthood of ancient Israel? After all, Jesus of Nazareth was not a Levite. According to both Luke and Matthew, he was of Davidic lineage, from the tribe of Judah (Matt. 1:2–3; Luke 3:33). The priesthood of Christ can be understood both in continuity and in discontinuity with the Levitical priesthood in three ways.

First, there is continuity in the order of grace. I noted above that the sacramental sacrifices of the Old Law were not causes of grace but signs of faith. If these sacrifices were conducted with living faith (in the Lord of Israel, enlivened by hope and charity), then they were conducive to the salvation and sanctification of the celebrants. However, the grace offered to the ancient Israelites was given in view of the one salvific atonement of Jesus the Christ, the incarnate Lord. Consequently, what these sacrifices *intimate* in the order of grace, the death of the Lord *instantiates* and *fulfills*.

Second, the ancient Israelites were not free from complicity with human sin: idolatry, betrayal of the covenant, greed, and moral weakness. The sacrifices of the old covenant signified, among other things, the ongoing need of the people of Israel for the mercy of God and the forgiveness of sins. As noted above, one use of the law is to convict the human person of his or her sinfulness and need for grace and mercy. Throughout Israel's history, the prophets repeatedly confronted Israel with its shortcomings in the face of the justice of God. Correspondingly, the appeal to divine mercy is inherent to the cultic life of the ceremonial law. In this sense, just because the sacrifices of the ceremonial law were not in themselves sufficient to convey the forgiveness of sins, the observance of these rites (which showed forth the moral limitations of the Israelites) pointed obliquely to a more ultimate priesthood of atonement and mercy that could effectively communicate grace to the entire world.

Third, the sacrifices of the Old Law were prefigurative of the anthropological structure of justification, sanctification, and glorification. The sin offerings of the Old Law were outward signs of the inward power of the grace of God to forgive sins and to render the penitent just. When the ancient Israelites performed sin offerings in faith and with true contrition, they received the infused grace of justification, given to them in view of the merits of the passion of Christ.[30] The peace offerings of the Old Testament were outward signs of the graces of sanctification. When ancient Israelites celebrated these sacrifices in a state of grace (which implies the habitual graces of faith, hope, and love directed toward the Lord), then they merited (only in and through grace!) progressive growth in the order of sanctification. The holocaust offerings of the Old Testament were prefigurative of the eschaton. In these sacrifices the entire victim was consumed by fire, symbolizing the entire offering of the subject to God and the holistic transformation of the human person by the glory of God. Thus in the sacrifices of the Old Law there was present a certain image of glorification, of the radical transformation of the human person in beatitude, both in body and soul. At the heart of the ceremonies of the Old Law, the dynamic process of human sanctification that Paul speaks of are present in a hidden way, under diverse representational forms. "And those whom he predestined he also called; and those whom he called he also justified; and those whom he justified he also glorified" (Rom. 8:30).

A final question that remains, then, concerns the degree of grace that is given in and through the sacraments of the Old Law, as distinct from that which is given instrumentally (*ex opere operato*) through the sacraments of the New Law. The sacraments of the New Law are instrumental causes of grace in a way that the sacraments of the Old Law are not. However, is there any change in the degree of sanctification that is given in either case? As Aquinas notes, "Greater is the

---

30. *ST* 3.84.7 corp. and ad 2. On this threefold division of the sacraments of the old law, see *ST* 1–2.102.3 ad 8, 3.22.2 corp.

effect of a thing already present, than of the hope thereof."[31] The sacraments that were instituted by Christ not only signify the salvific work of the Lord (as did the sacraments of the Old Law in figure), but they also communicate what they signify. It is fitting, then, that those sacraments that come after Christ should provide a more copious and intensive source of grace for the world than those that came before them, especially as they are directed toward the catholic and apostolic work of the sanctification of all human civilizations. This higher degree of grace is present in two ways.

First, the Christian sacraments of baptism, confirmation, and holy orders communicate "characters" or permanent ontological qualities (powers) that alter the spiritual soul of the recipient in a definitive manner; indeed, they can remain present in a soul even after a Christian has sinned gravely. These qualities do not effectuate sanctification automatically and do not assure the recipient of eternal salvation. However, the characters of these diverse sacraments do establish a permanent disposition within the soul of the recipient toward the cultic life of the Church so that the person is apt to receive freely (or offer freely, in the case of holy orders) the forgiveness of sins in the sacrament of reconciliation and the sanctifying grace of the body and blood of Christ in the Eucharist. Significantly, these sacraments are not communicated to one lineage of people alone (such as in the case of circumcision, which is reserved to the children of the ancient Israelites and their Jewish descendants). Rather, they are communicated to all peoples, opening up the saving covenant in Christ to all of humanity.

Second, the intensive degree of sanctifying grace communicated in the New Law and by the sacraments of the New Law is objectively greater. We must not ignore the saints of the Old Testament who became the greatest friends of God and who are far holier than many Christians. Significantly, the Catholic and Orthodox churches have always held this to be true of archetypal biblical figures like Abraham, Moses, and David. However, the sacraments of the New Law, as compared with the now defunct sacrifices of the Old Law, are far more advantageous means toward salvation and uniquely effective sources of grace than all that came before them. In general, the grace of the new covenant is more intensive. Generally speaking, the newer covenant has begotten more public saints and friends of God than the older covenant and is more extensive in effect, being catholic or universal in nature.

31. *ST* 3.70.4.

However, to conclude that the mystery of grace is absent in the Old Law is erroneous, and to think in this way is ultimately antichristological. "Salvation is from the Jews" (John 4:22). The ark and the tabernacle, the tent of meeting and the altar, the priesthood of Aaron, and the laws of sacrifice all prefigure Christ. In its deepest literal sense, the Old Testament cult was an expression of the covenant of grace in its concrete historical realization. At the heart of the ancient liturgy of Israel is a mystery of divine mercy, which ultimately flowers in the passion, death, and resurrection of the Lord.

The Ark and the Tabernacle (Exod. 25)

The Sanctuary of the Lord

25:1–9 "Let them make me a sanctuary, that I may dwell in their midst. According to all that I show you concerning the pattern of the tabernacle, and of all its furniture, so you shall make it" (25:8–9).

How should we understand the Torah's insistence on the dwelling of God with his people in the tabernacle? God is not embodied within the people of Israel, nor is he embodied within a place. The Torah does not endorse any version of pantheism or panentheism, whether overt or implicit. Rather, God the Creator is utterly transcendent—present in all that is as the total ontological cause of all that is. By that very fact, there is throughout the Torah an implicit ontological affirmation of the divine omnipresence.

If this is the case, what can it mean for God to "dwell with Israel" in a particular way, by a divine decision, and according to the terms of a covenant? Here Aquinas distinguishes a twofold form of divine presence: the presence of God by his effects of creation and the presence of God by his effects of grace.[32] The former presence pertains to God as the creative cause of all that exists. Because God gives creatures their very existence, God is more intimate to each thing than it is to itself; God remains the ever-actual giver of its very *esse* or act of being. The latter form of presence is that which pertains to God as the author of grace and divine adoption, which is given only to spiritual creatures (angels and human beings). This is the kind of presence that we are alerted to here. The Torah tells us that God dwells in Israel by a special elective choice. In a primarily internal way, God dwells within the mind and heart of the people of Israel by gifts of faith, hope, and charity. However, this internal indwelling of God is accompanied exteriorly by the

32. *ST* 1.8.3.

signs of God's presence: the law, the covenant, the tabernacle, and the priesthood. These exterior vehicles communicate a sense of the presence of God and permit Israel to respond effectively to the internal promptings of grace through external acts of recognition of the Lord.

Concretely, this "dwelling place for God" consists of the Holy of Holies (the inner sanctum of the tabernacle, containing the ark and the holy place, which includes the lampstand) and its outer courtyard (containing the altar for burnt offerings). Nevertheless, the concrete structure is clearly meant to denote something numinous and mysterious: a felt sense of the presence of God acknowledged in the minds and hearts of the Israelites, present in the temple and tabernacle. God dwells among the Israelites, with Israel, as they move through the desert, into the holy land, and throughout history in time and place.

A latent theological connection can be seen between this idea and the teaching of the New Testament that the God of Israel has become present to the world by taking on a human nature, body, and soul in the person of the Son incarnate, Jesus Christ. Aquinas rightly notes that this is a third kind of presence—a substantial presence of God in the flesh as a human being living among us rather than a presence effectuated either by creation of that which exists or by the gift of grace.[33] And yet this ultimate "fulfillment" of the sanctuary of the Lord occurs so that God can be encountered by all human beings (that is, the Gentile nations) in the fullness of grace. "The Word became flesh and dwelt among us, full of grace and truth. . . . For the law came through Moses; grace and truth came through Jesus Christ" (John 1:14, 17). This real presence of God among his chosen people is prolonged in the Eucharist, which is the substantial presence of the glorified Christ. Ordinary bread and wine are changed substantially in the words of consecration by a validly ordained bishop or priest, becoming the body and blood of Christ. Truly present in the Eucharist are the body, blood, soul, and divinity of the Lord. For this reason, it is appropriate that the Eucharist is reserved in the Catholic Church in a "tabernacle" that is purposefully meant to represent (however indirectly) the tabernacle of Exodus. Just as the Eucharist is the new manna from heaven that gives life to a messianic people, so the tabernacle that contains the real presence of God among us reminds us that the people of God are accompanied in their earthly pilgrimage through this world by the mysterious, abiding presence of the resurrected Lord.

33. *ST* 1.8.3 ad 4, 3.2.10 ad 2.

The Ark

25:10–22 "They shall make an ark of acacia wood; two cubits and a half shall be its length, a cubit and a half its breadth, and a cubit and a half its height. . . . Then you shall make a mercy seat of pure gold. . . . And you shall make two cherubim of gold; of hammered work shall you make them, on the two ends of the mercy seat" (25:10, 17–18).

There is no particularly good reason to deny the historical existence of an ark of the covenant. Peoples in the Near Eastern region of the purported era did typically attempt to depict the presence of the sacred in concrete objects or outward symbols. References to the Mosaic ark are found across subsequent epochs of ancient Israelite history, from the wanderings in the wilderness to the settlement, as well as in the Davidic monarchy and the era of the Solomonic temple (Num. 10:33–36; Deut. 10:1–5; 1 Sam. 3:3; 4:3–22; 6:1–7:2; 2 Sam. 6:2–17; 1 Kgs. 3:15; 6:19; 8:6; Jer. 3:16). The ark was lost in the destruction brought on by the Babylonian conquest and exile and was never recovered, so it makes little sense to consider it a mere contrivance of postexilic history.

The ark has three significant features. First, it contains the Decalogue, which is the heart of the covenant (Exod. 25:16; 40:20). Second, it facilitates a particular presence of the Lord among the people, both when they consult him prophetically and when he accompanies them into battle, with the ark acting as a kind of war palladium (Num. 10:33–36; 1 Sam. 4; 2 Sam. 11:11). Third, the ark is the mercy seat of God, symbolic of God's forgiveness of the sins of Israel (and through them all of humanity, whom they represent). This signification is depicted particularly in the ceremonies regarding the Day of Atonement in Lev. 16.

In its literal sense, the ark represents or instantiates the mystery of the law that is at the heart of the covenant. By the special gift of the covenantal law, God is made present to Israel, and Israel is able to live in the presence of God. This law stands over against Israel as a kind of judgment but also as the sign of God's perpetual offer of mercy. The claim that the ark is a "mercy seat" seems to suggest that God is truly present but also incapable of representation, which is acknowledged in his transcendent holiness by the cherubim on the ark but also concealed by them from human sight. All of this symbolism serves to signify simultaneously the authentic manifestation of God in his law and his perpetual hiddenness and mystery.

The moral sense of the ark is the law of God written on the hearts of the Israelites. Just as the people internalize the ark physically or sociologically as the heart of their civilization and temple worship, so God's moral law (expressed especially in the tablets of the Ten Commandments) is at the heart of their moral life. The external precepts are meant to be mirrored by a law written on the hearts of the people, just as "natural law" can be promulgated externally by civic legislation. The Decalogue recalls humanity's rational tendency toward the good and the obligation to refrain from human actions that are vicious or intrinsically evil. The ark represents the calling of Israelite society to spiritual and moral purity.

Typologically, the ark represents its counterpart in the New Testament: the Virgin Mary (a traditional claim of the Christian tradition). However counter-intuitive it might seem to those who have never considered the idea, it is based in fact upon a reasonable theological parallel between the old and new covenants and has a clear biblical warrant. In the old covenant the presence of God is maximal in the holiness of the law contained in the ark, making the ark the outward sign of the most intensive presence of God. In the new covenant the presence of God is maximal in the person of Jesus, who incarnates the law in his human actions and his ineffable holiness as God made man. Thus, the Virgin Mary with child is the outward sign of this most intensive presence of God among us. She is the "ark of the covenant" in whom the New Law of God is contained, Emmanuel, God with us (Isa. 7:14; Matt. 1:23).

In two places in particular, an explicit indication of this parallelism occurs in the New Testament. In Luke 1:35 the angel Gabriel tells the Virgin that she will be with child while remaining a virgin because "the power of the Most High will *overshadow* [*episkiasei*]" her (emphasis added). The Greek verb *episkiazō* mirrors the Septuagint use of the verb *epeskiazen*, which is employed to denote the glory of God "overshadowing" the ark of the covenant in Exod. 40:35. When the Virgin Mary, who is pregnant with Jesus, visits Elizabeth in Luke 1:41–43, she mysteriously communicates the presence of the Lord to her cousin and John the Baptist, who leaps in the womb. "Why is this granted to me, that the mother of my Lord should come to me?" (Luke 1:43). From this a similitude can be constructed: Mary is like the ark in the old covenant, bearing within herself the presence of the God of Israel. This imagery is present also in Rev. 11:19–12:6. There the "ark of [the] covenant" is seen in the temple of God in heaven. Superimposed on this image is that of a woman clothed in the rays of the sun, bearing the messianic child who is Christ (Rev. 12:1–2). This Marian figure crowned with twelve stars is also a symbol of the Church, who is persecuted by the dragon, "that ancient serpent" (Rev. 12:9). Thus the ark of God in heaven is both Mary and the Church, in whom the presence of God dwells in the person of Christ. For this reason the evil one persecutes the Church, not unlike Herod pursuing the Christ child. The dynamic that occurred in the old covenant when the ark was carried into battle is recapitulated here to denote the realm of spiritual warfare. The Virgin Mary is the figure who overcomes the ancient foe of humanity. In her, the holiness of Christ and his victory over sin are all-encompassing. She is the sign of the definitive victory of God over the enemies of Christ.

The mercy seat of the ark also prefigures Christ, which is an explicit teaching of Paul, who states in Rom. 3:25 that Christ has been put forth "as a propitiation" for the sins of the human race. Here, Paul makes use here of the Greek term *hilastērion*, which the Septuagint employs repeatedly to denote the mercy seat in the Torah (see Exod. 25:17; Lev. 16:2). The ultimate atonement for human sin is found in Christ. "They are justified by his grace as a gift, through the redemption which is in Christ Jesus, whom God put forward as an expiation by his blood, to be received by faith. This was to show God's righteousness, because in his divine forbearance he had passed over former sins" (Rom. 3:24–25).

Eschatologically, the ark represents the illumination of all the saints by the immediate presence of God in heaven, which occurs by virtue of the Lamb of God, who is Christ. "And I saw no temple in the city, for its temple is the Lord God the Almighty and the Lamb" (Rev. 21:22). Here the presence of the Lord is given without mediations, or rather only through the mediation of Christ crucified and glorified, so that by his grace the saints are able to perceive God himself—the "temple" or final dwelling place of his people. This ultimate presence is anticipated in this life wherever a soul becomes a special "ark" or bearer of the presence of God in the soul by faith, hope, and charity. Each Christian is invited to bear the presence of Christ within him- or herself out into the world in anticipation of the life of glory that is yet to come.

The Table and the Lampstand

25:23–40 "And you shall make a table of acacia wood. . . . And you shall set the bread of the Presence on the table before me always. . . . And you shall make a lampstand of pure gold. . . . And you shall make the seven lamps for it; and the lamps shall be set up so as to give light upon the space in front of it" (25:23, 30–31, 37).

Within the inner sanctuary of the tabernacle, alongside the ark, is a table that contains the bread of presence and a lampstand, typically depicted as a menorah with seven branches. The meaning of this "table of the bread of the Presence" (Num. 4:7) is difficult to interpret. The "showbread" was placed in two rows of six loaves each every Sabbath while frankincense was burned (Lev. 24:5–7). The following Sabbath it was replaced and eaten by the priests (Lev. 24:8–9). Does this mean that the bread represents an offering by the people to the God of Israel, or does it signify the gifts of the God of Israel to his people? Typically sacrifice in the Torah represents an exchange that moves in both directions, though with a distinction. The people offer to God all they have and are, acknowledging that all they receive from him is already a gift of God, who is the author of their being. Accordingly, the second signification is primal: we receive from God the bread of life. God gives us our very existence, and the "bread of presence" is the sign of his sustenance, which has been given to Israel throughout its history. God has no need of the sacrifices of Israel, and only an anthropomorphic conception of the deity could imagine otherwise. However, we have need—anthropologically and morally—to make an offering of ourselves to God through concrete symbolic actions, like offering sacrifice to God. These religious acts allow us to acknowledge our created dependency in a more fully human way.

The lampstand is a sign of the light of the presence of God in Israel; the light of the Torah shines in the darkness of the human conscience, illuminating human beings so that they become aware of the moral and spiritual law of God. The sevenfold character of the menorah is indicative of a "tree of light," a living source of illumination that gives life. Through the tree of the Cross, God ultimately gives this light, for Christ is the light that illumines all men. "When you have lifted up the Son of man, then you will know that I am" (John 8:28). "I am the light of the world" (John 8:12). When the light of God illumines the soul, it becomes a house of light, radiant with the virtues that stem from faith and charity, virtues that purify and elevate the human heart to live in the presence of God. Thus, the saints are houses of light in the Church in which God dwells in an especially intense way and in which his living law is clearly perceived. "You are the light of the world. A city on a hill cannot be hid" (Matt. 5:14). "But you are a chosen race, a royal priesthood . . . that you may declare the wonderful deeds of him who called you out of darkness into his marvelous light" (1 Pet. 2:9).

The Tent of Meeting (Exod. 26)

The Tent Cloth, Tabernacle Walls, and Veils

26:1–37 "Moreover you shall make the tabernacle with ten curtains of fine twined linen and blue and purple and scarlet stuff; with cherubim skillfully worked shall you make them" (26:1).

Exodus 26 details the various tent cloths, veils, and wooden frames needed to construct the tabernacle, the tent of meeting, and the inner sanctuary of the Holy of Holies. The first layer of cloth forms the inner lining of the structure (26:1–6), which is covered by a coarser outer lining of goat-hair cloth (26:7–13). The shape of the inner tent of the Holy of Holies is a perfect square. The entire structure (including the outer wall of the tabernacle) appears to be exactly one-half the size of the temple of Solomon and one-third its height, as depicted in 1 Kgs. 6:2.

Opinions of modern scholars differ widely on the question of what historical significance to afford this portrayal of the tabernacle in the wilderness. Some defend the possibility of a moving shrine in the desert, even of this size, while others ascribe the basic form to the subsequent shrine established in Shiloh after the settlement. Some associate it with David's tent for the ark in 1 and 2 Samuel while others think it is an idealized portrait of the Solomonic temple that depicts the wilderness tent as a prefiguration of the temple in Jerusalem. Still others claim that this depiction is a late (exilic or postexilic) depiction of the temple meant to prefigure either the reestablishment of the temple after exile or the possibility of a counter-alternative to the temple reestablished under Ezra and Nehemiah.

Whatever the redactional history of the text, the literal sense of the scripture must include each and every one of these interpretations, whether we take it to be a pure representation of the original structure or a purely postexilic idealization created by the Priestly writers. (My position is more moderate. I believe the text conveys a somewhat idealized portrait by the Priestly writers of a real, historical practice of ancient Israel, denoted by the wilderness traditions. While there was a tent of meeting, it is presented here in iconographic terms in light of the temple.) The wilderness worship of Israel is ontologically prefigurative of the later developments of Israelite religion in the monarchical and postexilic ages, much as the acorn prefigures the oak tree. This view of Israelite history is theological, which does not mean that that the event did not happen. On the contrary, the theological perspective, inspired by the Holy Spirit, tells us precisely what is operative in the depths of human history, as known by God and directed by him, beyond or below the range of the ordinary gaze of human observation. God orchestrated the exodus in view of the establishment of the monotheistic faith of ancient Israel.

The moral sense of this chapter concerns in particular the divinely inspired division of physical space so as to establish clear demarcations between the sacred and the profane. While some might see the distinction between sacred space and profane space to be a modern one, developed in a secular era, the distinction is inevitable in any truly religious society, even if it is also a relative distinction.

Even in the most intentionally religious society, not all actions can be oriented directly to God in equal degree. Actions that are oriented more directly to God (liturgical worship, communal prayer, sacrifice) typically have a privileged place for a twofold reason. First, they properly dispose the human community to the recollection or intentional action necessary for the exercise of the virtue of religion. Certain physical contexts incline people more readily to prayer and devotion, and the architecture of a religious society seeks to aid in this respect. Second, the architectural centrality of the sacred demonstrates the purpose of the more profane dimensions of existence. Thus the tent is at the center of the people of Israel in their pilgrimage in the desert, and the temple is at the center of the spiritual life of ancient Israel. In turn, the sacred space is relative itself because it is meant to inform the entire behavior of an authentically religious people in their more ordinary or profane everyday activities (the domestic sphere, human work, and so forth). The tent of meeting/the temple is at the center of Israelite society, but it is also the nexus that gives signification to all the moral and ceremonial laws of the Torah, including the many purity laws presented in Leviticus and Deuteronomy.

While most complex religious civilizations typically distinguish some space for the sacred in order to give meaning to the whole of the ordinary (profane) life of society, in the case of Israelite society the process is divinely inspired. On one level, the use of the tents, cloths, and partitions (and the subsequent walls of the temple with its inner sanctuary) are human inventions or the product of an archaic Near Middle Eastern society. However, this particularly human religious tradition was uniquely inspired by God for the sake of the human race so as to become the privileged locus of the revelation of the living God, who became present in a unique way in the ancient tabernacle and temple. This structure of partitions, then, is a work of divinity and humanity, grace and nature.

The structure put in place by Moses (and the priests of the monarchical era) sets conditions for the encounter with the Lord. In this way it is meant to "protect" the holiness of God from profanation by the people, but it also protects the people from God, from the danger of approaching God in either ritual or moral impurity. Behind this seemingly archaic mentality is something of universal significance for all humanity. The human race does not have a right to intimacy with God for two reasons, the first of which is the finitude of our created human condition before the infinite perfection and transcendence of God. The second is our moral imperfection and impurity, dynamically symbolized by the wide-ranging set of purity laws that encompass the people of Israel in the Torah. Behind the many laws that protect against profanation, the deeper metaphysical issue pertains to the transcendence of God and the justice of God.

Because of this twofold distance from God (our creatureliness and sinfulness, which obtains for all human beings), God sets the unique conditions for communion with God on God's own terms. While God truly does offer Israel habitual communion in the temple cult and the liturgy of sacrifices, God desires that this habituation take place in circumstances that inhibit human beings from taking the grace of God's presence for granted. The religion of Israel is meant to invite human beings to personal and communal transformation, not ritual control of the divine or vain attempts at magical manipulation.

Therefore, the "veils and walls" in Exod. 26 are ultimately spiritual. They represent the transcendence of God, the opaqueness of our understanding of God, and the hard-heartedness of our sin. We can transcend these distinctions or divisions when God invites us into the mystery of God's presence, God's unique holiness, and communion with him by mercy and grace.

Matthew 27:51 and Mark 15:38 both depict the renting of the curtain in the temple (which concealed the Holy of Holies) just after the death of Christ. Hebrews associates this curtain with the flesh of Christ (Heb. 9:3; 10:20), which unveils to us the pathway to heaven, the true sanctuary. The blood of Christ gives us access to this venue (Heb. 10:19). In his human death and resurrection, Christ is our "high priest" who has gone before us into heaven, into the Holy of Holies (Heb. 6:19–20). Through him, the veil is torn, giving us access to the eternal life of God.

The Altar (Exod. 27)

27:1–21 "You shall make the altar of acacia wood, five cubits long and five cubits broad; the altar shall be square, and its height shall be three cubits. And you shall make horns for it on its four corners; its horns shall be of one piece with it, and you shall overlay it with bronze" (27:1–2).

Exodus 27 is concerned principally with the altar of holocausts (27:1–8), as well as the court of the tabernacle (27:9–19) and the oil for the lamps of the sanctuary (27:20–21). Essentially, the narration moves "outward" from the inner sanctuary to the courtyard, at the center of which is the altar. While the ark and the implements in the Holy of Holies are made of gold, the altar is fashioned out of bronze, a change in metals meant to signify a descending degree of value or holiness. The courtyard is a place of more frequent interaction between Israel and God, at the heart of which is sacrifice. Neither acacia wood nor olive oil are substances that the ancient Israelites could have easily procured or produced in the wilderness. These facets of the narrative lend credence to the suggestion that the depiction of the tabernacle in this section of the Torah contains idealized elements from a historically subsequent era. Altars like the one depicted here (with four horns on the four corners) were in use in Israel during the epochs of the settlement and monarchy,[34] and the sacrifice procedures given in the Torah are very carefully scripted, making use of a variety of bronze implements: pots, shovels, basins, forks, and firepans (27:3). The text under consideration is meant to be interpreted in conjunction with Lev. 3–4, which details the various forms of sacrifice that are to be offered to God. As a whole, this text functions as a typology for temple sacrifices.

Modern commentators typically raise a key question here: Why does the Torah prescribe the sacrifice of animals (in addition to vegetative agricultural products)? Several ethical objections are frequently posed here: the killing of animals is intrinsically immoral; animal sacrifices of this kind imply innate cruelty on the part of human beings; this form of sacrificial religion inevitably depicts God as cruel, violent, and satiated in an arbitrary fashion by bloodlust; and human sacrifice of animals is a senseless activity with no intrinsically meaningful ethical function.

It is true that animal sacrifice derives typically from premodern cultures that were archaic both in their conception of reality and in their religious practices. Animal sacrifice is an archaic practice. Furthermore, some forms of animal sacrifice *might* have entailed cruelty and religious irrationality. Grave cruelty to animals and even the sacrifice of human beings were prevalent features in the history of human religion and were often allied with grotesque or idolatrous conceptions of the divine or the gods. Nevertheless, the Torah is not a continuation of this kind of unethical irrationality. The sacrifices of the Torah offer the human race a radical remedy: a rational form of religious worship that is based upon justice, mercy, and love—practices that are meant to heal and elevate the wounded religious dimension of human culture. These practices are expressed within the context of an ancient, archaic civilization, and they are temporally provisional or contingent, being ordered in time toward the unique sacrifice of Christ and the sacraments of the Christian religion. Nevertheless, if one considers the practices detailed in the Torah itself, the above-mentioned objections do not reasonably apply either philosophically or in light of the biblical revelation.[35]

34. See Durham 1987: 375.

35. For a developed philosophical consideration of physical and spiritual sacrifice in ancient Israelite religion and in Judaism, see Moshe Halbertal, *On Sacrifice* (Princeton: Princeton University Press, 2012).

First of all, according to the Torah it is not intrinsically immoral to kill and eat animals. Some speculate that according to Gen. 3:17–19, the human race would never have eaten animals had they never fallen into sin. Whatever one makes of such a theory, the Torah clearly does not treat the eating of animals as a sin, and its rationality on this point is entirely defensible. Nonrational animals have a dignity as living, sentient beings and must be treated with the proportionate respect that is due to them as creatures of God. However, they are innately mortal and can be used by human beings respectfully as a source of nutrition and manual labor. To deny a starving person the right to eat a nonrational animal, even if it would save the life of the person, is gravely immoral. This widely recognized moral truth is the sign that human beings, who are made in God's image by virtue of their spiritual souls, occupy a higher ontological status than that of the other animals, and they have the right before God and one another to make use of animals for the purposes of labor and nutrition.

Second, the sacrifice procedures of the Torah are not cruel. On the contrary, not only are the forms of life taking intended to be humane, but they are also meant to evoke a profound awareness that the animal is a gift of the creation of God. All life is received from God and must not be taken for granted or treated in a manipulative fashion as a mere human possession. Modern forms of mass production involving animal foods are often far less humane than the procedures of killing animals in ancient civilizations, including that of the Torah.

Third, the sacrifices of the law are not premised on a portrait of God as arbitrary, whimsical, or bloodthirsty. On the contrary, the canon of scripture clearly refuses any such viewpoint categorically. God does not need human sacrifices. He is not placated by them and cannot be manipulated. Furthermore, sacrifices are not magical and do not work in a mechanical way. Psalm 50:7–23 conveys how the observance of the moral law is essential to the inner spirit of sacrifice:

> "Hear, O my people. . . .
> I do not reprove you for your sacrifices. . . .
> For every beast of the forest is mine. . . .
> If I were hungry, I would not tell you;
>   for the world and all that is in it is mine. . . .
> Offer to God a sacrifice of thanksgiving,
>   and pay your vows to the Most High. . . .
> I will deliver you, and you shall glorify me."
> But to the wicked God says:
>   "What right have you to recite my statutes,
>   or take my covenant on your lips?

> For you . . . cast my words behind you.
> If you see a thief, you are a friend of his;
>   and you keep company with adulterers. . . .
> Your tongue frames deceit. . . .
> Mark this, then, you who forget God,
>   lest I rend, and there be none to deliver!
> He who brings thanksgiving as his sacrifice honors me;
>   to him who orders his way aright
>   I will show the salvation of God!"

This brings us to the final objection: offering animals in sacrifice to God is inherently meaningless or ethically vacuous. This objection stipulates either that true worship needs no external manifestation in physical gestures of sacrifice or that the offering of animals is in no way morally or symbolically meaningful. Against this objection, Aquinas stipulates that the offering of sacrifice is in keeping with the natural law. It pertains to our corporeal nature as animals that we should offer ourselves to God in ways that make use of visible and physical symbols, as embodied religious persons.[36]

The meaningfulness of offering animals and vegetables to God follows from the fact that they are sources of food for human persons and represent the dependency of humans beings upon the wider creation for their sustenance and life. In ancient cultures herd animals were employed in religious ceremonies as a sign that God has given all creatures life and has made us the stewards of creation, granting us the capacity to sustain life through the tending of animals. However, the animal offered in sacrifice is also an image of ourselves in our physical animality and mortality. It can also be a symbol of self-offering, embodying the real cost to oneself or one's family of offering something very valuable to the Lord. The offering is one of thanksgiving or reparation but also terminates with the consumption of the animal in gratitude to

36. *ST* 2–2.85.1:
> Natural reason tells man that he is subject to a higher being, on account of the defects which he perceives in himself, and in which he needs help and direction from someone above him: and whatever this superior being may be, it is known to all under the name of God. Now just as in natural things the lower are naturally subject to the higher, so too it is a dictate of natural reason in accordance with man's natural inclination that he should tender submission and honor, according to his mode, to that which is above man. Now the mode befitting to man is that he should employ sensible signs in order to signify anything, because he derives his knowledge from sensibles. Hence it is a dictate of natural reason that man should use certain sensibles, by offering them to God in sign of the subjection and honor due to Him, like those who make certain offerings to their lord in recognition of his authority. Now this is what we mean by a sacrifice, and consequently the offering of sacrifice is of the natural law.

God. Consequently, it is not an offering meant to deprive the human community of a source of nourishment but to underscore the divine gift of all resources, including the food "received back" from God on sacral terms, through sacrificial acts.

Human beings typically raise animals for consumption and kill them humanely for food. The Torah interjects into this practice a religious awareness of the fact that the entire cosmic and ecological order is a gift from God and must be used reverently by keeping this in mind. Both human and animal life are understood to be God given, each with a distinct degree of importance within the cosmic order.

Having said all this, we can make two caveats. First, a defense of the symbolic religious meaning and ethical rationality of the archaic practice of animal sacrifice need not entail the affirmation that this form of sacrifice is the highest or most reasonable form of religious worship. Christian theology has long affirmed that the spiritual sacrifice of Christ crucified is a higher rational form of ethical self-offering to God in the face of human moral evil. The eucharistic sacrifice, then, is a spiritual and rational sacrifice of a higher order that prolongs the real presence of the sacrifice of the Cross in such a way as to permit the Christian faithful to associate themselves in charity with the self-offering of Christ crucified.

Second, based on the reasonable metaphysical and anthropological arguments of Aquinas noted above, one may conclude that because God exists and because the human being is capable of acknowledging God in worship that is both corporeal and spiritual, sacrifice is natural and pertains to the heart of any rightly ordered civilization. Consequently, however archaic or alien we may take ancient animal sacrifice of the old covenant to be (it is primitive, to be sure), it nevertheless constitutes an objectively more rational and ethically more noble form of social existence than that of a society that has no form of religious sacrifice whatsoever. In other words, the temple sacrifices of the Torah are superior in ethical nobility and philosophical rationality to the modern secular ethos, which is denuded of any public reference to God in liturgical worship and collective religious sacrifice. Sometimes the primitive practice is the more human and rational.

The Priesthood of Aaron (Exod. 28–29)

The Priestly Vestments: The Ephod and Breastpiece

28:1–29 "These are the garments which they shall make: a breastpiece, an ephod, a robe, a coat of checker work, a turban, and a girdle; they shall make holy garments for Aaron your brother and his sons to serve me as priests" (28:4).

The historical development of the priesthood in ancient Israel is a topic of great complexity that is frequently characterized by controversial debate.[37] Did the earliest Israelite movement centered around Moses (presupposed here to be a historical reality) assign priests of some kind to officiate in sacrifices? Were there Levites even in this era or are they a tribe that dates primarily from a later time of the settlement? Were there Levitical shrines in the premonarchical era? Did the priestly family of Aaron originate from the Mosaic era, and if so, how did it maintain its legacy and heritage throughout the earliest phase of Israelite history? How did the eventual construction of the temple in Jerusalem and the centralization of the temple cult affect the relations between Levites and the priestly families that oversaw the temple sacrifices? Does the final redaction of the Torah reflect a postexilic phase of the priesthood in which "Aaron" is a foreshadowing type of the high priest?

Here I will not seek to answer these controversial questions, to which our answers, affirmative or negative, will remain probabilistic at best, and necessarily quite speculative. Instead, I will simply provide some general principles that allow us to think about the overarching theological and historical significance of the priesthood in ancient Israel.

First we should note that the office of the priesthood in ancient Israel is related most essentially to sacrifice, but that sacrifice is not wed necessarily to the priesthood. The patriarchs sacrifice, as do kings like Saul and David. This "inconsistent" biblical practice reflects a more general human pattern. Historically, religious sacrifices are not always performed by priests but can be accomplished by family members, ordinary citizens, elders, heads of tribes, kings, chieftains, and so on. In more sociologically complex civilizations of antiquity, however, it was not uncommon to establish a priestly caste to oversee the ritual functions of religious ceremonies, including sacrifices.

Second, the priesthood is an institution that is both divine and human in origin. Theologically, the religion of ancient Israel is fundamentally divine in origin and prophetically inspired. However, its inspiration was received into the collective life of a particular ancient people in a given time and setting that was already marked deeply by the sociological religious practices of their epoch. The revelation and its progressive transmission and development affected and informed this religious culture of the ancient Near East but did not create it ex nihilo. Consequently, reflected in the sacerdotal practices of ancient Israel are a

37. For two twentieth-century representatives, compare de Vaux 1997: 335–405 with Walther Eichrodt, *The Theology of the Old Testament*, 2 vols., trans. J. A. Baker (London: SCM, 1961), 1:393–436.

variety of phenomena derived from the generic religious culture of the ancient Near East. This does not mean that these practices have been adopted uncritically. On the whole, they seem to have been reinterpreted profoundly and transformed from within by the reception of divine revelation.

Third, one may certainly posit a complex development within the historical unfolding of the priesthood in ancient Israel in which the Levitical tribe played a major role, either during or after the settlement in Israel, and in which the priestly clan descended from Aaron was invested by the monarchy (repeatedly, at various stages) with significant responsibilities in the temple. This dynamic development gave rise in the postexilic situation to a reestablishment of the priesthood as the principal religious influence in ancient Israel (after the dissolution of the monarchy) in the newly reconstructed temple. It is probably to this group of people that we owe the text under consideration. The practices of Exod. 28–29 most likely have a prehistory that precedes the era in which they were written down, but they are also reflective of the epoch in which they are given. During the time in question, the priest was "consecrated," not unlike an ancient Israelite king and perhaps in substitution for the king who was absent from the life of the postexilic community.

Based on these three principles, there is little difficulty in maintaining theologically that the covenant or theologically inspired movement that began with Moses and his followers blossomed in Israel with the development of more complex and canonically stipulated forms of ritual sacrifice. This is not to say that sacrifice or priesthood were absent from the earliest movement. It is entirely reasonable to suspect that the primitive Israelite community did appoint officers to oversee ritual sacrifices to the Lord. However, whatever form sacrifice took in the earliest movement and after the settlement in Canaan, this dynamic of inspired religious offering made to the Lord developed over centuries into a set of patterns that was in turn codified and recodified in law and set into norms by the sacerdotal clan, particularly in the wake of the exile and the final redaction of the Torah. In some fashion, the entire process was inspired—much like a living organism undergoes a progressive development according to internally consistent patterns—in view of clear teleological ends. One, very central end of the Israelite religion is the offering of right sacrifice to the Lord in his temple in Jerusalem, something mandated by the Torah in very distinctive terms.

As I noted previously, the priesthood has a twofold order of ascending and descending mediation. In the ascending order, the priest represents the people of Israel as the one who either offers the sacrifices to God on their behalf or assists them in the offering of sacrifice. This ascending order is moral or impetrative, but it also requires ritual purity. That is to say, the priest represents the people by making an internal offering of prayer and devotion to God in his action of offering the physical sacrifice (animal or vegetable), and this inner moral cleanliness is meant to be reflected in all of the aspects of his life outside the sanctuary. Approaching the Lord in a morally unworthy manner is an act of profound spiritual hypocrisy. At the same time, the priest also must maintain a ritual purity. In this regard he represents the purification of Israel under the law and the terms set down in the Torah for approaching God in the sanctuary under external conditions of ritual purification. If he fails in this respect, he risks bringing down divine punishment on himself or the people for lack of attention to the conditions of ritual holiness prescribed by the law.

In the descending order, the priest represents God to the people, primarily by giving divine goods to the people in the forms of blessings, teaching, and practical counsel. In the old covenant the priest has some power of conferring the blessings of the Lord upon people (see Num. 6:22–27). Presumably the words and gestures of such blessings signify that God communicates grace to the recipients on the occasion of these blessings. In addition, however, the priest is meant to teach the law of God (the Torah itself) to the people and to give advice to them regarding contingent prudential questions of personal conduct.

I have briefly noted various theological issues pertaining to the priesthood as a prelude to commenting on the depiction of the ephod and breastpiece in Exod. 28:1–28 because the ephod is a privileged symbol of all that has been conveyed above: it vividly designates the office of the priest in ancient Israelite religion, particularly in the context of ritual sacrifice.

The ephod and the breastplate themselves probably had a complex history in ancient Israelite religion and bore resemblances to ritual garments used in other Near Eastern cultures.[38] However, the form depicted here (probably postexilic) is prototypical. The prevalence of gold (28:5–15) symbolically conveys the fact that the high priest is permitted to go into the Holy of Holies before the ark that is also made of gold. The twelve precious stones on the breastplate (28:15–21) represent the twelve tribes of Israel (28:21). The high priest, Aaron, bears upon himself the burden of leading the whole people of Israel and brings all of Israel with him into the sanctuary (28:29).

Within the larger context of the Torah, the robes of the priest should be understood against the backdrop of Gen. 3:21. After Adam sins, God makes

---

38. See de Vaux 1997: 349–53.

garments for Adam and his wife and clothes them to hide their nakedness. In Exod. 28, humanity is given this prototypical clothing of the priestly ephod. In Israel, Adam is clothed in glory before God, or put another way, Israel is the new Adam, particularly in the offering of sacrifice to God, which stands at the heart of the covenant and the center of creation.

The Urim and Thummim and Other Vestments

28:30–43 "And in the breastpiece of judgment you shall put the Urim and the Thummim, and they shall be upon Aaron's heart, when he goes in before the LORD; thus Aaron shall bear the judgment of the people of Israel upon his heart before the LORD continually" (28:30).

It is not clear what exactly the Urim and Thummim were or how they functioned. They seem to have been sacred lots, perhaps dice or contradicting signs (like "yes" and "no") that could be employed to respond to practical queries or prudential questions. Here the reader is confronted with something that bears clear resemblances to superstition or magical practice, which has been adopted (in some fashion) into the religion of ancient Israel. The casting of sacred lots need not be considered inherently irrational. In Acts 1:26 the apostles cast lots to determine who would replace Judas in the college of apostles (Matthias or Justus). While God can work through "the toss of a coin," the notion of sacred lots is something quite primitive, and recourse to such practices is never a substitute for acquired and infused prudence, both of which are more profound gifts of God.

The other vestments depicted here continue to fill out the portrait of the almost royal dignity of the priest as the emissary of the people before God and the emissary of God before the people. Most notably, Exod. 28:37–38 stipulates that a blue turban is to be worn on the head of Aaron and his sons and that "Aaron shall take upon himself any guilt incurred in the holy offering which the people of Israel hallow as their holy gifts; it shall always be upon his forehead, that they may be accepted before the LORD" (28:38). Aaron is depicted as a sin bearer who brings the sins of the people before God by ritual representation and offers sacrifice on their behalf. While this function is signified extrinsically in Aaron by his priestly vestments, it remains merely typological. In Christ, this act of offering for sin is intrinsic, due to the charity and merits of the human love and obedience of Christ. Christ suffers innocently, thus bearing on our behalf the penalties associated with sin (Isa. 53:11–12).

Aquinas notes that, figuratively, the priestly vestments represent the moral dispositions of the priest:

> The vestments denote the virtues of God's ministers. Now there are four things that are necessary to all His ministers, viz. chastity denoted by the breeches; a pure life, signified by the linen tunic; the moderation of discretion, betokened by the girdle; and rectitude of purpose, denoted by the miter covering the head. But the high-priests needed four other things in addition to these. First, a continual recollection of God in their thoughts; and this was signified by the golden plate worn over the forehead, with the name of God engraved thereon. Secondly, they had to bear with the shortcomings of the people: this was denoted by the ephod which they bore on their shoulders. Thirdly, they had to carry the people in their mind and heart by the solicitude of charity, in token of which they wore the [breastplate]. Fourthly, they had to lead a godly life by performing works of perfection; and this was signified by the violet tunic.[39]

Consecration and Ordination Sacrifices

29:1–46 Exodus 29 details the ceremonies of consecration for the priests who serve at the altar and in the Holy of Holies. First the priest is covered with the ephod and other vestments (29:1–9). A bull is then sacrificed as a sin offering to atone for the sins of the priest and the people (29:10–14). A first ram is sacrificed as a holocaust offering (29:15–18), and then a second ram is sacrificed; its blood is placed on the ears and hands and feet of the priests and on the altar. The priests are sprinkled with the blood (29:19–21), and a portion of the ram is returned to Aaron as a portion for the priest and his sons (29:26, 31–35). This process is continued for seven days (29:35b–36b). In addition, daily sacrifices are also prescribed for the altar: a lamb each morning and a lamb each evening, in perpetuity (29:38–42). If all this is done according to specification, God promises to dwell with Israel: "There I will meet with the people of Israel, and it shall be sanctified by my glory; I will consecrate the tent of meeting and the altar; Aaron also and his sons I will consecrate, to serve me as priests. And I will dwell among the people of Israel, and will be their God" (29:43–45). All of this is deeply interconnected with Lev. 8–9, where the actual rite is carried out for the first time and Aaron enters into the priestly functions on the eighth day, after these initial sacrifices are completed.

At this point, the ontology of priestly ordination in the old covenant should be mentioned. This is a typically Western Catholic theological question, based

---

39. *ST* 1–2.102.5 ad 10.

on the dogmatic teaching that priests of the new covenant are changed ontologically by ordination at the hands of a validly ordained bishop, who is a successor to the apostles. The notion that ordination to the priesthood of Jesus Christ imposes a "character" or permanent ontological mark upon the soul of the man who is ordained is grounded in the universal belief of the Catholic Church that (1) ordination cannot be repeated and (2) only a validly ordained priest has the power to perform certain functions (such as the consecration of the Eucharist). If a person is changed once and for all by ordination in a unique way, and has distinct capacities by that very fact, then the sacrament must have a particular ontological effect. At the same time, everyone recognizes that this change in the person cannot be equated with the grace of holiness, since an ordained person may be seriously morally deficient or gravely sinful. Analogous things can be said about the "character" of baptism or confirmation.

Different theories of the ontological status of the character exist in traditional Catholic theology. Aquinas posits that the character is an accidental property of the soul, a power received into the faculty of the intellect. It thus gives the capacity to perform sacramental actions but does not confer of itself any distinction of spiritual holiness or theological wisdom.[40] The grace of holiness that is given to a priest when he performs sacramental actions does not come from the character per se but is given only if and when the priest abides in the sanctifying grace of charity. This is why a priest may perform valid sacramental actions and still be in a state of sin. However, the character also allows a priest to act in a unique way *as a priest* so that he may become holy in a distinct way—by performing sacramental actions in charity.

This theology raises the question of the ontological status of ordination to the priesthood in the old covenant, which must be understood in terms that are both similar and dissimilar from the sacraments of the new covenant. Here, then, three things may be said.

First, it is clear that there is a fundamental difference between the two forms of ordination. The sacraments of the new covenant are both signs and instrumental causes of grace that confer the grace they signify, while the sacraments of the old covenant are principally signs of grace. They signify outwardly the inward graces of faith, hope, and charity that are meant to elevate the minds and hearts of the practitioners of Israelite religion. Consequently, ordination does not impart the power to sanctify others by actions that communicate grace instrumentally *ex opere operato*, merely by celebrating the sacraments.

40. *ST* 3.63.2, 3.63.4 ad 3, 3.63.5.

Second, the old covenant priesthood is not merely a natural priesthood, a religious sociological reality derived from human religious traditions. It is a reality instituted by God under divine inspiration in view of the sanctification of the ancient Israelites within a covenant of grace. Priests received the true power to bless, teach authoritatively, and (in some cases) speak prophetically. When celebrated in living faith, the rites of the old covenant were true occasions of grace for ancient Israelites. Furthermore, the activities of the priests of the Old Law prefigured typologically the one true priesthood of Jesus Christ, which suggests that some ontological change occurred in them as a result of ordination.

Third, then, the consecration of the priests of the old covenant did not confer an active power to communicate grace instrumentally, as we find in the New Law, but it did communicate an effective authority of office to officiate over divinely instituted rites. This power in the priests of the Old Law is analogous to that conveyed by "sacramentals" in the New Law (such as ordination to the lectorate or subdiaconate). That is to say, it conveyed a power residual in the recipient that disposed the priest to the habitual celebration of the rites of the old covenant. This allowed priests to be the continual, active sign of the presence of God's covenant with Israel through the faithful administration of the rites and symbols of the ceremonial law. Their priestly actions, to which their ordination disposed them, were the regular occasions for the sanctification of the people through sacred worship, as the people were moved inwardly by the love of God. The sacerdotal acts were not the cause of the grace of worship as such but rather its habitual sign, making manifest in a distinctive way the privileged status of Israelite worship.

Outward Instruments of Worship (Exod. 30:1–31:11)

The Altar of Incense

30:1–10 "You shall make an altar to burn incense upon" (30:1).

Incense was commonly used in religious ceremonies of this epoch. In practical terms, it masked the odor of the burning flesh of animals. There are approximately fifty references to incense in the Torah alone, so it seems to be of central importance in temple sacrifice. Symbolically it represents the beauty of prayers that rise up to heaven. "Let my prayer be counted as incense before thee, / and the lifting up of my hands as an evening sacrifice!" (Ps. 141:2). The book of Revelation (5:8; 8:3) equates it with "the prayers of the saints."

The Census Tax

30:11–16 "When you take the census of the people of Israel, then each shall give a ransom for himself to the LORD when you number them, that there be no plague among them when you number them" (30:12).

Taking a census in the ancient world could stir up tribal animosities and lead to warfare, persecution of minority groups, or political hardships. When interpreted in a religious light, it is sometimes associated in the Old Testament with disobedience to God and warrants divine punishment (see 2 Sam. 24). In this passage conditions are given for taking a census (perhaps in postexilic circumstances) that will allow funds to be raised in view of the ordinary maintenance of the tabernacle/temple.

The Laver

30:17–21 "You shall also make a laver of bronze, with its base of bronze, for washing. And you shall put it between the tent of meeting and the altar, and you shall put water in it, with which Aaron and his sons shall wash their hands and their feet" (30:18–19).

The bronze laver is associated with ritual purity. The priests must render themselves ritually pure in view of the observances of the ceremonies of the law. Old Testament scholars debate the extent to which "impurity" in the Torah should be understood as a kind of quasi-physical stain as well as the reasons that the purity laws have such a deep symbolic importance.[41] Modern anthropological theories about ancient Israelite notions of physical purity often seem quite reasonable. There is in Exodus and Leviticus a complex symbolic system of ritual purity that seems to have dense symbolic overtones. However, despite the importance of this dimension of the text, the appeal to purity laws should not be employed to undermine what remains a deeply intelligible moral or ethical dimension of Old Testament monotheism—namely, that the sacrifices conducted in ancient Israel essentially concern the relationship of human persons to God and to the love of neighbor. As Jesus notes, this is the essence of the law (Matt. 22:37). The less rationally intelligible, more highly symbolic features of ritual purity and "physical" ritual cleanliness are present in the Torah, but they overlap with and are embedded within a deeper ontological and moral vision of reality that is conceptually and semantically normative for a right interpretation of the law.

41. See Jacob Milgrom, *Leviticus 1–16*, Anchor Bible 3 (New York: Doubleday, 1991); Mary Douglas, *Leviticus as Literature* (Oxford: Oxford University Press, 1999).

The Anointing Oil

30:22–38 "You shall make of these a sacred anointing oil blended as by the perfumer; a holy anointing oil it shall be. And you shall anoint with it the tent of meeting and the ark of the testimony" (30:25–26).

The use of oil is portrayed here in a way that resembles a Catholic sacramental; the oil conveys the holiness that it signifies, perhaps in the form of a blessing. Central objects in the tabernacle are to be anointed, as are the priests. In this way they will attain to ritual purity. The persons who are anointed acquire ritual purity themselves, in view of the right administration of sacrificial rites of the law.

The Artisans

31:1–11 "See, I have called by name Bez'alel the son of Uri, son of Hur, of the tribe of Judah: and I have filled him with the Spirit of God, with ability and intelligence, with knowledge and all craftsmanship, to devise artistic designs, to work in gold, silver, and bronze, in cutting stones for setting, and in carving wood, for work in every craft" (31:2–5).

Blessings are required from God even to fashion the tabernacle. The natural talents of artists are a gift from God the Creator, and they can be placed in the service of the religious life of the people of Israel, contributing to the service of divine worship in the temple. In this passage, the consecration of artistic gifts occurs in accord with God's inspiration.

The Sabbath (Exod. 31:12–18)

31:12–18 "Say to the people of Israel, 'You shall keep my sabbaths, for this is a sign between me and you throughout your generations, that you may know that I, the LORD, sanctify you'" (31:13).

All of the instructions in Exodus concerning the ceremonial law terminate here in the injunctions concerning the Sabbath. This passage forms a kind of conceptual bookend with the creation narrative in Gen. 2:2–3, where God completes the creation on the seventh day and enters into his rest. The creation of the tabernacle procures the final "resting place" of creation. In Israel's sacred worship, it enters into the final rest of the creation, that is, the final purpose for which God created the world. Thus the Torah communicates to Israel the highest dignity given to any people: to bring to completion the ultimate purposes of God for the created order. Here the covenantal life of Israel is central to God's restorative purpose for creation as a way to bind fallen humanity back to God in faith and love. Because of this elevated vocation, the precept of divine worship through observance of the Sabbath is underscored here in the most vehement terms. The punition for failing to observe the precept is death (31:14–15). The transgression in question amounts to a profanation of the deepest vocation of Israel; consequently, the moral gravity of the issue is underscored in especially strong terms.

When studying the punishments of the Torah, it must also be kept in mind that the penalties in question may be considered *objectively merited*, but this does not mean they are *effectively applicable*. Laws such as this one are given to render human beings aware of the gravity of their errors, not in order to destroy them. The outward face of stern justice in the Torah is always the external expression of an internal divine love. In its purity and holiness, this love is "jealous" and wishes to receive in turn a reciprocal love from the elect people. The brilliant sternness of God is always accompanied by an associated mystery of loving mercy that continually invites human beings to recognize the gravity of their sins in view of true repentance and renewed love for God. This interpretation is not merely projected onto Exodus from the New Testament. The last and final section of Exodus, which I will address next, illustrates this dynamic most vividly. When Israel collectively fails to observe the law in the most grievous of ways, they receive the deepest mercy of God in view of a renewal of the covenant.

5

FALL
AND ESCHATOLOGICAL
RESTORATION

Exodus 32–40

The final section of Exodus is of capital significance and casts a new light upon all that has previously transpired. Israel has been liberated. The law has been given. The covenant has been ratified. The plans for the tabernacle have been revealed. And then almost immediately, Israel breaks the most fundamental commandment in the covenant by committing idolatry. This last section of the book, then, details this fall and restoration in which the mercy of God comes to light as one of the deepest mysteries hidden within the covenant of God with humanity. This event is understood within the larger context of the Torah to reflect back upon the original sin of Adam and Eve, whom God treated mercifully. It also points forward prophetically to the historical life of Israel and the Church, to whom God will continuously show mercy, renewing throughout history the covenant of grace.

What Is Idolatry? The Symbol of the Golden Calf (Exod. 32:1–6)

32:1–6 "When the people saw that Moses delayed to come down from the mountain, the people gathered themselves together to Aaron, and said to him, 'Up, make us gods, who shall go before us.' . . . So all the people took off the rings of gold which were in their ears, and brought them to Aaron. And he received the gold at their hand, and fashioned it with a graving tool, and made a molten calf" (32:1, 3–4).

Literal Sense

Numerous textual problems arise in the interpretation of Exod. 32. Exodus 32–34 can be treated as a unified literary source and is traditionally attributed to the Yahwist (though this is also frequently contested). However, even on this supposition, 32:9–14 and 32:25–29 seem to be expansions added in this chapter to the original source. In addition, even if 32:1–6 is treated as very ancient in origin, the cry in 32:4 is virtually identical with 1 Kgs. 12:28: "Behold your gods, O Israel, who brought you up out of the land of Egypt!" In this latter text King Jeroboam constructs gold calves for the people to worship as figures of the Lord. How are these two texts and the two histories they recount related? Are there two distinct incidents that lie behind them? If so, does this mean that the later authors added this phrase in Exod. 32:4 to suggest that the event in the wilderness was a prefiguration of the catastrophic error of Jeroboam, or does it suggest that the authors of 1 Kings purposefully chose to allude to this segment of Exodus? Furthermore, references to the event in Exod. 32 are found in Deut. 9:21; Ps. 106:19; and Neh. 9:18 (which utters the same cry as Exod. 32:4), while Hos. 8:5–6 and 10:5 refer to the incident of Jeroboam.

Here I follow the reasoning of Brevard Childs, who sees in the these texts references to two distinct events but notes that the two events have also been understood in light of one another typologically by the final redactors of the Torah. Why follow this reasoning? First, the account in Exod. 32 accords closely with what follows in Exod. 33–34, and these latter chapters seem to stem from a pre-Deuteronomical tradition. Consequently, the story in Exod. 32 does not seem to originate merely from 1 Kings. Second, the accounts in Exod. 32 and 1 Kgs. 12 are very different both historically and theologically. The story in Exod. 32 is not concerned primarily with the king or leader of Israel but with the whole people. Historically, the symbol of the calf works differently in the two contexts. Among the Egyptians, the bull represented Apis in the pantheon of gods, while among the Canaanites bulls represented Baal. Third, Aaron clearly is not a figure of Jeroboam in these passages, and yet his character is subject to independent treatment. Exodus 32–33 provides a complex but coherent account of Aaron's weakness and intentions, suggesting an autonomous tradition. Fourth, the interpolations in 32:7–14 and 32:25–29 may well stem from the Deuteronomical school because they seem to stand out against the background of an older narrative, suggesting that 32:1–6 was originally situated in continuity with 32:30–31. In all likelihood, we are dealing with an independent tradition.[1]

Presuming that the people fell into idolatry, one may wonder whether the calf that they fabricated was intended to represent alternative gods (whom they worshiped) or if it was meant to depict the Lord. The text suggests the possibility of syncretism. On the one hand, 32:1 depicts the people requesting that Aaron fashion images of false gods, but 32:5 notes Aaron's intention to make use of the golden calf to keep the people faithful to the Lord (he wants them to worship the Lord under this representation). Interestingly, this difference between the people and Aaron depicts typologically two distinct ways in which idolatry may occur, which I will return to below. One can worship false gods, or one can worship God in a false, superstitious way. The ambiguity of the text (which has given rise historically to many debates) is morally salutary. By leaving the nature of the sin somewhat open-ended, it invites us to understand that there is more than one way the human race can fall into serious religious error. In any case, it is unambiguous as to whether the people have broken the first commandment and violated the covenant at its core. Clearly they are still spiritually crude, confused, and uninstructed in the law. The external events surrounding their election have not yet penetrated into their hearts and minds, revealing the need for their forty-year "novitiate" in the wilderness, prior to entering into the promised land.

Moral Sense

Religious superstition is traditionally defined in two ways. It occurs most fundamentally when human beings worship something that is not God, ascribe divine attributes to what is not divine, or give to a creature the honor that is normally reserved to God alone.[2] This form of superstition is idolatry in the strict sense,[3] and it can only occur if and when human beings have some true knowledge of God. In an act of idolatry there must be enough knowledge of what God truly is that one can attribute what is proper to God alone falsely to what is not God.[4] The confused or perplexed character of this knowledge can be a sign that the error

1. Childs 1974: 560, 565.
2. *ST* 2–2.92.2.
3. *ST* 2–2.94.1.
4. *ST* 2–2.94.3–4.

of the practitioners is in some way morally culpable, since there is access to true knowledge of God that has been partially veiled or confined. This is clearly the implication in 32:1–6, and a similar teaching is found in Rom. 1:18–25.

A second form of superstition consists in the worship of the true and living God in ways that are inherently unfitting, unreasonable, or immoral.[5] For example, one cannot honor God by doing what is inherently evil or unethical. Human sacrifice offered to God is a classic example, as well as divination by the use of magical ceremonies. Religiously motivated suicide serves as a good modern example, especially when conducted in the name of political terrorism. Such activity is inherently irreligious since it is God's prerogative to take innocent human life (through the medium of natural death) and not the prerogative of human beings.

Exodus 32:6 clearly suggests that Aaron is engaged in superstitious activity even though he knows better. He accepts the people's idolatry, seeing it for what it is, but tries to direct it toward the Lord. This amounts to an inherently problematic (and perhaps syncretistic) way of worshiping God, which stands in direct violation of the prohibition on images of the divine. Exodus 32 depicts Aaron as weak and compromising. The degree of Aaron's innocence is a matter of traditional debate in both Jewish and Christian exegesis. In 32:22 Aaron demonstrates that he knows better when speaking to Moses: "Let not the anger of my lord burn hot; you know the people, that they are set on evil." However, he also tries to excuse himself from any wrongdoing: "I said to them, 'Let any who have gold take it off'; so they gave it to me, and I threw it into the fire, and there came out this calf!" (32:24). Here we see the echo of Adam in the face of his transgression of the divine commandment: "The woman whom thou gavest to be with me, she gave me fruit of the tree, and I ate" (Gen. 3:12). But God does not accept the excuse: "The LORD sent a plague upon the people, because they made the calf which Aaron made" (Exod. 32:35).

However innocent or culpable Aaron may be, it is clear that Exodus underscores (at least in this instance) the ineffective character of his priesthood. From a Christian point of view, this episode is understood to illustrate the provisional character of the Old Testament priesthood. While the priesthood of Aaron foreshadows that of Christ, it is also dependent upon morally fallible human beings—which is to be contrasted with the sinlessness of Christ. "Indeed, the law appoints men in their weakness as high priests, but the word of the oath, which came later than the law, appoints a Son who has been made perfect forever" (Heb. 7:28). Christ and his

5. *ST* 2–2.93.1–2.

ex opere operato agency in the sacraments of the New Law are of a superior order, and yet Aaron continues to function as an example of how the moral agency of the priest in the new covenant can either contribute to or undermine the health of the ecclesial body. The failures and compromises of priests are often the cause of systemic idolatry, which spreads among the people of God.

Typological Sense

Typologically, the golden calf incident points backward as well as forward. Recapitulating the fall of Adam, it signifies the universal weakness of human nature in the wake of the original sin. It points forward in Israelite history to the temptations to religious syncretism in the era of the monarchy (of which Jeroboam is an archetype). The punishment of the first people of Israel in the wilderness foreshadows the punishment of the Babylonian exile. In fact, what is depicted most profoundly is a permanent syndrome or perpetual temptation of Israel to forsake God or to reconceive their relation to God in perverse and confused terms. In Acts 7:38, Stephen points out that this systemic weakness in the life of Israel has become manifest once again in the rejection of Christ, though here the Church is also signified. As 1 Cor. 10:7 makes clear, Christians are also capable of religious indifference, idolatry, and superstition, especially when they show undue respect for the "gods" of this world and fail to take seriously the real presence of Christ in the Eucharist. The golden calf symbolizes, then, the permanent possibility that humanity may forsake God—even in seemingly religious ways—preferring the fabrications of sensual pleasure, material wealth, and temporal power.

From the earliest times, Christian commentators have noted that the crisis of the golden calf and the breaking of the tables of the covenant by Moses (Exod. 32:19) foreshadow the need for a "new covenant" based on the universal mercy of God given in Jesus Christ.[6] (In this respect see the prophetic announcements of the "new" and "everlasting" covenant in Jer. 31:31 and Ezek. 16:60; 37:36.) Irenaeus points out that the event of the golden calf binds together Christians and Jews more than it separates them since it demonstrates (against the gnostics) that the new covenant comes forth from the old. The fall of the Israelites is the occasion for Gentiles to receive inclusion in the covenant; they share with Israel a common human weakness and corresponding need for salvation by grace.[7] Neither Jew nor Greek is justified by the perfect observance of the law (Gal. 5:6). God

---

6. See, for example, *Epistle of Barnabas*, chap. 14.
7. Irenaeus, *Against Heresies* 4.27.3–4.

makes use of the limitations of Israel, then, to expand the sphere of the covenant in Christ, making it catholic. "For if their rejection means the reconciliation of the world, what will their acceptance mean but life from the dead?" (Rom. 11:15).

Meanwhile, Jewish commentators tend to read the text in a fashion that is diametrically opposed. Many Jewish commentators, both classical and modern, see the golden calf incident as the representation of a permanent metatemptation among the people of Israel, who are prone to discouragement and think that the Torah is insufficient or provisional. Consequently, they might be tempted to replace its mediator, Moses, with a substitute mediator or a materialistic form of religion based in syncretism.[8] In an indirect but clear way, the claim is being made here that the golden calf typologically prefigures the error of Christian belief in the incarnation, leading to the idolatrous errors of the New Testament.

As Christians we must respectfully take issue with our "older brothers," the Jews, whom we love most dearly. The fulfillment of the Torah by the person of Jesus Christ requires us to believe that Jesus is the ultimate mediator between God and man. However, this does no intrinsic violence to the teaching of the Mosaic law. The presence of God among us in Christ is no more scandalous to our shared monotheistic faith than the presence of God among us in the election of Israel. If Christ is too "particular" or "visible" a presence of God among us, then the Torah analogously must also be too particular a gift to a particular people. The mystery of exclusivity or the "scandal of particularity" is present in both cases. But if God has become present among us in a particular people, temple, and law, then God can also take on an individual human nature and a particular flesh. There is an inner trajectory to this historical development. As the covenant unfolds progressively in time, God reveals more profoundly both his transcendence and his immanent presence to the people of Israel. Seen in this light, the mystery of the incarnation complements the revelation of the Torah. It is not impossible for God to become a Jew.

The Torah clearly contains internal tensions or paradoxes that it cannot resolve itself and that call for resolution. The most evident concerns the universality of the covenant—that is, the promise made to Abraham is meant to bless all the nations (Gen. 17:4–5). Isaiah speaks of an everlasting covenant that will be opened up to all the Gentile nations (Isa. 61:8–9), which can only occur when the covenant becomes truly universal, expanding from out of Israel to all the nations. The Torah itself envisages something of this sort; even in Deut. 18:15–18, Moses promises another prophet who is to come, which must ultimately refer to the Messiah.

8. See, for example, Nachmanides, *Commentary on the Torah: Exodus* 32.1, who is typical in this respect and who cites other authorities such as Abraham Ibn Ezra.

Finally, there is a mystery of human sinfulness unveiled to the eyes of faith by the Torah, which concerns not only Israel but all humanity. The law teaches all human beings the truth about their moral failings and limitations in the presence of God. This teaching points toward our universal need for a Savior and the mystery of redemption by grace alone. "For God has consigned all men to disobedience, that he may have mercy upon all" (Rom. 11:32). Perceiving this frailty in the life of the people of Israel, Jeremiah and Ezekiel both speak of a new or everlasting covenant that is to come (Jer. 31:31; Ezek. 16:60; 37:36). In fact, this may be seen as the essential mystery of grace, mercy, and filial adoption, hidden in the old covenant and rendered fully manifest in the new. On the eve of his death, Jesus claims to fulfill these prophecies through his own passion, opening the covenant to all peoples (Mark 14:24; Luke 22:20). In this sense, Christ is the epitome of Israel as a "light to the nations" (Isa. 42:6; 49:6; 60:3). The apostolic Church is the light of Israel shining out into the world.

Divine Wrath and Atonement (Exod. 32:7–35)

32:7–14 "And the LORD said to Moses, 'I have seen this people, and behold, it is a stiff-necked people; now therefore let me alone, that my wrath may burn hot against them and I may consume them; but of you I will make a great nation.' But Moses besought the LORD his God, and said, 'O LORD, why does thy wrath burn hot against thy people, whom thou hast brought forth out of the land of Egypt with great power and with a mighty hand?'" (32:9–10).

Exodus 32:7–14 forms a unit that underscores the mystery of the wrath of God, and the mediating role of Moses in appealing to the mercy of God. Two questions arise in particular. First, what does the Torah mean when it refers to the anger or wrath of God? Second, what is the Torah suggesting regarding the "repentance" of God (32:14), wherein God is depicted as changing his mind?

In regard to the first question, anger is a passion of the soul whereby the sense powers in the human person react to a perceived threat, disorder, or injustice. In this way, anger is a movement of the soul dependent upon the body and proper only to animals with sense perception. God is not depicted in the Torah as literally having an animal body, despite the rich array of anthropomorphic metaphors that are employed. In the beginning, God is depicted as creating the whole physical world and is not subject to the constraints of time and place. Nor can God be depicted in images. Apophatically, the Torah denotes that God is incorporeal, so anger or wrath can be ascribed to God only metaphorically or figuratively and not in a proper or conceptually rigorous way.

That being said, metaphorical similitudes are not empty or meaningless; they have their own irreplaceable profundity and beauty.[9] In all metaphorical similitude the analogy is found in the effects. The king is like a lion because the lion acts as a "ruler" or dominant being over its given order. How then are the actions of God like those of the wrathful human being? God is said to respond to evil like a human being responds in righteous vindication and anger to a serious injustice. Rightly ordered anger seeks to restore order through a proportionally retributive justice. Punishment is given to demonstrate to the transgressor and to others in the public square that the moral order must be respected and that incorporation into the community is not an absolute right. Analogously, then, the goodness and wisdom of God are like sunlight that shines or wrath that burns intensively in the face of evil, casting the light of truth upon evil, unmasking it for what it is, and restoring order through the reassertion of divine justice. This ordering activity of divine justice is itself an expression of God's indomitable goodness and wisdom. The "punishments" or "chastisements" of God are in their own way both sublime and beautiful, no matter how terrifying they may be. They make manifest in some way the transcendent goodness of God and the deeper mystery of order in creation, which is suffused with divine wisdom. In addition, God's acts of justice in the Bible are typically therapeutic. They teach the recipient to order his or her life toward God and neighbor justly, in a radically truthful way. They seek to rehabilitate and redeem the human person.

Analogously, the images in the Torah of God "repenting" or changing his mind are beautiful images of the deeper power of God's omnipotent mercy, which "triumphs" in the heart of God. The text makes clear that the mercy that God "yields to" does not result from an inspiration Moses gives to God but from an inspiration God gives to Moses. The mercy of God is secretly at work in the saints, inspiring them to make intercession on behalf of others. In 32:10, God offers to "replace" Abraham with Moses in order to bring about a new people from Moses without historical connection to the patriarchs. Yet God leaves the door open to appeal, suggesting his deeper desire to undertake a new initiative of mercy. Moses then appeals to the covenant promises made to Abraham in Gen. 12:2 (which God has already alluded to in Exod. 32:10), thus going to the heart of the original covenant of faith with the people, which is very clever on Moses's part. Paul does

---

9. On this subject, see T.-L. Penido, *Le rôle d'analogie en théologie dogmatique* (Paris: J. Vrin, 1931), 42–46, 397–404.

the same thing in Rom. 4, going back before the law to find righteousness in the faith of Abraham. Jewish commentators speak here of God sparing Israel for the sake of the merits of the fathers. To accept this idea in an anti-Pelagian fashion, the merits of the saints must be understood as God's gifts, and infused charity (which is the principle of merit—faith working through love) must be seen as a gift of God that prepares the saints for God's predestined or foreordained benevolence of further grace. Everything, then, is a gift of God and stems from divine mercy. The grace of fidelity in the heart of Abraham is a created reflection of an even greater fidelity—that of God to Israel and the Church.

In Moses's argument with God he asks, "Why should the Egyptians say, 'With evil intent did he bring them forth, to slay them in the mountains, and to consume them from the face of the earth?'" (Exod. 32:12). If God forgives and saves the people, it will reveal to the world who God truly is, one who is merciful and just. The forgiveness of God for Israel is proleptic, foreshadowing the mercy that God will offer to all humanity in the atoning death of Christ. Moses the intercessor is a type of Jesus, who in his unique holiness and innocence intercedes for the world: "Father forgive them, for they know not what they do" (Luke 23:34).

32:15–35 "Moses' anger burned hot, and he threw the tables out of his hands and broke them at the foot of the mountain. And he took the calf which they had made, and burnt it with fire, and ground it to powder, and scattered it upon the water, and made the people of Israel drink it" (32:19–20).

If 32:7–14 is read as an alternative tradition or interpolation, then it is clear in 32:15–35 that Moses first punishes the people by burning the calf, grinding it into powder, casting it into water, and making the people drink it. Subsequently, God punishes them by sending a plague (32:35). In the interim (32:25–29) we encounter what may be another tradition or interpolation, in which the Levites join with Moses to put to death three thousand men who have participated in the activity of idolatry. Here the Torah depicts in various ways the notion of retributive punishment for serious sin.

Some form of punishment is an ordinary part of just relationships. Moderate discipline and proportionate retribution for injustices are elements of any natural human family, clan, city, nation, or kingdom, and this reality was widely recognized in the ancient world, even if moral standards and customs of punishment varied widely. Maintaining a just and proportionate punishment for transgressions in civic society accomplishes various goods. Not only is it a form of retribution that obliges the transgressor to acknowledge repercussions for his fault, but it can also be morally therapeutic, inviting those who undertake whatever wrongdoing to consider their error and change their patterns of behavior. Moreover, it serves to safeguard the common good by promoting justice and forewarning those who are inclined to transgress the moral law.

In Exod. 32, we encounter archaic images that are powerful and archetypal, such as the bitter image of drinking metallic ash or the fact that people are put to death for idolatry. However terrifying these images are, they also serve as vivid icons, denoting in pictorial gestures the mystery of divine punishment and its mediation through Israelite law.

Divine punishment signifies the mystery of transcendent justice, and it may be helpful here to note the imperfect and archaic nature of divine punishments in the Old Testament. However, this viewpoint should not be exaggerated too greatly. The New Testament emphasizes the real possibility of divine punishment no less thematically than the Old. God's chastisements typically take place through the medium of temporal goods in the Torah, whereas the New Testament emphasizes the possibility of eternal rewards and punishments in light of our eschatological judgment. Temporal punishment in the Torah is portrayed in largely therapeutic terms, with only occasional connotations of anything eternal or final. God punishes Adam and Eve in view of their eventual rehabilitation; the "skins" that he clothes them in after the fall are a sign of his continued providential care even after sin, foreshadowing the future "clothing" of grace in the incarnation (Gen. 3:15–24). Similarly, in Exod. 32 God sends a plague upon the people to evoke a sense of dread and responsibility but ultimately to stir up a yet deeper mentality of repentance, moral maturity, and love. We are not told here whether the punishment of death for three thousand men accomplishes any moral purification in its recipients. The zeal of the Levites does not necessarily stem immediately from God. How God might make eschatological use of their action for those they have killed remains hidden from view.

Ultimately, the scriptures do reveal that divine reprobation is a real possibility; eternal damnation is clearly not a therapeutic punishment since it is permanent. According to the repeated New Testament teaching of Christ, who is God, eternal damnation is a real possibility for every human being (Matt. 13:41–42, 49–50; Mark 9:43, 48–49). However, it results from a human initiative and not a divine one. The sin against the Holy Spirit that cannot be forgiven (Mark 3:29) is precisely the refusal of God's forgiveness of sins, stemming either from the callousness of presumption or the hidden pride of despair.[10] Presumption and despair are both

10. *ST* 2–2.14.1–2.

vices that destroy hope in God, and the tendencies toward these vices act as real temptations in all human beings, leading to the refusal of God's repeated offer of mercy and grace. As noted above, then, eternal loss stems from human rejection of God, not God's rejection of persons. Reprobation is a kind of divine response to unrepentant sin, as God judges all human acts in the light of his transcendent goodness, truth, and justice.[11] In reprobating the creature that has persevered in rejecting him, God reaffirms the truth about the human injustice of the rejection of God. Eternal reprobation is "merely" the divine confirmation that the creature cannot escape the truth about itself even after death, as all is brought to light before the face of God.

At the same time, the scriptures underscore that God governs the temporal order of the world uniquely in view of our relation to God, which is the primal theme of retributive justice in both Gen. 3 and Exod. 32. The retribution depicted in these chapters is understood to stem from the eternal goodness of God, from his mercy and his love for humanity and for Israel. The punishments are clement (they represent a softened application of justice in view of the rehabilitation of persons) and ordered toward the education of free creatures and their reinclusion into the covenant.[12]

Moses believes that he is familiar with God such that he can undertake "atonement" on behalf of Israel. "You have sinned a great sin. And now I will go up to the LORD; perhaps I can make atonement for your sin" (32:30). The word here for atonement (*kaphar*) is the word used thematically for atonement sacrifices in Exod. 29 as well as in Lev. 4–6 and 14–16. Clearly this event is theologically significant. Even before the sacrificial system for dealing with serious sin has been instituted it has been thwarted. The covenant must be renewed by something more primal than the cultic system, be it that of the tabernacle or that of the temple. Moses's friendship with God and his prophetic office as a mediator between God and man become the special locus of the "salvation" of Israel in the face of serious sin.

Morally speaking, this text poses a difficult question. On what grounds can Moses make atonement for the people by interceding with them before God? According to a Christian reading in which Moses foreshadows Christ, he is still truly interceding in some real way, by the grace that is given to him in view of the one saving sacrifice of Jesus. And yet Moses is only a creature—a flawed, imperfect person—no matter how great his friendship with God and his personal holiness.

11. *ST* 1.23.3 corp.
12. *ST* 2–2.157.1.

In answer to this question, the classical Christian tradition that distinguishes between "condign merit" and "congruent merit" proves helpful.[13] Condign merit is plenary in dignity and may be termed merit "in strict justice," whereby the one who makes propitiation for human sin possesses the dignity or moral worth proportionately adequate to atone for the sins of the human race. This is clearly possible only in the case of Christ, whose human prayer and impetration are of an infinite worth not by virtue of his human nature as such but by virtue of the dignity of his person, since he is the incarnate Word and himself the Lord.[14] Merit that is congruent, or "fitting," is a gift of God given to the saints who are friends with God by charity.[15] If God inspires some to pray on behalf of others, this in no way leads God to owe them some debt on account of their intercession. Rather, God moves his friends (the saints) to intercede out of charity and mercy on behalf of others so that God can answer the very prayers he inspires by grace. God does this not out of any need for the saints who pray to him but as a gratuitous gift, granting the saints a more intimate understanding of his own designs of mercy through a communion of love by which they are drawn more deeply into the life of Christ's saving charity. By moving them to pray for others, God moves them to become more like Christ and to reflect the concerns of Christ in the world, in the midst of human beings who learn from these "intercessors" what the presence of the charity of Jesus looks like when extended into the lives of his followers. "By this all men will know that you are my disciples, if you have love for one another" (John 13:35). It is this latter form of "congruous merit" that surfaces in Moses's intercession.

Of what type is the atoning intercession of Moses? First, it demonstrates symbolically that the Torah derived from Moses is of greater worth even than the temple or the tabernacle. Even when the latter are not operative or fail, the Torah is present to mediate between God and man. Second, it is a sign of the saints and prophets who are friends with God and who maintain the relationship of God and Israel in covenant, even in the face of Israel's worst sins and apostasy. Third, precisely because it is based on a kind of fittingness, the impetration of Moses is a sign of the need for a form of mediation between God and man that is perfect, which is accomplished only by the Redeemer, Jesus Christ, who is both God and man. The human imperfection of Israel in and through the entire biblical

13. See, for example, Aquinas in *ST* 1–2.109.6. Generally speaking, the use of the distinction is typical in scholastic theology.
14. *ST* 3.48.2.
15. *ST* 1–2.109.6 corp. and ad 2.

narrative is an archetypal image of the deeper imperfection of all humanity, and this points toward the need for a universal mediator in whom there is no sin and who is himself the Lord, the God-man who unites our humanity with his divinity. Moses's atoning intercession foreshadows the perfect atonement and intercessory prayer of Christ crucified.

Divine Mercy and Transfiguration (Exod. 33–34)

33:1–6 "The LORD said to Moses, 'Depart, go up hence . . . to the land of which I swore to Abraham, Isaac, and Jacob . . . and I will send an angel before you" (33:1–2).

Exodus 33 contains various traditions, the origins of which are difficult to determine. Exodus 33:7–11 seemingly forms a separate body of text from the rest, while 33:12–17 differs in theme from 33:18–23. Historically, the composition of the chapter is a subject of intense debate, with various modern interpreters ascribing the parts to either the Elohist or Yahwist traditions and with others attempting to refute these ascriptions. In its final redaction, however, the theme of Exod. 33 is clear. In light of the sin of idolatry, the people risk losing the manifest presence of God in their pilgrimage, and Moses seeks to fully restore the covenant and assure the continued presence of God with the people of Israel.

In Exod. 33:1–3, God repeats the promises of 23:20–33. God is sending the people into the promised land, where they will conquer their enemies. In addition, he will send with them "an angel" (23:20), which I discussed in the previous chapter. This figure might literally represent either Moses, Joshua, or God made manifest indirectly through the angelic host. It is also considered in traditional Christian commentary to be a typological representation of Christ. Here, however (in seeming distinction from Exod. 23:20), the promise of the angelic presence represents a kind of substitution: the angel will be present in the place of God himself. The Lord has spared the people due to the intercession of Moses (in Exod. 32) but will still withdraw his presence from them in some significant fashion in response to their sin. Moses makes clear in 33:12 that he does not understand who the angel is and that he wishes to procure instead the continued presence of God.

This text raises an important question central to ancient Israelite theology: Is the presence of God intensified in direct proportion to the presence or absence of creaturely mediators? Do creaturely mediations of the presence of God necessarily diminish God's presence? The Torah does not promote this kind of oppositional thinking. The designation of Moses as prophet and lawgiver takes place precisely so as to make God more manifest. The law and the prophets as well as the ceremonies of the tent of meeting and the temple function to make God more radiantly present and to manifest his glory to the people of Israel. There is no inherent rivalry between God and his revelatory mediations, just as there is no ontological opposition between the Creator and creatures. Because God is present in all things as the giver of their very existence, God can also make use of all that is to make himself manifest in the order of nature and in the order of grace, in various ways and to varying degrees of perfection. Nevertheless, it is possible for God to withdraw his presence from vehicles of mediation, just as God withdraws his presence from the temple in Ezek. 9–10. The promise of the accompaniment of a "mere" angel does not suggest the inherent limitations of mediations as such. Rather, it makes clear that the covenant is a gift. God is free to conceal himself should he wish to do so.

The moral sense of the text is conveyed in Exod. 33:4 and 6. The people no longer wear "ornaments," or rather God commands them to remove them (both ideas are conveyed, suggesting more than one textual tradition). It is not clear what these ornaments amount to. Spoils taken from Egypt? Gold meant for the construction of the tabernacle? While it is not possible to say definitively, the ethical meaning is clear. In the wake of Israel's sin, the people must do penance and adopt simplicity of life as a sign of repentance and fidelity to God.

33:7–11 "Now Moses used to take the tent and pitch it outside the camp. . . . When Moses entered the tent . . . the LORD used to speak to Moses face to face, as a man speaks to his friend" (33:7, 9, 11).

This section of the text is enigmatic. Most striking is the fact that Moses is said to speak regularly with God in a "tent of meeting" (Exod. 33:7) outside the camp of the Israelites. What tent is this? The prescriptions have just been given for the building of the tabernacle, which was interrupted by the incident of the golden calf. The tabernacle is going to be constructed for the first time in Exod. 35–40, which is imminent. Based on the internal logic of the narrative, this "tent" is not the tabernacle previously depicted. One possibility may be that the text represents an older tradition regarding the tent of meeting, which portrays the structure in different terms. There is no indication here that it is intended as a place of sacrifice. Be that as it may, the location of this section of the text is not incidental. The people have ruptured the covenant, and the building of the tabernacle is endangered. And yet Moses retains a unique proximity to God. His encounters with God in this tent are presented as a kind of echo of Sinai. He still speaks with God intimately as he once did on the mountain, and the people join in prayer with him (33:10), which seemingly incorporates them into his act of reparation.

The images of seeing and concealment in this passage are significant. The pillar of cloud is depicted again here, descending to the entrance of the tent (33:9). Again, God is concealed from ordinary human "sight" by a veil of thick darkness, implying that knowledge of God and illumination are gifts. At the same time, Moses speaks with God "face to face," which is the same expression used in Deut. 34:10 to denote the singularity of Moses: "There has not arisen a prophet since in Israel like Moses, whom the LORD knew face to face." Similarly, in Num. 12:5–8 God manifests himself in a pillar of cloud at the tent of meeting, confronting Aaron and Miriam on the question of the authority of Moses: "With him I speak mouth to mouth, clearly, and not in dark speech; and he beholds the form of the LORD. Why then were you not afraid to speak against my servant Moses?" (Num. 12:8).

Does Moses literally gaze on God in his glory? Is the text meant to denote here an immediate spiritual vision of the inner life of God? It seems not. Just after this passage, Moses asks to behold God's presence (Exod. 33:18) and is granted a fleeting glimpse of God in 34:6. Speaking with God "face to face" seems to denote a privileged intimacy and knowledge of God, particularly through the regular communication of prophetic understanding given to the human author of the law.

33:12–23 "Moses said, 'I pray thee, show me thy glory.' And [God] said, 'I will make all my goodness pass before you, and will proclaim before you my name "The LORD"; and I will be gracious to whom I will be gracious, and will show mercy on whom I will show mercy. But,' he said, 'you cannot see my face; for man shall not see me and live'" (33:18–20).

In 33:12–17 Moses implores God to remain with his people and to accompany them in their sojourn in the wilderness. In his plea he asks God to extend the favor God has shown him personally to the whole of the people and insists before God that this people alone are God's own people (33:13). It is only because God remains with and saves Israel that all the nations of the earth will come to know who God truly is (33:16). Once again the centrality of the intercession of Moses is clear. It is "priestly" in its own fashion. He is not merely the one through whom the law is given (descending mediation) but also the one who implores God on behalf of the people (ascending mediation). In 33:17, God consents. God's personal love for Moses is the point of contact from which God extends mercy to all of Israel: "This very thing that you have spoken I will do; for you have found favor in my sight, and I know you by name."

Throughout this narration Moses is a type of Christ who is to come, the unique mediator of all grace (descending mediation) and the one who impetrates before God in prayer on our behalf to make reparation for human sin (ascending mediation). Christ is not only the new Moses but also the one whose intercession is intended by God from all eternity prior to all else in the economy of salvation. All genuine forms of mediation are ultimately christocentric in nature. They depend upon his grace and are given in view of incorporation into the Church. "In many and various ways God spoke of old to our fathers by the prophets; but in these last days he has spoken to us by a Son . . . through whom also he created the world. . . . Jesus has been counted worthy of as much more glory than Moses as the builder of a house has more honor than the house" (Heb. 1:1–2; 3:3).

In Exod. 33:18–23, Moses asks to see God. "I pray thee, show me thy glory" (33:18). Aquinas notes that when we perceive the effects of a hidden cause, we naturally desire to know the cause directly.[16] The nobler and the more elevated the cause, the more avid the desire is. This is true particularly in the supernatural domain, where the effects by which God makes himself known are supernatural in kind and give a more excellent knowledge of God than is naturally available, communicating to us an inchoate understanding of who God is in his very essence. Here Moses exemplifies the life of the believer who is stimulated from within by the workings of grace to desire ardently to see God face-to-face. It is the hidden beauty and greatness of God in his incomprehensible mystery that Moses desires to contemplate.

In 33:19, God promises to reveal his name as Lord to Moses, echoing or recapitulating the revelation of 3:14: "I will make all my goodness pass before you, and will proclaim before you my name 'The LORD'; and I will be gracious to whom I will be gracious, and will show mercy on whom I will show mercy" (33:19). In Exod. 33–34, the mystery of God's covenant with Israel is being reconstituted from the beginning, with all of its essential elements. However, God is also making manifest something new in light of the sin of Israel: God is mercy, and that mercy is at the heart of the covenant. The framing of the revelation here is significant: "I will be gracious to whom I will be gracious" is an echo of "I AM WHO I AM" (3:14). In one sense this compounds the apophatic meaning of the divine name given in 3:14 so that, in essence, God is saying, "I will be who I will be and I am free to show grace and mercy to those who I choose." God is not determined by human failures or successes; God remains transcendent, free, and in a sense

16. *ST* 1.12.1.

radically unknown. This response also serves as a testimony to God's constancy, as if to say, "I will maintain the covenant on my terms as God and not on human terms, so as to preserve Israel in being." Nevertheless, there is an evident kataphatic sense of the phrasing here. In God's transcendent freedom, God reveals himself to be gracious and merciful. After all, God tells Moses that he will show him his "goodness" (33:19). It is precisely because God in his transcendent aseity has no dependence upon any creaturely being that he alone who gives existence to all things can continue to provide for creatures even in the face of their resistance to his grace and goodness, without any diminishment of his ineffable actuality of being. He who eternally is is he who is able to show mercy eternally. God alone can give without ever being diminished and without adding in the slightest way to his infinite glory. Consequently there is a certain sense in which, by being merciful in the face of sin, God is revealed even more profoundly in his immutable transcendent goodness as He Who Is for all eternity, in indiminishable, incomprehensible existence.

In 33:20–23, God tells Moses that he can see God's "back" but not his face, for "man shall not see me and live." Why can we not see God's face? And what does it mean here to say anthropomorphically that Moses can only see God's "back"? Regarding the first question, it is important to avoid a crucial error. One must not affirm that the soul is *metaphysically* incapable of seeing God face-to-face, for several reasons. First, the New Testament teaches that we are meant ultimately to see God face-to-face in the beatific vision (1 Cor. 13:12; 1 John 3:2; Rev. 21:23; 22:5). Second, natural reason cannot demonstrate that we are meant for the beatific vision, which is a grace transcending the scope of natural reason, but it can demonstrate that God exists; and since God remains only very imperfectly known by natural reason, we are able to desire naturally to know God perfectly and immediately, were this possible. Therefore, this form of innate desire of the human intellect cannot be understood as something pointless or alien to our nature. There is a natural desire to see God.[17]

This interpretation being excluded, what possibilities of interpretation remain available? The first is that human beings cannot see God face-to-face because it is not yet the time in which God has desired to reveal himself fully to humanity. This is the reading of Exod. 33:20 offered by 1 Tim. 6:13–16. God dwells in unapproachable light and will eventually make himself manifest to all the nations in

---

17. On this issue I am following a prominent strand of thinking in the Thomistic commentatorial tradition. See the argument in Thomas Joseph White, "Imperfect Happiness and the Final End of Man: Thomas Aquinas and the Paradigm of Nature-Grace Orthodoxy," *The Thomist* 78 (2014): 247–89.

the eschaton through the mystery of Jesus Christ. It is only in the light of the holy life, atoning death, and saving resurrection of Jesus Christ that human beings are invited into the supreme grace of the vision of God (see also 1 John 3:2; 4:12).

The second possibility is that we cannot see God face-to-face due to our moral unworthiness. We are in need of purification as a preparation to behold the beauty and goodness of God. This is why the souls of those who die in friendship with God but who are still in an imperfect state because of sin must be purified in the state known as "purgatory." This purification is a prelude to beatification, wherein the soul comes to perceive the essence of God intellectually in the immediacy of the beatific vision.

Third, the text may signify that the human being can in no way comprehend the mystery of God. God is utterly transcendent of the finite capacities and pretentions of all human understanding. This does not mean that human beings are constitutionally incapable of immediate knowledge of the essence of God (by grace), but it does mean that when God is perceived immediately (by the grace of the beatific vision), he is not understood by the intellect in a comprehensive way but is contemplated ecstatically and beheld.[18]

What, then, does the seeing of God's "back" signify? I have already treated this question in some detail in the commentary on Exod. 24:1–11. The image of God covering Moses with his hand and then revealing to Moses only his "back" seems clearly intended as an anthropomorphism or symbolic metaphor, even by the standards of the sometime archaic modes of communication employed by the authors of Exodus. There is a great deal of diversity of interpretation of this symbol of the "back" of God. Gregory of Nazianzus sees it as the imperfect mystical knowledge of God's essence that can be obtained in this life, especially through knowledge of God's effects of grace. The "rock" in which Moses hides represents the humanity of Christ, which gives us the most intimate knowledge of God's presence in the world:

> I was running to lay hold on God, and thus I went up into the Mount, and drew aside the curtain of the Cloud, and entered away from matter and material things, and as far as I could I withdrew within myself. And then when I looked up, I scarce saw the back parts of God; although I was sheltered by the Rock, the Word that was made flesh for us. And when I looked a little closer, I saw, not the First and unmingled Nature, known to Itself—to the Trinity, I mean; not That which abides within the first veil, and is hidden by the Cherubim; but only that Nature, which at

18. See *ST* 1.12.7–8.

last even reaches to us. And that is, as far as I can learn, the Majesty, or as holy David calls it, the Glory which is manifested among the creatures, which It has produced and governs. For these are the Back Parts of God, which He leaves behind Him, as tokens of Himself like the shadows and reflection of the sun in the water, which show the sun to our weak eyes, because we cannot look at the sun himself, for by his unmixed light he is too strong for our power of perception.[19]

As I have noted, Aquinas has a different view and thinks the symbol of the "back" may signify a momentary experience of the beatific vision.[20] Moses is given this "touch" of the deepest mystical union with God so that he will have sufficient perspective regarding who the Lord is and the grace of patience sufficient to lead the people of Israel over a long and arduous course. This is similar to Paul's mystical vision of God recounted in 2 Cor. 12:2–4. He was strengthened so as to endure many hardships as the apostle to the Gentiles.

Ultimately, whichever interpretation we take, what is most significant about this passage is that it introduces a central idea in divine revelation: the notion of beholding God, of seeing God by grace. In this sense, Exod. 33–34 lays the initial groundwork in scripture for the subsequent plenary revelation of the possibility of divinization of human beings by means of the grace of the beatific vision.

34:1–9 "The LORD passed before him, and proclaimed, 'The LORD, the LORD, a God merciful and gracious, slow to anger, and abounding in steadfast love and faithfulness, keeping steadfast love for thousands, forgiving iniquity and transgression and sin, but who will by no means clear the guilty, visiting the iniquity of the fathers upon the children and the children's children, to the third and the fourth generation'" (34:6–7).

Moses ascends to Mount Sinai once again (34:2), where he sees God. The name of God is uttered once again. Moses receives the law anew and descends from the mountain to restore the covenant between God and Israel; the theophany of Sinai is recapitulated and intensified. Arguably this is the core of the whole book, the summit of the revelation given in Exodus, particularly 34:6–7, where the divine name is reiterated in light of the mercy of God: "The LORD, the LORD, a God merciful and gracious, slow to anger, and abounding in steadfast love and faithfulness."

The central theological idea here is that God makes use of the transgression of Israel to reveal ever more profoundly who God is as God from all eternity, in

19. Gregory of Nazianzus, *Theological Oration* 2.3 (*NPNF*[2] 7:289).
20. *ST* 1–2.98.3 ad 2, 2–2.174.4 corp. and ad 1, 2–2.175.3 corp.

the depths of his eternal goodness and mercy. The divine name given in 3:14 is rightly taken by the tradition to signify, among other things, the divine aseity. God is pure act, an infinite ocean of subsistent being from whom all else derives its participated existence. This understanding is qualified rather than overturned by the new revelation of God's mercy. Precisely because of who God is from all eternity in his transcendence and incomprehensible plenitude of existence, God is able to give as no other is able to give and is able to show mercy in a way that no other is able to show mercy. The compassion of God in turn manifests the transcendent splendor and glory of his goodness, which is not a creaturely reality but the uncreated mystery of God's own being.

Strictly speaking, mercy is a form of love. It is the love of condescension that takes account of the sufferings or limitations of the other. Mercy seeks to remediate or take into account the difficulties another encounters and to meet those difficulties with charity and compassion. Divine mercy stems from the goodness of God and can be restorative in a unique way since God as the Creator is able to create anew, to grant divine forgiveness, and to heal and elevate creatures into friendship with him by grace. All of this is possible only for God, who is the Author of our being. Here, then, divine mercy is revealed to be the fundamental condition for the restoration of the covenant. Israel was initially freed from slavery in Egypt by mercy, and here Israel is restored to friendship with God by mercy. The election of the covenant stems from and is continually sustained in being by the living mercy of God. Far from being a disincentive from trust in God (who is not capricious), this revelation is meant to give Israel the deepest assurance. Israel's hopes rest with God, not with men. Because of God's fidelity to Israel, Israel can always rejoin or retain anew the living covenant, even in the midst of its ongoing errors or limitations. The condition sine qua non for the continuation of the grace of the covenant is not the impeccability of Israel but the willingness of Israel to rediscover God on God's terms, through genuine repentance, conversion of heart, and acknowledgment of the transcendent mercy and justice of God.

34:10-28 "And the LORD said to Moses, 'Write these words; in accordance with these words I have made a covenant with you and with Israel'" (34:27).

Exodus 34:10-28 contains renewed promises that God will accompany Israel into the promised land (34:11-16) and presents the concise body of law that is given to Israel to mark the renewal of the covenant in the light of Moses's intercession and God's pardon (34:17-28). Some of the laws are virtually identical with those given in 13:13-14 and 23:15-19. The Decalogue is also mentioned in 34:28, a verse that reiterates the notion that these moral precepts in particular are at the heart of the covenant with Israel.

Some interpreters understand the laws in Exod. 34 to represent a new legislation—one that is different from what is contained in the Book of the Covenant (Exod. 20:22–23:19) and is colored by the new situation of Israel in light of the transgression of the golden calf incident. In this case, the new law is more burdensome than the old, and its ceremonial precepts are intended in part as a penance for the people in the wake of their transgression. Personally, I see no sufficient foundation for this reading in the text. The succinct list of laws given here serves as a literary device and is to be taken as a representative symbol of the covenantal laws already given at Mount Sinai and elsewhere, as presented in previous chapters of Exodus. It is true that some material contained here seems original with respect to the rest of the book, but this is to be accounted for by the additional ancient legal traditions compiled by the final redactors of the law. The central theme of the chapter is recapitulative: the covenant is restored, and the Mosaic law regains its original prerogatives. Rather than being a burden, the presence of the law is a mercy for Israel, and even its burdensome, penitential aspects are meant to be borne in love, from living devotion to God. The Torah is imperfect when seen from the perspective of the New Testament, but it is still of divine origin.

34:29–35 "The people of Israel saw the face of Moses, that the skin of Moses' face shone; and Moses would put the veil upon his face again, until he went in to speak with [God]" (34:35).

The glory of God transfigures the face of Moses. If one takes this cryptic and singular passage of scripture to denote an actual physical miracle, then it should be understood that the visible countenance of Moses is irradiated with a mysterious quality of light, a radiance of splendor that results from his spiritual encounter with God. Other examples of this kind of charismatic grace can be found in the Christian tradition, most notably in the case of Seraphim of Sarov. There is no reason to doubt that such a miracle could have taken place with regard to Moses.

The deeper typological significance of the passage is more important, however. The direct encounter with the mercy of the Lord in 34:1–9 is seen to transform Moses, which is the work of the mercy of God: to save and transfigure the human being. This sign, then, is a promise of the transfiguration of all Israel. It is true that Moses covers his face with a veil (a mask?) so as to conceal the exceptional grace that is given to him alone (34:33). However, this grace also anticipates the glory of God that will dwell in the tabernacle and the temple, as depicted later in 40:34–38. God's presence among the people by virtue of the covenant is ultimately ordered toward their personal transfiguration both in soul and body. The radiance of splendor that shines out from the body of Moses is a prefiguration of the eschatological glory of the risen human body in the eschaton. The mercy of God will transform the entire cosmos through the medium of the covenant with Israel.

It is not surprising, then, that Paul applies this passage typologically to Christ and to the Church in 2 Cor. 3:7–18. The transfiguration of Moses is imperfect and temporal, a sign of the inherent imperfection of the older covenant apart from Christ. The transfiguration of the resurrected Christ, however, is perennial and enduring. Whereas the older Israel cannot perceive the glory of Christ and is blocked from viewing it by the "veil" of Moses, Christians perceive in Christ resurrected the plenary revelation of the presence of God. "And we all, with unveiled face, beholding the glory of the Lord, are being changed into his likeness from one degree of glory to another; for this comes from the Lord who is the Spirit" (2 Cor. 3:18). Gregory of Nazianzus rightly notes that this privileged illumination of the Christian stems from his or her baptism. This sacrament draws back the veil of obscurity so that one can perceive the luminous face of Christ. Jesus in his resurrection from the dead brings to fulfillment the knowledge of God that was initially given to Moses at the burning bush and at Mount Sinai. This knowledge is communicated to us in baptism and will be brought to perfection in the life of the resurrection.[21]

Building the Tabernacle as Prefiguration of the Temple and of Christ (Exod. 35:1–40:38)

35:1–40:38 "So Moses finished the work. Then the cloud covered the tent of meeting.... And Moses was not able to enter the tent of meeting, because the cloud abode upon it, and the glory of the LORD filled the tabernacle" (40:33–35).

21. Gregory Nazianzus, *Oration* 40.6 (*NPNF*[2] 7:361):
   A light typical and proportionate to those who were its subjects was the written law, adumbrating the truth and the sacrament of the great light, for Moses' face was made glorious by it. And, to mention more lights—it was light that appeared out of fire to Moses, when it burned the bush indeed, but did not consume it, to show its nature and to declare the power that was in it. And it was light that was in the pillar of fire that led Israel and tamed the wilderness.... Light was that godhead which was shown upon the mount to the disciples [on Tabor]—and a little too strong for their eyes. Light was that vision which blazed out upon Paul, and by wounding his eyes healed the darkness of his soul. Light is also the brilliancy of heaven to those who have been purified here, when the righteous shall shine forth as the sun, and God shall stand in the midst of them, gods and kings, deciding and distinguishing the ranks of the blessedness of heaven. Light beside these in a special sense is the illumination of baptism of which we are now speaking; for it contains a great and marvelous sacrament of our salvation.

In Exod. 35–40 the Israelites execute the commandments for the construction of the tabernacle given in Exod. 25–31. What was threatened by the incident of the golden calf has now been safeguarded and restored; the people are assured the continuing presence of the Lord among them. These two bodies of text are traditionally ascribed to the Priestly source, and they do clearly share basic theological presuppositions. Much of Exod. 35–40 consists of near-verbatim repetition of the earlier passages of cultic material, but what was commanded by God there is enacted by Moses and the Israelites here. Some of the marginal differences between the two texts have been studied in detail by modern commentators.[22]

Theologically speaking, however, there is a profound significance to the recapitulation of the cultic law that is finally enacted in this section. Most notably, this process follows the reconciliation with God that took place by virtue of Moses's intercession and friendship with God, which is depicted in Exod. 33–34. It also follows upon the plenary revelation of the name of God as mercy and loving-kindness.

The Literal Sense

The most evident literal sense of the passage concerns the restoration of the cultic life of Israel's covenant, even after its collective fall into sin. It is presupposed here that the worship of God embodied in the liturgical cult stands at the heart of the covenant. The cultic worship of the people constitutes the core of their obedience to the commandments, including the first three moral precepts of the Decalogue. The tabernacle and the temple are a preferential locus wherein God has promised to be radiantly present so that Israel may continually encounter him there.

In 40:27–29 Moses offers sacrifices that anticipate the prescriptive norms of Lev. 8 that are to be conducted by Aaron. Numbers 9:15 tells us that the glory of God accompanied the ark wherever the people traveled in the wilderness, a reality that is anticipated in Exod. 40:37–38. When the glory of God comes to rest upon the tabernacle in 40:34–35, the language employed closely resembles that of 1 Kgs. 8:10–11 regarding the presence of the Lord in the temple of Solomon.[23] Clearly, then, the literal sense of this passage is meant to convey the abiding presence of God with the people of Israel throughout the duration of their sojourn in the wilderness but also in the temple that is to be built in Jerusalem.

22. See, for example, Martin Noth, *Exodus: A Commentary*, trans. J. S. Bowden (London: SCM, 1962), 274–83; Childs 1974: 529–37, 634–38.
23. See Noth, *Exodus*, 282–83.

The Moral Sense

The moral sense of the passage is most evident in Exod. 35:4–36:7. Here the people take seriously the commandment of the prophet and act collectively to provide the materials for the construction of the tabernacle, contributing to the work of its edification. This is clearly symbolic of the collective responsibility of the people of Israel for their corporate worship. To employ the famous Thomist adage, one can see that grace does not destroy nature but acts to heal and elevate it. The grace of prophecy given to Moses does not exclude the natural collective life of the people of Israel. On the contrary, it is meant to be as collectively extensive and intensive as possible. All are not given the same tasks to accomplish; hierarchies of prophetic mediation and governance exist. But each human being and each family are called upon to enter into the work of the covenant collectively in concrete ways. The Torah is depicted as a source of political solidarity and authentic communion rather than a source of division. Behind these structures we can see the merciful face of God, who looks upon Israel with tenderness and calls all persons to respond to the grace of the covenant in so many diverse and variegated ways.

The Typological Sense

Typologically, this construction of the tabernacle after the devastating sin of Israel represents the reconstruction of the temple subsequent to its destruction during the time of the Babylonian exile. What took place in the wilderness in light of the mercy of God will take place later in Jerusalem. The restoration of the cultic life originates from the eternal mercy of God, and this mercy is made tangible by the restoration of the temple and the priesthood. God will remain with his people forever.

In another sense, the same text also signifies the new temple, who is Christ. In the Gospel of John, Jesus compares himself explicitly to the temple, using terms that suggest a kind of supersession. "Destroy this temple, and in three days I will raise it up. . . . He spoke of the temple of his body" (John 2:19, 21). On the night before he died, the Lord instituted the sacrament of the Eucharist as the enduring real presence of his body and blood and as the sacrifice of the new covenant. "This is my blood of the covenant, which is poured out for many for the forgiveness of sins" (Matt. 26:28). Here, as I have noted, the reference to Exod. 24:8 signifies that Christ's own death is the foundational sacrifice of the covenant and the source of unity of the Church, which is represented not by the twelve tribes of Exod. 24

but by the twelve apostles. In distinction from Moses, the background context for the sacrifice of Christ and his saving intercession is not only the incident of the golden calf (representative of Israel's continued imperfection and repeated infidelity to the covenant) but also the original sin of the first human couple and the universal presence throughout human history of fallen human nature. Christ is the new Moses who intercedes for all. He is the new temple in whom the presence of God is assured for all times and places by the new gift of his eucharistic body and blood. He is the new sacrifice, "the Lamb of God, who takes away the sin of the world" (John 1:29).

The Anagogical Sense

Anagogically, this passage signifies the abiding presence of God with the people in the most perfect and plenary of ways. The cloud of the glory of God descends upon the ark, and the people are irradiated by the glory of the Lord. This mystery of the transformation of Israel by the glory of God will come to its perfection in the resurrection from the dead and in the plenary knowledge of God that is given in the beatific vision. Spiritually, Exod. 35–40 clearly indicates the desire of God to manifest himself to Israel despite its limitations and faults and the desire of Israel to remain with God. Herein lie the seeds of the eschatological desire that animates much of the later prophecy of the people of Israel. In the face of Israel's repeated crises, the prophets begin to desire and to foretell explicitly an eschatological resolution to the drama of human existence: all the nations will be judged, Israel will be fully redeemed and restored, and God will reveal himself to all humanity in an unmediated and perfect fashion. Here, then, the deepest sense of the scriptures indicates the eschatological hope of Israel. Despite our sinfulness, we might come to rest in the mercy and peace of God, that his glory might shine upon us eternally and without end in the light of his radiant presence.

EPILOGUE

The Heavenly Temple and the Lamb Who Was Slain

The book of Exodus begins in darkness and ends in light. The Israelites are delivered from the darkness of slavery and enter into the luminous glory of the covenant. The vision of God granted to Moses in Exod. 34 illumines his visage and serves as a promise to all Israel: God wishes to share with Israel the knowledge of his own identity.

Or perhaps the imagery might be reversed. The book begins in the region of the light of man (represented by Pharaoh)—a world of reason marked by efficiency, calculation, and cruelty. As the people of Israel move out of Egypt they pass over into the darkness of God, represented by the cloud that always accompanies them. Even as the people are bound to God by law and worship, God remains hidden from them. The movement from Egypt to the promised land is an outward symbol of a deeper and more ultimate journey—of humanity into the knowledge of the very life of God. "I will espouse you to me in faith, and you shall know the Lord" (Hos. 2:20, my translation). The supernatural faith of Israel is obscure, but the light that Israel gathers from the law is the beginning of the vision of God promised to us on the last day.

> The glory of the LORD shall be revealed,
>   and all flesh shall see it together,
>   for the mouth of the LORD has spoken. (Isa. 40:5)

Genesis claims that the world was created in light as the first of God's creatures (Gen. 1:3). The Gospel of John reveals that this created light is the secondary refulgence of a more primal, aboriginal light—that of the uncreated Logos, through whom all things were made. "The true light that enlightens every man was coming into the world" (John 1:9). Thus the Father creates the world through his eternally begotten Word, God from God, the light who comes forth from light. It is this uncreated light of the Word that is revealed ultimately in the divine name of the Lord, which is revealed to Moses. It is the glory of this Word that fills the tabernacle in the wilderness, making manifest the presence of God. It is the light of this Word that shines upon the face of Moses on Mount Sinai, introducing him into the knowledge of God.

The book of Revelation recenters various themes from Exodus around their eschatological goal, making clear their anagogical sense: lamb, temple, glory, the divine name, seeing God face-to-face. At the center of heaven is the Paschal Lamb, Christ who was slain (Rev. 5:6). He is no longer dead but alive forever in the glory of the resurrection. Through him, the world is governed by God, and by him all nations will be judged (8:1; 21:27). The Church is the bride of the Lamb, and the apocalypse consists most ultimately in the wedding feast of Christ and the Church (19:7–9; 21:2, 9).

The new heaven and the new earth of the apocalypse contain a new temple. "[They] serve him day and night within his temple; / and he who sits upon the throne will shelter them with his presence" (7:15). As in Exod. 40:35, the temple of heaven is filled with the glory of God to such an extent that no one can enter until all God's final decrees come to pass (Rev. 15:18). At the same time, we are also told that there is no temple in heaven. "For its temple is the Lord God the Almighty and the Lamb" (21:22). The glorified body of Christ raised from the dead is the new temple. In Christ resurrected the presence of the Lord is made manifest to all the nations, to all of the redeemed.

Jesus also reveals the divine name of God. "He is clad in a robe dipped in blood, and the name by which he is called is the Word of God" (19:13). "On his robe and on his thigh he has a name inscribed, King of kings and Lord of lords" (19:16). This name of God is inscribed upon the minds of those who perceive God face-to-face in heaven. "They shall see his face, and his name shall be on their foreheads" (22:4).

At the same time, we see that this revelation of the name of God and this vision of God's face are also the perception of the glory of God. "The city has no need of sun or moon to shine upon it, for the glory of God is its light, and its lamp is the Lamb" (21:23). "And the night shall be no more . . . for the Lord God will be their light, and they shall reign for ever and ever" (22:5). The glory of God descends upon the people who behold the Lord with unveiled faces, and they in turn acknowledge the glory of the Lamb. "Worthy is the Lamb who was slain, to receive power and wealth and wisdom and might and honor and glory and blessing!" (5:12).

We see, then, both the *exitus* and the *reditus*, the going out and the return. All things proceed in creation from the uncreated, aboriginal light of the Word. Through him, in his incarnation, death, and passion, all things return to God. This pilgrimage to God, then, is the deepest subject matter of the book of Exodus. In the historical and spiritual liberation of the people of Israel, there is sown the seed of the final, eschatological exodus of Christ and the Church. Through him, the Paschal Lamb, we are invited to leave the Egypt of this world, to learn the divine name of God, to return to the Father by journeying in the wilderness of this life, and to enter into the temple of God, our eternal city. There we can perceive the glory of God shining on the face of the risen Lord, himself the Lamb who was slain.

CODA

The Divine Name and the Metaphysics of Exodus

I

Étienne Gilson famously notes that the divine name given in Exod. 3:14, "I AM WHO I AM," stands at the font of a rich tradition of Jewish and Christian metaphysical speculation.[1] Already the Septuagint translated the Hebrew *ehyeh asher ehyeh* as *egō eimi ho ōn*—"I Am the One Who Is" or even "I Am the One Who Is Being." Jerome's Vulgate similarly states: "Ego sum qui sum," that is, "I Am Who I Am." Authors such as Philo, Gregory of Nyssa, and Augustine but also Maimonides, Bonaventure, Aquinas, and Nachmanides all offer profound readings of the divine name that are similarly metaphysical in scope. In the words of Maimonides, the God of 3:14 is "the existing Being which is the existing Being, that is to say, Whose existence is absolute."[2]

Gilson rightly notes that however diverse the interpretations given in this "tradition" broadly conceived may be, the scriptures implicitly reveal to us something pertaining to the highest form of natural metaphysical speculation regarding God. Gilson's position is already advanced explicitly in the *Guide for the Perplexed* 1.63, by Maimonides, who argues that Moses taught the people by rational

1. The idea is discussed in many places in Gilson's work. See, for example, Étienne Gilson, *The Spirit of Medieval Philosophy* (London: Sheed and Ward, 1936), chap. 3; *Elements of Christian Philosophy* (Garden City, NY: Doubleday, 1960), 131–32; "Maimonide et la philosophie de l'Exode," *Medieval Studies* 13 (1951): 223–25; *Thomism: The Philosophy of Thomas Aquinas*, 6th ed., trans. L. Shook and A. Maurer (Toronto: PIMS, 1992), 95; *Introduction à la philosophie chrétienne* (Paris: J. Vrin, 1960), 58.

2. Maimonides, *Guide of the Perplexed*, 1.63 (Friedländer 1885).

demonstration as well as by miracle.[3] In *Summa contra Gentiles* 1.22, Aquinas suggests that the metaphysics of Exodus gives warrant to the affirmation of the real distinction between existence and essence in all creatures (which receive their being from God) and the corresponding nondistinction in God—for it pertains to God's nature to exist, and he cannot not exist.[4] These authors intimate that the revelation of the divine name itself calls humanity into a more profound form of philosophical rationality, one that might otherwise be forgotten or obscured under the defective leanings of fallen human reason in the religious polytheism of the ancient Near East, as well as in the nonbiblical philosophical traditions of the Greeks and Romans. Exodus 3:14, then, attains to a high plane of the cooperation between faith and reason. Biblically inspired philosophy at its highest apex can recognize that God is subsistent being, for God is "revealed" in the natural order by the gift of existence. However, God is also hidden by this same measure as God infinitely transcends the world to which he gives rise. Creation inevitably relates us back to its unseen source but also conceals God, who remains incomprehensible. This is the God of Abraham, Isaac, and Jacob. It is also the God of the philosophers.

The cooperation of faith and reason does not end here, however. For what is unique about the biblical revelation given to Moses and the people of Israel more generally is that God speaks personally to them. God reveals to them who he is personally within the context of a covenant of grace and by means of the gift of faith. This form of relationship depends upon the new initiative of God in what Thomism would call the supernatural order. It is something that unaided human nature can only anticipate inchoately in the darkness of natural reason (reaching out to God personally in unknowing) but cannot attain to immediately by its own powers. Alone, the human person cannot procure a personal encounter or intimacy with God. Therefore, the God who truly is speaks to Israel. He Who Is speaks under a personal name, a second name, which is given in 3:15—the name

---

3. Maimonides, *Guide of the Perplexed* 1.63.

4. Aquinas, *SCG* 1.22 (Pegis 1955):

> Everything, furthermore, exists because it has being. A thing whose essence is not its being, consequently, is not through its essence but by participation in something, namely, being itself. But that which is through participation in something cannot be the first being, because prior to it is the being in which it participates in order to be. But God is the first being, with nothing prior to Him. His essence is, therefore, His being. This sublime truth Moses was taught by our Lord. When Moses asked our Lord: "If the children of Israel say to me: what is His name? What shall I say to them?" The Lord replied: "I AM WHO AM. . . . You shall say to the children of Israel: HE WHO IS has sent me to you" (Exod. 3:13–14). By this our Lord showed that His own proper name is HE WHO IS. Now, names have been devised to signify the natures or essences of things. It remains, then, that the divine being is God's essence or nature.

designated by the tetragrammaton (YHWH) and uttered under the familiar col-
loquial expression "Adonai" in Hebrew, "Kyrios" in Greek, "Dominus" in Latin,
and "the Lord" in English. The idea is that we can encounter the God who is—who
has made all things—*personally* as the Lord, just as Moses did on Mount Sinai,
by virtue of the revelation given to the people of Israel. This encounter, in turn,
has its own form of light and darkness that is proper to the grace of supernatural
faith. Consider here the reading of Gregory of Nyssa, reproduced by figures like
Dionysius and Aquinas.[5] In the figure of Moses ascending Mount Sinai, Nyssa
perceives an image of the soul that is invited by contemplative faith into this yet-
deeper form of divine darkness, excelling that of the natural incomprehensibility
of God.[6] The supernatural darkness of Moses's encounter with the hidden essence
of God becomes manifest in the revelation given to Israel and given in Christ.
This new and higher darkness transcends the natural apophaticism of metaphysics and involves the purification of the intellect that is led into the perception
of the inner mystery of God. This darkness is accompanied by a corresponding
illumination by which the light of faith fills the soul with a mysterious personal
presence of God. One might say that both the light and darkness of faith are
deeper and more extreme than the natural light and darkness of our metaphysical
knowledge of God, but the two forms of knowledge copenetrate without being
confused. Metaphysically we might know the Creator as He Who Is, and as he
who is omnipresent but transcendent and utterly hidden. By the faith we know
personally He Who Is as the Lord who addresses us and calls us to live in and
with him in his hidden and radiant glory. Each form of knowledge is a support to
the other; grace presupposes nature, and nature is healed and elevated by grace.

II

All of this sounds very beautiful. But can it be held today in light of our best knowledge of the sources of scripture? After all, the modern paradigm of pentateuchal

5. Gregory of Nyssa, *Life of Moses* 2.22–26; Dionysius, *Divine Names* 1.596A; Dionysius, *Mystical Theology* 1.1001A.
6. Gregory of Nyssa, *Life of Moses* 1.46 (Malherbe and Ferguson 1978):
Since he was alone, by having been stripped as it were of the people's fear, he boldly approached
the very darkness itself and entered the invisible things where he was no longer seen by those
watching. After he entered the inner sanctuary of the divine mystical doctrine, there, while not
being seen, he was in company with the Invisible. He teaches, I think, by the things he did that the
one who is going to associate intimately with God must go beyond all that is visible and (lifting
up his own mind, as to a mountaintop, to the invisible and incomprehensible) believe that the
divine is *there* where the understanding does not reach.

studies took its point of departure from the divine names as well, though conceived in an utterly different fashion. According to the Graf-Wellhausen hypothesis, the passage in 3:1–15 is a blend of sources in which perhaps the Elohist insists on a new disclosure of the divine name, "the Lord" (YHWH), that was not made known in the time of the patriarchs, while the Yahwist tells the story of a continuity in the disclosure of the divine name from Abraham in Gen. 15:6 to Moses in this chapter (perhaps in Exod. 3:16–20). The Priestly source, meanwhile, attempts to blend the two traditions in the beginning of 6:2–8, where the story of progressive disclosure is again retold, a subsequent iteration of the Elohist tradition. This is at least one variant of the story.[7]

In truth, however, this complex of ideas (that I have only alluded to very briefly) leads us into a much more complicated set of questions. Today there is less scholarly consensus about the exact character of the pentateuchal sources and more dispute regarding the findings of archeology, especially with respect to the diversity of religious practices that took place in and around Palestine in the biblical period. Yahwism in ancient Israel is frequently depicted as something quite sociologically complex, while the Pentateuch is often envisaged as something edited or even largely composed only in exilic times.[8] Did Near Eastern Yahwism preexist the time period with which the exodus event is traditionally associated?[9] Did the primitive Mosaic religious movement, if there was one, stem in part from encounters with Kenite or Midianite Yahwist worshipers on the Sinai Peninsula in the region of Horeb?[10] Were there in fact forms of Near Eastern Yahwism dating back hundreds of years in the Palestinian region before the emergence of the Israelite monarchy? And perhaps more importantly, are there not clear signs of Yahwist syncretism in the early monarchical period, wherein the name denoted by the tetragrammaton is in fact given to one god among others in a pantheon or sometimes in a dual male-female relationship with Asherah, a tenth-century god of the Canaanites? In short, how pure is the monotheism of ancient Israel? To ask this another way, how did Israel come to develop such a pure form of monotheism? Is that monotheism the result of a religious development that took place only in the exilic and postexilic age? Is it this age in which the Torah was ultimately

7. See, for example, the analyses of Childs 1974: 47–89; Durham 1987: 27–41.
8. Consider the well-developed theory of David M. Carr, *The Formation of the Hebrew Bible: A New Reconstruction* (Oxford: Oxford University Press, 2011).
9. Mark S. Smith, *The Origins of Biblical Monotheism: Israel's Polytheistic Background and the Ugaritic Texts* (Oxford: Oxford University Press, 2003).
10. Joseph Blenkinsopp, "The Midianite-Kenite Hypothesis Revisited and the Origins of Judah," *Journal for the Study of the Old Testament* 33 (2008): 131–53.

redacted or even composed in view of the formation of biblical Yahwism that we have subsequently come to know?

It may well be that none of these questions can be answered in a scientifically compelling way that gains definitive scholarly consensus. There is the distinct possibility that scholarly trends will emerge, like waves of conventional consensus, only to break consecutively upon the hard shores of skepticism due to the lack of any truly sufficient evidence of the full shape of Middle Eastern culture in the Iron Age. Whatever real archeological and textual progress is made, it will probably never be enough to reconstitute a wholly adequate understanding of the real historical and intellectual culture of the period under consideration at this great distance in time. Historians and archeologists will also probably never be able to prove in any rationally compelling way that the basic delineations of biblical history as presented in scripture did not occur or could not have happened; nor can it be proved that they necessarily did happen. In other words, we should not expect historical reason in this domain either to confirm or disprove what we otherwise might believe or disbelieve about traditional biblical faith, based on the "givens" of the divine revelation. History rests upon likelihoods, and it is entirely possible and even reasonable to argue for the likelihood of an ancient Near Eastern religious movement, dating from as far back as the thirteenth century BC that might be called Israelite biblical Yahwism, which gave rise (through a complex process) to the culture that produced the Bible. The evidence for this history is primarily the Bible itself, which does after all exist and which remains our primary if not at times exclusive source of knowledge about the religious practices in Palestine during this period.

That being said, intensive historical study of the Bible and its cultures of origin can strongly condition how and what we believe the Bible to be telling us. Here a couple of poignant questions about the history of the two divine names in 3:14–15 and about the theological consequences of how we understand this history should be asked.

First, let us assume, as the archeologists tell us, that the history of religion in the pre- and postmonarchical times shows some signs (at least in discrete times and places) of very diverse concepts of the deity of God—polytheistic as well as monotheistic and proto-monotheistic. And let us also assume that the name YHWH or similar forms of the name was employed within a diversity of strands of religious practice in different times and places to denote either a local deity (such as "Yahwism" in the patriarchal age or Kenite religion on the Sinai Peninsula) or a god in a pantheon (such as certain forms of Yahwism in the early monarchical

era) or an exclusive attachment to the Lord, the God of Israel (I am thinking here
of the Deuteronomical reform and the first precept of the Decalogue) or God
the Creator (such as the theology of Second Isaiah, as subsequently reread in the
intertestamental literature and in the New Testament). Theologically speaking, if
biblical Yahwism is to be something coherent and real on a profound level, then
there must be a consistent grace of revelation that exists throughout Israel's history. In and through this history, the living God, the unique Creator of heaven
and earth, has come to the people of Israel to choose them as his unique people,
giving them access to him in personal intimacy under the sign of his distinctly
revealed name, the Lord (YHWH). What kind of continuity of theological truth
is required in biblical Yahwism for this claim to be true? And in what way might
we understand it coherently in accord with the historical claims about diverse
forms of Yahwism mentioned above?

Second, what should be made historically of the intriguing Hebrew name
of 3:14, "I AM WHO I AM," which is also rearticulated at times in succinct
form in Exodus as simply "I AM" (3:14b)? Does it matter whether this name
is articulated in an early tradition (the Elohist), possibly going back even to
Moses and the primitive Israelite movement?[11] If so, is the name not then
premetaphysical insofar as it reflects the religious mentality of an age that
preceded the rise of explicitly speculative questions regarding the being and
nature of the deity of God? If the development of the name is placed later—for
example, in the time of the exile—then the name can be read in light of the
Priestly theology of Gen. 1–2. The name might well be explicitly about creation
and the uncreated nature of the God Who Is. After all, God in Exodus does
liberate the people of Israel through signs and wonders that implicitly denote
an omnipotence that is proper to the Creator of all that exists. God is not to
be confused with the idols of the Egyptians, and it is God who alone is able to
foretell the future with certain knowledge, mold human free will throughout
history, act miraculously upon the being of the physical world, forgive sins,
and give the covenant with Israel that stands at the heart of creation.[12] Read
within this literary symphony of elements, the subsequent interpretation of
the divine name by the Septuagint, "I Am the One Who [truly] Is," seems
very fitting. In short, the question is, when did this name become explicitly
metaphysical in tone, if ever?

11. See Childs 1974: 64–70.
12. See, for example, the suggestive remarks found in Iain Provan, V. Philips Long, and Tremper
Longman III, *A Biblical History of Israel* (Louisville: Westminster John Knox, 2003), 127–29, 133–35.

Perhaps then our two questions can be recast more simply and more suc-
cinctly. One is about the development of Yahwism and the other about the
origin and meaning of the name I Am He Who Is. In the mature theology of
Israel and the Bible of Israel, the story we are told is a story about how He Who
Is, the one true and living God, became the God of Israel by revealing himself
to Moses under the name of predilection, the name of the Lord (YHWH).
The other story, however, is the story of the development of biblical religion.
How did the ancient Near Eastern deity whom we call the Lord (YHWH)
come to be known as He Who Is, the God who created heaven and earth? In
the end, both of these questions need to be answered theologically so that the
two answers cohere and are harmonious with one another theologically and
historically.

III

I would like to give some indication concerning how one might answer these
two questions by recourse to ideas from three authors: John Henry Newman,
Maimonides, and Thomas Aquinas. In doing so, I will make four points. They
address, in a limited but pertinent way, the two questions posed above.

First, Newman's basic claim about the relationship between Roman Catholic
dogma and the theological study of scripture should be recalled. He famously
claimed that the dogmas of the Catholic Church could not be *derived* scientifically
by the solitary reader through the study of scripture but that these dogmas could
be *confirmed* therein.[13] That is to say, one might not demonstrate empirically by
the study of scripture the textual necessity of the development of certain Catholic
doctrines. However, one might show from the development of doctrines that have
taken place historically through time the continuous presence of a single idea
that has developed down through the ages organically, having taken its origins in
scripture as read in the most primitive tradition and undergone adaptation and
expansion through time in a way that preserves the original "type" of the idea.[14] A
case in point is the doctrine of the Virgin Mary as the New Eve, which Newman
claims in his Letter to Pusey to be well-founded in Justin's and Irenaeus's readings of
Luke and which sets the foundation for the later doctrines of the divine maternity
and the sinlessness of Mary, as well as the idea of her merits and unique degree of

13. John Henry Newman, *Apologia Pro Vita Sua: Being a History of His Religious Opinions* (London:
Longmans, Green, 1909), 244–45.
14. Newman 1989: chaps. 5–6.

sanctity.[15] One cannot derive all of these ideas simply by reading scripture apart from the primitive tradition of the Church, but if one reads the scripture in the light of earliest tradition, the argument can be made for the coherent development of doctrinal thinking, from Luke through Irenaeus, Augustine, Aquinas, and down to the modern age.

My point here is not to defend any particular doctrines of Mariology but to claim that Christian theology must maintain something similar about a tradition of homogeneous development in regard to biblical Yahwism. One cannot easily go back to the earliest forms of Yahwism in order to demonstrate that they developed organically into the mature form of Israelite monotheism that emerges in Deuteronomy and in the period of postexilic Judaism. But one can offer an argument that the mature development has seeds that were planted in the initial Mosaic exodus movement and that these seeds developed in and through the early monarchical age. In fact, as R. W. L. Moberly rightly points out, the Torah is already doing something like this at a very primitive stage in the narrative of Exod. 3 with regard to the religion of the patriarchal age.[16] The contact with God among the fathers from this earliest period is purposefully being reread or reinterpreted by the Torah redactors as prototypical, in view of the plenary revelation given to Moses. The Lord (YHWH) who speaks explicitly to Moses was known in a more implicit fashion by the fathers. Meanwhile, the revelation given at the burning bush is itself archetypal for the revelations given to the prophets in subsequent ages, even until the time of the exile. On this theological reading of history, then, the Lord whom Israel progressively comes to understand as almighty God who created heaven and earth is apprehended implicitly, though perhaps less perfectly, from the beginning. There is a progressive rendering explicit through time of a revelation given implicitly from the beginning. One need not posit a fully conceptually developed form of monotheism from the initial age of the emergence of Israelite religion, but one must posit an implicit one, whether its development can be charted out historically or not. Continuity of idea must be maintained as a core affirmation of the divine revelation.

How does this square, then, with the idea I have posed regarding the diversity of forms of Yahwism in both pre- and postmonarchical times? For surely polytheism as such is an idea that is incompatible with the monotheism of Israelite religion at

15. John Henry Newman, *Certain Difficulties Felt by Anglicans in Catholic Teaching Considered*, vol. 2 (London: Longmans, Green, 1900), 26–76.

16. R. W. L. Moberly, *The Old Testament of the Old Testament: Patriarchal Narratives and Mosaic Yahwism* (Minneapolis: Fortress, 1992).

any stage in its development. I take it, at any rate, that this is the case. Here, then, some distinctions should be made. First, it is possible to affirm theological belief in a concrete historical origin of biblical Yahwism that was explicitly and prophetically revealed and that made exclusive claims on its adherents. The existence of a supernatural grace that *makes* explicit claims on the Israelites in antiquity is not something historically demonstrable or falsifiable, but it is historically demonstrable that they believed this revelation to have occurred. Marie-Joseph Lagrange speaks here of an implicit monotheism present even in the beginning, from the time of the exodus.[17] He perceives it in the requirements of exclusive worship denoted by the first commandment of the Decalogue and embodied even quasi-metaphysically in the prohibition on images. By both denying that God can be imagined in a corporeal form as something of this world and adamantly pursuing the worship of the Lord alone, this primitive movement was already implicitly monotheistic in orientation. This argument presupposes not only that there was a historical exodus event but also the antiquity of the Decalogue as a component of the initial movement. Such an argument has famously been defended by scholars like Roland de Vaux, based upon textual and archeological considerations.[18] It may be impossible to prove such an idea irrefutably, but it is just as impossible to disprove it. Theology here, I think, should remain firmly committed to a historical exodus event, insisting on the exclusive worship of the Lord (YHWH).

Second, a simple truth can be taken from Aquinas. A name itself can be used to denote diverse individuals, but this need not imply a continuity of ontological substrates.[19] The Zeus of the Greeks is not the Deus of the Vulgate, even though historically the names are genealogically related. Identical names take on new significations when ascribed in new contexts to new subjects. Thomas Jefferson is not Thomas the Apostle, and any claim to identity based on the name "Thomas" would be quite absurd. Likewise, there can be radically distinct and logically incompatible religious beliefs and practices that simultaneously denote God or the gods by using the term "YHWH." This could be the case even while these traditions are historically related to one another but structurally divergent. The archeological and textual presence of the name YHWH in a variety of religious contexts in the ancient Near East suggests that ancient Israelite religion did not fall out of the sky without any prior historical context. It was derived in large part

17. Marie-Joseph Lagrange, *Le judaïsme avant Jesus-Christ*, 2nd ed. (Paris: J. Gabalda et Fils, 1931), 2–3.
18. De Vaux 1978: 1:462–72.
19. With regard to the tetragrammaton, see *ST* 1.13.11 ad 1 and the study by Armand Maurer, "St. Thomas on the Sacred Name 'Tetragrammaton,'" *Medieval Studies* 34 (1972): 275–86.

in and through a particular cultural matrix. However, the religion of ancient Israel also refashioned that matrix radically, as much as or more than it was fashioned by it, and the signification of the name of the Lord took on a whole distinct meaning and theological set of associations based on the truly novel and internally coherent form of religion that emerged in biblical monotheism. Outside of that biblical and canonical context, the name of the Lord (YHWH) as used in Israelite religion becomes unintelligible.[20]

Third, syncretism has always existed in Judaism and Christianity, but the empirical fact of a syncretistic form of Yahwism (such as including the Lord within a pantheon of gods) need not imply that this form of religion was theologically normative at any given time. Genetic fallacies should be resisted. Syncretism does not always evolve into dogmatic religion; sometimes it devolves from it. In general, the practices of syncretism and the practices of dogmatic religion are mutually exclusive and inimical. One might argue from the prevalence of Arianism in the fourth century that Arianism is the normative form of ancient Christian doctrine, but that is a very problematic argument, whether it is examined historically or conceptually.[21] The truth about Christology must be measured against the deeper backdrop of Christian tradition both prior and subsequent to the fourth century. Yahwism might be considered in similar terms during the biblical age. The Bible says that it developed from something requiring exclusive worship, which is not something that historical study can readily disprove. Consequently, it is possible to hypothesize any number of potential "histories of biblical monotheism," saving all the facts of empirical study of the archeological record and the similitudes that can be gathered from diverse ancient Near Eastern religious traditions. Perhaps the idea of Israelite religion in such histories might pass only from the very implicit to the overt, through the dialectical passage of cultural debates, religious confusion, human forgetfulness, and the continually renewed interjection of prophetic revelation on the part of God, which leads in turn to doctrinal developments.[22]

Fourth, regarding the divine name in 3:14, "I AM WHO I AM," Maimonides rightly notes that it is simply impossible to exclude from this phrase any implicit

20. Consider this idea within the larger context of Brevard S. Childs, *Biblical Theology of the Old and New Testaments* (Minneapolis: Augsburg Fortress, 1993), and George Lindbeck, *The Nature of Doctrine: Religion and Theology in a Post-Liberal Age* (Philadelphia: Westminster John Knox, 1984).

21. Consider the counterproposals of Lewis Ayres, *Nicaea and Its Legacy: An Approach to Fourth-Century Trinitarian Theology* (Oxford: Oxford University Press, 2004).

22. In this vein of interpretation, see the heuristic typology of "orthodox," "heterodox," and "syncretist" forms of Israelite Yahwism developed by Patrick D. Miller, *The Religion of Ancient Israel* (Louisville: Westminster John Knox, 2000), 46–62.

form of metaphysical speculation.[23] Why is this the case? First, the verb "to be" is employed with regard to God, necessarily confronting us even grammatically with the very idea of the being of God. After all, it is God who "is," and so thinking about this title invites ontological reflection.

Second, there is the analogy of being: God is deemed here to be God the savior of Israel because of something pertaining to the way that God is who he is.[24] Here one might wish to follow the many modern exegetes who interpret the phrase to mean "I am present to you."[25] However, contained herein is the implicit affirmation that God *is* a God who saves because he is present and is *able always* to be present. Action follows upon being, or stems from what a given thing is, and so action always reveals being in some way.[26] The ontological dimension of the name is not effaceable, then, even if it is interpreted in an actualistic way. What is unique about God and about this God, the God of Israel, pertains to the way God is different in his very way of being. The analogy of being is located inexorably then, even in the most succinct version of the name: "I Am."

Finally, metaphysics is inevitable because of the copula and the predicate. What is different about God Who Is or God Who Will Be? That he is or will be the one who is or who will be. "I Am He Who Will Be." That is to say, as Maimonides notes, all beings other than God have a composite nature such that the predicate of a sentence denotes a quality or characteristic of their being, but in the case of God, his nature and qualities are identical with his being.[27] God is He Who Will Be because his predicates, such as existence or goodness, cannot be alienated from his very essence and are indeed identical with his essence. God is the one whose essence it is to exist. This idea might seem to us like an unlikely anachronism derived from the metaphysics of the fathers and medievals, which is unnaturally projected back onto an ancient Mediterranean text. But such an idea is implicitly encoded in the grammar of the phrase itself, however intuitive and archaic its original derivation. Consequently, it is entirely plausible to claim that the Septuagint interpreted the text in a permissible and feasible way, rendering the implicit metaphysical content more fully explicit. This is admittedly a great

---

23. *Guide of the Perplexed* 1.60 and 63.

24. See the helpful comments of Aquinas on this point in *ST* 1.13.5 and 11.

25. See, for example, Childs 1974: 69.

26. *SCG* 3.69 (Bourke 1956): ". . . agere sequitur ad esse in actu . . ."

27. *Guide of the Perplexed* 1.63 (Pines 1963): "The first noun which is to be described is *ehyeh*; the second, by which the first is described, is likewise *ehyeh*, the identical word, as if to show that the object which is to be described and the attribute by which it is described are in this case necessarily identical. This is, therefore, the expression of the idea that God exists, but not in the ordinary sense of the term. . . . He is . . . the Being whose existence is absolute."

deal to draw out of a grammatical structure of language, but I am simply suggesting that language is itself always metaphysically potent and that grammar, even in its most archaic forms, is not to be underestimated in its capacity to denote utterly profound truths.

IV

If what I have (suggestively) argued above is true, then it is possible to hold to the following idea: there is perhaps quite a complex developmental history behind the religion of ancient Israel and the development of Second Temple, postexilic monotheism. In addition, the text of the Torah regarding the divine names of 3:14–15 may well be marked by this developmental history in a myriad of ways, many of which might only be disputed hypothetically rather than delineated with certitude. Nevertheless, it is entirely feasible to defend and promote a notion of continuity in the development of biblical Yahwism that passes organically from the initial, primitive Mosaic movement on the Sinai Peninsula to the formation of the Yahwism of the Davidic monarchy and the supposed age of the Deuteronomic reform, through to the time of the exile and the final redaction of the Torah. Simultaneously, it is possible to see theologically in this history the story of how God, the unique Creator of all that exists, chose Israel and led this chosen people to a progressively developed, prophetically inspired awareness that they had been chosen by God, the Creator of all things. What is more, they were invited into an intimacy with God by faith that allowed them not only to know that there is only one God, who made all things, but also to know God personally and mysteriously as the Lord (YHWH), under the name by which he revealed himself to them in a definitive way.

I will conclude by saying a last word about Christology. Both of the names that have been under consideration here—"I AM WHO I AM" and "the Lord"— are recapitulated in the New Testament as names of Christ. In Paul's Letter to the Philippians, 2:6–11, Christ is referred to under the Septuagint euphemism "Kyrios," who is recognized in his resurrection as the Lord God of Israel. Before him "every knee shall bend and every tongue confess" (Phil. 2:10–11; Isa. 45:23), just as Second Isaiah foretold for the God of Israel, the Lord of Exod. 3:15.[28] Likewise, in John 8:28 Jesus tells his interlocutors that "When you have lifted

28. See the study of Richard Bauckham, "God Crucified," in *Jesus and the God of Israel* (Grand Rapids: Eerdmans, 2008), 1–60, esp. 41–45.

up the Son of man, then you will know that I am he," referring unambiguously to the name of God revealed in Exod. 3:14. Jesus is not only one with the Father (John 10:30), he is also the God of Israel: the Word who was "in the beginning" (1:1), He Who Is, even "before Abraham was" (8:58).[29]

Above, I mentioned the patristic notion of the divine name of Exod. 3:14 as presenting an implicit metaphysics of being, regarding the simultaneous presence and hiddenness of God the Creator, who is both known and unknown. By God's creation, we have evidence of his existence, but due to his transcendence, he is utterly hidden and incomprehensible. I also noted that the Creator is known personally to Israel in a new way under the name "Lord," which is revealed in 3:15. This knowledge stems from supernatural faith, and it gives us intimate knowledge of God, a yet greater illumination and a yet greater darkness than anything encountered in the realm of philosophical metaphysics. This intimacy reaches its greatest depth, however, in the crucifixion and resurrection of Jesus Christ, who is the God of Israel existing among us as a man. In Christ, God is most present to his creation and to his chosen people, and God illuminates us with the most intimate knowledge of his own trinitarian life. At the same time, He Who Is, the Lord, is also most hidden within the suffering and death of Christ, even within his cadaver, buried in the tomb. And God is present also, both luminous and hidden, in the resurrected, physical body of Christ, which is truly alive but no longer of this world. The glory of God, the Lord, is revealed in a new way in the face of Christ crucified and resurrected. The second testament itself invites us to recapitulate the truth about the God of Israel and the divine names of 3:14–15, rereading these names in the most ultimate light—the name of Jesus. The Cross is a new Sinai from which the divine name is spoken out in a definitive way to all of humanity, as a light to all the nations.

---

29. Bauckham, "God Crucified," 46–50.

BIBLIOGRAPHY

Frequently cited works are listed here. Other works are documented in the footnotes.

Anderson, Gary A. 2002. "'As We Have Heard So We Have Seen': The Iconography of Zion." *Conservative Judaism* 54: 50–59.

Anderson, James, trans. 1956. *Summa contra Gentiles* 2. Garden City, NY: Doubleday.

Bettenson, Henry, trans. 1972. *St. Augustine: City of God*. London: Penguin.

Bourke, Vernon, trans. 1956. *Summa contra Gentiles* 3. 2 vols. Garden City, NY: Doubleday.

Buber, Martin. 1958. *Moses: The Revelation and the Covenant*. New York: Harper & Row.

Cassuto, Umberto Moshe David. 2005. *A Commentary on the Book of Exodus*. Translated by I. Abrahams. Skokie, IL: Varda.

Catholic Church. 1995. *Catechism of the Catholic Church*. New York: Doubleday.

Childs, Brevard S. 1974. *The Book of Exodus: A Critical, Theological Commentary*. Philadelphia: Westminster.

Collins, Joseph Burns, trans. 1939. *Explanation of the Ten Commandments*. In *The Catechetical Instructions of St. Thomas Aquinas*, 67–116. New York: Wagner.

Denzinger, Heinrich. 2012. *Compendium of Creeds, Definitions, and Declarations on Matters of Faith and Morals*. 43rd ed. Edited by P. Hünermann, R. Fastiggi, and A. E. Nash. San Francisco: Ignatius.

Durham, John I. 1987. *Exodus*. Word Biblical Commentary 3. Waco: Word Books.

EDP (Fathers of the English Dominican Province), trans. 1947. *The Summa theologica*. New York: Benziger Brothers.

Friedländer, Michael, trans. 1885. *The Guide of the Perplexed*. London: Trübner.

Kitchen, K. A. 2003. *On the Reliability of the Old Testament*. Grand Rapids: Eerdmans.

Krailsheimer, A. J., trans. 1966. *Pensées*. London: Penguin Books.

Larcher, Fabian, trans. 2012. *Commentary on the Letter of St. Paul to the Romans*. Lander, WY: Aquinas Institute.

Lienhard, Joseph, trans. 2001. *Exodus, Leviticus, Numbers, Deuteronomy*. Ancient Christian Commentary on Scripture 3. Downers Grove, IL: InterVarsity.

Luibhéid, Colm, and Paul Rorem, trans. 1987. *Pseudo-Dionysius: The Complete Works*. Classics of Western Spirituality. New York: Paulist Press.

Malherbe, Abraham, and Everett Ferguson, trans. 1978. *Gregory of Nyssa: The Life of Moses*. Classics of Western Spirituality. New York: Paulist Press.

McHugh, John A., and Charles J. Callan, trans. 1949. *Catechism of the Council of Trent for Parish Priests*. New York: Herder and Wagner.

Newman, John Henry. 1989. *An Essay on the Development of Christian Doctrine*. 6th ed. Notre Dame, IN: University of Notre Dame Press.

O'Neil, Charles, trans. 1956. *Summa contra Gentiles* 4. Garden City, NY: Doubleday.

Pegis, Anton, trans. 1955. *Summa contra Gentiles* 1. Garden City, NY: Doubleday.

Pera, C., ed. 1950. *In librum beati Dionysii de divinis nominibus exposition*. Turin and Rome: Marietti.

Pines, Shlomo, trans. 1963. *The Guide of the Perplexed*. Chicago: University of Chicago Press.

Regan, Richard, trans. 2003. *On Evil*. Oxford: Oxford University Press.

Spaeth, Paul, trans. 1995. *Collations on the Ten Commandments*. Works of St. Bonaventure 6. Bonaventure, NY: Franciscan Institute.

Spiazzi, Raymundi, ed. 1949. *Quaestiones quodlibetales*. Turin and Rome: Marietti.

Vaux, Roland de. 1978. *The Early History of Israel*. 2 vols. Translated by D. Smith. London: Darton, Longman & Todd.

———. 1997. *Ancient Israel: Its Life and Institutions*. Translated by J. McHugh. Grand Rapids: Eerdmans.

Weisheipl, James, and Fabian Larcher, trans. 2010. *Commentary on the Gospel of John*. 3 vols. Washington, DC: Catholic University of America Press.

SUBJECT INDEX

NAME INDEX

SCRIPTURE INDEX

Ok Mar 21/17 H
ok Oct 30/17 et